Water from the ROCK

Daily Devotions *for* Disciples

VOLUME THREE

GREG HINNANT

CREATION HOUSE

WATER FROM THE ROCK: DAILY DEVOTIONS FOR DISCIPLES, VOLUME 3
by Greg Hinnant
Published by Creation House
A Charisma Media Company
600 Rinehart Road
Lake Mary, Florida 32746
www.charismamedia.com

AUTHOR'S NOTE: Some Scripture quotations have specific words and/or phrases that I am emphasizing. I have added italics to these verses to show that emphasis. Also, in some of the Scripture quotations, with the exception of the Amplified Bible, I have inserted in brackets explanatory text to help with the understanding of certain words and phrases.

Design Director: Justin Evans
Cover design by Terry Clifton
Copyright © 2014 by Greg Hinnant
All rights reserved.

Visit the author's website: www.greghinnantministries.org.

Library of Congress Control Number: 2014948487
International Standard Book Number: 978-1-62136-799-4
E-book International Standard Book Number: 978-1-62136-800-7

First edition

14 15 16 17 18 — 987654321
Printed in Canada

DEDICATION

To my faithful friends and tireless helpers at Greg Hinnant
Ministries. For helping me produce another book for
Christ's people and kingdom, thanks *ad infinitum*...

CONTENTS

*F*REE, FRESH, FLOWING water sustained Israel forty years in the wilderness. Miraculously its source was a rock that never ran dry and that released its priceless liquid when struck or spoken to. This "water from the rock" (Deut. 8:15, NLT) is speaking to us.

Interpreting, the inspired apostle Paul revealed "that Rock was Christ" (1 Cor. 10:4). After being smitten on the cross and spoken to by His disciples' prayers, the Rock released the living water of the Spirit at Pentecost. He still releases spiritual water when spoken to—whenever we ask Him for the Holy Spirit or His biblical illumination. The result?

Free, fresh, flowing water from the Rock—the Spirit and His reviving insights from God's Word—sustains us in the wilderness of this world. Spiritual water parallels natural water.

Natural water is the source of life. Wherever it goes, life arises.[1] Creation began with God's Spirit moving on "the waters" (Gen. 1:2). Water sustains life. When it dries up, life dies out. Water fills us. Our bodies contain up to 75 percent water. Water refreshes us. Engedi's springs often revived David and his men when they were weary. Water cools and warms us. Cool pools and warm baths are simple remedies for extreme temperatures. Water washes us. Whether we prefer baths or showers, water is essential to bodily cleansing. Water falls from above. Thus it's a taste of heaven on earth. Water travels far and goes deep. It traverses continents in rivers and fills vast lakes and oceans. Though naturally pure, water is corruptible. Stagnant water is unhealthy, even deadly. Water brings conflict. From marauding Amalekites to well-stopping Philistines to unscrupulous ranchers in the American West, blood has flowed for flowing water. When desert travelers lack water, fearful, they complain. Israel's nomadic murmurings were legendary. Water flows underground. Invisible aquifers sustain many American farms and farmers. Water is inexhaustible. Like its Creator, the water cycle is perfect; the sum of water in, on, or above the earth (liquid, mist, or frozen) never diminishes. What is God's nature saying to God's people?

Spiritual water—the insights flowing from God's Spirit-illuminated Word—is the source of our spiritual life. No one is born again without it. The same biblical insight sustains Christ's life in us. To avoid spiritual dehydration, we should regularly rehydrate our souls with the water of the

Word. If read, studied, and obeyed regularly, it will wash away our sin. It refreshes us when we are trial-weary, cools us when we are emotionally overheated, and warms us when faith or devotion grows cold. Our insights keep flowing freshly if we continue obeying and sharing them, but they stagnate and we corrupt if we don't. Seeking living water brings conflict as demons inspire modern Amalekites and Philistines to stop our wells of blessing through offenses, hostility, or threats. Will we succumb, or overcome by practicing Moses' steadfast prayer and Isaac's non-retaliation? Will we be Christ's humble, hidden aquifers, watering others freely with biblical insights with little or no recognition? Are we praising God that our "water from the Rock" is inexhaustible, that however hot, hard, or dry our way, it never ceases flowing? When thirsty, do we fear and complain or give thanks and quietly seek more Word-water? God knows we're thirsty in this wilderness.

"Thou shalt bring forth to them water out of the rock" was His directive to Moses (Num. 20:8). However feeble my efforts, I aspire to emulate Moses' wondrous watering of God's people. With its companion works, *Not by Bread Alone* and *Sweeter Than Honey*, this book completes my devotional trilogy. Together these works provide a full year of daily devotional studies. Bread, honey, water—may they be a balanced, nourishing, spiritual meal! Now about this book's spiritual water...

Speak to the Rock, asking Him to release all its blessings. May they warm, cool, refresh, wash, or rehydrate your spirit as needed. May they run deep in you and far through you. When conflicts arise to stop their blessings, endure. And don't let these waters stagnate! Let them flow through you by obeying them and sharing them with others. They're thirsty too.

—GREG HINNANT

Chapter 1

THE WAY OF PEACE

*T*HE "GOSPEL OF peace" proclaims the "God of peace" sent the "son of peace" to "[preach] peace" to unpeaceful people. Whoever believes receives "peace with God," the "peace of God," and enters the "way of peace."[1]

In this Christlike lifestyle, peace manifests in three ways: peace with God, peace with others, and peace within our souls. Let's focus on the last—our wondrous, powerful, sweet, flowing, inner tranquility, the "peace of God, which passeth all understanding" (Phil. 4:7). This new peace and Christ who gives it are inseparably linked within our souls. He controls it, giving, sustaining, increasing, decreasing, taking, and restoring it. Thus "he is our peace" (Eph. 2:14).

By steadily trusting Christ and obeying His Word in daily circumstances, we maintain our peace, with its freedom from agitation, anxiety, and anger, even in the most turbulent circumstances. If we turn from trusting and obeying Christ, we lose it. If we turn back and confess our sin, He restores it. If we deny our sin, He lets creeping restlessness trouble us—until we stop pretending and confess (Ps. 32:3–5). These are the simple but unchanging rules that regulate the "way of peace."

The presence or absence of our peace also reveals God's will. Peace marks the thoughts, words, activities, and relationships He approves; persisting confusion or agitation marks those He disapproves. Thus our peace is a sure, impartial judge, ruling our relationship to Christ with a perfect accuracy we can safely trust. Paul urges us to let peace "rule" our lives:

> Let the peace (soul harmony which comes) from the Christ *rule* (act as umpire continually) in your hearts [deciding and settling with finality all questions that arise in your minds...
> —COLOSSIANS 3:15, AMP

> Let Christ's peace *control* you...
> —COLOSSIANS 3:15, GW

> Let the peace of Christ *guide* all your decisions...
> —COLOSSIANS 3:15, PHILLIPS

Is God's peace ruling, controlling, and guiding you? Let's learn more about living habitually in the "way of peace."

Inner peace is part of the rich spiritual inheritance Jesus left us: "Peace I leave with you, my peace I give unto you" (John 14:27). It confirms we're experiencing true kingdom living, not mere religious rule-keeping.[2] It's a "fruit of the Spirit," or evidence the Spirit is present and having His way in us (Gal. 5:22). Like John the Baptist, God's true messengers "guide our feet into the way of peace" (Luke 1:79). We should therefore earnestly "pursue the things which make for peace" (Rom. 14:19, NAS). Jesus weeps when we ignore His appointed "visitations" of peace, or our opportunities to renew our peace by drawing near Him every morning (Luke 19:41–44).

Spiritual thinking—seeing our lives through the Bible's Spirit-inspired viewpoint—gives us "life and peace" (Rom. 8:6). While believing and obeying what Scripture teaches in every situation, we "live in peace" with others (2 Cor. 13:11) and Christ's peace remains "with" us (Phil. 4:9).

As we continue doing so, God continues to "fill" us with more of His peace (Rom. 15:13). It supernaturally "keeps" (guards) our minds, even in very stressful situations, if we steadily commit all cares to God through believing prayer (Phil. 4:6–7). Christ "speaks peace" to us by bringing Scriptures to mind that explain our adversities and reveal what He wants us to do (Ps. 85:8). God sends fresh supplies of peace to reassure us to stay faithful when others are abandoning Him (Ps. 125:5). He also renews our peace whenever we receive forgiveness or healing, do good works, win spiritual battles, complete tests, or witness God's fulfillments.[3]

Peace always accompanies God's wise guidance: "All her [wisdom's] paths are peace" (Prov. 3:17). Whoever sows God's Word will be "led forth with peace" (Isa. 55:12). Faithfully obeying God's commands brings "peace…like a river" (Isa. 48:18, NIV). Continuing peace confirms we're becoming spiritually mature, fully sanctified by the "God of peace" (1 Thess. 5:23). Meditating on God's faithfulness imparts "perfect peace" (Isa. 26:3). Loving God's Word prevents offense and imparts "great peace" (Ps. 119:165). Consistently yielding to Jesus' lordship brings "abundance of peace" (Ps. 72:7), ensuring we'll be "in peace" when He appears (2 Pet. 3:14). Ultimately we and our children will "delight" ourselves in peace—forever![4] Thus peace is a huge blessing.

Nothing is worth losing it. It kept Jesus tranquil through everything, long obscurity, public scandal, even the cross! And He's passed it on to us.

Have you received His peace? Are you pursuing "the things which make for peace" (Rom. 14:19)? Is peace ruling your decisions, activities, relationships, and controversies? Is it increasing, decreasing, or absent? Follow its stabilizing guidance until the gospel, God, and Son of peace establish you in the "way of peace."

Chapter 2

SOW RIGHT, SOW NOW, SOW MUCH, SOW ON!

*W*HATEVER WE SOW—PLANT in the field of life by our decisions, words, or actions—produces appropriate consequences, whether good or bad.

Paul declared, "Whatever a man soweth, that shall he also reap" (Gal. 6:7). Therefore the situations we're reaping, or receiving in our lives daily, are to some degree the result of our past decisions, words, or acts: "A man's harvest in life will depend entirely on what he sows" (Gal. 6:7, PHILLIPS). Let's examine this universal principle more closely.

It's proven—abundantly! Biologically, every kind of seed—whether from plants, animals, or humans—when planted or fertilized, reproduces "after its kind" (Gen. 1:11–12, 21, 24). Socially, human history repeatedly demonstrates we also reap what we sow toward other people: loving leaders are beloved, hateful oppressors are hated, deceivers are eventually deceived, and faithful servants faithfully promoted. Biblical history agrees. Haman is impaled on the pole he sharpens for Mordecai, Daniel's accusers die in the lions' den they appoint for him, and Ruth's loyalty to Naomi is returned by Boaz.

It's positive. Though this principle is usually taken negatively, as a warning against sowing sin or selfishness, it's equally optimistic. Every day spiritually minded Christians think, "Today I can sow good and increase my coming harvest of God's good blessings!" Thus, while seeing the negative, they choose to stress the positive.

It's practical. It calls for not only faith but also action. Paul applies it to various fields of life: sowing financial support for churches and ministers (Gal. 6:6–7); sowing good deeds of charity, mercy, or assistance to those in need (v. 10); sowing obedience to the Spirit's guidance, call, or correction (6:8); and not sowing to our old nature's selfish choices and carnal sins (6:8).

It's proportional. We reap not only what we sow but also how much. "He who soweth sparingly shall reap also sparingly; and he who soweth bountifully shall reap also bountifully" (2 Cor. 9:6). Therefore we should "always [be] abounding in the work of the Lord," sowing the most good possible (1 Cor. 15:58).

It's personal. Since we fully control our sowing, we each personally determine our own reaping—the blessings or punishments we receive in life and at our final harvest, Christ's judgment seat (2 Cor. 5:9–10). We'll never reap others' harvests, good or bad, nor will they reap ours.[1]

It's patient. Like seeds germinating underground, our acts usually take time to grow. There's no harvest on demand with God, so we must not expect to reap every afternoon what we've sown that morning. We must learn to wait patiently while our good decisions, words, or acts sprout, grow, and produce.

It's proactive. Or it can be, if we believe this principle, abandon passivity, and begin taking steps to create a future better than our past.

It's productive. If we proactively apply this principle, we'll eventually produce much fruit for Christ's kingdom and people and joyful returns for us and our families. Observe others and search history, and you'll discover fruitful Christians believe and apply this principle. Unfruitful ones doubt it and stagnate.

It's prophetic. Every seed, however small, is a prophecy of a harvest to come. Its type reveals exactly what fruit we'll reap many times over. Whenever we sow right decisions, words, or actions, we should prophesy, "This good seed will return to me, multiplied."

It perseveres. Like nature's harvests, ours come "in due season" (Gal. 6:9). Plants require different amounts of time to mature.[2] It's the same with our seed-acts. Some bear fruit sooner, others later, as stated above. James says we must sometimes have "long patience" for God's responses (James 5:7–8). God tests us by letting it look like we won't reap what we've sown, nor will our antagonists. But looks can be deceiving. It seemed sure Ahab was evading God's judgment and Job reaping the whirlwind, but "in due season" each received his due. So when God delays our or our adversaries' respective crops, and we grow doubtful, weary, and apathetic "in well doing," let's remember our harvest is sure if we "faint not" (Gal. 6:9). "Unless we throw in our hand, the ultimate harvest is assured" (PHILLIPS). And, reassured, let's persevere. Why did God inspire Paul, a prolific sower of good, to pen this principle?

To transform our sowing! Ponder this principle and sow right—to the Spirit, never the flesh. Sow now—without delay, confident of your coming harvest. Sow much—realizing the more you sow, the more you'll reap. Sow on—through storms, droughts, and the deep weariness caused by seemingly endless adversities, adversaries, and crop failure.

Yes, through it all, sow right, sow now, sow much, sow on!

Chapter 3

BY HIS SPIRIT

*W*HEN FACING A difficult task with mountainous opposition, Zerubbabel heard God say, "Not by might, nor by power, but by my Spirit, saith the LORD" (Zech. 4:6). Or, "You will not succeed by your own strength or by your own power, but by my Spirit, says the LORD" (NCV). Thus God promised His Spirit would do what Zerubbabel couldn't do.

Specifically Zerubbabel was rebuilding the Jewish temple to prepare for Messiah's first coming. If he would trust and obey God, His Spirit would supply every need and remedy every problem, flattening the "mountain" of stubborn Samaritan opposition and expediting the construction. Soon Judah would complete the temple, dedicate its capstone, and praise God's all-sufficient "grace" (Zech. 4:7). Thus their work, hindered fifteen years, would now succeed—not by their own strength, wisdom, or methods, but by the Spirit's assistance. And it did!

This shows that while our powers are limited and wisdom fallible, God's are not. He possesses divine wisdom, superior methods, heavenly plans, and supernatural strength in unlimited measure. Where we try and fail, He succeeds. When hindrances rise, He rises above them. If we'll trust and obey Him, the immortal Spirit will do what mortal spirits can't: "The things which are impossible with men are possible with God" (Luke 18:27). Let's consider His incredible works.

The Spirit converts people long hostile to Christ and Christians. He overwhelmed Saul of Tarsus with a vision of Christ, and suddenly the church's worst enemy was humble and pliable in God's hands. He gives repentance to those long prodigal. In Jesus' parable of the lost son, the Spirit's influence caused the long wayward, wasteful younger son to suddenly "come to himself" and his father (Luke 15:17). He relieves those long oppressed. When Jesus spoke to a Jewish woman long bound and burdened by Satan, the Spirit instantly delivered her. He converts nations long given to paganism. When Jonah preached to Nineveh, the Spirit drew the whole nation to God. He heals those long crippled. When Peter ordered a man crippled from birth to rise and walk, the Spirit miraculously enabled him to do so.

The Spirit redeems regions long given to idolatry. During Paul's three-year ministry in Asia Minor, the Spirit worked so powerfully that "almost...all Asia" turned from false gods[1] to Christ (Acts 19:26). He causes lifelong rationalists to joyfully believe biblical revelation. Even in Athens, a center of Greek learning, the Spirit convinced some philosophers that Paul preached the truth. He liberates those long held in religious legalism. Scripture implies the Spirit drew Nicodemus, a Pharisee, into spiritual rebirth and liberty.[2] He transforms lifelong thieves into philanthropists. The Spirit in Christ changed Zacchaeus' criminal covetousness into Christian charitableness: "The half of my goods I give to the poor" (Luke 19:8). He emboldens those long timid. Without the Spirit Peter was cowardly; with Him he was courageous, even bold (Acts 4:13).

He liberates people long deceived by occultism. In Samaria and Ephesus Philip's and Paul's preaching released the Spirit—and lifelong occultists became loyal Christians. He cleanses and rehabilitates lives long given to promiscuity. The woman of Sychar and people of Corinth lived immorally until the Spirit moved them to love Christ's presence more than illicit pleasures.[3] He transforms judgmental religious zealots into gracious, long-suffering ministers. The Spirit influenced the apostle John to stop desiring his enemies' judgment and start compassionately ministering to them.[4] He melts long-held prejudices. The Spirit gave corrective words and visions to the early church—and Hebrews and Hellenists, Jews and Samaritans, and Jews and Gentiles came together.[5] He revives and raises churches—spiritual temples—long hindered by worldliness, carnal attitudes, and lukewarm faith. Just as the Spirit inspired and guided the reconstruction of Zerubbabel's temple before Christ's advent, so He'll revive and raise the end-time church before Christ reappears. God made all these impossibilities possible...by His Spirit.

What persistently difficult task, person, or problem do you face today that tempts you to say, as perhaps Zerubbabel said when viewing the unfinished temple, "That's impossible," "There's no way," or "I've tried everything and nothing's worked"? Don't let apparent impossibilities overwhelm your faith in God's clearly revealed will. Keep believing in the Spirit's awesome power. Look at your unfinished "temple" again and say, "Truly, we can't do this by mere human might or strength—our raw willpower, many people, financial resources, political influence, academic wisdom, innovative methods, or excellent organization. But by His Spirit it can be done!" And it will!

That is, if you humbly obey, persist in duty, and pray until His Spirit falls, revives, guides, and shows again that God can do what we can't do...by His Spirit.

Chapter 4

FAITHFUL TO THE LORD

*M*OVED BY THE apostle Paul's preaching, Lydia asked if he considered her "faithful to the Lord" (Acts 16:15). His response showed that, indeed, he did. Why?

To answer this, let's examine faithfulness, unfaithfulness, and the benefits of faithfulness.

A faithful Christian is true in his statements, promises, and pledges. He (or she) speaks accurately and honestly, promises only what he can perform, and takes pledges and vows seriously, never forgetting but ever fulfilling them. He is loyal, steadfastly standing by his Lord, faith, family, friends, and fellow Christians, even in the worst adversity. When Paul's Christian friends turned away, Onesiphorus loyally stood by: "He often refreshed me, and was not ashamed of my chain" (2 Tim. 1:16). He is reliable, discharging tasks, duties, or ministries correctly and thoroughly. Philemon was so reliable Paul predicted he would "do more than I say" (Philem. 21). He is trustworthy, never carelessly damaging or presumptuously misusing others' property or funds in his control. And he's accountable, ready to report to authorities, patrons, or stockholders how he's managed their organizations, donations, or investments, knowing he'll ultimately "give account of himself to God" (Rom. 14:12). But some Christians aren't true, loyal, reliable, trustworthy, or accountable.

Just the opposite, they're unfaithful. Their words, promises, vows, or pledges can't be trusted, because they're too often untrue. Loyal only to themselves, their steadfastness to the Lord, His truth, and His people wavers when sin and unbelief abound. Unreliable, their work is consistently incorrect or incomplete. Unworthy of trust, they frequently misuse, neglect, or steal monies, goods, or merchandise entrusted to them. And they resist giving account to their superiors, patrons, or government. Thus when God tests their faithfulness, they fail.

God also tests us regularly, as Paul examined Lydia, to see if and to what degree we're faithful to the Lord. He begins with small, not large, tasks, knowing, "he that is faithful in that which is least is faithful also in much" (Luke 16:10). He examines our trustworthiness first in natural, not spiritual, responsibilities. If we're honest with this world's "unrighteous money," He'll entrust us with the "true riches" of His truth, people, churches, and missions

(v. 11). He observes how we help others run their businesses or ministries. If we're dutiful in "another man's" work, He'll give us "that which is your own" (v. 12). But if we fail these tests, we forfeit the benefits of the faithful—which branch out widely to bless God, others, and faithful Christians.

God gains much by His faithful ones' efforts. Their loyal reliability enables His work to succeed and His kingdom—presently the church—grow. Thus every faithful Christian in this unfaithful world pleases and honors God significantly.

Many people are also benefitted. When we're true, trustworthy, and accountable, our actions, jobs, and ministries bless and help others—and sometimes save them! Because Joseph remained faithful in a long, unjust, humiliating test, God raised him to "save" Egypt, many nations, and Jacob's family from starvation (Gen. 50:20). Today our faithful prayers, preaching, and testimonies help redeem and transform individuals and through them save families, businesses, churches, cities, and nations from problems, pitfalls, and perdition.

Faithful Christians also receive rich benefits. Faithfulness gives us moral authority to teach God's Word as "faithful men...able to teach others" (2 Tim. 2:2). Faithfulness increases our influence from overseeing "few things" to "many things" (Matt. 25:21). Faithfulness increases our joy. Christ foretells of one day charging His faithful servants, "Enter thou into the joy of thy lord" (v. 23). Faithfulness wins God's call to ministry. Paul wrote Christ "counted me faithful, putting me into the ministry" (1 Tim. 1:12). If we remain faithful in seasons of suffering, God crowns us with seasons of enhanced spiritual life. Jesus promised Smyrna's sufferers, "Be thou faithful unto death, and I will give thee a crown [reward] of life" (Rev. 2:10). Faithfulness reserves a place for us in Jesus' army and glorious victory at Armageddon: "They that are with him are...faithful" (Rev. 17:14).

Faithfulness' highest reward, however, is the honor of being made like God Himself, whose character in a word is utter faithfulness. Of the Father, Paul wrote, "God is faithful" (1 Cor. 10:13). Of the Son, John wrote He is "called Faithful and True" (Rev. 19:11). Of the Spirit, Jesus declared He will "abide with you forever" (John 14:16).

Faithful to the Lord, Lydia exemplified this faithfulness and enjoyed its benefits. Her humble request for Paul to assess her faithfulness suggests faithfulness to God—being true, loyal, reliable, trustworthy, and accountable to Him—was her chief aim in life. Make it yours too.

Be faithful to the Lord.

Chapter 5

PREACHING AND PRACTICING THANKSGIVING

*T*HE APOSTLE PAUL never stopped thanking God for the Ephesians' faith and love: "Wherefore I...cease not to give thanks for you" (Eph. 1:15–16). He also persistently preached thanksgiving.

Paul penned three of the New Testament's four most memorable exhortations to thanksgiving:[1]

> In everything give thanks, for this is the will of God in Christ Jesus for you.
>
> —1 THESSALONIANS 5:18, NKJV

> Giving thanks always for all things unto God and the Father in the name of our Lord Jesus Christ.
>
> —EPHESIANS 5:20

> Whatever ye do in word or deed, do all...giving thanks to God...
>
> —COLOSSIANS 3:17

Note the all-inclusive terms he used: "everything," "always," "whatever." This word choice reveals God wants thanksgiving to fill our souls and days. Why?

Thanksgiving releases many rich blessings for us, others, and God. Let's review them.

Since it's His will, thanksgiving pleases God: "This [thanksgiving] is the will [pleasure] of God" (1 Thess. 5:18). Our thanks acknowledges our Father's loving faithfulness and watchful care. This deeply gratifies Him and moves Him to respond more readily to our prayers. Thus Paul teaches we should always close prayers "with thanksgiving" (Phil. 4:6). Such abundant thanks glorifies God abundantly (2 Cor. 4:15).

Thanksgiving also frees us from our harmful complaining habit—those invisible shackles that hinder us from walking closely with God and spoil so many days, opportunities, and blessings. By training us to embrace and make the best of every circumstance, thanksgiving gives us a consistently positive, can-do attitude. This enables us to stay attuned to the Holy Spirit so He can give us timely wisdom, guidance, and correction.

And thankfulness always grows. The more we give thanks, the more reasons for thankfulness we discover.[2] Paul wasn't born super thankful. By training himself to give thanks, he grew to become an extraordinarily thankful man. And thankfulness to God also cultivates thankfulness toward people for the good they do us and others (Rom. 16:3–4; 1 Tim. 2:1).

Furthermore, thanksgiving distinguishes us from the murmuring, sour, mixed multitudes in our churches and this "unthankful" last-days generation (2 Tim. 3:1–2). It humbles us. The opposite of boasting, thanksgiving yields all credit to God and what's left to those who pray for or help us. It draws us near God. We "enter into his gates with thanksgiving" (Ps. 100:4). It prompts God to deliver us. As we "offer…thanksgiving" and fulfill our vows, God rescues us in the "day of trouble" (Ps. 50:14–15). Giving thanks makes us excellent role models. Our good attitude draws sinners to Christ and Christians to thanksgiving—and spiritual growth. Thanksgiving keeps us connected with the Vine, who refills us with His Spirit (Eph. 5:18–20), and we enjoy His loving comfort, power, and hope daily. When ministers and parents give thanks for their congregants and children, as Paul did, they find it easier to patiently love them and avoid the pits of irritation or discouragement. Thanksgiving revives our spirits, enabling us to rise above adversity and endure sufferings. It powered Paul through many long, hard trials.[3]

Chiefly, thanksgiving molds us into Jesus' image. He constantly thanked His Father—for revealing spiritual truths to childlike hearts; for miraculously feeding His disciples; for the Communion cup He shared with them; for miracles He expected.[4] These are the reasons Paul preached thanksgiving.

And practiced it! Over and over, situation after situation, day after day, Paul thanked God in trusting acknowledgment of His ceaseless fatherly care for him and those for whom he prayed. Why? He realized practice makes perfect. And, indeed, by practicing the thanksgiving he preached, Paul became spiritually perfect—a consistently thankful, Christlike man. His persistent expressions of thanksgiving fill the New Testament.

Paul thanked God for the faith of the Roman Christians (Rom. 1:8) and again when he met them (Acts 28:15). He thanked God "always" for the Colossians' faith and love (Col. 1:3–4) and the Corinthians' abundant, victorious grace (1 Cor. 1:4; 2 Cor. 2:14). He thanked God "upon every remembrance" of the Philippians and thanked them for giving to his ministry so faithfully (Phil. 1:3; 4:14–15). He thanked God "always" that the Thessalonians' faith and love grew vigorously during their many persecutions (2 Thess. 1:3–4). He thanked God "night and day" for his ministerial protégé Timothy and fellow minister Philemon (2 Tim. 1:3; Philem. 4). He thanked God for every meal (1 Tim. 4:3–4) and pleased Him "well" by often praying or singing thanksgiving "with the Spirit" (1 Cor. 14:14–18). This repetitive practice perfected thanksgiving in Paul. It will in us too.

We already observe a Thanksgiving Day. Why not observe thanksgiving every day? And preach it. Then, like Paul, we'll be preaching and practicing thanksgiving.

Chapter 6

Are You Clinging?

*W*HEN ANONYMOUS EVANGELISTS preached Christ to the Greeks in Antioch, "a great number believed," turned to Christ, and founded a large, dynamic church (Acts 11:19–21).

Hearing of this, the Jerusalem church sent Barnabas to Antioch to evaluate the new Gentile assembly. Once convinced of its authenticity, Barnabas, a gifted minister, "exhorted them all, that with purpose of heart they would cling unto the Lord" (v. 23). In the Greek, "cling" means "to stay further" or "remain in a place, with a person"; or "adhering to, continuing with, or persevering in"[1] a place, relationship, or activity. So one of the first sermons Antioch's new converts received urged them to "cling" to Jesus with a fixed heart, or stay in this new place with Jesus, adhering to, continuing with, and persevering in a close walk with Him. It was a serious charge by a serious minister to a serious people concerning a serious issue: their new, wondrous relationship to their Savior!

Do we take this seriously? Do we realize we too should cling to Him? The truth is, some Christians—Christ's truly committed disciples— are clinging, but others are flinging. They're thoughtlessly flinging away this most important relationship by neglecting it. Let's review how to cling to Christ.

We should cling to Him and our "so great salvation" (Heb. 2:3) as if to our only lifeline while adrift at sea. In the wide, raging ocean of this fallen world with all its false gods and their purported lifelines to heaven, only One can ultimately safely prevent us from drowning in sin and judgment. Christ our Lifebuoy said, "No man cometh to the Father, but by me" (John 14:6). Peter added, "Neither is there salvation in any other" (Acts 4:12).

We should cling to Christ as if to vital nourishment and refreshment in a desert. Like our bodies, our souls need water and nourishment to survive this spiritually hostile environment. Convinced "man shall not live by bread alone, but by every word of God" (Luke 4:4), the wise disciple clings to his (or her) biblical reading, study, and instruction, feeding daily on the bread of life and spiritual "meat in due season" (Ps. 145:15). Knowing water is the source of life, he also clings to his secret place of prayer, where he drinks in the invigorating living water of the Spirit.

We should cling to Jesus as if we've found the most valuable substance. Gold, silver, diamonds, and pearls are among earth's most valued metals and gems and are often found in hidden treasures. But life's most valuable treasure is not earthly but heavenly, not material but spiritual. It is daily personal fellowship with Jesus. This hidden kingdom—life with the King—is the true disciple's "[hidden] treasure" and "pearl of great price" (Matt. 13:44–46). He will sell everything, if necessary, to gain, hold, or recover it.[2]

We should cling to Jesus as if to the sweetest lover in the most ideal romance. Truly blissful marital love is the most desired yet least found human relationship. Whether married or single, Christians have an even sweeter, more satisfying, and never failing Lover, the immutably lovely one, our eternal spouse, Jesus. We can "be content with such [worldly] things" as we have, because He said, "I will never leave thee, nor forsake thee" (Heb. 13:5). His mercies are new every morning, and in His "presence is fullness of joy" (Ps. 16:11).

We should cling to Jesus as if some hostile force or person were trying to take Him from us—because it is! Scripture warns that our "adversary, the devil" (1 Pet. 5:8) is bent on spoiling our relationship to Jesus and its potential kingdom fruitfulness. Jesus warned, "Hold fast [tightly] that which thou hast" (Rev. 3:11) so no person or demon will steal the living and written Word we hold or the rewards we seek.

While in these ways many cling to their fellowship with Jesus, others fling it away by neglecting Him in many different ways. They fail to seek God daily, continue practicing sin, neglect to study or obey God's Word, ignore self-examination, refuse to suffer rejection for Christ, crave worldly things more than spiritual, cling obsessively to other people or interests, or in other ways consistently disobey Christ. They need to learn a profound lesson from Jacob.

After foolishly wrestling against God's will, Jacob, broken and penitent, finally clung to God, acknowledging he needed Him desperately (Gen. 32:24–26). Are we there yet? It's time to stop wrestling, flinging, and just cling—gripping our Lifeline, grasping our Nourishment, clutching our Treasure, and embracing our Lover. Closely. Firmly. Forever.

Are you clinging?

Chapter 7

It's Time We Fear Him

*I*NNATELY WE ALL want people to respect us, and we're hurt when their words or actions reveal they don't. In this we mirror our Creator. He also wants respect.

And He's supremely due it. In loving wisdom and awesome power He created us and this wonderful earth—and we rebelled! Yet, in amazing grace, He redeemed us—by His Son's blood! Such love deserves our deepest respect. Are we giving it?

The Bible calls this profound God-esteem "the fear of the Lord." More than mere "reverential trust," the fear of God is a deep, loving respect for God that causes one to stand in awe of His awesome power, believe everything He says (promises and warnings), and turn from whatever displeases to whatever pleases Him. Instead of driving us from Him, this sin-killing, life-giving holy dread of the holy One draws us to Him and inspires joyful obedience, praise, and service. Put simply, it's ultimate respect for God, the true spirit of worship.

Paradoxically, when this fear enters, all others depart. We stop dreading people, harm, loss, or failure. No longer avoiding God, we now crave to be with Him, search His Word, and pursue His call.[1] This fear inspires integrity and accountability. No longer dreading judgment, we eagerly take steps to reorder our lives so we'll be approved when He evaluates us (2 Cor. 5:10–11). Thus motivated, when tested we draw back from sin and walk forward in obedience. But sometimes this fear manifests as physical terror.

In God's presence sinners and saints have experienced trembling, immobility, even fainting. A. W. Tozer wrote:

> Always there was about any manifestation of God something that dismayed the onlookers, that daunted and over-awed them…This terror…is…the deep reaction of a fallen creature in the presence of the holy Being the stunned heart knows is God.[2]

When the church realized Judge Jesus had miraculously intervened to remove Ananias and Sapphira from their midst, "great fear gripped the entire church and everyone else who heard what had happened" (Acts 5:11, NLT). When Daniel, Saul of Tarsus, and John saw Christ's full glory, they were overwhelmed—instantly broken, willing, and silent at His feet. Whether overwhelming or undergirding, this powerful respect for God has many beneficial effects. Let's explore them.

Fearing God enables us to begin building a personal knowledge of Him and learning His "wisdom," or excellent decision making (Prov. 1:7; 9:10). It is an essential characteristic of good leaders (2 Sam. 23:3) and fair-minded judges (2 Chron. 19:7, 9). It prompts us to submissively cooperate with other believers, lest our disunity or strife displease Christ (Eph. 5:21). It moves us to seek fellowship with other God-fearers "often" (Mal. 3:16). It motivates respectful obedience to all authorities, yet disobedience when in rare cases their commands defy God's or harm His people. It causes us to "hate" sin (Prov. 8:13) yet retain compassion for sinners. It inspires us to "cleanse ourselves" from not only acts but also thoughts of sin and walk in true holiness (2 Cor. 7:1). And the benefits don't stop with these.

By inspiring right living, God-fearing leads to an array of rich personal blessings. We receive strong security, spiritual refreshment, deep contentment, deliverance from debt, financial blessings, honor, fulfilled desires, families, God's watchfulness, His mercy and pity, His protection, His approval, His secret friendship, biblical insights, deliverances, promotions, and longevity.[3] This spiritual "treasure" chest (Isa. 33:6) of blessings is ours—if we fear God.

If we don't, these preferred blessings will never appear, nor will the aforementioned godly characteristics develop in our lives. Our obedience will remain slack, our praise tepid, and our worship superficial—and unacceptable to the One who seeks true worshippers. Most importantly, God will be deprived of the deep respect He so richly deserves and requests of us: "Oh, that they had such an heart in them that they would fear Me...that it may be well with them and with their children forever!" (Deut. 5:29, NKJV).

Today far too many Christians think lightly of God, sin, Christ's return, and our coming judgment. We want ministers who tell us what we want, not what we need. We judge others constantly and ourselves rarely. We take God's grace for granted and test His patience by our stubborn selfishness and sins. These visible flaws betray one invisible cause: we don't fear God! The secular world will never fear Him.

But we can. And should. Now! Peter commanded, "Fear God" (1 Pet. 2:17). In the tribulation angels will call sinners to "Fear God" and glorify Him (Rev. 14:7). Ultimately "all the ends of the earth shall fear him" (Ps. 67:7). Then why wait? It's time we fear Him.

Chapter 8

JESUS' INTERESTS

ARE YOU INTERESTED in Jesus' interests? Or do you find other matters more interesting? This subject interested the apostle Paul.

In Rome he lamented, "All seek their own, not the things which are Jesus Christ's" (Phil. 2:21). The "things" Paul speaks of are Christ's interests: "They all seek their own interests, not those of Jesus Christ" (ESV). Other translations render "things" as, "what matters to Jesus Christ" (NLT), "the work of Jesus Christ" (NCV), and "the cause of Jesus" (PHILLIPS).

Jesus' "things," or interests, speak of what's dear to His heart, what occupies His thoughts and stirs His emotions. They're what He dreams of, longs for, looks for, and focuses on. They're His goals, the ends toward which all His plans and providences are working every hour of every day. His are not mere intellectual interests.

They're consuming—He shed His blood to obtain them! Isaiah promises Christ's self-sacrifice wasn't in vain: "He shall see of the travail of his soul, and shall be satisfied" (Isa. 53:11). But how will His interests be accomplished and heart "satisfied" if His own people don't share His interests? This explains Paul's lament, "Everyone looks out for his own interests, not those of Jesus" (Phil. 2:21, NIV), and his joy at finding one young minister who shared Christ's interests.

His name was Timothy—Paul's best student, ministerial assistant, and friend. Like Paul, Timothy recognized Jesus' prime interest is His people. So Paul informed the Philippians that Timothy "genuinely" cared for "your welfare" (Phil. 2:20, ESV). Timothy focused on Christ's focus: Christians' spiritual condition. Therefore Paul appointed him as his messenger to examine, evaluate, and edify the Philippian church. He knew Timothy would faithfully serve not his own concerns but "what matters to Jesus" (v. 21, NLT).

Using Scripture as our source, let's identify some of Jesus' interests, the causes, concerns, and works that really matter to Him.

As Savior, He's passionately interested in not rejecting but redeeming the lost (2 Pet. 3:9). He came to "destroy the works of the devil" (1 John 3:8)— sin and all its deceptive, destructive influence—in our souls and societies by the power of His salvation, Word, and Spirit. He wants to save Christians from not only sin's ultimate consequences but also its present control (Matt. 1:21). He wants to see the fulfillment of His high priestly prayer (John 17) and Paul's inspired visions of the church as a holy temple, mature man, and gloriously purified bride.[1] He wants us to fulfill our commissions to preach the gospel, teach disciples, and be His witnesses worldwide.[2] He wants us to study and obey His Word and walk in His ways (spiritual life disciplines) so we'll live close to Him, sense His hand and voice, receive His correction, and follow His guidance daily. He wants to sanctify us wholly and unify us perfectly. He wants to change our motives, goals, and attitudes until we're conformed to His character "image" (Rom. 8:29).

He wants us to pursue our predestined "good works," whether vocational, professional, charitable, or ministerial (Eph. 2:10). He wants to steadily increase our faith, hope, and love (1 Cor. 13:13) and teach us to offer "true," or pleasing, worship (John 4:23–24). He wants to thoroughly test us to prove our faith, obedience, and loyalty; purify our hearts, habits, and hopes; and demonstrate His great faithfulness in our lives. He wants to revive us, personally and corporately, whenever we grow lukewarm or cold. He wants to reveal His glory—beautiful character and manifest presence and ministry—among us by His Spirit to draw and convert unbelievers (John 17:22–23). He wants to accomplish these goals in us now and then remove us before this world's seven-year final test. He also wants to reestablish God's order in society—but after, not before, He returns. Interested in these things?

If not, there's a reason. Other interests are crowding out "the things that are Jesus Christ's." Some likely distractors are money-making, pleasure, leisure, material things, business or professional ambition, seeking religious acclaim, promoting denominations or dogmas, seeking popularity or political power, institutionalism, social activism, or other personal passions and preoccupations. These concerns, causes, and crusades consume us. They captivate our thoughts, stir our emotions, sap our energies, steal our time, crowd our agendas, and usurp our dreams. We long and look for them. They matter greatly to us—but not to Jesus. I suppose Paul's still lamenting.

But over twenty-first-century, not first-century, Christians. Like Paul's peers, too many of us are obsessed with our own interests and are ignoring Christ's. To adopt His interests, we must abandon ours. Are you willing? Ready to cultivate new interests? Let's get interested, and stay interested, in Jesus' interests.

Chapter 9

GOD HAS A PLAN!

HEN THE APOSTLE Paul visited the Jerusalem church, he discovered he had a problem: his teaching had been misrepresented and many Jewish Christians doubted his ministry (Acts 21:17–26). But God had a plan.

God revealed His strategy to the church leaders: discredit the lies that discredited Paul! To do so, Paul would not just declare but openly demonstrate his loving respect for Old Testament truth and custom by helping several Jewish Christians fulfill their Nazirite vows. This would prove he wasn't against Moses or the Law, as some claimed. Paul's acceptance, without the Spirit's check,[1] implies he recognized, and the Spirit confirmed, that this was God's plan. Paul knew that for every divine purpose God has a plan to achieve it.

God's purposes are revealed in biblical promises and prophecies. As we walk closely with God and study His Word, He reveals His purposes. As we subsequently seek God's plans, He reveals them—specific strategies to accomplish His purposes. Like God, His plans are irresistible. The Bible repeatedly shows them prevailing over all problems, persecutions, and postponements.

God had a plan to prepare Joseph for high office, and neither his brothers' betrayal, his low status (as slave, prisoner), nor his two-year delay in prison could stop it. God had a plan to save Egypt—and Jacob's children and coming Messiah—from a great famine and revealed and executed it through Joseph. God had a plan to release the Hebrews from Egyptian slavery and accomplished it through Moses, despite Pharaoh's obstinate resistance. God had a plan for Israel's worship and showed Moses the tabernacle's design, service, and priesthood to facilitate it. God had a plan for Israel to conquer Jericho and told it to Joshua: "March around it." God had another for taking Ai: "Set an ambush!"

Later, God had a plan for His temple and revealed who was to build it, when, where, and with what materials. God had a plan for Jesus' birth and timed Caesar's tax registration so Mary would give birth in Bethlehem, not Nazareth. God had a plan to protect young Jesus from Herod's murderous plot by sending Joseph's family to Egypt. God had a plan to get Israel ready for Jesus' ministry and sent John to "prepare

19

his ways" (Luke 1:76). God had a plan to grow the early church dynamically and sent the Spirit's power to increase its miracles and membership. God had a plan to expand the church throughout the world and used its first persecution to initiate this (Acts 8:1–4). God had a plan to maximize Paul's ministry in the key city of Ephesus and so delayed his visit there until Paul and the Ephesians were perfectly ready. Church history continues showcasing God's plans.

God had a plan to reform the medieval church from its sins and errors and raised Wycliffe, Hus, Luther, and others to accomplish it. God had a plan to periodically revive the reformed church and sent Pietists, Moravians, Methodists, and the Great Awakenings to fulfill it. In these last days of the church age God has a plan to reawaken, teach, train, test, and transform us before Christ appears, and He already has remnant ministers, ministries, and churches prepared and in place, ready to lead. No human resistance will thwart His plan. No matter how confusing, stubborn, strange, mean-spirited, demonic, or seemingly successful the opposition, if we continue trusting and obeying His plan, God will complete it.

Indeed, by resisting God's plans, our enemies only further them! As Paul obeyed God's plan in Jerusalem, unbelieving Asian Jews (not the Judean Christians Paul's actions were intended to influence) falsely accused Paul of sacrilege and caused his arrest by the Romans. But God used this persecution to serve His larger plan to send Paul to Rome! The Jews' subsequent prosecution of Paul resulted in the Romans housing, feeding, transporting, and guarding him all the way to Rome (Acts 21–28). So instead of foiling Paul's ministry, they furthered it. But this doesn't always happen.

God has no plans for our selfish purposes. As long as we chase our prideful desires and vain dreams in life, work, or ministry, God's only plan is, "Stop and return to My purposes and plans!" Have you abandoned your purposes yet?

Are you pursuing God's purposes in your family, church, ministry, or work? Do you know His plan? Pray till He reveals it, and then pursue it. Will opposition come? Yes, like Paul you'll meet obstinate critics, perplexing problems, situational impasses, persisting needs, and surprising defeats. But if you patiently pray and persist in God's plan, it will ultimately succeed. It must, because "God is faithful" (1 Cor. 10:13).

So cheer up: God has a plan!

Chapter 10

How He Makes Champions

*S*HOW ME A champion, and I'll show you a challenger. Show me a great champion, and I'll show you a skilled, strong, focused, relentless challenger. Why am I so sure?

That's how champions are made, whether on the fields of war or sport. Or Christianity. In every generation challengers develop new champions. As they repeatedly clash, challengers help make champions great and great champions even greater. How?

Challengers push champions to be their best, because they realize if they don't, they'll be defeated. So by becoming smarter, stronger, and more skillful, challengers drive champions to improve themselves by learning, self-discipline, and training. By occasionally defeating champions, challengers stun and force them to humbly self-examine, face their weaknesses, and eliminate them. Challengers' increasingly effective efforts force champions to increasingly summon more strength, new strategies, and every supplemental aid available. Ultimately it takes a champion's best effort—everything he (or she) has—to best his challengers. Thus their persistent pursuits have been a catalyst for his improvement, driving him to seek a higher level of performance and tenacity. His adversary's quest to defeat him has made him undefeatable—a champion!

Wherever we find famous champions in war, sports, or biblical and Christian history, we also find formidable challengers. And the grittier the challenger, the greater the champion.

In war, the Persians challenged the Greeks until Alexander decisively conquered them. The Carthaginians harried Rome until its legions became legendary. The Muslims bullied the Spanish for centuries, until the battle-hardened Conquistadors defeated them and turned to the New World. The Spanish Armada repeatedly challenged England's navies until they emerged masters of the seas.

In sports, Arnold Palmer was pressed to golfing excellence by Jack Nicklaus. The Green Bay Packers earned football fame by subduing tenacious Cowboys, Vikings, and Bears. Joe Frazier gave Muhammad Ali all he could handle.

In biblical history, Moses' long, tedious standoff with the Pharaoh made him a wiser, stronger, more patient leader. Elijah's greatness was forged by the constant pressure of Ahab's and Jezebel's resistance. King Saul's relentless assaults made David a more confident believer, effective warrior, and gracious king. The Samaritan's persistence and craft drove Nehemiah to become even more persistent and discerning.

In Christian history, Paul's debates with the heretical Judaizers only made him a sharper, more effective teacher. Church leaders' rejection of John Wesley's teaching helped make him and his lay preachers champions of English and American evangelicalism. Billy Graham's rejection by certain small-minded factions of fundamentalists only made him a stronger, larger-than-life evangelical leader. We call these biblical champions "overcomers."[1]

Jesus repeatedly promised the Christians in Asia Minor, and us, a wide array of enduring rewards and honors if we become overcomers: "To him that overcometh will I..." (Rev. 2:7).[2] Like a master craftsman, God uses "all things," including a wide array of human tools, to make overcomers: "We know that God causes all things to work together for good to those who love God, to those who are called according to His purpose" (Rom. 8:28, NAS). If you devotedly love, obey, and follow the Lord, He wants to make you an overcomer. That's why He has sent adversaries and critics into your life to challenge your devotion, faith, love, and commitment to your God-given gifts and work.

Who's challenging you? Questioning your knowledge—and driving you to study Scripture more? Trying to hinder your spiritual walk—and prompting you to walk with a steadier trust and obedience? Tempting you—and driving you to pray more for the grace of holiness? Trying to distract you with entangling interests and causes—that make you refocus on Jesus and His will? Battering you with offenses—that force you to practice forgiveness more perfectly? Occasionally defeating you—and awakening you from the deadly sleep of pride, indifference, or indolence? Probing you with criticisms—that prompt you to reexamine your heart, change your attitudes, and confess sins quicker? Determined to bring you down—thereby provoking you to be more determined to rise above them? Pressuring you relentlessly—yet only making you more peacefully efficient at committing your anxieties to God in prayer?

Whoever these challengers are, they're no accident. God put them in your life for His higher purposes: to get everything out of you He put in you—your very best in Christ—and propel you to the highest levels of faith, knowledge, grace, and faithful service. If God has given you one persistent challenger, He wants to make you a champion; if two or three, a great champion.

Let Him! Forgive your challengers, embrace their presence in your life, and continue overcoming, thanking God that you know how He makes champions.

Chapter 11

GREATNESS IN GALATIA

OOKING FOR AN example of spiritual greatness? Extraordinary Christian character? Look no further. Paul's first mission to Galatia spotlights spiritual greatness (Acts 13–14).

Though divinely appointed, Paul's Galatian ministry was tough going. In Antioch the leading citizens expelled Paul and Barnabas. In Iconium the city leaders plotted to execute them. In Lystra they succeeded, stoning Paul! Yet, amazingly, Paul revived and persevered, walking fifty miles to Derbe, where, finally, he and Barnabas experienced fruitful ministry without persecution. There they made a great decision.

Despite deadly opposition on their first visit, "They returned again to Lystra, and to Iconium, and Antioch" (Acts 14:21). This choice demonstrated great courage. Cowards would never return to enemy-infested territory. It also showed great faith. They believed that God's grace would see them through whatever opposition arose, as it had before. Furthermore, they evinced great commitment. They were utterly dedicated to their kingdom-building work, whatever their personal cost. Their motivation also was the greatest.

Pure love moved them. Their passion for Christ prompted them to adopt His passion: "Feed my sheep" (John 21:15–17). Young in the faith, unorganized, inexperienced in suffering, and without strong leadership, the newly converted Galatian Christians were highly vulnerable to Satan's wiles. Paul and Barnabas were the only ones nearby who could give these exposed lambs spiritually mature oversight, edifying teaching, and strong comfort in suffering. So like their Chief Shepherd, these under-shepherds were "moved with compassion" to, with great risk and without rewards or honors, nurture these unshepherded sheep. This was great leadership in action.

On this second pass through Lystra, Iconium, and Antioch, theirs was surely an underground ministry. Banned from all three cities, they kept close to the house churches where they lodged and ministered, avoiding public exposure. This demonstrated great wisdom, specifically discretion.

Discreetly but diligently, from house to house, they discharged their ministerial duties: "confirming" (rooting) the Christians in their faith by teaching, counsel, prayer, and fellowship meals; warning them that they too would face "much persecution"; exhorting them to "continue" in their walk and work; pointing them to hope, not in Rome's present empire, but in God's coming "kingdom"; appointing "elders" to lead in every church; and by prayer committing them to the Chief Shepherd's faithful care (Acts 14:22–23). This was great ministry.

And a great witness. Paul and Barnabas embodied the great Lord, love, truth, and lifestyle they preached. We naturally consider Paul's great character first, because he was the mission leader (Acts 13:13), primary speaker (vv. 16, 45; 14:9, 12), miracle worker (vv. 9–10), stoning victim (v. 19), and most famous apostle. Most teachers, therefore, focus on Paul's physical courage, indomitable spirit, undeterred perseverance, and unquenchable love. And rightly so! But Barnabas also showed greatness.

When Mark abandoned Paul (Acts 13:13), Barnabas persevered, facing every threat, slander, and violent attack alongside Paul. Scripture asserts that in Antioch, Paul "and Barnabas" were bold (v. 46) and persecution arose against Paul "and Barnabas" (v. 50). Both were ignominiously "expelled" (v. 50), and Iconium's angry leaders fully intended to stone not just Paul but "them" (Acts 14:5). Barnabas also surely helped nurse Paul through his brutal injuries and assist him on the long walk to Derbe (v. 20). And that's not all.

Barnabas' greatness is seen chiefly in his humility. Before their mission, Barnabas was apparently the presiding elder in the Antioch (Syria) church and Paul a junior leader (Acts 13:1–2). Today, Barnabas would be a senior or lead pastor and Paul his associate pastor. Though Barnabas began their apostolic mission in this leading role (v. 7), after leaving Cyprus their roles changed: Paul became the leader and Barnabas his associate. Luke describes them as "Paul and his company" (v. 6). Why the reversal? Both apparently remembered Paul's special call, gifting, and preparation for ministry to Gentiles (Acts 9:15, 27), and, like Christ, Barnabas humbly acquiesced in the Father's will. When proud, ambitious thoughts tempted him to resist his role, he remembered that neither his nor Paul's preferences mattered, only the Father's. His will must be done and His plan followed. This was great thinking!

Specifically, Barnabas was "spiritually minded" (Rom. 8:6), neither envying nor resenting but loving Paul. During their mission and after returning to Antioch (where Barnabas had presided), rather than competing, Barnabas complemented Paul. This sweet humility fostered church unity and mission success. This greatness was spiritual, hidden from undiscerning eyes yet treasured by Jesus. For his meekness, Barnabas will be rewarded equally with Paul (Matt. 10:41).

This greatness in Galatia was nothing less than Christ's character manifesting in Paul and Barnabas. Do you love their great decisions, courage, love, leadership, ministry, wisdom, witness, humility, and thinking? Then live it! Manifest your own greatness in Galatia.

Chapter 12

LIKE THE CORNERSTONE

SCRIPTURE REPEATEDLY IDENTIFIES Jesus as the church's Cornerstone: "Jesus Christ Himself being the chief cornerstone" (Eph. 2:20, NKJV).[1] Let's consider ancient cornerstones and what they reveal about Jesus, the church, and us.

Cornerstones founded buildings. They completed foundations and began their superstructures. Jesus' life, teachings, and works founded or established the Christian way that began officially at Pentecost. Are you following your Founder and His established ways of living and ministering? Are you building on His rock-solid Word or this world's shifting, sandy ideas?

Cornerstones supported. Like foundations, of which they were a part (1 Cor. 3:11), cornerstones supported the structures resting on them. After establishing His church at Pentecost, Jesus continued supporting it by providing its needs and answering its prayers. Are you leaning and resting on His faithful help for all your needs and problems (Phil. 4:6–7)?

Cornerstones prophesied. If able to speak, they would have announced, "A structure will be built on me according to the architect's design." Jesus prophesied, "Upon this rock I will build my church" (Matt. 16:18), and declared believers would be His witnesses "unto the uttermost part of the earth" (Acts 1:8). After Pentecost the apostles began fulfilling the Cornerstone's prophecies and the Architect's (Father's) plan for His "holy temple" (Eph. 2:21). Do you know Jesus' prophesies and plans for His church? Believe they'll be fulfilled before He appears?

Cornerstones joined. Whether set dry or mortared, they joined the three main sections of a building—its foundation and two primary walls. Thus they held buildings together. When obeyed, Christ's great commandment, "That ye love one another; as I have loved you," binds churches together (John 13:34). Are you strengthening or breaking your church's "bond of perfectness" (Col. 3:14)?

Cornerstones located. They assigned buildings particular locations. Wherever they were set, buildings rose. Jesus ministered and suffered "in Zion [Israel]" (Isa. 28:16), God's natural kingdom. Soon His spiritual kingdom, the church, arose there. Do you understand your placement in Christ's spiritual kingdom? Your position "in Christ," enthroned in "heavenly places" (Eph. 2:6)? Are you longing for heavenly ends or earthly things (1 John 2:15–17)? Exercising or ignoring your prayer authority in Jesus' name?

Cornerstones bestowed honor. Often inscribed with the construction date, builder's name, or references to one's deity, they brought a sense of distinction or honor. We're highly honored to be associated with Christ's name and elected to His church! Are you honoring Him by Bible study, obedience, thanksgiving, Communion, cross carrying, and confidence that He'll honor you for so honoring Him by your discipleship?[2]

Cornerstones were associated with prayers and sacrifices. They were sometimes laid with dedicatory prayers and rites.[3] Just before Jesus' sacrificial death, He prayed for the spiritual temple it would establish (John 17). Only days later His disciples' earnest prayers (Acts 1:13–14) marked the Cornerstone's heavenly dedication (exaltation). Have you studied the Cornerstone's dedicatory prayer for His temple? Are you praying it? Working for it? Ignoring it?

Cornerstones were weighty. Solid rock, they were extremely heavy and thus dangerous, even deadly, if dropped on builders' bodies or limbs. Though He desires only to build, our Cornerstone also breaks (Luke 20:18). Are you letting Him build your faith, hope, and love? Or are you forcing Him to break your stubborn pride, sins, or selfishness?

Cornerstones were level. They were carefully leveled so the walls they supported would be vertical and neither lean nor fall. Jesus our Cornerstone is perfectly level—truthful, faithful, and without deceit or error—and nothing built on His Word will fall, however severely the winds of adversity blow (Matt. 7:24–25). Are you living safely on the level—honestly, faithfully, uprightly? Or leaning dangerously with dishonesty, malice, carnality, injustice, or ungodliness, and about to fall into unbelief or judgment?

Cornerstones aligned. Once set, they determined the line or direction of the primary walls. Thus the laying of a cornerstone "was crucial because the entire building was lined up with it."[4] Wise masons never deviated from the direction the cornerstone set. Are you aligned with Christ, living in joyful, submissive conformity to His sound, sure Word and His ways, decisions, guidance, prophecies, and plans?

If so, the Cornerstone is growing in you. As you become increasingly like Him, "ye also, as living stones" (1 Pet. 2:5) will found and support kingdom works, foretell God's prophetic plan, hold relationships and churches together, help believers understand their position in Christ, honor and be honored by Christ, make sacrifices for His work, pray His will, speak weighty words that build believers' faith and break sinners' unbelief, and set a spiritually straight (upright and true) example others can safely build their lives by. So keep growing.

Be like the Cornerstone.

Chapter 13

THE VOICE ABOVE ALL OTHERS

*W*HEN OTHER VOICES challenge God's voice in your life, how do you respond? Julius, the Roman officer commanding Paul's ship, responded wrongly. His test came at a Cretan port.

Though not a perfect winter anchorage, Fair Havens was the fairest available haven for Paul's ship, a large Alexandrian grain vessel bound for Rome (Acts 27:8). Seeing a huge storm system approaching, and only hours away, the Holy Spirit's voice warned Julius through Paul that the ship shouldn't depart: "Sirs, I perceive that this voyage will be with injury and much damage" (v. 10). The voice of common sense agreed. Every mariner knew since it was now autumn, "sailing was now dangerous" in the Mediterranean (v. 9). But other voices disagreed, confusing the issue.

The voice of experience spoke first. Through the ship's "pilot" (v. 11, NIV), a seasoned nautical authority, it urged Julius to sail immediately for Phoenix, a better winter anchorage nearby. The voice of business spoke next. Through the ship's owner it agreed wintering at Phoenix—a harbor surrounded by promontories sheltering vessels from high winds—would better protect his considerable investment in the ship, cargo, and crew (v. 11). Convenience also spoke up. The mariners informed Julius that Fair Havens' "unsuitable" (v. 12, NIV), or more exposed, harbor would require more work to protect the ship from storm damage and to resupply their food from Lasea, eight miles away (v. 8). Then the voice of the majority gave counsel. "The greater part" voted "to depart" (v. 12). Finally, the voice of cautious disobedience whispered its shrewd advice. It suggested they sail for Phoenix, but within sight of land, "close by Crete" (v. 13). If Paul was right, they could still avoid being blown out to sea toward the dreaded North African (Libyan) shoals (v. 17). After all these voices spoke, Julius spoke.

Sadly, he took the last option, disregarding the Spirit's voice. Within hours, after the storm overtook them, he regretted but couldn't reverse his decision (vv. 13–15). Paul later said, "You should have hearkened unto me, and not have loosed from Crete" (v. 21). Happily, Christians don't have to repeat Julius' error.

He was once born; we're twice born. He was carnally minded; we can think spiritually. He wasn't Spirit-filled; we can be. He didn't have God's Word; we do. God hadn't spoken to him; He speaks to us. He didn't know God's ways; we can. He didn't fellowship with God; we can. He never experienced the Spirit's checks; we have. His discernment was dull; ours can be sharp.

If when facing issues we don't know God's will, we should prayerfully seek it until He speaks—through the Bible, circumstances, open or closed doors, counselors, pastors, prophets, or His "still, small voice" in our hearts (1 Kings 19:12). Once sure He's spoken, we should obey immediately. "After he had seen the vision, immediately we endeavored to go...assuredly gathering that the Lord had called" (Acts 16:10). Then we'll know He'll accompany and assist us, however difficult our path.

Acts 27 illustrates, however, that when other voices—common sense, experience, business, convenience, impatience, greed, family, friends, the majority, or cautious disobedience—challenge God's, if we obey them, we'll meet unnecessary troubles. So we mustn't yield! "Trust in the LORD with all thine heart, and lean not unto thine own understanding" (Prov. 3:5). David vowed, "I shall not be moved" (Ps. 62:6). Many have held fast.

Micaiah rejected the voice of the majority of ministers and told Ahab the truth. Esther rejected her fearful reasonings to obey God's call to save her people. Isaac overruled his business interests to obey God's call to accept quietly the Philistines' unjust use of his wells. Peter abandoned the shores of cautious disobedience when Jesus' challenged him, "Launch out into the deep" (Luke 5:4). Finney disregarded the voice of experience to boldly practice new evangelistic methods the Spirit revealed. Why? They discovered that the love and wisdom of God's voice surpasses that of any other voice.

Omniscient, the Spirit knows our future. Just as He foresaw a great storm about to overtake Paul's ship, so He knows our "weather" tomorrow—and every tomorrow! Eternally wise, His voice ever calls us to the smartest path, never erring. Faithful, it never deceives. Loving, it always serves not only God's but also our and our children's best interests. By obeying God's voice, even the simplest believer becomes a wise overcomer whose decisions always please God, build his church, and bless others. Listen, God is calling.

"Obey my voice, and I will be your God" (Jer. 7:23). Learn from Julius' error and respond correctly. Stay in "Fair Havens"—God's present will. Don't yield to other voices. Wisely, obey the voice above all others.

Chapter 14

MESSIAH PLEASERS

RILLIANT YET SIMPLE, the apostle Paul discerned Christians are either man pleasers or Messiah pleasers. There's no middle ground.

After rebuking the Galatians for exchanging the true gospel for a false one, and anathematizing those who misled them, Paul asked, "For do I now seek the favor of men, or of God? Or do I seek to please men? For if I yet pleased men, I should not be the servant of Christ" (Gal. 1:10). One version reads:

> Do you think I am trying to make people accept me? No, God is the One I am trying to please...If I still wanted to please people, I would not be a servant of Christ.
>
> —GALATIANS 1:10, NCV

Paul was comparing his motives with those of the "Judaizers," Jewish Christians with Pharisaic backgrounds who taught Gentiles had to be circumcised and keep Jewish customs (thus "Judaized") to be saved (Acts 15:1). Their grace-plus-works salvation implied Jesus' sacrifice on the cross wasn't enough. To be right with God, Gentiles also needed to keep Jewish laws and traditions. Paul quickly discerned this heresy—and its advocates' motive. They desired to please not Christ but men, specifically, the Pharisees, and, thus approved, avoid their persecution: "They [Judaizers] constrain you to be circumcised...lest they should suffer persecution for the cross" (Gal. 6:12).

Paul, however, asserted he wasn't man-pleasing. The Judaizers claimed Paul didn't require Gentile Christians to convert to Judaism because he was trying to appease their traditionally anti-circumcision, Greco-Roman views. But Paul's gospel was motivated not by timidity but truth—Christianity *was* a totally new thing, not merely a new twist to Judaism.[1] From the first, Paul had had only one aim in ministry: pleasing Messiah Jesus! Some teachers taught what they wanted. Others taught what the people wanted. Still others, like Paul, taught what Christ wanted. If their hearers were displeased, well, that was acceptable, as long as Jesus approved their message. Why? They were His "servants" entirely (Gal. 1:10).

Typically, servants' loyalties and objectives are one: to please their masters! Therefore, Christ-pleasing is at the heart of our Christian servantship and Christ's lordship in our lives. As Jesus did everything to please His Father (John 8:29), we should always seek first what pleases Jesus and do it—if we call Him Lord and ourselves His servants! Then, no matter who's dissatisfied with us, we'll remain satisfied, knowing Jesus is pleased.

If we don't do this, we'll live on an emotional roller coaster—up when we have our way and down when we don't, up when others are happy with us and down when they're not. And we can't honestly say we're serving Jesus. Instead, like the Judaizers, we're serving ourselves—always trying to appease people so they won't turn and trouble us. At base, therefore, man-pleasing is self-pleasing. We appease others so they won't reject, criticize, or oppose us.

But man-pleasing creates its own troubles. Specifically, it brings burdens, bondage, torment, discontent, distraction, and, ultimately, spiritual failure.

Seeking everyone's favor burdens us with much extra work and anxiety. We spend lots of energy, money, and time ensuring they're pacified, yet even then we worry they may still disapprove. This puts us in bondage. Those we must please become our masters and we their approval-slaves. In every situation we're bound to do whatever they want—and thus kept from doing whatever God wants. We're also tormented. Even when we satisfy people today, we're constantly tortured by the dread of displeasing them tomorrow, the day after, or the next, and this "fear involves torment" (1 John 4:18, NKJV).

Frustrated and joyless, we're discontent. We feel we can never do enough to have our human master's full, lasting approval—and rest. Thus ours is a distracted life. We've lost sight of our central purpose—pleasing our Messiah—and have refocused on a convenient satanic substitute: seeking people's favor. This distraction leads to spiritual failure. Focused on pleasing others, we never discover and complete the "course" of service Christ appoints for us (2 Tim. 4:7). Ultimately, at the judgment, we'll be unpraised and unrewarded while single-minded, Christ-pleasing servants receive His glowing commendations and rich rewards. Why? Like Paul, they're committed Messiah pleasers. Paul had it right.

Everybody's seeking somebody's favor. Our need for approval is innate, constant, and strong. The only question is, whose favor will we seek? Man pleasers dream the impossible dream—that they can keep everyone happy! Messiah pleasers ponder and chase only one vision—to do what Jesus wants and live to hear Him say, "Well done, thou good and faithful servant" (Matt. 25:21). Don't waste your life slavishly appeasing people. Be brave.

Be a Messiah pleaser!

Chapter 15

THOSE POSITIVE CHECKS!

*T*HE APOSTLE PAUL asserted, "As many as are led by the Spirit of God, they are the sons of God" (Rom. 8:14). Or, "The true children of God are those who let God's Spirit lead them" (NCV). So to live and labor like God's "true children," and His Son, we must respond to divine guidance. For that, we must recognize spiritual "checks"—God's quiet warnings not to continue in a particular path, activity, calling, or relationship.

These inward restraints are subtle, yet undeniable; intuitive, not intellectual; sensed, not calculated; revelations, not reasonings; of the Spirit, not of ourselves; ignorable, but persistent. We usually view these inspired urgings to stop or change course as being negative since they contradict our choices and spoil our plans. But they're neither negative nor dishonoring.

Checks don't imply we're ignorant, carnal, rebellious, or divinely disapproved. God checks even His wisest, godliest, and most spiritual children. Jesus' handpicked apostle to the Gentiles, Paul, was checked during an apostolic mission not once but twice. Abraham's son of promise, Isaac, was checked while attempting to relocate in Egypt. The extraordinarily wise leader Joseph was checked when he objected to his younger son receiving Isaac's blessing. The mighty prophet Samuel was checked when he expressed confidence that God had chosen Eliab, not David, as king. Joseph of Nazareth, God's chosen guardian for Jesus, was checked while contemplating divorcing his shamefully pregnant espoused wife, Mary.[1] If God checked these outstanding saints, He'll surely check us. Their experiences prove there's no shame in receiving checks, only in rejecting them!

Why would any reasonable Christian reject divine checks? Yes, they spoil our plans, contradict our choices, and frustrate our desires. But from God's perspective they're thoroughly positive and praiseworthy. Consider these four check-facts.

First, checks redirect us. When God closes doors and we humbly accept the check and prayerfully wait on Him, He always leads us on to an open door. That's why He checked us! He had another path, work, friend, or mission in mind and wanted us to discover it. Paul thought of going to Asia, but God checked! So he started trekking toward Bithynia, but, again, God checked! After waiting for God's direction, God graciously flung open a new door: "Come over into Macedonia" (Acts 16:9)! Now God's will was clear. That the envisioned Macedonian was urgently "begging" help (v. 9, NIV) convinced Paul God wanted him in Macedonia—"immediately" (v. 10). Similarly, God's check led Joseph to understand God's greater favor rested on Ephraim, not Manasseh. It led Samuel to see that David, not Eliab, was God's anointed. And it led Joseph to discern God wanted him to marry, not divorce, Mary. Though mysterious, all these checks were reasonable. God's checks are always not only reasonable but also perfectly wise.

Second, checks reassure us. God promised to check us when we turn away from His will: "Thine ears shall hear a word behind thee, saying, This is the way, walk ye in it, when ye turn to the right hand [or]...the left [leaving God's will]" (Isa. 30:21). This promise implies God constantly watches over us, as an attentive, loving father does a toddler, to alert us whenever we leave His perfect plan. How comforting it is to realize Father is watching! When checks come, we should feel loved, secure, and thankful that Father has rejected our proposed paths. When He opens doors, we should pursue them joyfully, confident that, in His loving wisdom, Father has chosen them and will therefore accompany, protect, provide for, and assist us.

Third, checks are always amazingly timely, coming just before, after, or as we err. The Spirit restrained Paul just before he departed to minister in Asia and, later, just after he left for Bithynia, necessitating a reversal of course (Acts 16:6, 7–8). Like Paul's, our checks are timed with great precision.

Fourth, checks are personalized, coming in ways we are individually most inclined to recognize. For instance, by:

- Irrecoverable loss of inner peace
- Bible verses brought to mind or quickened in reading
- Pastors' or elders' counsels, or friends' exhortations
- Visions or dreams (Gen. 20:3)
- Prophecy[2]
- Unrelenting inner convictions
- Persisting unfavorable circumstances (Rev. 3:7)

Why so many ways? We're all different and taught or inclined to prefer different divine methods. So God graciously uses the ways we best understand individually.

Do you now understand how positive God's checks are? Redirecting, reassuring, timely, and personalized, they're nothing but good. They contradict our choices, but reveal God's. They frustrate our plans, but fulfill His. Obeying these inspired restraints marks us as God's true, Spirit-led children. That's all positive.

So start praising God for those positive checks.

Chapter 16

APOSTOLIC ANGER MANAGEMENT

EPLORE OR DENY it, everybody gets angry, often daily. Even God is "angry with the wicked every day" (Ps. 7:11). So the question isn't if but when and why we'll become irritated—and how we'll manage it.

The apostle Paul advised us, "Be ye angry, and sin not; let not the sun go down upon your wrath; neither give place to the devil" (Eph. 4:26–27).[1] Knowing we all experience indignation at offenses and injustices suffered or witnessed, Paul realized our responses are crucial. We either handle these offenses or they handle us. We arrest anger or it rests in us. We conquer it and grow wiser, or it conquers us and makes us fools.

A Bible scholar, Paul understood holding anger leads to foolish behavior: "Anger rests [lodges, resides[2]] in the bosom of fools" (Eccles. 7:9, NKJV)! Fools often act rashly, not considering the consequences before acting or speaking, and therefore regularly provoke, wound, or stumble others. They're also their worst enemy. By behaving badly, they cause themselves grief, spoil their blessings, and hinder their works. This is the folly of sinners—and Christians—who let anger "rest" in them. They also displease and dishonor God.

"Human anger does not produce the righteousness God desires" (James 1:20, NLT). Always harmful, unchecked anger creates hasty decisions, sharp words, pointless arguments, and, if indulged, violent rage. If suppressed, it creates moodiness, discouragement, depression, and sometimes psychosomatic illnesses. However justified our anger may seem, we can't afford to hold it. It's destructive!

Paul commands, "Don't go to bed angry" (Eph. 4:26, GW), adding we'll give Satan "place" (v. 27, KJV) if we do. The Greek word here means "place, passage, position, possibility."[3] So holding anger gives Satan:

- Space in our souls, to hinder our spiritual growth
- A passage or corridor of access, to trouble and confuse our minds
- A position or seat of spiritual authority, to influence or control us

- A possibility or opportunity, to hinder or harm us and others through us

In this condition, instead of pleasing and honoring Christ, we misrepresent, disappoint, and dishonor Him and hinder His kingdom work.

"Foothold" further implies we permit Satan to put his foot on our necks and walk all over us. Why? By holding anger we disobey God and imitate the angriest rebel, Satan. By following his example, we submit to his authority. He then quickly and legally influences us to serve his malicious plans—and check God's. God intends us to be "more than conquerors" (Rom. 8:37), with our feet firmly on Satan's neck, trampling him daily by rising above his opposition, snares, and temptations. Paul warns us to never indulge anger, especially unforgiveness, lest we reverse this plan and give Satan the "advantage" (2 Cor. 2:11), an "opportunity to work" (Eph. 4:27, ISV), or "a way to defeat you" (NCV). So we must never indulge or suppress but ever stop our anger. Every time. And quickly! How?

When openly or inwardly angry, privately acknowledge it. Telling yourself the truth liberates you from self-deception (John 8:32); telling God brings forgiveness (1 John 1:9). Recall God's key biblical commands regarding anger: "Fret not thyself [at evildoers, evil deeds]" (Ps. 37:1). Most importantly, "Cease from anger, and forsake [abandon] wrath" (v. 8). To "cease" is to halt, disallow, quench, terminate! To "forsake" is to walk away and not return. With conviction, think and say, "I *refuse* to hold anger!" This submission to God's Word, combined with your determined confession to disallow anger, saves you from anger's power[4]—and Satan's foothold! Immediately you're free, in the Spirit, your foot on Satan's neck, and walking all over his crafty plans, hidden pits, alluring temptations, and cruel persecutions. If personally wronged, forgive your offenders, abandoning your desire for revenge and right to retaliate. God will confirm your obedience is complete by giving you His peace. When angry thoughts return, "[cast] down imaginations" (2 Cor. 10:5) by quietly repeating this simple, scriptural process. Then anger can't manage you; you'll manage it! For total victory, always face why you're angry.

"If you are angry, be sure that it is not a sinful anger" (Eph. 4:26, PHILLIPS). If truly wronged, your initial anger is justified—though, as stated, you must not hold it. But if you're angry "without a cause" (Matt. 5:22), acknowledge it. For instance, if "soon [quickly] angry" (Prov. 14:17), you may have already been irritated about something beforehand. Other common causes of unjustified anger are envy, pride, unmercifulness, impatience, greed, selfishness, and so forth.[5] If you don't humbly confess these sinful angers, you'll deceive yourself. And give Satan place.

Don't do that! Ever! Abandon folly and practice apostolic anger management.

Chapter 17

THE RECORD KEEPER

AUL INFORMED THE Philippians, "God is my record" (Phil. 1:8, KJV). Or "God knows," God "is my witness," or God "can testify."[1] Thus Paul affirmed God knew his record, that he sincerely loved the Philippians, and would testify of it.

God often testified about His people in the biblical record. He gave witness of Job's righteousness, Abraham's faithfulness, King Saul's disobedience, the Israelites' idolatry, and Eli's permissiveness.[2] Having studied under Gamaliel, Paul knew these divine testimonies were on the record. They may have been on his mind when he wrote, "God keeps my records too," or "God is my record keeper." Why is this important?

Through the centuries this world's records of the lives and works of God's servants have often been inaccurate. This world's prince—the "father" of lies (John 8:44)—often inspires unfair descriptions of the children of truth.

To this day Jewish records declare Jesus a false messiah, His resurrection a hoax, and His disciples deluded. The Roman Catholic Church's histories wrote up some pre-Reformation dissenting groups as heretics, misrepresenting their beliefs and destroying their writings, when they were in fact heroes. The same Roman annals characterize Wycliffe, Hus, Luther, Tyndale, and other enlightened reformers as subversive troublemakers! Beside religious records, there are legal and historical ones.

Human justice systems occasionally produce injustice. Thus criminal records are sometimes criminally wrong. I'm sure somewhere there's an ancient Egyptian papyri describing Moses as a disloyal royal son banished for murder and treason. Persian law once described the Jews as hopelessly lawless (Esther 3:8). Rome's archives stated Jesus, Peter, and Paul were executed, and John banished, for treason. Roman historians described the early Christians as arsonists, unpatriotic, and antisocial. England's courts twice adjudged John Bunyan a lawbreaker worthy of prison. Recently DNA evidence has proven innocent many Americans pronounced guilty by shoddy prosecution.[3] Other courts have declared suspects innocent who should have been incarcerated. In civil suits, divorces, and custody actions the right side sometimes gets the wrong judgment. And we could give more examples of flawed humans writing flawed records. Besides these, there are unofficial records kept daily in the court of public opinion.

Often Christians are grossly misunderstood and misjudged when in fact they're innocent—or not at all like their unflattering description. Jesus pronounced us blessed and instructed us to "rejoice" when "all manner of evil" is spoken against us "falsely, for my sake" (Matt. 5:11–12).[4] Sometimes our bitter adversaries say or do things that look good in the unofficial public record only to win favor and turn others toward them—and against us. They've forgotten that God keeps His own records. They don't believe He knows their motives or will eventually reckon with them, so they attack committed Christians without hesitation: "Suddenly do they shoot [bitter words] at him and fear not" (Ps. 64:4). Today unsubstantiated rumors are posted all over social media websites, as the Internet has now become the de facto records vault for the court of public opinion. Now back to Paul.

Paul was a man often grossly misrepresented in religious, legal, and social courts. False apostles swore his apostleship, not theirs, was false. Philippian occultists alleged he and Silas, not they, were corrupting their city. One Roman governor publicly pronounced him insane. The Athenian intelligentsia dismissed him as an unintelligent babbler. The Maltese public misjudged him as a murderer. Jewish leaders alleged he denounced their law and desecrated their temple. How blessed he was to know that God, not these people, keeps the records that count!

His affirmation gives us another triumphant confession. With David we joyously confess, "God is my light," "my strength," "my fortress," and "my rock" (Ps. 27:1; 31:3). Now with Paul we declare, "God is my record keeper," and breathe in new confidence and hope.

When misrepresented, officially or unofficially, we need not fear or be discouraged. Our heavenly Father knows everything—our actions, words, and motives, and also those of our adversaries.[5] He knows how we've privately responded to His Word's high standards and His Spirit's calls, leadings, and checks—and been slandered or misunderstood for doing so. He recalls the crosses and thorns we've accepted for His sake and all the pain and grief they've caused. He remembers all the gifts, prayers, and sacrifices of praise we've offered Him. He has witnessed our perseverance in the duties, works, and ministries He has assigned us. It's all written in His records. One day He'll vindicate us, convict our accusers, and set the earthly record, however long and maliciously twisted, straight. And His record will stand. Forever!

So if you're being misjudged, follow Paul's example and Jesus' instruction. Rejoice that you know and trust the Record Keeper.

Chapter 18

DREAMING…

*W*HEN ISRAEL'S CAPTIVES returned, the psalmist exclaimed, "We were like them that dream" (Ps. 126:1). What induced this dreamlike state? Who were these "captives"? Where had they been?

They were Jews returning from the seventy-year Babylonian captivity. The psalmist recalls them coming home to Jerusalem to rebuild their lives, temple, capital, and worship. Those experiencing this, including the psalmist, were so overjoyed they didn't know if they were awake or dreaming!

Similarly many postmodern Christians, especially in America, have been long held by worldliness, sin, or selfishness. For these stubborn faults God has exiled us from "Zion"—our heavenly, close walk with Jesus—to "Babylonia," a spiritually distant, fruitless life serving false gods and values. But, like the Jews, we'll soon come home to God and His truth, ways, and eternal purposes. This last-days revival will be so wonderful we'll be "like them that dream."

Our dreams, whether night visions or daydreams, reveal things about us. While sometimes meaningless, dreams also expose suppressed emotions and ardent hopes. In trouble on earth, Jacob dreamed for a ladder of salvation to heaven. Full of himself, Nebuchadnezzar envisioned a dazzling image of his greatness. Humble and hungry for insights to bless his people, Daniel dreamed of their trials and triumphs in the end times. Eager to please his father's God, Joseph envisioned his heavenly Father's grand plan for his life.

God often reveals His plans, prophecies, guidance, and correction through dreams. Peter's vision unveiled God's plan to accept Gentiles. A Midianite soldier's dream foretold his nation's impending defeat by Gideon's army. Joseph's dreams guided Mary and Jesus to Egypt and back. Elihu asserted God uses dreams to dissuade people from wrong paths.[1] Yet some err because of their dreams.

They envision wrong purposes and goals. They aspire only for riches, power, popularity, worldly achievements, pleasures, or other purely selfish ends. Never do they envision God's wide and wonderful will for His people and world. Let's be different. Let's do a little dreaming after God's own heart: What will it be like when Christians fully come home to Jesus?

I dream revived Christians won't live for income or assets. We'll seek spiritual riches—richness in biblical insight, fullness of the Spirit, and trust in Christ's unfailing provision, guidance, and grace. We'll abandon all our prejudices. We'll love, respect, and receive every Christian, regardless of their race, socioeconomic standing, nationality, occupation, education, or gender. Denominationalism won't hinder us. Scripturally minded, we'll affirm the universality of Christ's body and deny any petty partisanship needlessly dividing it. We'll address but not obsess over political or nationalistic issues. We'll focus instead on kingdom goals, values, and labors.

Spiritually minded, we'll not envy individuals, pastors, churches, or ministries. We'll all respect, assist, and pray for each other, no longer comparing and competing for religious results. We'll emphasize God's Word and Spirit. Scripture will rule us, and the Spirit and His gifts will teach, guide, correct, and comfort us. Not craving pleasures, we'll long to fully know God and finish His will—and suffer whatever rejections and hardships come for pursuing that "mark" (Phil. 3:14). We'll focus on our blessed hope. Everything we do will be motivated by our desire to be spiritually mature, tested, and ready to leave this world to meet Jesus, and hear, "Well done...good and faithful servant" (Matt. 25:21). Undistracted by this information age, we'll crave the knowledge of God, not useless or trivial information. To gain this profound knowledge of Christ, we'll wait upon Him daily in the secret place of private prayer, Bible study, and worship.

For this distinctly different worldview and purpose we'll be opposed by secularists and unrevived Christians, who prefer living for self-will or sin. But we'll pray for strength and courageously stand, "perfect and complete in all the will of God," unmoved by Satan's wiles and works (Col. 4:12). I dream this God-vision day and night.

Yet a recurring nightmare also troubles me. Daily I see American culture sliding further into Sodom-like immorality, greed, and pride—while too many Christians, lukewarm and visionless, sleep. "Where there is no vision, the people perish" (Prov. 29:18). But this terrible dream will pass and God's inspiring vision visit.

History describes many victorious dreamers. Joseph's dream came true at last. Constantine envisioned the cross and conquered. Bunyan's dream inspired *The Pilgrim's Progress.* Martin Luther King Jr.'s dream of a prejudice-free America is growing. These visions changed our world, yet they pale before that of Christ's returning captives.

When Peter received a sudden deliverance from captivity, he didn't think it was real, "but thought he saw a vision" (Acts 12:9). We'll soon feel just like him. Just dreaming...

Chapter 19

FRIENDLY FIRE

NLIKE MILITARY PERSONNEL, most civilians are unfamiliar with the term "friendly fire." Let's examine it.

Whatever their nationality, all military units fight "the enemy"—their current adversaries. When enemies are wounded or killed by guns, bombs, artillery, missiles, drones, or hand-to-hand fighting, though sad, such losses are expected. But friendly fire isn't expected.

It occurs when combatants accidentally wound or kill their own people. Typically this happens when undergoing live-fire training, fighting at night, friendly and enemy forces intermingle, air or artillery strikes are inaccurate, or allies are mistaken for adversaries. Unfortunately, friendly fire has troubled military forces from ancient to modern times.

Understanding this, after exhorting the Galatians to walk in love (Gal. 5:14), Paul warned them, and us, of the danger of spiritual friendly fire:

> But if [instead of walking in love] ye bite and devour one another, take heed that ye be not consumed one of another.
>
> —GALATIANS 5:15

He knew Christians are called to stand and fight the "good fight" of faith (2 Tim. 4:7) by obeying God's Word, following His call, sharing the gospel, teaching Bible truth, witnessing against sin and injustice, and, clad in God's full armor, interceding for saints and sinners. Thus we fight unitedly against "the enemy"—Satan and the demonic "rulers of the darkness" (Eph. 6:12) —to enlarge, edify, and establish Christ's present kingdom, the church. But infighting ends this good fight. Instead of conquering our common foe, we become "consumed one of another" and never complete our commission for Christ and His kingdom (Gal. 5:15). Wisely Paul realized if we pull ourselves down, we do Satan's work for him and leave ours undone—to Satan's delight, God's grief, and our dishonor. So he warned us.

Spiritual friendly fire is unjustified and harmful opposition of other Christians. It typically arises when our wrong attitudes[1] toward believers, ministers, churches, or movements prompt adversarial words or acts that injure Jesus' love and unity among us.[2] These attacks spoil relationships, break unity, quench the flow of God's Spirit, and render our kingdom witness and work ineffective. Why? We're fighting the wrong enemy...and dividing God's house.

Jesus taught, "Every...house divided against itself shall not stand" (Matt. 12:25). Israel forgot this, split into two nations, and self-destructed. The church has also forgotten it. Down the centuries many Christians have fired on their own kind, as Roman Catholics persecuted the pre-Reform movements, Reformers denounced other Reformers, and later Protestants harassed other Protestants. All these self-inflicted wounds injure Christ's body. Others improve it.

When professing Christians promote fundamental error, especially concerning Christ, Scripture, or salvation, or impenitently practice clearly defined sins, we must protest to check falsehood's harmful influences and preserve the church's holiness, unity, and power. But all other infighting is friendly fire.

It occurs when we unfairly gripe and snipe at more popular ministers or churches; misjudge teachings, movements, or leaders before fully examining their beliefs and practices; reject Christians because of differences in politics, ideology, manner of worship, or form of church government; oppose them due to their nationality, race, or culture; or retaliate when they fire at us! Such misdirected religious combat ruins unity, grieves the Spirit, and weakens us in our ongoing spiritual battles.

If in minor differences of teaching or practice we honestly believe fellow Christians are wrong, we should offer biblical reproof, or pray and let God send correction in His time and way (1 John 5:16). If unsure, we should "judge nothing before the time" (1 Cor. 4:5). But we should never denounce or demonize other Christians, or shun them for such petty differences.[3] This small, simple adjustment will stop our friendly fire and leave us stronger to stand against our common enemy, Satan, and the various agents who promote his atheism, false religions, and heresies, and oppose our faith, gospel, and what the Spirit is saying and doing in the church.

Summarizing, let's no longer delight Satan, grieve God, and wound ourselves by infighting. If we're born-again, Bible-believing followers of Jesus, we're on the same side in the war of salvation. We're in the same spiritual body, under the same Lord, trusting the same Word, guided by the same Spirit, pursuing the same commission, rejected by the same world, awaiting the same Second Coming, and bound for the same eternal kingdom. So let's stop reproaching and start receiving each other. Instead of attacking and undermining, let's respect and support one another. Then we'll fight foes only, never friends. Instead of consuming each other, we'll cooperate—and complete our mission! It's time for a cessation of hostilities.

Let's make peace, not war, with our own kind and be forever free from friendly fire.

Chapter 20

THE ESCAPIST

*I*N ANCIENT TIMES magicians wowed superstitious, illiterate crowds with trickery or demonic powers. That's how Simon Magus fooled the Samaritans and Elymas influenced Cyprus' governor. The public's infatuation with magicians, mystics, and illusionists from Rasputin to Houdini to Harry Potter persists.

All these counterfeits prove there is a real article, a real jaw-dropping, crowd-wowing wonder worker. He is our God, the Escapist. No dark, secret, or fraudulent arts, His all-powerful, perfectly timed interventions bring His people "escapes"—merciful releases from distressing confinements, pitiless pursuers, or looming dangers.

His Word proclaims His unique ability to plan and execute extraordinary escapes:

> God is faithful, who will not permit you to be tempted above that ye are able, but will, with the temptation, also make the way to escape, that ye may be able to bear it.
>
> —1 CORINTHIANS 10:13

God makes ways to escape by increasing our grace in trouble or freeing us from it. Some translations emphasize His increased grace: "At the time you are put to the test, he will give you the strength to endure it" (GNT). Others stress the exits He creates: "When you are tempted, he will also provide a way out" (NIV) or "will show you a way out" (NLT). The Old Testament showcases the Escapist's amazing work.

He famously rescued Rahab, Jehoshaphat, Hezekiah, Daniel, and many others from disaster. But He helped David avoid the jaws of death more than anyone else, opening paths to safety from Philistine giants, plotting Ziphites, marauding Amalekite raiders, a javelin-throwing father-in-law, and his own rebellious son Absalom! The benevolent Escapist also released others less deserving than David. When Sodom was initially captured and again when it was destroyed, God delivered wayward Lot for Abraham's sake. His wonders continue in this age.

Perhaps the most dramatic Christian escape was Peter's angelic, unofficial "discharge" from Herod's death row (Acts 12:5–12). The Escapist's greatest beneficiary, however, was the apostle Paul. His evasions of harm

and death fill the Book of Acts, including flights from plotting city leaders, angry rabbis, rioting pagans, dark dungeons, violent temple mobs,
and conspiracies between Roman governors and Jewish Sanhedrists—
and robbers, hurricanes, shipwrecks, and snakebites! "And so...they all
escaped safely to the land" (Acts 27:44). No wonder Paul—the great es-
capee—assured us "God is faithful" to "make a way to escape"! Besides
saints, Saviors also need the Escapist's assistance.

Jesus evaded unjust arrests, traps, even attempted murder. When
His synagogue angrily tried to execute Him, the Escapist miraculously
parted the crowd, and Jesus passed through to safety. Similar encoun-
ters with deadly snares and plots followed, "but he escaped out of their
hand" (John 10:39)—until His time. But though great, these weren't the
Escapist's greatest rescues.

They are Noah's ark, the Red Sea parting, and the Rapture. The
world mocks the first, Israel glories in the second, and the third is
Christianity's blessed and purifying hope. If we watch and pray, and
walk worthily, we'll "escape all these things that shall come to pass" in
the Tribulation (Luke 21:36). But these extraordinary exoduses aren't for
everyone. Some forfeit the Escapist's help by:

- NEGLECTING FELLOWSHIP WITH GOD: "How shall we
  escape, if we neglect so great salvation" (Heb. 2:3).

- REJECTING GOD'S CORRECTION: "For if they escaped not
  who refused him that spoke on earth, much more shall
  not we escape if we turn away from Him that speaketh [to
  correct us] from heaven" (Heb. 12:25).

- SELFISHLY TURNING COWARD: "Mordecai commanded...Esther: Think not within thyself that thou shalt
  escape in the king's house [if you won't help your people]"
  (Esther 4:13).

- RETURNING TO SINFUL LIVING: "They [who revel in
  works of darkness] shall not escape" (1 Thess. 5:3; see also
  vv. 6–7).

- ARRANGING THEIR OWN ESCAPES: David's unbelief-
  induced, self-led flight into Philistia led not to escape but
  to a deceptive sixteen-month detour ending in the Ziklag
  disaster (1 Sam. 27:1–7; 30:1–2).

If, however, we don't make these errors, yet the Escapist leaves us unhelped, there's only one reason: our work is finished, as John's was when Herod seemingly ended his life prematurely. Yet even then we escape—into His presence. "Today shalt thou be with me in paradise" (Luke 23:43). That's comforting.

So if you're hindered, besieged, or embattled, take heart! If God made these ways to escape where there were none, He'll make yours. However impossible your dilemma, the Escapist will immediately empower you with His grace and ultimately release you. He's promised this in His Word: "I will even make a way" (Isa. 43:19). Ask Him persistently to do so: "Cause me to escape" (Ps. 71:2). Then expect His response.

Today obey, petition, believe, and praise the Escapist.

Chapter 21

LYDIA CHRISTIANS!

IVINELY SENT TO Macedonia, Paul was probably disappointed when his evangelism in Philippi initially converted only "a certain woman, named Lydia" (Acts 16:14). But his first European convert was special.

Lydia's attributes were outstanding. Her name means "bending,"[1] suggesting a heart inclined to submissive faith in God and a will easily bent to His. She was a God-fearer, or proselyte "who worshiped [Israel's] God" (v. 14). So she stood in awe of God and worshipped Him acceptably. She was one of "the women who resorted" to a riverside prayer meeting near Philippi every Sabbath (v. 13). So she prayed regularly. The riverside chapel she frequented was 1.5 miles from Philippi. That she regularly walked this far for prayer and fellowship shows she was deeply committed to God. "Whose heart the Lord opened" (v. 14) indicates she was personally touched by God's Spirit, or spiritually reborn, when she heard Paul's gospel, and thus enabled to understand Scripture.[2] This "opened heart" also indicates she was open-minded, and therefore not closed-, small-, or dull-minded.

Furthermore, she "attended to the things" Paul spoke (v. 14). So she was an excellent disciple, listening to, studying, and obeying God's Word, as is seen by her immediate baptism, hospitality, and request for Paul's examination (v. 15). The latter proves she wasn't judgmental—obsessively applying spiritual truths to others instead of herself (Matt. 7:1–5). Why? Nobody does both simultaneously. Those busily judging others aren't examining themselves, and those seriously examining themselves aren't preoccupied with examining others!

After conversion "she was baptized" (Acts 16:15). So she submitted to Christ's ordinances (Matt. 28:19). She also influenced "her household" (Acts 16:15) to do the same. So she was a godly leader, influencing her family and servants to receive and obey Christ. She asked Paul, "If ye have judged me to be faithful to the Lord, come into my house" (v. 15). So she humbly invited her minister's examination, ready to accept his correction when necessary. She hoped Paul would assess and declare her "faithful to the Lord." This was very likely her life goal. Paul's acceptance of her hospitality confirmed that he, and the Spirit in him, indeed found her "faithful." She asked, "Come into my house, and abide" (v. 15). So she was unusually hospitable, offering to lodge not one but four ministers—Paul, Silas, Timothy, and Luke!

She "constrained us," writes Luke, to accept her offer (v. 15), wishing or sensing it was God's will. So, like the Syro-Phoenician woman, Lydia was persistent in righteousness, or matters of God's will. Her guests were an apostolic ministry team. By ministering to ministers' needs, therefore, she was exercising her newly received gift of "helps" (1 Cor. 12:28). She continued this vital assistantship even after Paul and Silas suffered shameful public abuse. After leaving Philippi's jail, they "entered into the house of Lydia" (Acts 16:40), where, by receiving them, Lydia demonstrated rare Christian loyalty—the willingness to suffer with others who suffer shame, misunderstanding, or mistreatment for Christ's sake. The fledgling Philippian church also met in "the house of Lydia" (v. 40). So Lydia was generous, letting believers use her home several times weekly for meetings. Her vocation discloses more excellent characteristics.

She was a "seller of purple" from the "city of Thyatira" in Asia Minor (v. 14). So Lydia was a sales agent for a Thyatira-based business selling prized red or purple dye, fabrics, and garments. This and her ownership of a home large enough for four guests proves she was wealthy, implying strongly she was a successful businesswoman. Therefore she had to be intelligent, diligent, and faithful in business and financial transactions. Her previous devoutness as a Jewish proselyte is also illuminating.

The place of prayer Lydia visited regularly was situated "by a riverside" (v. 13) so she and others could regularly undergo ceremonial washings symbolizing their desire for holiness. Thus we may infer that, once converted, she continued seeking sanctification and heart purity. She regularly examined herself, confessed her sins, and "washed" in the river of Jesus' blood. She also regularly studied and obeyed God's Word to wash her soul in its rivers of living water.[3] Why did God inspire Luke to tell us all this about Lydia?

God wants more Lydia Christians—in this world but not of it! Believers of both genders find plenty to consider and emulate in Lydia's brief but telling biblical biography.

Are you bending your will to God's? Seeking sanctification to please Jesus? Deeply fearing and freely worshipping Him? Studying His Word with an open mind and judging yourself, not others? Seeking and receiving your minister's correction? Cultivating godly influence? Faithful in business? Persistent in God's will? Loyally assisting sufferers? Helping ministers?

Arise, Lydia Christians!

Chapter 22

DECLARE THE UNKNOWN GOD!

W HEN THE APOSTLE Paul arrived, Athens was a center of not only education but also religion. Filled with temples, altars, and statues of every conceivable deity, it was the world's most idolatrous city.

On every street, hill, and public square Paul saw the city "wholly given to idolatry" (Acts 17:16). Deeply distressed, he immediately began evangelizing the city's synagogue and marketplace. Some curious listeners invited him to address the Areopagus, Athens' high court governing religious issues.

Paul began with his impressions of their city:

> I perceive that in all things ye are very religious. For as I passed by, and beheld your devotions [objects for worship], I found an altar with this inscription, TO THE UNKNOWN GOD. Whom, therefore, ye ignorantly worship, him declare I unto you.
>
> —ACTS 17:22–23

Paul used this altar to the "unknown god" as a springboard for presenting the gospel to Athens' learned Epicurean and Stoic philosophers. Did he know the altar's story?

Many years earlier a deadly plague gripped Athens. Seeking relief, Athenians offered sacrifices to every known god—but the plague continued! Assuming there must be another deity yet unsatisfied, they built this "unknown god" an altar, offered sacrifice, and the plague immediately ceased.[1] Thereafter they continued this worship, hoping to prevent future catastrophes.

Thus informed or not, Paul knew the heavenly Father was the true "unknown God" who mercifully ended their plague despite their misguided sacrifices. So Paul compassionately and bravely undertook to describe Him to those who didn't know Him. Twenty centuries later we're still doing this.

Today Jesus of Nazareth is the most famous, influential, and studied figure in Western history. All Christian churches claim Him as their Savior and worship Him in fact or form. His name and acts are known throughout Christian nations, but His character, ways, purposes, and plans are not. Tragically, even millions of born-again believers worship Him "ignorantly." Why?

Like ancient Athens, modern "Athens," this pluralistic world order founded on Greco-Roman values and ways, is "wholly given" to idols— people or things that usurp God's rightful place in our hearts. On every avenue of our souls we've erected invisible shrines and altars to these distracting loves that dominate our affections, decisions, and behavior. For example, loving or trusting in money; acquiring material things; seeking fulfillment in human relationships; pride in wealth, knowledge, accomplishment, skill, or beauty; sexual gratification; athletics; entertainment; leisure and comforts; technology; religious rituals; and many others loves. In their proper place many of these are fine, but in first place, they're idols, stealing God's worship. By avidly giving them our time, thoughts, and energy, we cease seeking God. So we never know Him, because to know Him we must seek Him.

Even born-again, Spirit-filled, Bible-taught Christians don't know the "unknown God" until we abandon our dead idols and start avidly seeking, worshipping, studying, and obeying the living God. Paul challenged the Athenians to "seek" God, promising they would "find Him," since He was "not far" from them all (Acts 17:27). Are we seeking Him? Paul had to seek Christ regularly to know Him deeply and declare Him accurately. So must we. How do we seek, know, and declare God?

To seek and know Him, we must spend sufficient time with Him daily in private devotions, prayer, worship, and Bible study. We should also participate in church life, fellowship, and, whenever possible, ministry. And we should trust and obey God in our tests daily, examine ourselves frankly, confess our sins faithfully, and intercede for others persistently. Then we'll grow in the knowledge of the unknown God.

And we'll declare Him by our comprehensive witness. Specifically, by our:

- LIFE WITNESS—letting "Athenians" see us walk humbly and peacefully with Jesus daily

- LIGHT WITNESS—living by the light of "His righteousness" (Matt. 6:33), not other standards

- LOGOS WITNESS—submitting to His Word's authority in every issue and decision

- LABOR WITNESS—doing "whatever" we do "heartily, as to the Lord" (Col. 3:23)

- LIP WITNESS—telling others Jesus is the world's only divine Light (John 8:12), Savior, and coming Judge (Acts 17:31)

- LECTURE WITNESS—teaching, preaching, or counseling biblical truths in churches and public forums

- LOVE WITNESS—patiently understanding and forgiving "Athenians" who reject or mock us (Acts 17:32)

- LOYALTY WITNESS—remaining true to the "unknown One" and His truth, call, and people, even when suffering for it[2]

Christians who release these witnesses declare the unknown God to our generation's pitifully lost, blind Athenians every day. Will you be one?

Is your spirit, like Paul's, distressed over the gross idolatry filling modern-day Athens? Then seek, know, and declare the unknown God!

Chapter 23

BE BEREAN!

FTER BEING LEGALLY banned from Thessalonica, the apostle Paul was undoubtedly disappointed. But not long. He found some outstanding believers in the next city (Acts 17:10–15).

The Jews in Berea were, in Jesus' words, "good ground" for God's Word (Luke 8:15). Berea, meaning "place of many waters,"[1] had springs nearby. Like their city's terrain, the Bereans' souls were well watered— not in water fountains but in God's Word, Spirit, and ways. Consider their outstanding qualities.

They received God's Word with "all readiness of mind" (Acts 17:11). This mental readiness reveals they were excellent Bible students, hungry and zealous for truth. It further implies they were "open-minded" (v. 11, NLT). Thus they weren't closed-minded—so proud or prejudiced they assumed they already knew enough. Nor were they dull-minded—so incurious they were thoughtless. Yet their openness to new knowledge was balanced by childlike faith in the absolute truthfulness of Scripture. So they were really biblically open-minded, or open to any reasonable, factual teachings that harmonized with God's Word, but not those that contradicted or questioned it.

They "searched [studied] the scriptures daily" (v. 11) in a synagogue Bible study group. Devotionally thirsty, they read to nourish their souls while praying for insight. Intellectually curious, they longed to know everything possible about God and His purposes. They studied and researched biblical characters, events, issues, and prophecies not weekly but "daily."

Wisely they tested all teachings and teachers. After Paul proposed Jesus was Messiah, they researched "whether those things were so" (v. 11). Perfectly balanced, they were teachable, but not gullible. They listened willingly, but verified thoroughly, knowing deceiving religious spirits and wolves in sheep's clothing abounded. Their testing confirmed Paul and his gospel were true!

Together these traits made them "noble" (v. 11)—not common, ordinary, or low in character but honorable, distinguished Christians, "vessel[s] unto honor" (2 Tim. 2:21). Born again by God's Spirit and seed, they were now of "more noble" birth, or better spiritual stock, than unbelievers. They developed a noble mind by renewing their thinking with God's Word until they became "spiritually minded" (Rom. 8:6). And they built noble characters—like God's Son—by consistently obeying God in their tests of faith, patience, and endurance.[2]

Furthermore, their daily Bible studies produced a stronger faith. Better read, their faith was better fed. More nourished with spiritual milk, bread, and "meat in due season," their confidence in God became stronger than others less well fed. Consequently, not some but "many…believed," Jews and Greeks (Acts 17:12).

Strong in their faith and sure in their knowledge, they weren't swayed by errors, slanders, or fads. When deceived, disgruntled Thessalonican Jews came slandering Paul, denouncing his teaching, and "stirring up" others with lies, the Berean Christians stood loyally by God's man and message (v. 13). Unmoved, they continued helping Paul spread Jesus' truth (vv. 14–15). And their teachers were the best available.

While itching-ear churches listened to ear-tickling uncommitted, ignorant, or egotistical ministers, God gave the Bereans His wisest, humblest, and most knowledgeable instructor, Paul (v. 10). This was God's reward for their excellent scholarship and noble characters: He sent His best students His best teacher!

As their church grew up, conditions "stirred up" (v. 13), not only for their founding pastor but also for his flock. Soon Paul's persecution became theirs. Then as now, churches that diligently study, obey, and spread God's Word eventually meet "tribulation or persecution" for the Word's sake (Matt. 13:21). For living godly they're loathed greatly.[3]

But the Bereans remained hospitable. They graciously received, hosted, and protected Paul in their city for an unspecified period of time. And there's more.

They produced Christian armor bearers—believers who assist spiritual leaders in their ongoing spiritual warfare. When Paul hastily left Berea, they sent men, probably with church funds, who "brought him unto Athens," over 140 miles away (Acts 17:15). These travel companions gave Paul financial support, fellowship, and a first-class courier service. And their presence helped shield him from the pursuing Thessalonicans until he arrived safely in Athens.

All these noble characteristics are recorded so we will ponder and practice them in our lives. Are you willing to be good ground, spiritually well watered? To seek and drink the waters of God's Word and disperse them generously to others?

Then be ready for teaching, or biblically open-minded. Study Scripture daily and test teachers and teachings by its unerring truths. Since you're of noble spiritual rebirth, develop noble thinking and character. Build strong faith—be better read and better fed. Refuse to be swayed by errors, slanders, or fads. Seek and study under the best teachers. Accept difficulties arising for the Word's sake. Be hospitable, especially to ministers. Be an armor bearer.

Or, put simply, be Berean!

Chapter 24

GOD, HIS GOLD, HIS GLORY

*H*ISTORIANS AGREE THAT the New World's explorers and conquistadors had three primary motivations: God, gold, and glory. But not necessarily in this order.

These famous adventurers—Columbus, Magellan, Cortez, Pizarro, De Leon, De Soto, and others—claimed devotion to God, yet the evidence shows gold and glory were their stronger passions.

The alluring yellow metal the Americas yielded gripped and entranced them. If not this gold, then another—the precious spices of the East—spurred them to endure storms, disease, starvation, combat, shipwreck, and mutiny on long, dangerous explorations. Gold, they dreamed, would enrich their kings' and nations' treasures. And theirs.

Glory also drew them. They wanted the honor of claiming islands and continents, founding treasure cities, and above all, discovering a passage to the Spice Islands.[1] This would forever distinguish their sponsoring kings' and nations' names. And theirs.

But, double-minded, they also wanted to honor God. Steeped in Catholic tradition, the conquistadors spread their church's universal call to submission by force of arms. Though tragically wrong, they hoped this coercive evangelism would honor the pope, Peter—and the Prince of Peace, Peter, and popes!

Which motive was greatest? One simple question exposes it: Would they have risked life, limb, and liberty to do Christ's will alone, without the prospect of wealth or fame? If so, He was their motivation. If not, they were selfish, not saintly souls, and unexceptional pioneers. The exceptional ones came later.

Those great hearts were humble folks of faith who probed new lands and conquered new adversities for higher motives, such as political freedom, missionary work, or relief from religious persecution. First came the Catholic friars intent on converting Native Americans. Later English Separatists, French Huguenots, German Moravians, Baptists, and other religious pilgrims crossed the Atlantic solely to live, worship, and honor God according to their biblical convictions. But the initial explorers weren't so large hearted.

Neither were many Catholic popes and bishops. Corrupt, greedy, and perverted, Martin Luther's prime adversary Pope Leo X shamelessly justified his opulent lifestyle, "Since God has given us the papacy, let us enjoy it."[2] Recoiling from such ecclesiastical excesses, many devout monks, mystics, and reformers quietly took the road less traveled. They quested to seek and please God and conquer spiritual enemies—and forgot worldly gold and glory. Knowing and pleasing God was their gold, and they gloried in it. Many were imitating the apostles.

They remembered Peter and John testified, "Silver and gold have I none," yet were rich in spiritual power, truth, and grace (Acts 3:6). They read that Paul solicited Gentile churches' "gold," or Roman denarii, but only for a unifying love gift to the Jewish churches in Judea. Additionally, Paul quested for glory, but for God, never himself: "Unto him [God] be glory in the church" (Eph. 3:21). Thus the apostles' gold was to do God's will, and their glory lay in honoring Him.

Tragically, most conquistadors never acquired this vital spiritual viewpoint. But we can—and spend the rest of our days questing for God, His gold, and His glory.

We begin our extraordinary spiritual expedition by making God Himself, not His temporal blessings, our goal. Is knowing, pleasing, and walking and working closely with Jesus the "new world" of which we dream?

We continue by answering Jesus' call to seek spiritual gold: "I counsel thee to buy of me gold tried in the fire, that thou mayest be rich" (Rev. 3:18). Spiritual gold consists of the most precious kingdom valuables, such as proven faith, experiential knowledge of God, godly character, rich love, spiritual insight, biblical wisdom—all purified and made permanent in fiery tests.

We go further by living only to glorify Christ. We commit ourselves to honor Him daily by obedience and worship, and rejoice when He honors us with His presence, peace, and answers to prayer (1 Sam. 2:30). This is our glory, gold, and God.

And our expedition. Every Christian is a spiritual explorer and conqueror in this fallen world. Daily we sail by faith into the intimidating circumstances of our unknown future, exploring new and strange trying experiences. By steady obedience we conquer our King's most immediate enemies—our sins, selfishness, and worldliness—and then build His kingdom by sharing His Word and fame with all.

On this mission no other god rules us. Just Jesus. No other gold entrances us. Just His. No other glory motivates us. Just His. In all their travels the explorers never found this spiritually rich land. Will you seek it? Endure storms and mutinies to discover it? Conquer hindrances and distractions to explore and settle in it? Then launch today.

Seek God, His gold, His glory.

Chapter 25

Reckon, Yield, and Walk to Victory

OWEVER POWERFULLY CONVERTED, every born-again Christian eventually confronts the same frustrating problem. We have two natures struggling to control us. It's a very private, inner war between our flesh and God's Spirit.

The flesh is our old unspiritual self or sin nature with its higher and lower ways of manifesting. Refined flesh is proudly upright, religious, and educated, but worldly in values. It always serves self-will and ignores God's will. Unrefined flesh serves our lower instincts, urging us to indulge selfish desires in excessive or obviously sinful ways (Gal. 5:19–21).

The Spirit, conversely, is our new Spirit-born, spiritually minded nature—the very life of Jesus miraculously given us by grace through faith at conversion. It urges complete reliance on God and honors and serves Him by devotion, obedience, and worship. Just as Esau and Jacob grappled in Rebekah's womb, these two natures constantly wrestle to control our will and everything we think, say, and do in the body.

The apostle Paul warned us of this frustrating conflict, "For the flesh lusteth [strives] against the Spirit, and the Spirit against the flesh; and these are contrary the one to the other, so that ye cannot [always] do the things that ye would" (Gal. 5:17). He also experienced it.

At one time Paul simply couldn't understand himself. What he knew he shouldn't do, he did! And what he knew he should do, he didn't (Rom. 7:15–16). His frustration eventually grew into despair, and, exasperated, he was ready to abandon his quest for spiritual maturity: "I am carnal, sold under [hopelessly captive to] sin" (v. 14). But instead of quitting, he prayed: "Oh, wretched man that I am! Who shall deliver me?" (v. 24). God responded by delivering him and giving him a body of teaching to pass on to us regarding this universal flesh-versus-Spirit problem.

In Romans and Galatians Paul asserted it's not acceptable for us to continue obeying our sin nature.[1] Or advantageous! If we "walk in" (consistently practice) the flesh:

- We'll be led, controlled, and used by sin's master, Satan (Rom. 6:16).

- We won't be led, controlled, or used by the Spirit
  (Rom. 8:14).
- Our character won't bear the Christlike "fruit of the Spirit"
  (Gal. 5:22–23).
- We'll lose our spiritual inheritance, or eternal rewards
  (Gal. 5:21).
- We risk early death (Rom. 8:13; Gal. 6:7–8; 1 Cor. 11:30).

So instead of letting our flesh rule, we must crucify the old tyrant and crown our new spiritual nature king of our lives. How? Paul reveals a concise plan for victory over the flesh that God gave him. It's encapsulated in three simple steps: reckon, yield, and walk.

When our sin nature suggests disobeying God, whether in higher or lower ways, we "reckon" it dead. "Reckon ['consider,' NAS] ye also yourselves to be dead indeed unto sin" (Rom. 6:11). Reckoning involves remembering and confessing our faith in God's Word. We remember we died with Jesus on the cross—Paul says, "We...are dead to sin" (v. 2)—and confess aloud, "I'm dead to sin," or, "Sin is dead in me." Affirming this truth releases the Spirit's power to make it real in us. Thus by His power we deaden ("mortify," Col. 3:5) the impulses of our sin nature.

Then we yield. "Yield yourselves unto God" (Rom. 6:13). This surrender of our heart and body to God enables the Spirit to energize our will to obey. Yielding is easy. The weakest, feeblest Christian can surrender.

Finally, we walk. "Walk [on] in the Spirit, and ye shall not fulfill the lust of the flesh" (Gal. 5:16). To "walk" is to move forward or go farther. "In the Spirit" implies walking with or alongside the Spirit, neither rushing ahead nor falling behind, filled and controlled by Him. This union requires obedience to God's Spirit-inspired Word and the Spirit's spontaneous prompts and checks. Walking in the Spirit also means moving on in spiritual living. We pursue studying Scripture; walking in God's ways, including prayer, worship, and fellowship; and fulfilling our God-given work or ministry. Paul testified, "I follow after...I press toward the mark [of my calling]" (Phil. 3:12–14). As we move ever forward, we grow ever fuller of the Spirit—who inspires us to easily overrule our flesh.

Walking in the Spirit also implies we don't go backward—to old worldly ways, errors, sins, or wrong relationships. Nor do we stand still—spiritually idle, indifferent, or indolent. There is no standing still in the Christian life. Whenever we try to stand still, we slip back.

Are you, like Paul, frustrated by your flesh? Worried you can't control the monster within? Don't despair. Reckon, yield, and walk to victory.

Chapter 26

BEEN REFILLED LATELY?

RESHLY SPIRIT-BAPTIZED, PETER declared the outpouring at Pentecost was due to Jesus' glorification: "This Jesus...being by the right hand of God exalted [glorified]...he hath shed forth this" (Acts 2:32–33). This shouldn't surprise us.

John's Gospel foretold it. After John records Jesus promising "rivers of living water" to those who believe, come unto Him, and "drink," he added the explanatory note, "But this spoke he of the Spirit, whom they that believe on him should receive; for the Holy Spirit was not yet given, because Jesus was not yet glorified" (John 7:39).

Together these two texts reveal, as A.W. Tozer taught, that *wherever Jesus is glorified, the Spirit is given.* How do we glorify Jesus? In the same way He glorified His Father—by doing His will, or simply obeying Him. Jesus reported to His Father, "I have glorified thee on the earth; I have finished the work which thou gavest me to do" (John 17:4). Peter later affirmed God gives the Holy Spirit "to them that obey him" (Acts 5:32).

Initially, this means when a sinner obeys God's call to repent and believe on Jesus, he becomes a candidate for the baptism with the Holy Spirit (Acts 2:38)—but not the sinner who refuses to humbly believe and receive Christ. Cornelius obeyed God's instructions to call Peter to come preach to him. Cornelius' friends also obeyed his (and God's) invitation to come hear Peter. Then the Spirit fell on these obedient ones who believed the good news of salvation by grace. But our text reveals more.

It also hints that every time we as established believers obey the Lord, we receive more of His Spirit. Fresh anointings follow every fresh act of surrender and compliance with God's Word, guidance, correction, or call to service. Why? Yielding our wills to God's will glorifies, or exalts, Jesus again in our lives. It lifts Him up as our sovereign Lord, and puts us in joyful subjection to Him. Then "being by the right hand of God exalted" again by our obedience, and "having received from the Father" more of the promised Holy Spirit, He "sheds forth" a fresh outpouring on us (Acts 2:33).

We see these ongoing refillings in the Book of Acts. Christ released fresh anointings of the Spirit when Peter bravely testified to the Sanhedrin (Acts 4:8) and again when the church prayed for power to endure, not evade, their persecutions: "They were all filled with the Holy Spirit, and they spoke the word of God with boldness" (v. 31).[1] Again, this shouldn't surprise.

We already know numerous practical ways to receive new impartations of the Spirit: by praying; reading or studying our Bibles; praising or worshipping God; discussing spiritual things with other disciples; or attending worship services, Bible study groups, or prayer meetings. But here's another sure way: every time we yield and obey God in daily life, fresh anointings of the Spirit follow! Why? The reglorified Baptizer refills us!

So Jesus didn't just baptize those in the Upper Room. Acts shows He continued this work by baptizing many others: the Samaritans, Saul of Tarsus, Cornelius and company, and Paul's Ephesian converts.[2] And He's still the Baptizer—and refiller—with the Holy Spirit.[3] Enthroned beside His Father, He searches daily for those who glorify Him by fresh obedience so He may release more of His Spirit upon them.

Conversely, this principle implies Christ withholds refillings of His Spirit from those who withhold their obedience. Why? The Holy Spirit won't bless sin. He'll convict and correct us, if we'll let Him, but He won't descend on anyone who impenitently continues in sin.[4] All sin dishonors Christ. Instead of lifting Jesus up in his (or her) life, the sinning Christian lifts up his self-will—and puts Christ down from a sovereign to a subordinate position in his heart and life. Should Christ refill such a Christian, in effect empowering him to continue dishonoring Him? As long as this continues, Christ rightfully withholds His Spirit. And the disobedient Christian, deprived of living water, gets drier. And drier. And drier.

Until the instant he humbles himself, confesses his sins, and calls for God's mercy. Immediately the Spirit rushes back in to fill every nook and cranny of his parched soul with precious, reinvigorating heavenly water. Why? By surrendering and obeying Christ's call to repent and be reconciled, he's glorified Christ again. So Christ pours out His Spirit upon him again.

"Jesus Christ, the same yesterday, and today, and forever" is still at the Father's right hand (Heb. 13:8). This very moment He's longing to "shed forth" His Spirit upon you—again, anew, afresh! You know the way. Take it! Been refilled lately?

Chapter 27

BE FULLY OBEDIENT

*T*HE LIVING WORD fully obeyed His Father, "Obedient unto death, even the death of the cross" (Phil. 2:8). The written Word urges we do the same: "Work out your own salvation" (Phil. 2:12). How obedient are we?

The Bible exhibits God's people rendering Him varying degrees of obedience. Most were partially obedient, opting to stop short at some point in their walk with God. Others, however, went on to full obedience, never saying no to their Sovereign. Among them were Joshua and Caleb. While for forty years their Hebrew brothers obeyed God partially, these two overcomers obeyed "wholly" (Num. 32:12).

With these examples in mind let's consider Christians' varying degrees of obedience to God.

Every Christian will obey when God's biblical orders, guidance, or call are sweet, or delightfully easy and joyful. Most will obey when they're suitable, or conveniently requiring no changes in our attitudes, habits, or lifestyle. Many will readily obey if they're sensible, or in agreement with societal norms and reasonable expectations. Many will obey if they're safe, or sure not to create enemies or troubles. While most Christians obey these sweet, suitable, sensible, or safe divine directives, sadly, many refuse to go farther.

They won't obey if God's pathway adds mental, emotional, or physical stress to their lives. They'll halt if going farther requires separating, or painfully parting ways with hindering nonbelieving friends or carnal Christians or family members.[1] Others turn aside when obedience is self-effacing, requiring them to endure a season in the humbling "dust" of obscurity or the mortifying "dunghill" of reproach and rejection (Ps. 113:7). Still others draw back over sacrificial obedience, when finishing God's will means they must suffer painful injustices, defeats, and losses. Stress, separation, self-effacement, and sacrifice—these mileposts measure our spiritual progress on Obedience Road, revealing accurately whether we're partially or fully obedient. The Bible describes both.

Aaron obeyed, served, and worshipped God excellently—until he was separated from Moses for forty days. Then he crumbled and compromised with Israel's carnal congregation, building them a golden calf. Though personally obedient, a dutiful priest, and an excellent mentor to young Samuel, Eli refused the stresses of disciplining his sinful sons, separating from them if necessary, or risking their possible retaliation. King Saul was an effective head of state, military leader, and occasional prophet—until God ordered him to kill "all" the Amalekites and their flocks. He immediately balked at God's seemingly unreasonable orders. Orpah was loyal to Naomi, her God, and her gospel for years, but turned back to seek a husband rather than humbly glean wheat with Judah's poor as Ruth did. Mark helped Paul and Barnabas faithfully—until strong opposition at Paphos brought the prospects of suffering and sacrifice to their previously peaceful mission. But just where these quit, others persevered.

The Levites stood with God even when it meant standing against, and thus executing, their own impenitently idol-worshipping family members (Exod. 32:26–29). Though as queen of Persia Esther was personally safe, she willingly risked her life to obey God's call to help her distressed people. Abraham obeyed the Lord's orders even when it meant sacrificing his beloved son, Isaac, and all the divine promises he embodied. These fully obedient ones received full rewards. So will we, if we follow their examples.

We'll receive the supreme joy of delighting God's heart. Abraham's full, sacrificial obedience enraptured God (Gen. 22:15–18). Oswald Chambers said, "The spirit of obedience gives more joy to God than anything else on earth."[2] Since our complete obedience honors God, He will honor us: "Them who honor me I will honor" (1 Sam. 2:30). God will restore all our losses in His time and way. In an unexpected turn He restored Isaac to Abraham immediately (Gen. 22:12–14). He will confer blessings upon our "seed"—children, students, teachings, works—and multiply them as He did Abraham's (v. 17). And He'll make us and our seed a blessing to many. He assured our father in faith, Abraham, "Thou shalt be a blessing" (Gen. 12:2) and "in thy seed shall all the nations of the earth be blessed, because thou hast [fully] obeyed my voice" (Gen. 22:18). Will you fully obey? "I wrote to you...to...see if you would fully comply with my instructions" (2 Cor. 2:9, NLT).

Sadly, many Christians won't. But God still needs fully obedient ones to complete His kingdom work in these trying last days. Are you obedient in everything? Or have you stopped short because obedience will require stress, separation, self-effacement, or sacrifice? God's challenging you to go beyond what's sweet, suitable, sensible, and safe. Be like Joshua, Caleb, Abraham, and Jesus. Today, in the issue before you, be fully obedient.

Chapter 28

OUR DOCTOR'S ORDERS

*I*F ASKED, MOST Christians would claim we're more concerned about our immortal souls than our mortal bodies. But evidence suggests otherwise.

We visit physicians numerous times during our lives. Upon arrival, the doctor typically examines us, touches certain areas of our body, listens to our heart, measures our respiration and blood pressure, and occasionally takes blood, X-rays, or tissue samples. Then he examines our lives, probing us with questions about our diet, work, activities, and stress. We'd take offense if others asked such personal questions, but we don't mind our doctor doing so. We understand it's necessary—if we want help. Diagnosis follows, as our medical seer, avoiding euphemisms, plainly tells us what illnesses or infirmities we suffer and what's causing them. Finally he issues his most important message: his orders.

Based upon his knowledge of medical science and our bodily condition, he orders medication, treatment, or surgery. Or he'll recommend changes in our diet or exercise, since these life habits are so vitally linked to our health, quality of life, and longevity. He may, for instance, suggest a lower cholesterol diet; less caffeine, salt, carbohydrates, or food in general; more exercise, such as walking twenty-minutes daily. Our response?

We submit to his examination, accept his diagnosis, receive treatments or medications and, most significantly, change our diet or exercise as needed. And usually without fussing! Humbled but happy, we now anticipate a better, longer, more active life. Why? We've complied with doctor's orders. Meanwhile, another Doctor looks on.

When on earth, this Great Physician ran a mobile health clinic that restored countless sick bodies and souls throughout Israel. While we understandably emphasize His miraculous physical healings, His soul cures were equally successful and of greater importance and duration. Let's review His gospel files and revisit His practice.

His examinations were thorough: "Jesus, having fixed his searching gaze upon him...said" (Mark 10:21, WUEST). His questions probed deeply: "Do you want to be healed?" (John 5:6, ESV). His diagnoses were precise: "Take heed, and beware of covetousness" (Luke 12:15). His orders were clear: "Sin no more, lest a worse thing come" (John 5:14).

The New Testament contains His direct orders to us: "Love one another, as I have loved you," "Have faith in God," "Seek ye first the kingdom of God," "Come unto me," "Ask…seek…knock," "Watch and pray."[1] His staff of apostles wrote other prescriptions He inspired posthumously: "Study to show thyself approved unto God," "Fear God," "Be anxious for nothing, but in everything by prayer," "Be ye angry, but sin not," "Pray without ceasing."[2] Besides these general orders, Dr. Jesus gives us very personal prescriptions.

They come through His current clinical staff of pastors, teachers, elders, and mentors. As they live close to Him and are full of His Spirit, He—their heavenly Head—uses them as His healing eyes, ears, and hands. In His stead they examine, question, diagnose, and order soul treatments for willing believers. By His express instructions our soul care is largely in their hands. One of His wise clinicians taught: "Obey them that have the rule over you, and submit yourselves; for they [ministers] watch for your souls" (Heb. 13:17). This prompts some crucial questions.

Will we cooperate with our ministers as freely as we do our doctors? Will we respond positively when their teaching or counsel prescribes changes in our spiritual diet—the thought stuff we're feeding our minds regularly? Or when they attempt to change our spiritual exercise—prescribing specific biblical responses to the stressful tests challenging us? Do we realize this cooperation is required for better spiritual health? Christians unwilling to comply typically avoid challenging, spiritually active pastors and churches.[3] It's time for some hard questions.

Do we want spiritual wellness as much as physical health? Our professions and prayers affirm we do. But how badly? How badly do we want to cure our spiritual weakness and sicknesses? How urgently do we desire a close, healthy walk with Dr. Jesus?

Enough to follow His direct orders in the Gospels? Enough to obey His prescriptions in the epistles? Enough to submit to His spiritual diagnoses through Spirit-led ministers and elders? Enough to not deny but rather confess and abandon our spiritual faults and un-Christlike habits? Enough to change our spiritual diet to take in more spiritual nourishment through personal Bible study and less "junk food" through worldly media, trivia, and entertainments? Enough to exercise our souls more by daily devotions, thanksgiving, intercession, fellowship, and biblical conduct?

If so, it's true. We want healthy souls as much as healthy bodies and appreciate ministers as we do doctors. And we're proving it daily by following our Doctor's orders.

Chapter 29

GOD'S BELIEVER-TEMPLES

*T*HE APOSTLES DECLARED and reformers reaffirmed that all Christians are believer-priests.[1] But there's more. We're also believer-temples—and the apostle Paul was adamant that we know it.

"Do you not know that your body is a temple of the Holy Spirit, who is in you?" (1 Cor. 6:19, NIV). Being a Jew, Paul used "temple" to refer to the historic Jewish temple.[2] By calling us God's temples, he implied the various features of the historic Jewish temple and its courts represent things that should be present in our bodily lives. Let's review the temple's assets and activities.

In the temple courts there was prayer. Devout Jews observed two hours of prayer daily (9:00 a.m., 3:00 p.m.). Initially, the exclusively Jewish Jerusalem church kept these times faithfully: "Peter and John went up together into the temple at the hour of prayer" (Acts 3:1). Praise and worship were present. Levites recited psalms and sang praises, especially at festivals. After Pentecost Christians continued daily "in the temple…praising God" (Acts 2:46–47). Teaching was widespread there. Like other rabbis, Jesus taught God's Word in Solomon's Porch (John 8:2), as did the apostles (Acts 2:46). Giving occurred there. Faithful Jews brought their tithes and offerings to support their temple and its ministers. Jesus watched with interest to see what and "how" they gave (Mark 12:41–44). Separation was emphasized. Walls, warnings, and gates separated Jewish and Gentile worshippers and public proceedings from the awesome Presence within.

Correction occurred there. Jesus famously drove merchants and money-changers from the Royal Porch, rebuking them for disregarding His Father's will for His "house of prayer" (Matt. 21:13). Healings and miracles manifested there. By Jesus' hands and believers' prayers, God's compassionate power made many temple-goers whole. Prophets and prophecies were there. Baruch read Jeremiah's prophecies and pleas aloud to all who would listen (Jer. 36:5–6, 8). God's authoritative written Word was there. The Torah was read in the temple, and the most holy place contained the ark of the covenant with its Ten Commandments inscribed on stone tablets. The mercy seat—the ark's lid and God's earthly throne—was there. The high priest sprinkled atoning blood on it yearly to transform God's seat of righteous judgment into a throne of saving grace. Fresh bread was there. Every Sabbath the priests removed the old loaves of showbread from their table and replaced them with new. Light was there. Lamplight filled the holy place, and glory-light the most holy, guiding the priests' steps and labors.

Sacrifices abounded there. Daily priests submitted worshippers' offerings to please and honor God. Gold was plentiful there. From its inner sanctum to roofline, and its utensils to columns, the temple was adorned with various gold coverings. Living water was there. During the Feast of Tabernacles, the priests drew water from the spring-fed Pool of Siloam[3] and poured it out at the altar, symbolizing the water from the rock that sustained Israel in the wilderness. Chiefly, the glory—God's very presence—was there! No other temple had the Creator dwelling within it! Consequently, joyful gatherings occurred there. All seeking the glorious One's presence, righteousness, and blessing were drawn to it, especially during festivals. What do these facts tell us?

Christians should pray often in the courts of our bodily temples, at appointed times and spontaneously. God's praise and worship, especially thanksgiving, should ascend from the altars of our lips "continually" (Heb. 13:15). We should seek and sit under Spirit-illuminated Bible teaching—and share with others what we're learning and living. We should willingly give financial support to our churches and ministers to please Jesus, who is watching. We should faithfully maintain spiritual walls of separation from practicing sinners—and our besetting sins![4] We should receive Christ's correction, seek His healing, and stay open to genuine prophecy. We should remember the Bible's authority, receive forgiveness when needed through Christ's atoning blood, and seek the fresh bread of biblical insight from the tables of personal Bible study regularly.

We should also fill our inner man with the light of God's Word and Spirit and follow its guidance. We should offer sacrifices daily, accepting crosses and thorns in the flesh as we obey God's Word and call. We should persistently trust and obey God in fiery trials to "buy" and cover ourselves with the precious "gold" of proven faith, knowledge, and wisdom (Rev. 3:18). Daily we should draw the living water of the Spirit from Christ, our Rock, and pour it out in loving service to God and others. We should seek the glorious One's presence often so others, drawn by the Spirit, will gather round to discover and walk with Him. Then we'll not just be believer-priests.

We'll also be God's believer-temples.

Chapter 30

THE POWER OF SONG

*J*EWISH AND CHRISTIAN history, the Bible, and life have some vital counsel for you: you won't make it without a song! What do they mean?

God has so designed Christianity that we won't walk very well or far with Him without the power of songs in our hearts and on our lips. Not pop, folk, or romantic tunes, but God-given, Spirit-filled songs of adoration for Jesus. Let's consider the evidence.

The Bible's longest book is Israel's hymnal, the Psalms. Why? God is telling us we need inspired songs to live biblically—and He desires our worship in song! "Children, here's a very large songbook, so sing to Me!" Or, as Psalms repeatedly exhorts, "Praise *ye* the Lord!" God's Spirit and songs work hand in hand. As we raise our voices in song, the river of the Spirit rises and flows in our hearts (John 7:37–39), refilling and reinvigorating us. The whole Bible confirms this. Its sermon on songs begins with Moses' victory song and the Israelites singing for water and doesn't end until the redeemed are in heaven singing worshipfully before God's throne.[1] Israel's way of life, especially its festivals, was filled with songs. Church history, in and after Acts, shows saints singing God-songs in every situation.

Why do we need Spirit-filled songs?

- THEY REFILL US WITH THE HOLY SPIRIT (Eph. 5:18–29).
  So Paul advised us not once but twice to sing to the Lord (Col. 3:16). These refillings refit us for our daily stresses.

- THEY BRING REASSURING AWARENESS OF GOD'S PRESENCE IN OUR CHURCHES. When congregations give Him powerful praise, He releases His powerful presence to indwell their praises (Ps. 22:3).

- THEY'RE A GREAT WAY TO RENDER THANKS FOR VICTORIES. Moses, Deborah, and David demonstrated this.[2]

- THEY PROMPT GOD TO STOP OUR PERSECUTORS (2 Chron. 20:21–22).

- THEY SEE US THROUGH SUFFERINGS. David composed and sang songs throughout his many wilderness trials. Jesus sang a hymn before His sufferings, Paul sang in Philippi's jail, and Jon Huss sang psalms while being led to the stake. As we sing, God sends strength—and gives sweet songs to sustain us in our bitter trials.

- THEY ACCOMPANY REVIVALS. The Reformation and the Wesleyan, Evangelical, Pentecostal, and Charismatic revivals "rained" fresh psalm and hymn singing. Every revival releases many new inspired worship songs.

- THEY EVANGELIZE EFFECTIVELY. David believed the inspiring "new song" God gave him after his "horrible pit" trial would cause "many" to "fear" and "trust" God (Ps. 40:1–3). Not only the sermons of Dwight Moody and Billy Graham but also the biblical songs of Ira Sankey and George Beverly Shea saved many.[3]

- THEY REPEL DEMONS. Demons loathe worship songs so much, they leave (1 Sam. 16:23)!

- THEY PREPARE US FOR OUR ETERNAL VOCATION: WORSHIPPING GOD! The more we "praise the LORD with the harp" (Ps. 33:2) in this life, the more ready we'll be to join in "the voices of harpers harping with their harps" in the next (Rev. 14:2).

Got a harp? A piano, guitar, or other stringed instrument? Strum and sing to God! Or if you prefer worshipping without instruments, use your inner harp, your vocal chords, and sing a cappella. Learn new songs periodically: "Sing unto him a new song" (Ps. 33:3). Solomon wrote over a thousand![4] Worship often until you sing and "play skillfully" (v. 3). Sing thoughtfully, with feeling, worshipfully focused on the Lord: "Sing praises with understanding" (Ps. 47:7, NKJV). Sing not just about but to Him: "Singing…to the Lord" (Col. 3:16). After singing verses as written, sing them again altering the words to address the Lord directly: "I'd rather have Jesus" becomes "I'd rather have You, Lord." Then you'll fully experience the power of song.

While singing to your Strength, His Spirit will strengthen you, calming, healing, re-inspiring, and carrying you. The power of His indwelling presence will transform your trials, cooling you in your fiery furnaces, steadying your steps on your high places, and clearing your thoughts in your chaotic, confusing storms. Don't feel like singing?

Neither did Jesus, Paul, David, or Hus at times, I'm sure. But they sang anyway, and God blessed and kept their souls. When you want to sing the least is when you need to the most—and when God is most pleased and sure to reveal His love most powerfully. It's easy to lose your song in the stress, rush, and noise of life. Lost yours?

If so, reclaim the wonder of worshipping in song. The song of the Lord always brings the Lord of the song. You already know the power of His Word in Bible study and His Spirit in prayer. Learn, and live in, the power of song.

Chapter 31

THE PROPER POSITION FOR PRAYER

FTER EXHORTING THE Ephesian elders, Paul "knelt down, and prayed" with them (Acts 20:36). Why did he kneel? That's the proper position for prayer. Right?

Yes, kneeling is the physical posture most often associated with prayer in the Bible. Paul knelt often to pray: "For this cause I bow my knees unto the Father" (Eph. 3:14).[1] This physical posture—lowering one's stance and bowing one's head in God's presence—symbolizes vital truths. It demonstrates God's sovereignty over us, as we assume a position beneath Him. It shows our submission, the bending of not only our knee but also more importantly our will to God's will. It acknowledges God's thoughts and ways are far above ours (Isa. 55:8–9), and thus we bow not only our heads but also our minds to His, trusting His wisdom with all our hearts and leaning not to our own understanding (Prov. 3:5). And it exhibits our servantship, that we're ready to receive His commands, commissions, and corrections and rise to do His pleasure. But kneeling isn't the only biblical posture for prayer.

Scripture shows many others. Elijah prayed crouched over with his face between his knees and sitting on the ground under a tree. Daniel prayed regularly facing Jerusalem and once down on his hands and knees. King David prayed sitting in a chair and lying in his bed. Joshua and Jesus supplicated lying facedown. Moses prayed barefooted and covering his face. King Hezekiah begged God's mercies with his face against a wall. Peter called for help while sinking in stormy waters. Jonah prayed while being tossed around in a fish's stomach.[2] Jesus and Paul authorized us to pray standing.[3] King Solomon prayed standing with hands spread toward heaven. Abraham's servant prayed standing—while his camels kneeled! Jesus prayed standing in a river. Adam and Enoch prayed often while walking with God. Though all these petitioners' bodily positions were different, their prayers were equally successful, because they all enjoyed the peace of God's presence and received open answers to their private petitions. What does this suggest?

Simply that God isn't focused on our physical position when we pray. It's our inner position, the spiritual posture of our heart and life before Him, that counts: "Man looketh on the outward appearance, but the LORD looketh on the heart" (1 Sam. 16:7). And what spiritual posture does He desire?

The Bible reveals the inner stance of successful petitioners as fully as it describes their outward poses. They have humble hearts: "He forgetteth not the cry of the humble" (Ps. 9:12). The chains of their tyrannical self-will broken, they now desire God's will only: "The LORD is near to those who have a broken heart" (Ps. 34:18, NKJV). Their hearts are "perfect," or perfectly reliant on God: "The eyes of the LORD run to and fro throughout the whole earth, to show himself strong [answering prayers] in the behalf of them whose heart is perfect toward him" (2 Chron. 16:9, see v. 8). Perfect also implies spiritually mature, or consistently obedient to God: "Whatever we ask, we receive of him, because we keep his commandments, and do those things that are pleasing in his sight" (1 John 3:22). Christians praying in this spiritual condition may expect the Lord to receive them into His presence and respond to their petitions in His time and way. Why?

That's the proper position for prayer! And it's far more important than any physical posture we assume. Indeed it's our inner man—our soul posture, where our inner spiritual man stands, the closeness and richness of our fellowship with Jesus—that determines the quality of our communion and regularity of our answers in prayer. Some examples may help.

If Job, Daniel, or Noah prayed while skipping rope, doing calisthenics, bathing, or eating a meal, God would delightedly draw near, bless them, listen, and respond to their requests. But if Ahab, Nabal, or Herod Antipas knelt so long their legs and necks remained permanently bent, God would withhold His peace and deny their petitions however passionately and persistently they supplicated! Why?

God seeks substance, not symbols. He wants reality, not show. So let's not overemphasize outward things and forget what really counts. It's fine to pray kneeling, but kneeling—or any other religious posture, symbol, object, person, or fixed prayer—won't open heaven's gates or win its King's favor. Only Jesus' blood opens our "new and living way" (Heb. 10:20), and only the correct inner posture for prayer—humility, trust, a broken will, and an obedient life—enables us to walk in it successfully.

Are you in the proper position for prayer?

Chapter 32

PASSING BY THIS WORLD'S WONDERS

C HRONICLING PAUL'S THIRD mission, Luke notes Paul passed by Rhodes: "We came by a straight course to Cos, and the next day to Rhodes, and from there to Patara" (Acts 21:1, ESV). This is interesting.

At the time the great Colossus of Rhodes lay in ruins near the harbor entrance. An image of the Greek sun god, Helios, the Colossus was a wonder of the ancient world. Like its fame, its dimensions were superhuman.

Originally built atop a fifty-foot marble pedestal, the shiny brass Colossus was massive, about 106 feet tall, and stood beside Rhodes' harbor entrance.[1] Though twelve years in construction, the giant idol's glory was short-lived. An earthquake in approximately 226 BC made it snap at the knees and collapse—where it lay in pieces for 800 years! Even in ruins the crippled Colossus, with fingers larger than most statues, still drew tourists. Many tried to wrap their arms around one of its thumbs. But Luke's record reveals Paul wasn't among them. Why did he bypass this worldly wonder?

It wasn't because Paul was small-minded or incurious. Scholarly, observant, culturally sensitive, and well traveled, Paul fully appreciated human art, architecture, and achievement. In Athens, he thoroughly examined the city's numerous religious statues and shrines: "As I walked around and looked carefully at your objects of worship" (Acts 17:23, NIV). Yet, keeping things in perspective, he wasn't awed by man-made wonders, however beautiful, religious, ingenious, or massive. Why?

His sense of wonder was thoroughly captivated by God and His wonderful works and will. Beside God and His wonders, every worldly wonder paled.

Also, at the time Paul was pursuing God's will of church unity. To help heal the lingering, prejudice-and-heresy-driven rift between Jewish and Gentile Christians, Paul hastened to deliver the Gentile churches' love offering to the largely Jewish Jerusalem church.[2] After this, he planned to focus on pursuing God's will at the next stop on his ministry itinerary, Rome (Acts 19:21).

Besides these fascinations, Paul was firmly gripped by the greatest wonders—not man's but God's works! Scripture describes them.

With David, Paul wondered at God's incomprehensively vast creation, including our sky, the planets, and deep space: "When I consider thy heavens, the work of thy fingers, the moon and the stars...What is man?" (Ps. 8:3–4). The sea and its amazingly diverse creatures enthralled him: "They that go down to the sea...see...his wonders in the deep" (Ps. 107:23–24). He marveled at the human body's amazing design, systems, and abilities: "Thank you for making me so wonderfully complex! Your workmanship is marvelous" (Ps. 139:14, NLT). He revered the control over the elements God displayed in the Exodus: "The LORD brought us forth out of Egypt with a mighty hand...with wonders" (Deut. 26:8). He wondered at the stunning power of Christ's miracles in the Gospels—"The multitude wondered, when they saw the dumb to speak" (Matt. 15:31)—and when the Spirit duplicated them in his ministry (Acts 19:11–12). To Paul, these God-wonders rendered the Colossus a dwarf!

God agreed. By prompting the earthquake of AD 226, He made Helios fall before Him as Dagon had, demonstrating again that no false god can stand before the true God (1 Sam. 5:1–4). The brassy Colossus' demise also foreshadowed the coming, sudden, end-time judgment of Gentile world governments revealed symbolically in Nebuchadnezzar's prophetic dream (Dan. 2:31–45). Together these famous collapses show us that whatever fallen man creates without God, however wonderful, will eventually fall! So while we may appreciate their temporary function, value, and beauty, we mustn't be overawed by the temporary works of mere men. That holy wonder should be reserved for God's works, which, like His Word, "stand forever" (Isa. 40:8, ESV). What fascinates you today?

Like Paul's, our world is captivated by man-made wonders. Our modern "Colossuses" are science, technology, communications, the Internet, transportation, arts, entertainment, sports, rich or famous people, powerful nations, heads of state, space exploration, skyscrapers, engineering marvels, advanced weaponry, precious metals, and fabulous jewels, to name a few. Will we appreciate these people, products, substances, and entities without being awestruck? Will we see or use them and pass by? Or do they preoccupy us so much they eclipse the eternally greater wonder of God and His wondrous works, will, and Word?

God's wonders will soon reappear. The ultimate wonder—*Jesus* in all His fascinatingly tender love, soaring truth, amazing grace, and awesome power—will revisit and revive Christians by an outpouring of the Spirit in these last days. It will grow until the church's final glory exceeds its first (Hag. 2:6–9)! Then the whole world will wonder at God's wonders! Shouldn't we do so now?

Today follow Paul in passing by this world's wonders.

Chapter 33

OUR HOUR IS NEAR

*W*HEN IN GETHSEMANE Jesus said His "hour" was "at hand" (Matt. 26:45), He was referring to His divinely permitted period of persecution, the "hour...and the power of darkness" (Luke 22:53).

Earlier He had ministered freely throughout Israel, even among His religious enemies: "I sat daily with you teaching in the temple, and ye laid no hold on me" (Matt. 26:55). Though they repeatedly tried to arrest Him, they failed because it wasn't yet His "hour," or time to suffer. But in Gethsemane things suddenly changed. Now His enemies had their way, swiftly betraying, arresting, and executing Him. Did this evil power play evade His Father's notice or control? No, the whole sordid affair was in His hands. He personally planned, began, controlled, and ended Jesus' "hour." The Resurrection and Ascension proved that.

God did the same with Israel. After the Hebrews enjoyed a season of favor in Egypt in Joseph's day, God turned public opinion against them: "He turned their [the Egyptians'] heart to hate his people, to deal subtly with his servants" (Ps. 105:25). Why? He was testing His children and using their enemies' strong opposition to prepare them for their great deliverance, the Exodus. He sent others such hours of supreme testing.

Joseph's hour began when his brothers sold him into slavery. David's began when King Saul drove him from his home, wife, and military office. Job's began when he suddenly lost his children and possessions. Peter's began when Herod Agrippa "stretched forth his hand to vex certain of the church" (Acts 12:1). The early church's hour began when Nero accused Christians of burning Rome. God controlled all these hours, beginning, regulating, and ending them as He willed. His ways haven't changed.

This last-day generation of Christians will also have its hour. Jesus declared, "If they have persecuted me, they will also persecute you" (John 15:20). As God revives us and Christ's teaching and works worldwide, He'll also permit Christ's sufferings to visit our lives during Christianity's final "hour and power of darkness." Genuine believers will be rejected, ostracized, reproached, and in some cases attacked for our beliefs, obedience, witness, and ministries. But only for a season.

Like all such hours, God will control and ultimately end ours. But it must first begin.

Already a spiritual turn is underway in America. There's a groundswell of anti-Christian sentiment due to growing societal secularization and the nearness of Jesus' appearing. Things may feel like they're getting out of hand, but they're not. They're in our Father's hands! He's permitting the hearts of numerous "Egyptians"—secularists and worldly Christians—to turn against His remnant. Why? He must test us before He takes us: "We must through much tribulation enter into the kingdom of God" (Acts 14:22). But don't dread.

This challenge comes with a comfort. If we endure our hour of troublesome testing, we won't experience the next—the terrible seven-year Tribulation. Jesus promised the thoroughly tested Philadelphians exemption from that final test designed for Israel and the nations: "Because thou hast kept the word of my patience [endurance], I also will keep thee from the hour of temptation, which shall come upon all the world, to try them that dwell upon the earth" (Rev. 3:10). If we have their experience, we can claim their exemption! Still, a larger question looms.

Why does a loving God allow such difficult hours? As we faithfully trust and obey, He uses them to accomplish His eternal purposes in us, such as:

- Teach us to wait perfectly for Him—contentedly, expectantly, dutifully, joyfully (James 1:4)

- Purify our hearts of wrong thinking, desires, and motives (Job 23:10)

- Develop in us deep, persevering faith in His unfailing faithfulness (1 Cor. 10:13)

- Reveal more distinctly His sensed presence (Dan. 3:25)

- Teach and establish us in His "ways" (disciplines, methods) (Ps. 84:5–7)

- Give us clearer biblical insight and spiritual discernment (Heb. 5:14)

- Conform our characters to the image of Christ, who also suffered injustice patiently (Isa. 53:1-4)

- Create in us the compassion and ability to comfort others (2 Cor. 1:3–5)

- Give us the experience-born wisdom (good judgment) necessary to rule with Christ (2 Tim. 2:12)

- Qualify us to receive our full spiritual inheritance (Rom. 8:17)

This is why our Father will, He must, turn our easy day of favor into a challenging night of adversity. So get ready.

Walk closely with Jesus by giving thanks and studying and obeying God's Word. Put on God's "whole armor," and pray "always" (Eph. 6:10–18). Be faithful, generous, and loving, especially to Christians. Believe our hour will achieve God's purposes in you. And don't delay! Our hour is near.

Chapter 34

INSPIRED INTERCESSIONS

*T*HE NEW TESTAMENT not only calls us to pray, but it also assumes we will pray. Let's review its summons.

Jesus called, "Come unto me" and urged us to "Ask...seek...knock" for God's help in prayer (Matt. 11:28; 7:7). He warned prayer was a necessity, not a novelty: "Watch and pray, that ye enter not into temptation" (Matt. 26:41). A praying man, Jesus assumed serious Christians would follow His example and thus taught us not "if" but "when thou prayest..." (Matt. 6:6).[1] The original Christians were serious and "continued with one accord in prayer" until, suddenly, the Spirit filled them and birthed the church.[2]

If we're serious, we'll ask four questions: Where, when, how, and what should we pray?

Where? The first believers obeyed Jesus' instructions to pray daily in their "inner room" (Matt. 6:6, NAS). But they also prayed publicly: in temple courtyards, streets, ships, deserts, islands, prisons, and so forth. So "where" is, everywhere!

When? Following Jewish tradition, early Christians prayed regularly at 9:00 a.m. and 3:00 p.m. Some, like David and Daniel, prayed "evening, and morning, and at noon" (Ps. 55:17).[3] Others imitated Jesus, praying before daybreak (Mark 1:35). Paul insisted we stop and pray whenever tempted to anxiety (Phil. 4:6-7) and encouraged us to make our entire lives one long prayer by teaching us to pray "always" and "without ceasing" (Eph. 6:18; 1 Thess. 5:17). So "when" is, anytime!

How? Jesus gave us an inspired format for prayer—the Lord's Prayer (Luke 11:1-4). It instructs us to recognize God is our Father (v. 2); begin prayer by worshipping Him (v. 2); seek His kingdom and will before our needs and desires (vv. 2-3); pray about one day's needs at a time (v. 3); forgive offenders lest we offend our Forgiver (v. 4); request discernment to avoid temptation and strength to endure testing (v. 4). Through Paul, Christ later advocated we pray in both our native and prayer languages (1 Cor. 14:14-18). So "how" is, as He taught us!

What? While Jesus fully authorized abiding Christians to ask "whatever you wish" (John 15:7, NAS), John added complete "confidence" comes when praying "according to His will" (1 John 5:14-15).

The New Testament, which declares God's will, records many sample prayers. John 17, Jesus' prayer for His church, is the greatest and the Holy Spirit's focus in this age. But the other New Testament prayers, being Scripture, are equally inspired and reflect the Spirit's personal thoughts and prayers.[4] As we pray them for individuals and churches, we can be sure we're praying God's will—and He'll answer. So "what" is, according to God's will!

Knowing that will, Paul—and the Spirit inspiring him—prayed for Christians to:

- Receive heavenly "revelation" to deeply know God, our hope, God's inheritance (the glorified church), and God's supernatural power available to us (Eph. 1:15–21)

- Allow Christ to "dwell" in our hearts, "root and ground" us in God's love, reveal its immensity, and fill us "with all the fullness of God" (Eph. 3:13–19)

- "Abound" in the knowledge and wisdom of God, live "without [causing] offense," and be "filled with the fruits of righteousness," thus glorifying God (Phil. 1:9–11)

- Be "filled with the knowledge of his will [God's plan]," "walk worthy" of Christ, "fruitful" in every good work, and "strengthened with all might" to endure sufferings with patience, joyfulness, and thanksgiving (Col. 1:9–14)

- "Stand perfect and complete in all the will of God" (Col. 4:12)[5]

- "Do no evil," but rather steadily progress toward "perfection [spiritual maturity]" (2 Cor. 13:7–9)

- Receive new "spiritual gift[s]" to further "establish" our churches, and be "comforted together" by fellowship (Rom. 1:9–12)

- "Perfect" our faith and "increase" our love until we consistently live "unblamable in holiness" (1 Thess. 3:10–13)

- Fulfill everything God wants and experience "the work of faith with [divine] power" (2 Thess. 1:11–12)

- Be established in "every good word and work" (2 Thess. 2:16–17)

- Have "peace always" and "grace" (2 Thess. 3:16–18)

- Receive God-given "utterance [words]," "boldness," and "doors [speaking opportunities]," especially ministers (Eph. 6:18–20; Col. 4:2–4)

- Be "delivered from unreasonable and wicked" people to minister God's Word and mercies freely (2 Thess. 3:1–2)

- Pray impartially for "all" government leaders so our society enjoys peace and God's "truth [gospel]" spreads (1 Tim. 2:1–3)

Unchanging, the Spirit still prays these inspired intercessions. Notice neither He nor Paul prayed we would receive great wealth, power, fame, or other temporal, selfish ends. Serious about intercession?

Turn wholly from selfish to scriptural praying. Seek God's will for His people. Ponder the objectives of these inspired prayers. Memorize and pray their key phrases. Persist in this, with faith, thanksgiving, and expectancy, knowing God always answers inspired intercessions.

Chapter 35

NO REST UNTIL HE RESTS!

RIMARILY, PSALM 132 spotlights David's passion for God's "rest"—the permanent establishment of God's ark of the covenant, temple worship, and kingdom in Jerusalem. It also laments Israel's long season of defeat, disunity, and despair after the Philistines took the ark from Shiloh: "Lo, we heard of it [the ark] at Ephrathah; we found it in the fields" (Ps. 132:6). But there's more.

This psalm reveals God had a plan to achieve His "rest." Rest implies cessation from work, travel, or unsatisfied desire.

Previously God's earthly throne, the ark of the covenant, traveled incessantly—through the wilderness, to Shiloh, to Philistia, and back to Israel. Also, God worked ceaselessly after appearing to the Jews on Sinai, training them to be true, or God-pleasing, worshippers. Meanwhile His heart's desire—to dwell among His chosen people in His chosen place, Zion[1]—remained unsatisfied. So He was left in a sense restless, yearning to love and be loved by them in worship, illuminate them with spiritual insight (Ps. 132:17), prosper their labors (v. 15), fill them with joy (vv. 9, 16), and defend them (v. 18), all under benevolent Davidic leadership (vv. 11–12). When this happened briefly during David's entire reign and part of Solomon's, God and His people enjoyed ideal rest, their hearts' desires sweetly fulfilled. God revealed this rest-plan to David.

Once enlightened, David focused on God's plan, vowing not to "sleep," forget or lose consciousness of the divine plan, until it became a reality (v. 4). Nor would he "slumber," or recline spiritually into a self-serving or self-indulgent lifestyle pursuing his own purposes. Captivated by God's longing, he vowed:

> Surely I will not come into the tabernacle of my house, nor go
> up into my bed; I will not give sleep to mine eyes, or slumber
> to mine eyelids, until I find out a place for the LORD...
> —PSALM 132:3–5

Or paraphrasing, "I'll take no rest till He rests!" Thereafter David lived to establish God's ark, temple worship, and kingdom in Jerusalem—and for nothing else! God responded in kind.

He too made a vow, promising to give David rest, or the satisfaction of his heart's desires, specifically a ruling dynasty and share in the Messiah's family line. Thus God honored with rest the one who honored His rest. Why study God's Old Testament "rest" and its promoter?

Today God has a new plan to achieve His "rest"—and new promoters. Jesus' high priestly prayer presents God's new covenant rest succinctly. God's ministers will stop traveling, His Spirit cease training worshippers, and His heart's desire be satisfied when Christ's followers are: sanctified by obeying God's truth (John 17:17), deeply unified (vv. 21, 23), bearers of God's glory (v. 22), practicing God's love (v. 26), and, finally, translated to heaven (v. 24). The apostle Paul—our "David"—enlarged our understanding of God's new rest.

Paul's writings portray Christians as a living temple founded on Christ, His apostles, and the prophets, and indwelt by God's Spirit (Eph. 2:19–22). He also sees us as a mature man, a body of committed believers worldwide having a mature, Christlike "faith," "knowledge" of God, and "fullness" of ministry (Eph. 4:11–16). Such believers discern and reject false teachers (v. 14), speak God's truth frankly but kindly (v. 15), enjoy clear communication with their Head, Jesus (v. 15), and work together perfectly, everyone helping another (v. 16). They reached this spiritual maturity by the persistent prayerful labors of five-fold ministers, who, like David, seek God's rest (vv. 11–13). Finally, Paul sees the true body as a purified bride (Eph. 5:25–27), a submissive, holy people deeply cleansed by obeying biblical teaching and counsel, free from "spots" of habitual fleshly thinking and living and "wrinkles" of new worldly methods, spurious teachings, and religious fads. Having proven their faithfulness to their Bridegroom in this age, these eternal soul mates of Christ are ready for presentation to Him in heaven after the Rapture, which Jesus promised, prayed for, and prophesied posthumously through Paul.[2] The apostle John adds another portrait.

On Patmos John beheld the wondrous end of God's rest—God personally living among His chosen people in His chosen place, the ultimate "Zion," heaven.[3] There Father, Savior, Spirit, and saints will revel in ideal rest, their mutual hearts' desires satisfied forever. This is God's new rest-plan, and Davidic Christians focus on it!

So let's stop seeking rest in other plans, programs, or passions. No other cause—national, political, economic, institutional, social, or personal—however desirable, must captivate us. Today God yearns for

Christians with Davidic hearts, and He pledges to give rest to all who pursue His rest, without "sleeping" in indifference or "resting" in self-centered living, until it's realized. It's pledge time.

With David let's vow, "I'll take no rest until He rests!"

Chapter 36

SPEAKING OF LEADERS...

URPRISINGLY, CHRISTIANITY'S GREATEST leader—who taught us to respect leaders[1]—once spoke disrespectfully to a leader. Acts 23:1–5 describes this ironic twist.

Standing before the Jewish council, Paul testified he had always maintained a clear conscience before God (v. 1). The high priest, Ananias, immediately and illegally ordered him to be slapped. Stunned, Paul retorted angrily, "God shall smite thee, thou whited wall" (v. 3). It was an uncharacteristically ungracious response from the usually gracious apostle. Clearly he was caught off guard.

But the high priest's attendant wasn't. Overlooking his superior's error, he instantly focused on Paul's fault: "Revilest thou God's high priest?" (v. 4). Now collected, Paul responded with equal sharpness, citing the precise scripture he had hastily broken: "I knew not...that he was the high priest; for it is written, Thou shalt not speak evil of the ruler of thy people" (v. 5).[2] Thus he quickly confessed and corrected his sin.

Paul's error was not that he retorted but that he reviled his leader. Though emotionally justified, his sarcastic expression was excessive and unacceptable to God. Truly, the high priest was a "whited [whitewashed] wall," or falsely religious exterior whitewashing or masking a corrupt interior, but Paul shouldn't have said so! Jesus Himself called the scribes and Pharisees "whited sepulchers" and worse ("hypocrites," "fools," "serpents"), but He was addressing them generally, not personally, and especially not the high priest in a public hearing (Matt. 23:13–33). So Paul's emotions got the best of him, but only briefly. This reveals seven truths about him.

First, though very spiritual, Paul had his human moments. By hastily popping off, he shows he too had an "old man," or fallen human nature with the same pride and anger we suffer. Second, he deeply respected God's Word. By citing Scripture as the cause of his apologetic about-face, he confirmed it ruled his conduct as well as his faith. Thus he honored the Word by obeying it. Third, he focused on what God wanted him, not others, to do. Though mistreated, he knew he had spoken "evil" of his leader—so he promptly dealt with his own fault. Fourth, he had amazing self-control. That after yielding to his selfish will Paul so quickly overruled it demonstrates that, by habitually yielding to God in the past, Paul had mastered his self-will. He was ever ready to forgo his will to fulfill God's. Many "not my will but thine" experiences had taught him to submit to God's ever-perfect will sooner with joy rather than later with regret!

Fifth, his rapid repentance demonstrates humility. To save face, a proud man would have kept resisting such humiliating abuse—from the nation's highest cleric! But Paul meekly accepted it, submitting to the biblical authority of the high priest's office, though the high priest himself was corrupt and arrogantly remorseless. Sixth, Paul trusted God's justice. Though spoken hastily, "God shall smite thee" expressed Paul's abiding confidence that, as Jesus taught, God would ultimately "avenge" Christians of impenitent offenders (Luke 18:1-8).[3] Seventh, Paul's actions confirmed his testimony: he *did* maintain a clear conscience before God! Though passion had briefly moved him to misspeak, he quickly obeyed his conscience, reversing himself for the Word's sake. What lessons may we learn from this?

Ananias' error proves religious leaders sometimes err. Though history confirms Ananias was corrupt, most religious leaders—superintendents, bishops, pastors, elders—are not. Yet human, they occasionally err, fail, sin, or come short of our expectations. Even Paul did!

But Paul's disrespectful retort warns us, "Thou shalt not speak evil of the ruler of thy people!" We may disagree with leaders, but not dishonor them—if we want to please and honor God. However disappointed we are in our leaders, we shouldn't speak "evilly"—falsely, hatefully, or abusively—of them, publicly or privately. Have your emotions, like Paul's, gotten the better of you and moved you to speak disrespectfully of a leader?

Then follow Paul's recovery. From now on, disagree when necessary with religious or political leaders, including presidents, governors, legislators, and justices, but don't disrespect them. Question them without castigating them. Discuss issues without demeaning them. Voice objections without flinging abusive epithets, accusations, or imprecations. By reversing your abusive rhetoric, you'll show that, like Paul, you are deeply respecting God's Word, focusing on what you should do, growing in self-control, becoming humbler, trusting God's justice, and maintaining a clear conscience before God. To complete your recovery, pray often for the very leaders you've been reviling, so peace, order, and godliness may thrive in your church and land! Paul taught us this also (1 Tim. 2:1-4)!

Remember and practice these lessons from Paul's life the next time you're speaking of leaders...

Chapter 37

VISION VENGEANCE

*P*HYSICALLY ABUSED, UNJUSTLY jailed, and alone, the apostle Paul received an uplifting night vision from Jesus assuring him he would minister in Rome (Acts 23:11). The very next morning murderous conspirators targeted Paul (vv. 12–13). Why?

This was vision vengeance—Satan's revenge for the encouraging vision and word Paul received.

Paul's vision helped him greatly. It reassured him of Christ's presence and strengthened him with His word, a sweet promise that Paul wouldn't remain incarcerated or be executed but would live to minister again—in the world's capital! Oh, Paul was "of good cheer" again (v. 11)! But Satan was angry and responded with vision vengeance, a spiteful counterattack against Paul's fresh vision and its sustaining word. We too receive visions.

Since Jesus speaks and is God's Word (John 1:1), our visions of Him are most often new insights into God's Word. Usually received during Bible reading or study, they cheer or edify us. They often come by night, or when spiritual darkness surrounds and tests us. They may be Bible promises, principles, or patterns that the Holy Spirit quickens to our heart, as if saying, "This promise, principle, or pattern applies to you in your present situation." Or our visions may bring other kinds of spiritual light or comfort: timely guidance, calls to ministry, revelations of God's plans, enlightening teachings or counsels for God's people, reassurances of Christ's presence in our distresses, helpful corrections, and so forth. These blessings bring Satan's backlashes.

Let's examine more closely the hellish vengeance that followed Paul's heavenly vision.

Though not stated, the origin of Satan's revenge was the work of his agents, this world's invisible and insidious "rulers of darkness" (Eph. 6:12). Its timing was swift, arising early on the morning after the vision. Its nature in this instance was a conspiracy, as many enemies "surely gather[ed] together" (Isa. 54:15) to quench Paul's hope. Its size was large, with "more than forty" conspirators (Acts 23:13). Its fervor was hot, the conspirators vowing to fast till they prevailed (v. 14). Its strength was imposing, with the nation's highest religious leaders (Sanhedrin) participating (vv. 14–15). Its seriousness was grave, the plan being not merely to harass but to murder Paul (v. 12). Its commitment was total, as the conspirators were prepared to die fighting the Roman soldiers guarding Paul just to kill him. Its consequences were costly, as their oath invoked a death curse if they failed (v. 14). Its demise was swift, as God out-planned its planners by quickly exposing their plot and inspiring the Roman tribune to immediately send Paul to Caesarea, escorted by 470 soldiers (vv. 16–33)! But God did more than defeat Satan's vengeance. He used it.

It tested Paul's devotion to Jesus and His call, thus further approving Paul. It revealed Jesus' great faithfulness, as He again saved Paul in an apparently hopeless crisis. It spotlighted Jesus' complete control, as He easily exposed a hidden plot and turned an apathetic tribune's heart to aggressively protect His servant. It showcased Jesus' providence, or "hidden hand," using a most unlikely person—Paul's young nephew—as a deliverer (v. 16). It revealed afresh Jesus' unbreachable protection, as there were more soldiers with Paul than conspirators against him.[1] And it demonstrated God's wondrous ways, or amazing methods of operation, as He subsequently used the Romans to help Paul, housing, feeding, transporting, and protecting him from the Jews until he finished his course of ministry! By thus blessing Paul and building his and our trust in Jesus' amazingly faithful and complete care, God not only routed Satan's revenge but also reversed it, turning a curse into a blessing! He'll do the same for us.

Are you experiencing hellish backlashes for receiving, ministering, or helping minister heavenly "visions" of Christ, His Word, or His will? If so, ponder this lesson well.

Reexamine the elements of Paul's vision vengeance—its origin, nature, timing, size, strength, fervor, seriousness, commitment, consequences, and demise—noting all valid parallels to your experience. Review also how wonderfully God turned Paul's curse into a blessing and believe He'll do something similar for you. Renewed in faith, resolve to seek not less but more visions of Christ—insights into biblical promises, principles, and patterns; the "light" of God's guidance, call, plans, or correction; enlightening teachings or counsels; or reassurances of Christ's presence. Reset your heart to neither waver nor quit but pursue your course of discipleship or ministry at all times, in all seasons, all the way to your "Rome," or divinely appointed goals. Be confident Christ will reverse whatever vision vengeance you meet. Finally, offer Him praise by faith.

Today, while people and demons still oppose you, praise God for routing and reversing your vision vengeance.

Chapter 38

HE FAITHFULLY HELPS THE HELPLESS

*W*HEN VIOLENTLY ASSAULTED in the temple courts, the apostle Paul, though faithful, suddenly found himself in grave trouble, alone, and helpless. But when his friends couldn't help, and others wouldn't, Jesus faithfully "stood by him" (Acts 23:11).

Christ's loyal assistance was prophetic, providential, and personal.

Prophetically Jesus had already helped Paul. For months prophets had repeatedly warned him "bonds and affliction" awaited in Jerusalem (Acts 20:22–23). This forewarning forearmed Paul emotionally for his ordeal, helping him not panic when suddenly assaulted in the temple, arrested, and jailed without cause.

Providentially Jesus helped Paul through the actions of a Roman officer and even the Pharisees! The officer intervened three times to save Paul: first, when the Jews were beating Paul; second, when the next day the Sanhedrin turned on him; third, when the morning after the Jews conspired to assassinate him.[1] The Pharisees' help was surprising, even humorous. To defend their pet doctrines against their theological rivals, the Sadducees, they sided with Paul, "We find no evil in this man" (Acts 23:9)—unaware that former members of their sect[2] were busy attacking Paul's teachings in synagogues and churches around the Mediterranean! Thus Christ moved disinterested and even hostile parties to assist Paul.

Personally, Christ appeared to Paul that very night to promise that, despite his troubles, he would still get to Rome. To make His pledge even more sure and comforting, Jesus spoke imperatively: "So *must* thou bear witness of me in Rome" (v. 11). This revealed Paul would not die in Jerusalem, be left in jail there, or be denied further ministry. To the contrary, it confirmed he was headed for the world's most exciting field of service, Rome! This greatly relieved Paul, who was facing the dark prospects of contentious legal wranglings, execution, or extended imprisonment. He knew once Jesus spoke, that was it. His sovereign promise had to follow in His time and way. No longer a maybe, now Rome was a "must"!

Thus prophetically, providentially, and personally Jesus faithfully helped His helpless one—who also was faithful!

Indeed, Paul's loyal devotion and reliable service to Christ is a big part of this story. Consistently obedient, Paul experienced this trouble due to his ministry, not mischief; his righteous living, not rebellion. Though Christ repeatedly warned him of adversity lurking in Jerusalem, He never once said, "Don't go."[3] Paul's purpose in visiting Jerusalem was to promote unity in the body of Christ by delivering the Gentile church's love offering to the largely Jewish Jerusalem church. His Jewish temple vow was meant to dispel lies about his teaching that were hindering his ministry to Jerusalem's Jewish Christians (Acts 21:20–24). Thus he acted in faithfulness. If unfaithfulness had caused Paul's trouble, Christ would have corrected him before encouraging Him. But Jesus' message only commends and comforts Paul (Acts 23:11). This wasn't the only time Jesus helped Paul.

As Paul sailed for Rome about two years later, Jesus stood by him during a powerful, seemingly inescapable storm. Speaking through an angel, Christ repeated His imperative language: "Fear not, Paul, thou *must* be brought before Caesar" (Acts 27:24). During the two years following Paul's arrival in Rome, he again found himself in grave trouble, alone, and helpless while awaiting trial before Nero. All his friends who should have supported him withdrew—except One: "At my first defense...all men forsook me...Notwithstanding, the Lord stood with me, and strengthened me, that by me the preaching might be fully known" (2 Tim. 4:16–17). Thus repeatedly the Lord faithfully helped His faithful servant. Paul's experience speaks of ours.

When our faith and courage are tried in deep troubles, short-lived or long-lasting, some who could and should help, even some of our Christian friends, won't. But One will always stand by. He has vowed, "I will never leave thee, nor forsake thee" (Heb. 13:5), and "I am with you always, to the very end of the age" (Matt. 28:20, NIV). If like Paul we've been faithful, He'll comfort and reassure us. If unfaithful, He still won't abandon us. Instead He'll reprove us with a frank description of our sin, and then graciously reassure us that if we'll repent, He'll redeem—and give us strength and grace to endure whatever consequences we must face.

Are you in a "Jerusalem" of difficulties? Facing turbulence, opposition, uncertainty? Helpless? Alone? Seek Jesus' faithful assistance and expect it: providentially, through friends, strangers, even enemies; prophetically, through Spirit-inspired utterances or sermons that "show you things to come" (John 16:13); and personally, through clear, timely dreams, or Bible portions you read or remember with the Spirit's quickening. Why expect this?

You're sure now He faithfully helps the helpless.

Chapter 39

READY FOR TERTULLUS

*U*PON ARRIVAL IN Caesarea, the apostle Paul had already overcome many adversities and adversaries—angry Pharisees, synagogue expulsions, violent mobs, beatings, incarcerations, and dangerous journeys to name a few. Now he faced a new foe.

Tertullus! Described only in Acts 24:1–9, Tertullus was the attorney the Sanhedrin appointed to present their case against Paul in the court of the Roman governor, Felix. Tertullus embodied all the characteristics of unethical attorneys who skillfully twist fiction around facts to create false impressions of innocent people—in this case a godly, fruitful Christian—in jurors' and judges' minds. More than a professional liar, he was the attorney from hell, a judicial incarnation of the diabolical "accuser of the brethren" (Rev. 12:10). His name confirms this.

Tertullus means "triple-hardened, liar, impostor."[1] A world-class liar with a thoroughly hardened conscience, Tertullus set a global record for falsifying information in his opening statement against Paul. Almost every word he spoke was fabricated or twisted.

He characterized Paul as a "pestilent fellow" (Acts 24:5), or a malicious disease ("plague," ESV), infecting society with trouble. Actually Paul's ministry cured society's maladies, specifically its sin pandemic. He called Paul a "mover of sedition among all the Jews," or someone constantly disturbing the peace by stirring Jews to rebel against Rome. Insurrection was a capital offense and plausible. At the time Jewish nationalists were fomenting rebellion and assassinating Jewish collaborators, but Paul wasn't among them. He promoted a spiritual, not a political kingdom and advocated peacefully obeying, not defying authorities (Rom. 13:1–7). Tertullus alleged Paul defiled the Jewish temple by bringing Gentiles into the Jewish courts. In fact, Paul accompanied four *Jewish* Christians there to obey Jewish purification rites. Tertullus correctly claimed Paul was a ringleader of a Nazarene cult. This he was. Most Romans saw Jesus' "way" as a Jewish sect, and thus a branch of legally recognized Judaism. If proven a separate religion, its "ringleaders" could have been executed for promoting an unauthorized religion.[2] His falsehoods persisted.

Tertullus also boldly indicted Jerusalem's presiding Roman officer, Claudius Lysias, claiming the Jews were trying to give Paul a fair hearing when Lysias illegally and violently intervened (Acts 24:6–7). This insinuated Lysias obstructed justice and used excessive force. Yet it was the Jews who were acting illegally and violently by denying Paul due process and summarily beating him, an untried Roman citizen, outside their temple gates (Acts 21:27–37). And they continued this misbehavior in their hearing the next day (Acts 23:8–9) and by plotting Paul's assassination the day following (vv. 12–15). Meanwhile Lysias consistently upheld Roman law and order by stopping the mob's violence; trying to discover what crimes, if any, Paul had committed; halting Paul's scourging when informed of his citizenship; and removing Paul to Caesarea to prevent his assassination. Tertullus further implied Lysias acted unethically if not illegally by moving Paul's trial from Jerusalem to Caesarea (Acts 24:8). Yet this was only to protect Paul's legal right to a fair trial. Finally Tertullus announced with a straight face he could prove all these lies. And the Jews' audaciously amened his falsehoods: "The Jews also assented, saying that these things were so" (v. 9). Thus the villains vilified the victims. This is one of Satan's common strategies.

The father of lies often uses lying villains to vilify their victims in order to vindicate themselves. King Saul falsely accused David of his very crime: conspiracy to murder (1 Sam. 22:6–8)! This strategy is often effective—temporarily.

Saul's slander hindered David for a decade. Tertullus' lies caused Paul many hardships. He was treated as a criminal, denied freedom over four years, misjudged and abandoned by Christian friends, exposed to storms, shipwrecks, and snakebites, and kept from the traveling ministry he loved. But Paul overcame all this! How? He refused to be offended with Jesus, forsook anger at Tertullus, sought and worshipped God daily, ministered whenever possible (Acts 28:30–31), patiently endured slander, and believed God's promise to "bring forth thy righteousness as the light, and thy justice as the noonday" (Ps. 37:6), thus keeping the word of Christ's enduring "patience" (Rev. 3:10).

Are you willing to face your "Tertullus," or triple-hardened liar who persistently maligns you and whoever loves or helps you? He (or she) may be a lawyer from hell, estranged spouse, rebellious child, hateful parent, unscrupulous business partner, former friend, envious minister, or hostile neighbor. Are you willing to be vilified by these villains and endure the fallout from their vicious mischaracterizations for Jesus' sake? Will you, as Paul did, cease from anger, refuse offense at Jesus, seek and worship Him daily, serve Him whenever possible, believe His promises, and endure till He delivers you?

If so, you're ready for Tertullus.

Chapter 40

PROACTIVE PROVIDENCE

SCRIPTURE OFTEN REVEALS Satan working preemptively to thwart God's works before they're established. Or in some cases, before they've even begun!

For instance, Herod the Great tried to kill Jesus as a child, before He could grow up to be a mature Messiah. Adonijah moved to usurp David's throne before Solomon, God's chosen successor, could be crowned. Pharaoh had all the Hebrew male infants murdered just before their long-awaited deliverer, Moses, was born. But Satan isn't the only one sensing upcoming events and making preparations to check or minimize them.

In Acts 23:11–35 we see God's proactive providence on display. He worked proactively by helping the apostle Paul escape an assassination plot before it was hatched. And His method of operation was providential. He worked not by a miraculous intervention but through seemingly ordinary people and events to accomplish His purpose. Let's review His proactive providence.

After a most chaotic day filled with false allegations, a wild mob, violent abuse, sudden arrest, and his surprising spontaneous evangelism of thousands in the temple courts, Paul finally got some sleep in Jerusalem's jail. But as he rested, his enemies wrestled—with irrepressible vengeful impulses. They hated Paul so greatly they couldn't rest in peace until he did! As Solomon noted, "They [the wicked] sleep not...their sleep is taken away, unless they cause some to fall" (Prov. 4:16). Thus stirred, over forty of Paul's Jewish enemies rose "in the morning" (Acts 23:12, NCV) to plot his assassination before daybreak. Their plan was simple: the corrupt high priest, Ananias, would request another hearing and, while Paul's guards transferred him from jail to the council chamber, ambush the guards and kill Paul (vv. 13–15). But their early morning plans omitted one rather big factor.

Matthew Henry notes that Christ had risen even earlier than Paul's enemies that eventful morning, long before dawn, to tell Paul *His* encouraging plans. Acts states, "The night following the Lord stood by him, and said, Be of good cheer...as thou hast testified of me in Jerusalem, so must thou bear witness also in Rome" (v. 11)! After daybreak, Jesus initiated this plan.

By unspecified means He caused Paul's nephew to discover the

Jewish plot and report it to the Roman commander, Claudius Lysias. The prospects of either Paul's (a Roman citizen-prisoner) assassination or anti-Roman riots sparked by Paul's super-zealous Jewish enemies[1] so disturbed Lysias that he took extraordinary measures. He sent Paul to the provincial capital of Caesarea with a 470-man military escort that very night—before the conspirators could spring their trap. When they finally discovered Paul's escape the next morning, he was thirty miles away in Antipatris, much too far for a successful pursuit (vv. 16–35). Thus God's proactive providence saved Paul. And this wasn't the only time.

God rescued Paul through proactive providences no less than six times.[2] Why did Jesus go to such lengths to save Paul?

He was in Christ's royal family and plan. As a redeemed son of heaven's royal family, Paul was due royal treatment…and got it. Moreover he was a specially anointed, enlightened, and committed agent of God's kingdom plans—to evangelize sinners, train Christians, and prepare Christ's bride church—and was therefore valuable to his King. That's why God sped Paul out of harm's way with a military escort fit for an imperial prince or distinguished general, as if angels stood by all night warning would-be assassins, "Make way, King Jesus' royal son and anointed leader must complete his mission! Stand back! Neither harry nor hinder us!" The King does the same for us when we need it.

Provided, of course, we're born-again Christians committed to His plans! Spiritual rebirth puts us in God's royal family, "no more strangers…but fellow citizens with the saints, and of the household of God" (Eph. 2:19). And as Paul was predestined to minister in Rome, we are "created in Christ Jesus unto good works, which God hath before ordained that we should walk in them" (v. 10). So our Shepherd-King goes ahead of us, proactively and providentially clearing our new pastures of predators and dangers: "When he putteth forth his own sheep, he goeth before them" (John 10:4). How comforting!

Got enemies? Angry, active, threatening, scheming adversaries? Are they making plans against you or your church, family, ministry, mission, or movement? Then remember God's proactive providences for His royal children and committed servants. Every day Jesus gets up before your enemies. Before they plot, He plans for you. Before they slander, He favors you. Before they rob, He rewards you. Before they close, He opens doors.

So don't dread your adversaries' plans. Believe in Christ's plans and watch for His proactive providences.

Chapter 41

UNREASONABLE!

*P*ONDERING HIS MOST recent decision to grant Paul's appeal, the Roman governor Porcius Festus concluded, "It seemeth to me unreasonable to send a prisoner [to Caesar's court] and not signify the accusations laid against him" (Acts 25:27). Thus he judged justly his own court's unreasonable injustice. Let's look closer.

Though persistently accused of lawbreaking by the Jewish leaders, the apostle Paul was innocent. He declared, "Neither against the law of the Jews, neither against the temple, nor yet against Caesar, have I offended" (Acts 25:8). Yet, respecting the law, he pledged to submit to even capital punishment if proven guilty (v. 11). When asked to consent to transfer his case from Caesarea to Jerusalem, a venue he knew from past experience was both biased and dangerous, Paul declined, insisting Caesarea, the Roman capital of Judea, was the appropriate place for his trial: "I stand at Caesar's judgment seat, where I ought to be judged" (v. 10). Believing he had no other recourse, Paul then exercised his right of appeal as a Roman citizen (v. 11). All his decisions were reasonable.

But his enemies' decisions weren't! The high priest initially begged Festus to execute Paul without a hearing (Acts 25:15). Festus responded this would breech Roman law (v. 16). Unmoved, the Jews stubbornly continued insisting Paul "ought not to live any longer" (v. 24), yet presented no proof—witnesses, exhibits, or other evidence—Paul committed any crimes (vv. 7, 25). Theirs wasn't the only unreasonableness Paul faced.

Having heard Paul and his accusers, Festus recognized Paul's innocence. During a public forum, with King Agrippa II present, Festus conceded, "I found that he had committed nothing worthy of death" (v. 25). Yet Festus still prepared to send Paul on appeal to Rome rather than simply release him—and risk offending his volatile Jewish constituents! Since Agrippa was Jewish, knowledgeable of Jewish law, and overseer of the Jewish temple, Festus asked Agrippa to examine Paul. Maybe he could identify some legal charges he could bring against Paul (vv. 26–27). But this too was illogical—and illegal. Paul's due process was inverted. Indictments should precede, not follow, arrests and trials! Exasperated,

Festus then admitted to Agrippa, "It seemeth to me unreasonable..." Though unreasonable, at least Festus was honest!

Thus Paul was a reasonable man caught in an unreasonable mess filled with unreasonable enemies and authorities. How surprising! We might expect uneducated Jewish mobs to be wild and unsensible, but not their highest councilors and most learned religious leaders! We can understand how Roman rabble might treat God's messengers unreasonably, but not Roman governors! However immoral some were, Roman governors carefully defended Roman laws and rights—or lost their right to rule!

The madness of Paul's prosecution reminds us of Pilate's court. Pilate publicly proclaimed Jesus innocent three times, yet ordered His execution![1] If Paul's and Jesus' persecutions were unreasonable, ours will be also. Are we willing to face adversaries who treat us not only unkindly but also unreasonably?

Are yours doing this? Before you say hello or shake their hand, they frown or scowl. You execute your job excellently, but they're still dissatisfied, critical, or curt. You've long loved and helped them, but they persistently misjudge and exclude you. You share their beliefs, yet they claim you teach and practice error. You persistently try to make peace, but they're consistently contentious. You help them financially, but they're unthankful and resist being responsible or accountable. You're very understanding and truthful with them, patiently explaining your actions, but they distort your motives and accuse you of being hasty, untruthful, and hard to please. They're so enraged they feel you "ought not to live any longer" and tell their twisted story to every gullible soul they meet, yet they can't prove their accusations. Soon you realize, no matter what you say or do, they'll find an excuse to reject and defame you—while posing as compassionate, reasonable people, even Christians! Why this unreasonableness?

Naturally, it's without cause: "They...fought against me without a cause" (Ps. 109:3). But spiritually, there's a cause. You're a light-bearer, studying, living, and sharing God's Word and revealing Christ's life and love to others daily. You're a fruit-bearing branch in Christ's vine, enlarging God's kingdom through intercession, evangelism, and other ministries. For these reasons you're wrestling against not just earthly people but "evil spirits in the heavenly places" (Eph. 6:12, NLT). Demonic forces are stirring unreasonable opposition to offend you, halt your fellowship with Jesus, and end your usefulness. So don't faint!

Forgive your unreasonable "Jews" or "Festuses." Carefully trust God and obey His Word yourself, believing He'll faithfully deliver you in His time and way. Meanwhile, be reasonable. Accept that, like Jesus' and Paul's cross experiences, yours is, well...unreasonable!

Chapter 42

You'll Never Fail

ESIDES DECLARING "GOD IS LOVE,"[1] Scripture describes the distinctive characteristics of God's love—and concludes those who walk in it will never fail.
First Corinthians 13:4–8 says God's love:

- "SUFFERETH LONG, AND IS KIND." Patient, love is willing to suffer long to help, bless, save, or deliver others. How? By intercession, hard work, care-giving, counsel, forgiveness, and other ministerial acts. Yet even when long frustrated, love refuses to be bitter. How? It's supernaturally renewed by God's gracious Spirit daily as we fellowship with Him. So wherever impatience or bitterness is, love is not.

- "ENVIETH NOT." Love recognizes envy is satanic, "not from above…[but] demoniacal," and that wherever it is, "there is confusion and every evil work" (James 3:15–16). So whenever envy arises, love moves us to quickly expel it. We confess envy, reject it, thank God for our blessings, and commend Him for blessing the very ones we've envied! Where envy is, love is not.

- "VAUNTETH NOT ITSELF, IS NOT PUFFED UP." Because love adores God, it detests whatever He hates—especially pride! So love doesn't boast or shamelessly self-promote. It's humble and doesn't think of itself too highly. Where pride is, love is not.

- "DOTH NOT BEHAVE ITSELF UNSEEMLY." Knowing God desires good behavior, love inspires it. Abandoning rude, offensive, immoral, or illegal behavior, it pursues excellent conduct. Where misbehavior is, love is not.

- "SEEKETH NOT ITS OWN." Love isn't self-centered. God-centered, it focuses on satisfying His pleasure and plans and eagerly helps build the kingdom of Christ, not self. Where selfishness is, love is not.

- "Is not easily provoked." Or, "easily angered" (NIV).
  God's love is understandably displeased with all that spoils
  His benevolent will. Yet it's consistently slow, not quick, to
  anger. Where irritability is, love is not.

- "Thinketh no evil." Equating thoughts with acts, love
  screens ungodly thoughts to keep its mind pure and pleasing to God. Forgetting whatever it forgives, it "keeps no
  record of being wronged" (NLT) and so "it is not... resent-
  ful" (ESV). Where evil thoughts are, love is not.

- "Rejoiceth not in iniquity [injustice, wrongdoing]."
  Holy and just, love can't be glad when sin or injustice prevails. It helps change what it can, prays, and patiently
  waits for the just One to set everything else right. Where
  sin or injustice is celebrated, love is not.

- "But rejoiceth in the truth." Or, "whenever the truth
  wins out" (NLT). Why? Passionately truth-seeking, love cel-
  ebrates every phase of truth—honesty, reality, faithfulness,
  and God's Word. Where lying, pretense, infidelity, or error
  is cheered, love is not.

- "Beareth all things." Supremely strong, love carries all
  burdens encountered in God's will, for love of Him and by
  His "sufficient" grace (2 Cor. 12:9). Wherever we refuse to
  "bear ye one another's burdens" (Gal. 6:2), love is not.

- "Believeth all things." Or, "always trusts" (NIV). Love
  believes everything God says—the Bible's history, revelation,
  prophecy, promises, and warnings—because it's convinced
  He's utterly faithful. Where doubt of God is, love is not.

- "Hopeth all things." Or, "always hopes" (NIV). Resting
  in God's faithfulness, love always expects the fulfillments
  of His Word. Even during periods of perplexing, persisting contradictions, it chooses hope over despair, joyfully
  anticipating a tomorrow divinely made better than today.
  Where discouragement is, love is not.

- "Endureth all things." Or, "always perseveres" (NIV).
  Love's faith and hope inspire it to endure whatever

hardships God sends to mature us however long they last. Whether tested by long delays, persisting persecutions, or protracted injustices, love steadily walks on keeping "my command to endure patiently" (Rev. 3:10, NIV). Wherever we refuse to endure further hardships, love is not.

- "LOVE NEVER FAILETH." Though gentle, meek, and patient, love isn't weak. Quite the contrary, it's the strongest grace. Loving others strengthens us: "Love edifies" (1 Cor. 8:1, NKJV), or "It is love that strengthens the church" (NLT). As we bear, believe, hope, and endure all things, we gradually develop more of love's amazing, invincible power. Whatever the obstacle, we eventually rise above it. Where weakness is, love is not.

Are you walking in this kind of love?

If you're a born-again, Spirit-baptized Christian, it's already "shed abroad" in your heart (Rom. 5:5). Jesus said this love identifies His true disciples, ordered us to love each other, and asked His Father to help us do so.[2] So release God's love by loving those who are near you daily. Replenish it by seeking regular refillings of the Spirit who makes love easy. Grow it by continuing to think, speak, and practice it.

Then, filled with and sustained by love's invincible strength, you'll never fail.

Chapter 43

THE GOADS OF GOD

*J*ESUS TOLD SAUL of Tarsus he was futilely and perilously resisting God's "goads" (Acts 9:5). But what were they?

In ancient Israel goads were long poles (eight feet) sharpened on one end and having a wide metal blade on the other, used primarily to prod animals to obey their masters' commands. While used on other animals, including sheep, goads were typically used on oxen during plowing. Being long, they easily reached their subjects. The blade end was used to dig, especially to remove dirt, roots, and thorns from the plow.[1] All this facilitated the plowing process, preparing hard uncultivated ground for planting and harvests. Goads also served as weapons, helping win wars against God's enemies. Shamgar slew 600 Philistines with an "oxgoad" (Judg. 3:31).

Historically, then, goads were used to prod to obedience, plow hard ground, dig away dirt, and slay God's enemies, all to produce rich harvests or win God's battles. But what did Jesus mean by "goads" (Acts 9:5)?

Spiritually, God's goads are His words or will communicated by wise Christians: "The words of the wise are like goads" (Eccles. 12:11). These "words of truth" (v. 10) prodding us to do God's will are "given by one Shepherd," Jesus (v. 11, NAS). He shows the "wise" (God-fearing, Spirit-led Christians, ministers) corrective, lifting, or guiding words revealing His will (Isa. 50:4). Always they're timely and motivating. To "kick against the goads" is to resist these inspired promptings to obey God, like an ox kicking against its master's sharpened goad and injuring its heels.

Like physical ones, spiritual "goads" prod, plow, dig, and slay—and bring harvests and victories.

They prod our consciences to obey God when we're procrastinating. They plow us, disturbing our lukewarm devotion, overturning our proud self-confidence, and breaking up our hard wills to respond softly to God. They dig deep, penetrating our conscious and subconscious minds to remove the "dirt" of sin, "roots" of bitterness, and "thorns" of selfishness and worldliness. As they "discern" our wrong "thoughts and intents" God further purifies us (Heb. 4:12), if we humbly confess them and repent. As we yield to God's goads—biblical teachings, counsels, corrections, and exhortations—they also slay God's enemies within us, mortifying the control of our "flesh," or old self-serving nature (Rom. 8:12–13). With this Goliath slain, we're ready for spiritual fruitfulness and conquests. Such goading isn't comfortable.

It isn't supposed to be. Goads are designed not to comfort but to change oxen's minds and actions, fields' conditions and fruitfulness, and Christians' souls and obedience! And that's exactly what God's goads do.

They're long, reaching our consciences even when we're living far from God! They're sharp, quickly dividing and clarifying our confusing problems. They plow effectively, changing our hard, barren hearts into soft, fruitful fields and turning our spiritual defeats into victories—if we humbly receive their uncomfortable but vital work. Observe our Master's goads, or "the words of the wise," in action.

The gospel prods unbelievers to repent and receive Jesus. Teaching on discipleship stirs converts to diligently study, practice, and share biblical truth. Testimonies and prophecies spur disciples to prepare for Christian service (1 Tim. 4:14). Godly counsel prods us to follow God's paths at life's crossroads. Spirit-led reproofs motivate us to abandon our recurring faults. Stirring exhortations move us from indolence to diligence. Spirit-empowered teaching inspires us to research key or timely biblical topics. Rebukes move us to turn from reckless backsliding to God's secure, peaceful ways. Teaching on occultism prods us to "Ephesianize," or remove all symbols or books promoting witchcraft or magic (Acts 19:13–20). Expositing end-time prophecy stimulates us to prepare *now* for Jesus' appearing. Teaching on charity and worship inspires us to dedicate more money to the needy and praise to the Savior. Preaching against worldliness nudges us to exchange temporal pursuits for more time with Jesus. If we respond to these goads, they cease. If we resist, they persist.

And bring more difficulty. And more futility. And more chastening! Jesus warned Saul of Tarsus, "It is dangerous and it will turn out badly for you to keep kicking against the goad [to offer vain and perilous resistance]" (Acts 9:5, AMP). Wisely, Paul yielded and stopped kicking against God's will—specifically, His Son Jesus, His gospel, and His people! Though temporarily blinded (v. 8), he avoided further chastening. Amazing kingdom harvests and conquests followed.[2] Is Saul's Master goading you?

Is He urging you, His sheep, to some change, path, duty, ministry, or sacrifice? Let His goad prod, not pierce you. Let Him turn your trouble into a triumph. Let Him make you His harvester and conqueror. Stop kicking and start obeying the goads of God.

Chapter 44

LOST YOUR FOCUS?

*A*RE YOU SPIRITUALLY focused? Often the difference between fulfilling and failing God's will is simply our concentration. While focused, the apostle Peter easily did the impossible.

One stormy night the apostles saw Jesus walking on Galilee's churning waters toward their wave-battered boat. Peter immediately asked permission to approach: "Lord, if it be thou, bid me come" (Matt. 14:28). Surprisingly, Jesus authorized him: "Come" (v. 29). Assured, Peter left the boat and, amazingly, duplicated Jesus' mastery of the impossible—with his attention carefully focused on Jesus: "When Peter was come down out of the boat, he walked on the water, [looking] *to go to Jesus*" (v. 29). Everything went well, with sufficient grace abounding, while Peter maintained his spiritually minded, Christ-centered focus. Then something changed.

Specifically, his focus. Instead of gazing at his inspiring Helper, he began concentrating on his imposing hindrances...and sinking: "When he saw the wind boisterous, he was afraid; and beginning to sink..." (v. 30). Though scared, he prayed, "Lord, save me" (v. 30). Mercifully Jesus quickly stopped his sinking and started his studying—what had happened, and why, so it wouldn't happen again. Succinctly, Peter's demise began when he became distracted by the enveloping "boisterous" contradictions he saw, heard, and felt (waves and winds; v. 30). The moment he yielded to their pressure, turning his attention from the faithful, living Word to the ferocious, large waves, he began to "doubt" his authorization (v. 31), unwisely reconsidering what Jesus had plainly said. The more he rethought his problem and doubted Jesus' leading, the lower he sank, in fear and water. Overwhelmed, instead of fulfilling Christ's will—to continue walking stably on the turbid waters—he failed. This didn't have to happen.

If Peter had recognized his distraction and quickly refocused, he could have maintained his overcoming position and fulfilled Jesus' plan. To avoid Peter's error, let's consider the importance of focusing, the power of distractions, some typical spiritual distractions, and how to refocus.

Concentration is essential to all success, worldly or spiritual. To excel, we must harness our mental powers and keep them fastened on the tasks before us. The dentist's eyes focus on the tooth he's drilling and the surgeon's on his incision. The singer concentrates on enunciating her words and staying on pitch. The politician's advisers remind him constantly to stay on message. Thus focused, these fulfill their missions. So will we.

To walk with God, keep our faith, and finish our course, we must be spiritually focused. Jesus gave us a clear focal point: "Seek ye first the kingdom of God, and his righteousness" (Matt. 6:33). Are we seeking the King and His kingdom purposes first every morning? In every decision? In every test? If so, we'll build a spiritually focused life. We'll experience close, sweet fellowship with Jesus, live by strong, stable trust in His faithfulness, and enjoy unshakable confidence in His Word. With such closeness and certainty, we'll rise above all the "waters"[1] that challenge us. Unless we're distracted.

In this world, distractions are everywhere and powerful. In war, an army attacks one city to draw enemy forces from another, which it then successfully assaults. In athletics, a tennis player stands at net with racket raised for an overhead slam, only to tap the ball just over the net at the last moment so his opponent can't return it. In court, the clever defense attorney attacks the prosecution witness' credibility to divert the jury's attention from his client's guilt. While driving, the motorist looks away from the road briefly to send a short text message—his last! Behold the power and consequences of worldly distractions.

And spiritual distractions. Anything or anyone that unduly interferes with our walk and work with Christ is a distraction and a threat to our spiritual success. Some common spiritual diverters are politics, moneymaking, relationships, pastimes, entertainment, investments, houses, automobiles, the Internet, technology, weaknesses, faults, failures, disagreements, financial needs, health issues, delayed promises or visions, church programs or activities. Presently American Christians are grossly distracted with political controversies and economic worries. If these or other spiritual waves are overwhelming you, it's time to refocus. Know how?

Do whatever gets you closer to Jesus and stronger in spirit. Examine yourself, confessing and forsaking all sin. Take extra time to feed on God's Word—slowly, thoughtfully pondering and noting timely promises, passages, and references: "Stand thou still a while, that I may show thee the word of God" (1 Sam. 9:27). Pray more, pouring out your heart to God. Offer a sacrifice of praise and worship. Return to faithfully pursuing your church or ministry duties. This will refocus you spiritually.

Thereafter, periodically ask yourself if you've lost your focus.

Chapter 45

TARGET CHURCHES

EVER ONE TO leave God's work unchallenged, Satan attacked the first Christians early and often. After stirring persecution outside, he began troubling the saints within their ranks with secret sin, divisive prejudice, and finally, heresy.[1]

False teaching first invaded the Antioch (Syria) church through the Judaizers—Pharisaic Christians who insisted Gentiles had to become Jewish proselytes to be "saved" (Acts 15:1–2). Why the attack in Antioch? Why at this time? The reason is simple: Antioch's church was full of spiritual excellence and thriving growth. Matthew Henry wrote, "If ever there was a heaven upon earth, surely it was in the church at Antioch at this time."[2] Let's examine their excellent features. They began at the top.

Antioch's leaders were spiritually mature (apostolic), culturally diverse (Acts 13:1), and shepherdly, as seen in their constant watchfulness, sharp discernment, and brave determination to refute error (Acts 15:1–2). Their teachers—the backbone of strong churches—were as good as they come, including Paul and Peter, whose biblical insights and exhortations still feed and challenge us.[3] Their elders were spiritually disciplined, always addressing problems and launching works first by prayer and fasting (Acts 13:3). Therefore the congregation experienced dynamic growth. Spiritually they matured steadily, and numerically they added disciples steadily and in spurts (Acts 11:21, 24). God's invisible "hand"—the awesome power of the Holy Spirit—worked dynamically through their preaching and prayers (v. 21). As Mark later wrote, "The Lord [Himself] working with them" (Mark 16:20). They heard God's voice clearly, as the Spirit directed their works with unerring guidance and, as needed, strong checks (Acts 13:2, 4). And this wasn't all.

They had a heart for true worship. Their leaders regularly "ministered to the Lord," praising, thanking, and worshipping Christ in spirit and in truth, and urged the people to also do so (vv. 1–2). They were zealously committed to missions. Not occasionally but regularly they gave themselves to intercede for, support, receive, and hold accountable missionaries (Acts 14:26–27), even releasing their best ministers for the Messiah's missions (Acts 13:3). Not false but true prophets ministered to them. Their preaching edified and their prophetic utterances were accurate and confirmed by undeniable fulfillments.[4] Their charity was real and Spirit-led. As needs arose, they gave compassionately and freely (Acts 11:28, 29–30). Their relationships with other churches and ministers were excellent. In Christ's desired unity, they lovingly received other churches' messengers and ministers and humbly sought their counsel and assistance as needed.[5] They all ministered. Not just their elders but every congregant attended, waited upon, and served souls through evangelism, intercession, assistance, sharing God's Word, and most importantly, by demonstrating Jesus' character and ways of living daily. Thus their spiritually excellent, Christlike life-witness drew many to Jesus and earned them a distinctive reputation as being "Christians," or *Christ's loyalists*: "The disciples were called Christians first in Antioch" (Acts 11:26).[6] Predictably, these delightful qualities drew Satan's determined opposition.

But if the Antiochians had been compromised by worldliness, lukewarmness, sinfulness, or error, the adversary wouldn't have attacked them. When churches are spiritually substandard, he likes and leaves them as they are. Since, however, the Antiochians maintained a high level of spiritual excellence, he targeted them. This tests us.

No right-minded leaders or congregations want to be targets! Yet we should desire spiritual excellence so much that, even if it means facing periodic satanic attacks—from reproach to ostracism to harassment to heresy—we'll stay the course God's Word, Spirit, and call set for us. During such times we receive strength from remembering that, if we react rightly, opposition only makes us stronger, wiser, and more discerning, transformed, compassionate, approved, and prepared for Jesus' appearing. Paul went so far as to declare heretical and other controversies "must" come to accomplish this spiritual growth: "Of course, there must be divisions among you so that you who have God's approval will be recognized" (1 Cor. 11:19, NLT). And these attacks occur in proportion to our spiritual condition. The more excellence we walk in, the more challenges we walk into—and the more spiritual growth and divine approval we gain. Pause and ponder this.

And ponder well Antioch's spiritual excellence: mature leadership, excellent teaching, disciplined prayer, dynamic growth, God's "hand" working, His voice heard clearly, true worship, a commitment to missions, accurate prophecy, real charity, everyone ministering, cooperation with other churches and ministers, and a Christian reputation springing from Christlike living! That's awesome—wonder at it. It's attainable—God's done it before. It's available—He can do it again. If we ask...

So humbly ask God to make your church spiritually excellent. Keep asking, believing, and thanking Him until He does it! Then maintain your spiritual excellence. And when tests come, give thanks: you're one of Christ's target churches!

Chapter 46

BOUND FOR A CERTAIN ISLAND

*O*F ALL PAUL'S trials, his voyage to Rome was the most tumultuous. For two weeks his vessel, a large Alexandrian grain ship, appeared totally out of control.

When a powerful Mediterranean storm suddenly "caught" the ship, its pilot tried unsuccessfully to keep navigating: "When the ship was caught, and could not bear up into the wind, we let her drive" (Acts 27:15). Besides high winds, cloud cover made navigation impossible. Ancient mariners relied on celestial observation to determine their position and course. After not seeing the "sun nor stars in many days" (v. 20), the pilot had no idea where the ship was located or headed. Thus it was relentlessly "driven up and down" (v. 27) at the mercy of the merciless powers of the air. Not man but wind was now commanding.

Yet while the dark, swirling chaos seemed to do what it would with Paul's ship, God was still in control and Paul on course. An angel revealed the heavenly Pilot was guiding Paul's troubled ship to a "certain island" and it "must" reach it (v. 26). Why? God foresaw the storm and devised a plan to use it for His purposes.

Earlier Jesus revealed His plan to send Paul to Rome—or send the world's greatest apostle to the world's greatest city to address the world's greatest leader (Acts 23:11). Now the angel revealed a second, more immediate part of Christ's plan: Paul will also visit a "certain island" (Acts 27:26).

Acts 28 discloses that island was Malta. There Christ planned to:

- Grant an attesting miracle giving Paul favor with the chief official (vv. 1–7)

- Reveal Jesus' compassion by healing the official's father and others (vv. 7–9)

- Evangelize the Maltese (v. 9)[1]

- Honor Paul, whose faith had honored Him in the storm (v. 10; cf. 1 Sam. 2:30)

- Give Paul a well-deserved, three-month sabbatical (Acts 28:11)

- Use these impressive signs, healings, and honors to give
  Paul more influence with the centurion Julius, who later
  delayed his mission a week just so Paul could visit the
  Puteolian Christians (vv. 13–14)[2]

Though the terrible storm had seemed to delay Paul's travel itinerary, his arrival on Malta was perfectly timed.

God's coordination of events was exquisite. On Malta He worked everything for good. The chief official's bedridden father needed immediate healing. The people, though superstitious, were ready for Paul's gospel. Julius needed another ship to transport his prisoners to Rome and found one wintering there (v. 11). And exhausted from the ordeal, Paul needed the three months' rest. So during the wild, cold, and wet two-week northeaster, everything had remained in God's hands and on His schedule.

When the Alexandrian ship's pilot sat down, the heavenly Pilot stood up to keep Paul's ship in a clear channel through the dense chaos. Though the mariners couldn't fix their position on the sun, the Sun of righteousness was fixing their position from above. While they looked anxiously for the deadly Libyan shoals, God was faithfully leading them toward Malta. Though they lost "all hope" (Acts 27:20), their future was still very hopeful. Though they appeared headed for certain death, they were headed for a "certain" island. Why? God's faithful servant, Paul, was on board and praying to the heavenly Pilot.

Ever faithful, that Helmsman has led many of His faithful, praying servants through storms of uncertainty to certain places of service or blessing. He guided David through a dark, sunless wilderness to a shining place of leadership; Philip through a strange call to the desert to evangelize a key Ethiopian official; Ruth through a starless night of sorrow to a new day of love, fruitfulness, and security; John the Baptist through years of lonely separation to a popular riverside ministry that converted thousands; the oppressed English Separatists through a stormy North Atlantic passage to a free, rich new world; and the fifth-century missionary, Patrick, through cold, choppy seas to a literal "certain island"—Ireland! He's the same benevolent Helmsman today.

Like Paul, are you "caught" and "driven up and down" in a dark, confusing trial? Have you seen no lights of reassurance or guidance for "many days"? Have you lost confidence that you're still on course and in God's plan? Are things spiraling out of control, seemingly at the mercy of the cruel "prince of the power of the air"?[3] Don't despair! The heavenly

Pilot is still guiding your life-vessel on a clear channel through your chaotic situation. Keep trusting, serving, and obeying Him—and praying, until He brings you, and those sailing with you, with perfect timing, to the certain place of service or blessing He's chosen. So don't mourn.

Rejoice! You're bound for a certain island.

Chapter 47

BOUND BY HOPE

*T*HE APOSTLE PAUL told the Roman Jews, "For the hope of Israel I am bound with this chain" (Acts 28:20). What was the "hope of Israel" that bound Paul?

It was Israel's great expectation of Messiah's coming, the establishment of His kingdom, and the resurrection of the dead. It was because Paul preached this—that Messiah Jesus had come, risen from the dead, and initiated His spiritual kingdom, the church—that he found himself persecuted and bound to a Roman soldier day and night.

Today we also hope for Messiah Jesus' coming—not to the earth but to appear above it to resurrect dead Christians, catch up living ones, receive us all into His heavenly kingdom, and, seven years later, return with us to establish His earthly kingdom for a thousand years. For this "blessed hope" we eagerly await and diligently prepare (Titus 2:11–13). So does Jesus!

The Rapture will be the first time Jesus fully gathers and embraces His beloved bride church, all those He gave Himself to redeem, purify, teach, transform, and live with forever. "Bound"—gripped, motivated, and guided—by His great desire to meet us, Jesus is eagerly preparing living quarters, blessings, and new kingdom responsibilities for us in heaven: "I go to prepare a place for you" (John 14:2). Paul urged us to respond by "setting" our hearts on meeting Jesus, not on worldly ends: "Seek those things which are above...set your affection on things above, not on things on the earth" (Col. 3:1–2). Then we'll know we'll be taken when Jesus appears: "[And] when Christ...shall appear, then shall ye also appear with him" (v. 4). If we obey Paul, we'll be "bound" by the same hope that motivated him and grips Jesus!

As Jesus' appearing draws closer, this hope will bind us to:

- "Walk with God" ever more closely so, like Enoch, we'll be taken (Gen. 5:22–24)

- Fully trust God, so we avoid doubt, unbelief, and apathy (Rev. 3:15–16)

- Steadily discharge our divinely appointed duties, so we'll be found "faithful" (Matt. 25:21)

- Diligently study God's Word, so we'll know and share His will, plan, and prophecies (2 Tim. 2:15)

- Live faithfully in our earthly marriages in preparation for our heavenly marriage to Christ

- Submit to all authorities so Christ may give us authority now and in His kingdom (Rom. 13:1–7)

- Perfect our gifts by use, so we may honor Christ now and receive rewards and greater responsibilities at His judgment

- Steadily pursue our "high calling," avoiding entanglement with lesser causes (Phil. 3:13–14)

- Righteous living, since Christians living in sin, like Lot's wife, won't escape when Jesus appears (Luke 17:32–36)

- Quickly confess and forsake our sins, so we walk in the light of God's truth and guidance daily (1 John 1:5–9)

- Prayer, so we'll be "watching," "praying," and spiritually "worthy," instead of indifferent, indulgent, and unfit when Jesus appears (Luke 21:34–36)

- An invincibly positive outlook that lifts us above despair or bitterness as our culture declines in these last days

- Fellowship with and exhort other believers daily, so we'll all maintain spiritual readiness (Heb. 3:13)

- Fulfill our ministries, to help Jesus' beloved bride church "make herself ready" (Rev. 19:7; Matt. 25:10)

- Patiently endure tests, knowing those who do so will be "kept from" the tribulation period (Rev. 3:10)

- Increasingly praise and worship God, since we'll be doing so in heaven forever (Rev. 4–5)

- A sweet consolation, when believing relatives or friends pass, knowing we'll see them again at Jesus' appearing (1 Thess. 4:13–18)

- Tell others about Jesus' saving grace and appearing, so they'll also prepare to escape the coming wrath (1 Thess. 5:9–10)

Thus gripped, motivated, guided, and limited daily, we'll be truly "blessed." This hope-influenced living isn't novel.

Everyone's bound by some hope. Joyful anticipations of pleasant changes, expectations of tomorrows better than today, these longings drive all people. We hitch our life-wagons to stars or visions of desire and travel longingly toward them. Even the hopeless are bound by a hope. They expect a tomorrow worse than today, and slowly, sadly plod toward it. And non-expectation usually gets its expectations!

But the hope Jesus offers only blesses—lifting, inspiring, cleansing, guiding, and unifying us: "Every man that hath this hope in him purifieth himself" (1 John 3:3). It never deceives or disappoints: "Unto them that look [eagerly] for him shall he appear" (Heb. 9:28). Knowing this, Satan has a very different hope.

He desires to confuse, refute, and spoil our "blessed hope" and leave us burdened, miserable, and bound by hopelessness. Escape his designs today. With Paul, be bound by hope.

Chapter 48

PRISON MINISTRY—PAUL'S WAY

ODAY "PRISON MINISTRY" usually refers to Christians ministering to prisoners. We visit jails and prisons to evangelize,
teach, encourage, or aid the incarcerated. Many churches
sponsor these open doors behind locked doors.

The apostle Paul received prison ministry, most notably from
Onesiphorus. Of his sweet help in bitter times Paul wrote touchingly,
"The Lord give mercy unto the house of Onesiphorus; for he often re-
freshed me, and was not ashamed of my chain, but, when he was in
Rome, he sought me out very diligently, and found me" (2 Tim. 1:16–17).
Yet to Paul, "prison ministry" meant more.

It included prisoners ministering to others, incarcerated or free. For
a chained prisoner Paul's ministry was surprisingly unbound.

For instance, during his two-year detention in Caesarea, though
bound to a guard, Paul had liberty to minister. Though restricted to a
cell in Herod's judgment hall (Acts 23:35), he was free to receive and
converse with anyone who called (Acts 24:23). Thus, though imprisoned,
he ministered freely and frequently. And without prejudice.

Paul told King Agrippa he busied himself "witnessing both to small
and great" (Acts 26:22). An egalitarian, Paul considered all souls equally
dear to God. He didn't seek audiences with the rich and powerful, yet received them when they came calling. He evangelized prisoners as gladly
as princes. He shared Jesus with everyone who listened—genuinely or
disingenuously. The Roman governor Felix summoned Paul frequently,
seemingly eager to hear the gospel, but secretly hoping for a bribe (Acts
24:26)! Despite Felix's duplicity, Paul still shared Christ with him. Why?
He knew Christ died for all and wants all to know Him, even deceivers!
Paul's free and unbiased prison ministry didn't begin in Caesarea.

It started in Philippi. There Paul ministered hope to hopeless
prisoners, who "heard" his prayers and praises ascend from the "inner
prison" and saw God's stunning response (Acts 16:25–26). He ministered
salvation and baptism to the jailer and his household (vv. 27–34). And
he ministered correction to the unprincipled city magistrates (vv. 35–40).
All this occurred while Paul was in custody.

During his voyage from Caesarea to Rome, Paul continued

ministering in chains. He dispensed guidance to the commanding centurion, exhortation to his discouraged shipmates, healing to Malta's sick, fellowship and teaching to the Puteoli church, and an amazingly bright, Christlike life-witness to the "other [condemned] prisoners" sailing with him (Acts 27:1)—some of whom were scheduled for execution in Rome.

Under house arrest in Rome, Paul persevered. Beginning with the local Jewish leaders, he "received all" who visited him, teaching them about Jesus without interference from political or religious authorities (Acts 28:17–31). Still unbiased, he continued witnessing to "small and great," from the socially undistinguished servants and guards of the emperor's palace to Nero himself and his family (Phil. 1:13; 4:22). He also penned his four inspiring and instructive "prison epistles"[1] while in Rome. Others practiced prison ministry Paul's way.

The Bible highlights two extraordinary examples. Joseph ministered excellently in prison by interpreting the dreams of Pharaoh's incarcerated butler and baker. The apostle John wrote for us his monumental Book of Revelation while exiled on the Isle of Patmos. Church history reveals more prison ministers.

For nineteen months John Knox demonstrated courageous, uncompromising faith to the captive oarsmen suffering alongside him in a French galley. During the ten months Martin Luther spent hidden in Wartburg castle—his unofficial prison-refuge after Charles V declared him an outlaw—he translated a much-beloved German New Testament. Though imprisoned twelve years in Bedford jail for preaching without a license, John Bunyan continued preaching by penning his inspiring and comforting allegory, *The Pilgrim's Progress*. Like Paul's, these examples call us to practice prison ministry, literally or figuratively.

And many have. More recently, Watchman Nee, Corrie ten Boom, Dietrich Bonhoeffer, Richard Wurmbrand, and countless thousands less known have continued ministering while imprisoned by anti-Christian authorities. Despite cruel detention, they helped others by intercession, exhortation, evangelism, writing, teaching, or example. But your incarceration may not be literal.

Instead your chains may be figurative—inflexible circumstances, people, duties, finances, or other restrictive conditions that limit your opportunities to minister as freely or often as you wish. Whatever your prison or house arrest, follow Paul's grand example. In your bonds refuse to succumb to self-pity, abide close to Jesus daily, and faithfully pour out

His Word, hope, mercy, and help to everyone around you small and great. As Paul and the others above did this, despite their limitations, God's unlimited grace helped them: "Having, therefore, obtained help from God, I continue unto this day, witnessing..." (Acts 26:22).

He'll do the same for you as you practice prison ministry—Paul's way.

Chapter 49

ANGELS STAND BY

*W*HEN PAUL SAILED for Rome from Caesarea, God prompted two believers to accompany him (Acts 27:2). Apparently Luke's and Aristarchus' mission was to stand by Paul as he stood before Nero. En route they could also provide sweet fellowship as Paul faced the bitter prospect of execution. But something challenged God's plan.

"Euroclydon," a massive storm system, mercilessly battered Paul's ship for "many days" (vv. 14, 20). Eventually Luke and Aristarchus' hope failed: "When neither sun nor stars in many days appeared...all hope that we should be saved was then taken away" (v. 20). Doubtful and discouraged, their fellowship no longer blessed and supported Paul. Thus instead of standing by him, they stood down from their assignment, leaving Paul in grave peril, without help, and seemingly abandoned by Christ.

But when Paul's friends stood down, Christ's angel stood by, continuing to comfort and support Paul as he continued to pray about his situation. Paul testified, "There stood by me this night an angel of God...saying, Fear not, Paul, thou must be brought before Caesar [as promised]" (vv. 23–24). No accident, Jesus had promised this unfailing support: "I will not leave you comfortless; I will come to you" (John 14:18). How does Jesus come to us?

Exactly as He did with Paul. When we face stormy or bitter difficulties, Christ stands by us through believing friends. Their faith helps calm us in our storms. Their sweet fellowship helps make our bitter trials palatable. Their presence with us helps make us stronger in our adversaries' presence. Why? Christ in them helps steady and strengthen Christ in us. But Satan will challenge this plan.

When pressed by long, dark stormy tests of faith, our Lukes may lose hope in God's faithfulness and, discouraged, stand down from helping us. Though called to stand by Paul and Barnabas on their first mission, Mark stood down from his calling. Others will stand off from us when our prolonged adversities seem to prove Christ has forsaken us. During Paul's second Roman imprisonment, many Christians stood off: "Everyone from the province of Asia has deserted me" (2 Tim. 1:15, NLT). Or when we stand on God's Word against sin or false teachings, and God withholds signs of His approval, some will stand undecided. On Mount Carmel, Elijah rebuked the Israelites' indecision in the face of his conflict with idolatry: "How long halt ye between two opinions?" (1 Kings 18:21).

In our adversities others will be forced to stand separated from us, desiring but unable to help. When Herod Agrippa held Peter in prison for execution, the Jerusalem church wanted to stand by him, but couldn't due to Herod's tight security. So they stood by in spirit: "Prayer was made without ceasing by the church unto God for him" (Acts 12:5). Some close to us may stand up to defy us. When David was old and vulnerable, his son Absalom cruelly usurped David's kingship. Such rebellions breed betrayers, as some switch loyalties to stand on the side of those who appear to have defeated us. When David heard Ahithophel, his closest friend, was "among the conspirators with Absalom," his heart broke (2 Sam. 15:31).[1]

In all these troubles, not only our friends but also Jesus' angels faithfully stand by to see us through! How do angels "serve those who will inherit salvation" (Heb. 1:14, NIV)? As we pray, Christ dispatches them to:

- Speak encouragement to our hearts—or ears (Acts 27:23–24)

- Strengthen us physically (Luke 22:43)

- Release us from unjust spiritual or literal bonds (Acts 12:7)

- Guide us providentially, personally, or in visions[2]

- Confuse those who threaten or plot against us (Gen. 19:11)

- Close lying mouths that would devour our good name (Dan. 6:22)

- Surround us with an impassable "hedge" of protection (Ps. 91:10–12; Job 1:10)

- Teach us vital insights as we study Scripture (Dan. 10:20–21)

- Visit and fellowship with us in human form (Heb. 13:2)

- Rescue us by stopping our hardened persecutors (2 Chr. 32:20–22)

Thank God that, however distressed, confused, lonely, misunderstood, hindered, or hated we are, friends and angels are standing by to help—if we pray, as Paul did in his storm! A word on angels.

Never obsess over, seek to contact, or venerate angels. But when in stormy trials others stand down, off, undecided, separated, against, or on the other side, never hesitate to ask Christ to dispatch them: "Lord, please send angels to help us!" Then give thanks and rest in faith in your storm.

Is a spiritual Euroclydon mercilessly battering you? Rejoice! There's never cause for offense, self-pity, panic, or despair when angels stand by.

Chapter 50

REMEMBER THE HUGUENOTS!

*H*OW WE SEE our sufferings determines how we endure them. If we imagine our troubles are the worst, we're the worse for it.

I know one Christian sister who was told by a prophetess, "No one has ever suffered like you have." Poor dear, she believed it, pitied herself, and stopped growing. How do I know this "word" wasn't correct?

It contradicts God's Word. Scripture says, however severe they may feel, our sufferings are not unique but are rather "common to man" (1 Cor. 10:13). Or, "The temptations in your life are no different from what others experience" (NLT). It also ignores the grave sufferings in biblical biographies—the harried lives of Joseph, Moses, David, Hannah, Paul, and others. It further disregards church history's catalog of martyrs, confessors, exiles, and others defamed, detained, deported, or tortured during Jewish, Roman, Catholic, and Islamic persecutions. Additionally it overlooks current Christian sufferers in lands or provinces hostile to Christianity—North Korea, China, India, Africa, Islamic states, and others.

Conversely, studying other Christians' troubles, rejections, and losses for Christ's sake makes ours seem easier, especially when theirs are obviously much worse. Such meditations may even embolden us. Paul noted:

> It has become known…that my imprisonment is for Christ. And…the brothers, having become confident in the Lord by my imprisonment, are much more bold to speak the word without fear.
>
> —PHILIPPIANS 1:13–14, ESV

So let's consider one Christian group whose afflictions far outweigh ours, so we'll be heartened to preach the good Word and fight the good fight more vigorously. Our sample sufferers, whose distresses rivaled those of early Roman Christians,[1] are the Huguenots.

"Huguenot" was the derisive nickname given French Protestants during the Reformation. It was first used in Tours, where Protestants met illegally at night near a gate purported haunted nightly by the spirit of mythical King Huguon. Thus local Catholics hinted Protestant beliefs and activities were as strange and suspicious as Huguon's appearances!

The Huguenots, however, accepted the insult and went on to produce, nurture, or support many outstanding leaders, such as, Calvin, Farel, Beza, and Viret. But living and ministering in Catholic France was no easy calling.

After the Peace of Augsburg (1555) European countries followed the religion of their kings. For the next three centuries French monarchs pulled the Huguenots back and forth with their waffling Edicts of: Nantes (1598), granting them toleration; Fontainebleau (1685), retracting it; and Versailles (1787), reestablishing it! During their long tribulation period Huguenots suffered acutely under two especially oppressive rulers.

Their first antichrist, Catherine de Medici ("Madame le Serpent" to many), ordered the brutal assassination of the Huguenot leader Coligny in 1572, sparking the Saint Bartholomew's Day massacre, during which Catholic zealots slaughtered over 12,000 Protestants throughout France.[2] Resilient, the Huguenots survived and began growing again.

Their second beast was worse. Not content to harass, Louis XIV aimed to exterminate French Protestants. His persecution was systematic, cruel, and relentless.

Initially Louis harassed Huguenots with restrictions: banning daytime funerals; limiting ministers to one church; disallowing psalm singing (a Huguenot delight) outdoors, or even indoors when Catholic processions passed by; reserving seats in Huguenot churches for Catholic observers, who interrupted and challenged the pastor's teaching at will. Then Louis' pressure increased.

He excluded Huguenots from key trade guilds and public offices, forbade them from having Catholic servants, closed their ministers' schools, and ordered their church buildings demolished! Unsatisfied, Louis raged on.

He sent Catholic soldiers (dragoons) to live with Protestant families to "encourage" conversion to Catholicism. Ruthless, the dragoons terrorized Protestant communities, destroying books, ransacking personal belongings, breaking windows, riding horses through shops and homes, and threatening worse abuses. Then came Louis' final stroke.

His Edict of Fontainebleau (1685) outlawed Protestantism, forcing Huguenots to convert. Or, if caught worshipping in France or attempting to flee the country, they were imprisoned, sent to the galleys, deported to the Caribbean, or executed. Thousands converted, but thousands more stayed faithful in their fiery trials in prisons, galleys, exile, or dangerous flights to Switzerland, the Netherlands, England, America, and elsewhere. And we think we're suffering?

Are you weary of your woes? Convinced no one's suffered like you? Pitying yourself? Pouting at God? Ready to stop seeking and serving Him and revert to unbelief or lukewarm religion? Don't do it. Stay faithful in your fires by laying off your hindering spiritual "weights" (Heb. 12:1) and receiving the uplifting ministry of memory.

Remember 1 Corinthians 10:13. Remember the "cloud of witnesses" above—in biblical biographies, church history, and current Christianity (Heb. 12:1). Remember Jesus, who "endured such contradiction of sinners" (v. 3). And remember you haven't yet "resisted unto blood," as they did (v. 4). Still weary?

Remember the Huguenots!

Chapter 51

GET BACK TO GOD'S WORD!

*I*N PSALM 19 David preached this gospel: Get back to God's Word, and all will be well with your soul! But all hadn't been well with David.

Feeling the Sun of righteousness' "heat" of conviction (vv. 4–6), David was deeply troubled by his sins, specifically his "errors, secret faults, presumptuous sins," and unacceptable "words" and "thoughts" (vv. 12–14). Distressed, he sensed he was slipping spiritually, or losing control—and his sins were gaining it: "Don't let them control me" (v. 13, NLT). Feeling helpless he cried: "Who can understand his errors?" (v. 12). But, a fighter, David didn't give up.

With determination he sought God for release from sin's power (v. 13), resumption of his righteous living (v. 13), and restoration of God's full approval for intimate fellowship and fruitful service (v. 14). And, a man of faith, he confidently confessed the Lord would again be his "strength" and "redeemer" (v. 14). But how?

By God's Word! Let's ponder David's instructive commentary on God's Word.

"The law of the LORD [today our whole Bible] is perfect" (19:7), or spiritually complete, revealing all we need to know about God and walking closely with Him. It "[converts] the soul" (v. 7), turning our hearts, minds, and ways of living back to God, and "reviving the soul" (ESV) and "restoring the [whole] person" (AMP) whenever we read and obey it. It's "right" (v. 8), or factually correct and inerrant in its original form.[1] Though neither a scientific nor exhaustive work, the Bible is spiritually accurate, morally exemplary, and historically sufficient. Thus it's "sure" (v. 7). Proven faithful for many centuries, all its principles, proverbs, warnings, promises, and prophecies are certain to occur. It "[makes] wise" (v. 7), imparting the highest good judgment—God's own spiritual, moral, and practical decisions—to anyone who studies and practices it, even unpromising "simple" ones (v. 7).[2] And David continues.

"Rejoicing the heart" (v. 8), Scripture imparts God's supernatural, inspiring gladness, His irrepressible joy that lifts us in even our lowest moments and longest, saddest valleys of "Baca" (Ps. 84:6). Because they're "pure" (Ps. 19:8), God's commands teach us God's purity or holiness.[3] As we read, sit under, and obey biblical teaching, it washes us until we consistently manifest Christ's holiness. "Enlightening" (v. 8), Scripture illuminates the inner "eyes of our understanding" with insight into God's character and ways, our life purpose, God's guidance at life's crossroads and crises, and perplexing people and problems. The ultimate reality check, the Bible imparts the enduring "fear of the Lord" (v. 9) by repeatedly describing God's awesome immensity, power, and unchanging principles of judgment. After reading it, we stand in awe, draw back from displeasing God, and believe His warnings as confidently as His promises. Its ordinances are "true and righteous" (v. 9), or perfectly just, fair, and impartial. If adopted, they'll make us as unbiased as "God," who "is no respecter of persons" (Acts 10:34).

Additionally, David says we're "warned" (Ps. 19:11) of all life's dangers, spiritual and worldly, by God's Word. It faithfully alerts us of sin and judgment, hell, the futility of worldliness,[4] false teachers and prophets, and the approaching tribulation period. If we stay full of the Word, the Spirit will bring appropriate portions of it to mind to warn us when personal danger lurks.[5] Since it reveals the true God, salvation, eternal truth, and way to fulfillment in life, the Word is worth more than anything, even "much fine gold" (v. 10). As life's most valuable asset, therefore, "All the things thou canst desire are not to be compared unto her [the wisdom of God's Word]" (Prov. 3:15). The ultimate soul satisfier, Scripture is antiquity's sweetest sweetener, even "sweeter than honey" (Ps. 19:10). Indeed, trusting and obeying it sweetens our hearts so thoroughly even the bitterest people, experiences, and seasons become tolerable—and springs of sweet, new truths!

If we continue studying and practicing God's Word, God will be so pleased He'll grant us "great" rewards (v. 11), such as:

- Friendship with God, with its "sweet, satisfying companionship of the Lord" (Ps. 25:14, AMP), timely counsels, and growing understanding of His plans and purposes

- Increasing awareness of God's voice and hand in our lives

- God's approval for higher, more fruitful service

- Eternal blessings so great no mortal eye or ear has yet discovered or imagined them (1 Cor. 2:9)

So David concludes God's Word is "more to be desired" (Ps. 19:10) than anything!

Do you desire it most? Or have you forgotten God's written Word links you vitally to His living Word, Jesus? Is sin reasserting its control and the Sun of righteousness increasing His convicting "heat"? Then seek again your most valuable valuable and sweetest sweetener. And remember David's gospel: all will be well when you get back to God's Word!

Chapter 52

ESTABLISHED TO GROW

*L*ORD, ENLARGE US" is the passionate prayer of many churches. And rightly so. While spiritual growth—our character transformation into Christ's image (Rom. 8:29)—is our most essential goal, numerical growth is also important and desirable. But our motives must be right.

Sadly, some church leaders want more congregants for wrong reasons: religious prestige, community pride, rivalry with other pastors or churches, larger revenues, political clout, etc. Others want church growth for pure motives: Jesus commissioned us to "teach [disciple] all nations" (Matt. 28:19). That's a large work, and we want to fulfill it! But how?

Acts illuminates the way: "So were the churches [of Galatia] established in the faith, and increased in number daily" (Acts 16:5). Note the order in this verse. The Galatian churches were "established" first, and then steadily "increased." This is growth through spiritual strength and establishment. But these Gentile churches weren't always strong.

Their confidence had been badly shaken by false teachers insisting that to be "saved" Gentiles must first become Jewish proselytes (Acts 15:1). But the Jerusalem council's "decrees" (Acts 16:4) that Paul distributed to the Gentile churches settled this controversy: Gentiles were saved by grace through faith alone, without Jewish rituals (Acts 15:23–29)! Paul's and Silas' preaching and teaching further strengthened these congregations. Thus strengthened, they steadily grew and gradually became "established" in their walk and work with God (Acts 16:5). Then they increased with more new members! The pattern here is *strengthening-establishment-increase.* But some churches may be strengthened without being fully established.

Before visiting Galatia, Paul ministered in the churches of Syria and Cilicia. His work there was "confirming" (Acts 15:41) or spiritually "strengthening" (NIV), yet stopped short of fully establishing them as mature assemblies. His work in the Galatian churches, however, went further. It "established" them (Acts 16:5), meaning the Galatians were not only strengthened but also became consistently strong, founded, fixed in God and His work, and no longer moved by sin, false teaching, or persecution.[1] Thus "established," the Galatian churches subsequently grew, or "increased in number daily" (v. 5). This pattern persists.

Today the purest numerical growth still occurs when our churches are spiritually established. In that condition our spirits are strong, we're full of the Word, the Spirit moves regularly, we're walking closely with Jesus, our conduct is pure, our attitudes are right, our doctrine is sound, our vision of God's purposes is clear, we walk in God's ways habitually, our fellowship is sweet, and our unity unbreakable. That's a stable, strong groundwork for Christ to build on! He can send us young converts, growing disciples, or penitent backsliders, knowing we'll love, feed, counsel, correct, and model His ways for them, just as He would. That's increase God's way.

But if we're spiritually weak with carnality, error, strife, or divisions, we would inevitably misrepresent Christ and mishandle, mislead and miserably fail those He sends. We would only reproduce our own kind: more weak, confused, contentious, lukewarm, un-established Christians! Or, if desperate, we completely compromise and begin seeking anyone and everyone regardless of the sincerity of their repentance and faith, we may increase, but only with miserably "mixed multitudes" of unconverted, spiritually uninterested people—and all the hindering troubles they bring.[2] That's not increase God's way.

As in Syria and Cilicia, our churches may be strengthened without becoming established. We may be spiritually improved by edifying teaching, preaching, counsel, and other blessings, yet come short of the spiritual consistency typical of truly established churches. Why? We allow serious faults, weaknesses, divisions, or other deficiencies to remain. "Established" suggests all necessary stabilizers are present and destabilizers removed. All root sins, fundamental errors, and divisive attitudes are corrected, and the leadership, discipleship, worship, stewardship, and other key ministries are in place, tested, and up to biblical standards. On such spiritual bedrock God can build new layers of Christians, knowing they'll be well led. Let's get even more specific.

To be minimally "established," congregations must be firm in these areas: the gospel; faith; hope of Christ's appearing; love; thanksgiving; pastoral focus; sound doctrine; holiness; obeying God's Word; good works; godly separation; prayer; praise and worship; right attitudes; and fair judgment.[3] This spiritual stability will sustain numerical enlargement. As we increase in these essentials, God can increase us with new, hungry disciples "daily"—or any day He pleases (Acts 16:5).[4] And those He adds won't go away. Are we seeking increase God's way, or another way?

We may seek numerical growth through new programs, special appeals, advertisements, demographic research, or other novel methods, but enlargement through establishment remains a pure, proven New Testament method. Let's be simple.

Let's focus on strengthening and establishing our churches, and trust God to increase us when we're established to grow.

Chapter 53

GOD'S OPPORTUNISTS

*A*FTER A LONG, difficult voyage, Paul finally arrived in Rome. There, once again, he found himself in adversity—still in custody on false charges trumped up by his Jewish enemies. But though he longed to resume his missionary work, Paul made the best of his bad situation for two years (Acts 28:30–31). How? He saw opportunity in his adversity.

He recognized the captain of the Roman guard's decision—to confine him in a house, not a cell—was God's providential plan. His "rented house" (Acts 28:30, NKJV) could serve as a ministry center or school of Christ in which he could help anyone God sent: Christians, Jews, pagans, officials, students, citizens, slaves, travelers, merchants, and others. Perhaps Paul remembered how useful Tyrannus' lecture hall had been in Ephesus (Acts 19:9–12). A mighty river of evangelism, teaching, healing, and newly trained disciples flowed out from Paul's ministry there, impacting not only Ephesus but also all Asia Minor (v. 26). Ephesus was a large and influential city; surely Rome, the world's largest and most influential, would prove even more fruitful!

Whatever his initial thoughts, Paul soon recognized new doors opening in Rome. Continually protected by Roman guards, Paul enjoyed a rare season of peace and quiet perfect for writing. Over the next two years he penned four inspired letters[1] that still bless Christians today. With his guards changing every six hours, many soldiers heard Paul's prayers, counsels, and gospel teachings. Through this exposure and Paul's prayers, many surely converted. And since they were Nero's imperial guards, they spread word of Paul's situation and Savior to the other guards, servants, and family members of "Caesar's household" (Phil. 4:21–22). Thus God's royal messenger informed Rome's royal family of heaven's royal Son and family. These heavenly designs elevated Paul in his low valley.

Inspired, he settled down and went to work amid his woe:

> Paul dwelt two whole years in his own hired house, and received all that came in unto him, preaching the kingdom of

138

God, and teaching those things which concern the Lord Jesus
Christ, with all confidence, no man forbidding him.
                                                —ACTS 28:30–31

Instead of sitting idly, he sowed God's Word daily. Rather than
grumble, he grew. Rather than waste time, he redeemed it. Rather than
rave at his enemies' schemes, he rejoiced in his Father's plan. Rather than
fret, he farmed his valley of testing and reaped rich, eternal fruit for the
Lord of the harvest! What a spiritual opportunist!

Worldly opportunists are intensely selfish, quick to perceive chances
to take advantage of situations to further their own desires, often without
regard for ethics, laws, or others' welfare. God's opportunists are delightfully different. They're quick to recognize God's designs in their disappointments and do their best to serve them in even their worst times, to bless
God and His people. A seasoned spiritual opportunist, Paul did this often.

Shipwrecked on Malta, he used the three-month layover as an opportunity to minister to the islanders (Acts 28:1–11). Unjustly jailed in
Caesarea, he used his two-year incarceration to minister to Christians
who visited him. When denied his planned missions to Asia and Bithynia,
he quickly accepted God's preferred plan to minister in Macedonia (Acts
16:6–10). Opportunely, Paul turned these adverse circumstances to God's
advantage without murmuring, slacking, or rebelling. David did the same.

When King Saul suddenly drove David from his home, marriage,
and military career into the wilderness, David could have self-destructed
with rage, self-pity, and bitterness. But David saw opportunities in his
offenses. Saul's persecution was his pathway to destiny: God was using Saul's opposition to grow and perfect David's faith, character, and
leadership skills. So David promptly pursued this! Instead of being indolent, David worked industriously, meditating on Scripture, building a
prayer life, worshipping God, writing psalms, teaching six hundred men
God's ways, and ministering to everyone he met, even Nabal![2] When he
emerged from his wilderness years, David was mature in character, rich
in knowledge of God, full of the Spirit, and ready to fulfill his predestined higher service. Why not follow David's and Paul's examples?

When for a season you don't get your way, look for God's way.
Prayerfully discern His designs in your disappointments. Perceive His
plans in your persecutions. Seize His opportunities in your adversities.
Make the most of your "rented house," "lecture hall," or "wilderness"
for Jesus' honor. Don't grumble; grow! Don't waste time; redeem it! Be

industrious, not indolent! Instead of fretting over what you can't do, focus on what you can do.[3] Then go do it—with faithfulness, perseverance, prayer, worship, joy, and contentment, expecting to bear rich, eternal fruit for the King of the harvest. Why?

You're one of God's opportunists.

CHARACTERISTICS OF THE HOLY SPIRIT

*H*ISTORICALLY, GENESIS 24 chronicles the search of Abraham's servant for Isaac's bride. But there's more here. Symbolically, this chapter foreshadows the Holy Spirit's mission in this age—how the Father has sent Him to find Jesus' bride, the true church. Abraham symbolizes God the Father, his servant Eliezer represents the Holy Spirit, and Isaac represents Jesus.[1]

Let's examine Eliezer to discover eight of the Holy Spirit's characteristics reflected in his behavior:

1. HE PRAYS WITH AMAZING EFFECTIVENESS. Eliezer's request to discover the divinely appointed woman was answered with amazing speed and specificity. Before he finished praying, God's answer—Rebekah—appeared, and she did precisely what Eliezer asked, offering to water his camels (Gen. 24:12–19). Like Eliezer, the Spirit prays very effectively: for us, as He prays independently in our bodily temple prayers we can't understand (Rom. 8:26–27); assisting us, as we pray in our native tongue about people and needs He brings to mind; through us, as we pray in our prayer language with the utterance He supernaturally gives.

2. HE'S ENTHUSIASTIC AND INSPIRES ENTHUSIASM. When Eliezer realized Rebekah was God's answer, he moved quickly to confirm this. Neither ambling nor strolling, he "ran" toward her (Gen. 24:17). Energetic about everything he did, his enthusiasm was infectious. After seeing Eliezer run to her side, Rebekah "ran" to share the news of his arrival (v. 28). Soon Laban also "ran" with joy (v. 29). Wherever the Spirit visits, believers revive, abandon apathy and lethargy, and enthusiastically run to seek, obey, and serve God—and inspire others to do the same.

3. HE'S A PERFECT GENTLEMAN. Though enthusiastic, Eliezer didn't barge into Rebekah's home uninvited. Rather, he politely asked permission to lodge there (v. 23) and

patiently "stood by" the well, waiting until Laban invited him in (v. 31). As Eliezer respected Laban's free will, so the Spirit is never pushy or rude in presenting Jesus, Himself, or His gifts (1 Cor. 12:4–11).

4. HE GLORIFIES ONLY THE FATHER AND SON. When "evangelizing" Rebekah, Eliezer boasted only of Abraham and Isaac, not of himself or anyone else (Gen. 24:34–36). Similarly, the Spirit never excessively exalts or praises anyone other than the heavenly Father and Son—not Mary, popes, saints, or specially gifted or successful Protestant ministers.

5. HE'S A WORSHIPPER. Every time Eliezer recognized God's answers or favor, he stopped and worshipped, once after God confirmed Rebekah was His choice (Gen. 24:26–27) and again after Bethuel accepted Eliezer's proposal, sealing his mission's success (vv. 51–52). Likewise, the Spirit inspires worship, teaches us how to worship acceptably, and prompts us to stop and give thanks every time we recognize God's hand, voice, or answers.

6. HE'S VERY FOCUSED. Superbly mission-minded, Eliezer wouldn't even eat until he presented his proposal to Bethuel (v. 33). Similarly, from Pentecost to the Rapture the Spirit is focusing like a laser on His great mission—fulfilling the Father's request to find His Son's bride (vv. 2–9) and fulfilling the Son's prayer to prepare and retrieve His bride (John 17:13–26).[2]

7. HE'S NOT FANATICAL. Though focused, Eliezer was no fanatic. Immediately after Bethuel's consent assured his success, Eliezer relaxed, enjoying Bethuel's banquet and a much needed night's sleep (Gen. 24:54). A fanatic would have refused these pleasures and returned home immediately. The Spirit inspires hard work, persistence, and self-discipline, but never asceticism, wild emotionalism, or extreme labor. Perfectly balanced, He knows zeal must be controlled, and He teaches us when to work and when to rest.

8. HE DISCERNS HINDRANCES. The next morning Laban suggested extending his hospitality ten days. Eliezer immediately declined, pleading, "Hinder me not" (v. 56). Just as quickly the Spirit alerts us—inwardly, quietly, but persistently—when people, activities, or interruptions hinder our Christian devotion, separation, ministry, or mission.

Why did God reveal these characteristics of the Spirit in Genesis 24? He wants them reproduced in every born-again, Spirit-filled Christian. How?

Remember, "Eliezer" is in you. Believe He's always praying effectively for you, and ask His assistance and utterance whenever you pray. Wait on God in Bible reading, prayer, and worship daily until the Spirit's enthusiasm permeates you. Then do everything "heartily" as to Christ (Col. 3:23). Be patient, not pushy, when presenting Jesus and spiritual things. Respect others' free will, and never try to force their compliance. Exalt God alone, never people, however prominent, powerful, wise, gifted, or spiritual. Be a habitual worshipper. Whenever you recognize God's help or voice, stop and thank Him. Be mission-minded. Focus on your great life mission—to know Christ and fulfill His calling. Correct any fanatical excesses. And when the Spirit reveals hindrances, quickly eliminate them. Then Father, Son, and Spirit will rejoice! Why?

Like Eliezer, you're demonstrating daily the characteristics of the Holy Spirit.

Chapter 55

MASTERFUL PATIENCE

*W*HILE MANY LAUD Paul's significant ministry in Rome, his most productive period of ministry by far occurred in Ephesus—thanks to his masterful patience! Let's revisit Paul's patient march toward Ephesus.

Three years earlier Paul planned to visit Asia Minor, and its most influential city, Ephesus, but the Holy Spirit checked him (Acts 16:6). While no reasons for this check are stated, Acts 16-18 imply that Ephesus wasn't ready for Paul's gospel and Macedonia and Achaia were. So Paul faithfully occupied himself ministering to the Macedonian and Achaian cities of Philippi, Thessalonica, Berea, Athens, and Corinth, while Ephesus remained in his thoughts and prayers.

When divinely released from his service in Corinth, Paul promptly "came to Ephesus," where he "entered into the synagogue, and reasoned with the Jews" (Acts 18:19). To his delight this Ephesian "field" was now ready for sowing. And eager! The Jews "desired him to tarry a longer time" and further explain the Scriptures proving Jesus was their Messiah (v. 20). But Paul declined their offer. Why?

God was calling him to visit Jerusalem during the festival to deliver the Gentile churches' donations to the Judean churches: "But [Paul] bade them farewell, saying, I must by all means keep this feast...in Jerusalem" (v. 21). Still Ephesus remained on his heart: "But I will return again unto you [Ephesians], if God will" (v. 21). Surely Paul felt frustration. Earlier he was ready for Ephesus, but it wasn't ready for him. Now Ephesus was calling, but God called him away! Though he wished to remain, he obediently "sailed from Ephesus" to Jerusalem (v. 21).

After visiting Jerusalem, Paul returned to Ephesus overland, ministering along the way to Syrian, Galatian, and Phrygian churches. When he "came to Ephesus" (Acts 19:1), Paul discovered his arrival was divinely timed— and blessed! Over the next three years he evangelized widely, taught many disciples in Tyrannus' lecture hall, sent them evangelizing and discipling throughout Asia, worked astounding "special miracles" (v. 11), significantly reduced Ephesus' idolatry-driven tourism economy,[1] and convinced many locals to renounce magical arts, for which their city was famous (vv. 1–29). Luke triumphantly proclaims, "So mightily grew the word of God, and prevailed" over everything and everyone arrayed against it (v. 20)!

While many factors contributed to this extraordinary season of ministry, Paul's willingness to wait God's perfect time was key. His was a masterful patience. He perfected the rare art of waiting for God, as did our Master Himself, Jesus, who waited thirty years in Nazareth until the very moment His Father released Him to begin ministering in His power to His people. Others also demonstrated masterful patience.

As Noah's long, dark year in the drifting ark drew to a close, I'm sure he felt a bit antsy. When he finally saw dry land, he must have had mixed emotions, his eagerness to exit the ark checked by his awareness that God hadn't yet released him (Gen. 8:13). But, an expert spiritual survivor, Noah waited fifty-eight more days till God spoke: "Go forth from the ark" (v. 16).

Moses certainly experienced his share of frustration, doubt, and discouragement during the latter years of his long, demanding desert sojourn. But, skilled at meekly following God, he didn't leave Midian until "forty years were expired" and an angel summoned his return to Egypt (Acts 7:30).

As Elijah's water supply dwindled daily, he must have wondered when the God who called him to Cherith would call him away. But, proficient in patience, he waited daily in deep, sustained communion with God until "the word of the LORD came," releasing and redirecting him to Zarephath (1 Kings 17:8).

The apostles also showed expertise in self-control when, despite their burning desire to fulfill the Great Commission, they obeyed the Great Check—Christ's explicit order that they defer their earthly mission until they received heavenly power.[2] Church history offers more examples.

George Mueller's patient endurance was one of the most masterful. He often prayed with steady, expectant faith for weeks, months, sometimes years, about the spiritual, financial, and material needs of his orphanages, schools, and other ministries. However pressing his needs, Mueller always prevailed by more prayer, more patience, more waiting on God.

All these mastered waiting for God. Do you want to?

Then follow their examples. Stay close to Jesus daily, heeding His checks and following His guidance, knowing your wisdom is suspect but His is perfect. Willingly wait and occupy faithfully in your "Macedonia," knowing God's time is always best for everything: "He hath made every thing beautiful in his time" (Eccles. 3:11, KJV). Finally, be confident Paul's Master will lead you to your "Ephesus" season of fruitful ministry or fulfillment—if you'll commit yourself to practice His masterful patience.

Chapter 56

HIS SHINING FACE

*I*NVOKING AARON'S BLESSING, an anonymous psalmist prayed, "God be merciful...and cause his face to shine upon us" (Ps. 67:1). His plea wasn't unique.

Numerous psalmists petitioned God to smile on them. David prayed, "Make thy face to shine upon thy servant" (Ps. 31:16). Three times in one psalm Asaph pleaded, "Cause thy face to shine" (80:3, 7, 19). Psalm 119's author begged, "Make thy face to shine upon thy servant" (v. 135). Rephrasing this request, David asked, "Lift thou up the light of thy [shining] countenance upon us" (Ps. 4:6). Ethan proclaimed "blessed" are those who "walk...in the light of thy countenance" (Ps. 89:15). What does God's shining face symbolize?

It portrays Him releasing spiritual light beams—light- and life-giving rays of His favor, hope, guidance, biblical illumination, knowledge, presence, and healing. Let's examine these God-rays more closely:

- FAVOR. When pleased, we smile. Similarly, when our Creator is pleased with us, He smiles, releasing invisible and visible rays of His favor. Inwardly we feel the Sun of righteousness' invisible but warm reassuring touch, the sense of His loving approval confirming all is well between us. His love-rays also give us visible favors with others, as He turns people's hearts to openly approve us. Friends show love, employers advance us, sales come our way, judges side with us, our advice is adopted, and our labors prosper—all because Father is smiling. We need this favor, as Joseph needed Pharaoh's approval, to fulfill God's will.

- HOPE. When stormy trials bring persisting thick clouds of adversity that block all bright prospects for a blessed future, we need the light of hope. As our heavenly Father's face shines, quickened Bible verses, messages, signs, dreams, counsels, and prophecies are released, reminding us "God is faithful" (1 Cor. 10:13), and, however bad things look, the best is still yet to be.

- GUIDANCE. Even when faithfully trusting and obeying God, we sometimes "[walk] in darkness," temporarily unsure what to do or where to go next (Isa. 50:10). If we pray, Father will smile on us with a revelation of the next step in His wise plan. "Arise, get thee to Zarephath" (1 Kings 17:9). Or, "Call for...Peter...he shall tell thee what thou oughtest to do" (Acts 10:5–6).

- BIBLICAL ILLUMINATION. Many read the Bible sincerely but blindly—understanding neither its meaning nor application. When Father smiles, His Spirit releases illumination, and we receive insight into His words, wonderfully edifying awareness of its literal and figurative meanings and how they apply to our hearts, tests, and times. The psalmist asked for this illumination: "Make thy face to shine...teach me thy statutes" (Ps. 119:135).

- KNOWLEDGE OF GOD. Our facial expressions reflect our souls' condition—our thoughts, emotions, and character. Thus by reading our countenances, people may know us. As we behold God's face through prayerful Bible study and pondering His characteristic dealings in our lives, other lives, and history, His Spirit gives us an increasingly full knowledge of God—His complete person or character, including His attributes, purposes, values, decisions, and methods. By persisting, we come to know God's character fully, like Moses, "face to face" (Exod. 33:11).

- PRESENCE. Before photographs, films, and teleconferences, seeing someone's face required their presence. To "seek God's face," therefore, implies having audiences with Him, or spending time in His presence: "Seek his face evermore" (Ps. 105:4). Conversely, to run from God is to avoid His face or presence: "Adam and his wife hid themselves from the presence [face[1]] of the LORD" (Gen. 3:8). When God smiles, He releases to us His stimulating manifest presence: "He that hath my commandments, and keepeth them...I will love him, and will manifest myself to him" (John 14:21).

- HEALING. Matthew described Jesus' ministry as the long-awaited rising of Israel's "Sun of Righteousness" with healing in His "wings [sunbeams]" (Mal. 4:2). This "great light" (Matt. 4:16) was God's smile radiating His mercies, especially in Jesus' wondrous healing ministry. Wherever Father's face shines, relationships, marriages, families, and bodies are healed.

But He doesn't always smile. Scripture reveals Father sometimes "turns" His face in disapproval, "hides" His face by withholding prayers, and sternly "sets" His face with determination to punish stubborn evil-doers.[2] These non-smiling conditions deprive us of God's favor, hope, guidance, insight, knowledge, presence, and healing.

To spare us this suffering, God calls us to seek His shining face. David heard Him and promptly responded: "When thou saidst, Seek ye my face, my heart said... Thy face, LORD, will I seek" (Ps. 27:8). God is calling you too, Christian. Will you respond and bask in the warm rays of His smile? Today seek, find, and delight in His shining face.

Chapter 57

THE WORLD WILL KNOW

RESENTLY THE SECULAR world doesn't acknowledge God's existence. Or if it does, it's unsure which professed deity—Jehovah, Allah, Buddha, Hindu gods, indigenous gods—is truly God. But before we're gone, the world will know who God is. Why am I so sure?

God has promised. Through the psalmist He declared, "I will be exalted among the nations, I will be exalted in the earth" (Ps. 46:10). Through Habakkuk He reveals the wide scope of this God-consciousness: "The earth shall be filled with the knowledge of the glory of the LORD as the waters cover the sea" (Hab. 2:14). Ultimately all will not come to Him, but all will know He exists and who He is—the God of Israel and the church.

God first implied this when promising to bless "all families of the earth" through Abraham (Gen. 12:3). He reiterated it when demonstrating His presence and power at the Red Sea: "I will be honored over Pharaoh...that the Egyptians may know that I am the LORD" (Exod. 14:4). Since Egypt symbolizes the world, God here promised to reveal Himself not only to Egypt but also to all nations. That's why He saved and sanctified Israel.

His law revealed this central purpose to fill the Hebrews with His glory that through them all peoples would know Him: "The LORD shall establish thee an holy people unto himself...And all people of the earth shall see that thou art called by the name of the LORD" (Deut. 28:9–10). Throughout Scripture key Jewish leaders and prophets repeated this theme of revealing God to the world.

Joshua said this was why God miraculously opened the Jordan River: "That all the people of the earth might know the [mighty] hand of the LORD" (Josh. 4:24). David testified this was why he challenged Goliath: "The LORD [will] deliver thee into mine hand...that all the earth may know there is a God in Israel" (1 Sam. 17:46). Twice King Solomon declared this was why God established His temple, with its otherworldly Shekinah glory, and answered prayers offered there: "That all the people of the earth may know thy name, to fear thee...[and] that the LORD is God, and...there is none else" (1 Kings 8:43, 60). Twice Scripture says it's why King Hezekiah asked

God to save Jerusalem from Sennacherib's armies: "Save thou us out of his hand, that all the kingdoms of the earth may know that thou art the LORD God, even thou only" (2 Kings 19:19).[1] These witnesses weren't alone.

Isaiah said God raised King Cyrus to end Judah's captivity to show the world God's supremacy: "That they may know from the [east to]...the west, that...I am the LORD, and there is none else" (Isa. 45:6). Ezekiel added this was why God restored Judah after the captivity: "[Then] the nations shall know that I am the LORD...when I shall be sanctified in you before their eyes" (Ezek. 36:23). Daniel cited this as the reason God so publicly disciplined King Nebuchadnezzar and included his testimony in Scripture: "This matter is...to the intent that the living ['everyone,' NLT] may know that the Most High ruleth in the kingdom of men" (Dan. 4:17). Ezekiel stated three times this is why God will so publicly and powerfully destroy Antichrist's armies at Armageddon: "Thus will I magnify myself...[and] be known in the eyes of many nations, and they shall know that I am the LORD" (Ezek. 38:23).[2] All these servants understood and declared God's heart. So did Jesus.

Jesus' high priestly prayer reveals His and His Father's heart. In it Jesus requested that His followers be sanctified and unified to reveal His glory: "That the world may believe...[and] know that thou hast sent me" (John 17:21–23). So the church's central mission, like Israel's, is to enable the world to know who God is—Jehovah, revealed in His Word, manifested in His Son, living in His people, working by His Spirit, sovereign, unchanging, eternal, and without equal. Are we pursuing this mission?

Are we remembering who and all our God is? Our Savior? Lord? Father? Refuge? Deliverer? Vine? Teacher? Shepherd? Friend? Husband? Helper? Coming King? If so, we'll joyfully study His Word, easily obey His will, confidently follow His guidance, humbly receive His correction, restfully trust His provision, and passionately worship Him. Then the aura of His glorious deity, power, truth, love, faithfulness, and righteousness will shine over and through us and our churches ever more brightly and broadly. Before Jesus comes, this—His glorious beauty—will be seen in our personal lives, works, and ministries.[3] Seeing it, many will come to Him. Others will not.

But in that day, be assured, the world will know.

Chapter 58

TRAVAILING FOR TRANSFORMATION

AUL INFORMED THE Galatians he was travailing in prayer for them again (Gal. 4:19). Earlier he had prayed for their conversion. Now he was praying they would turn from error and grow to spiritual maturity. Several translations illuminate his prayer.

One states Paul was praying Christ in them would be "fully developed" (NLT). Another, that He'd be "completely and permanently formed (molded) within" them (AMP). Another, that he was praying, "Until you truly become like Christ" (NCV). Another paraphrases, "Until Christ's life becomes visible in your lives" (THE MESSAGE). Summarizing, Paul was praying for a complete character transformation in the Galatians. Let's also consider the various ways Paul "travailed."

Primarily, he spoke of travailing in regular intercession. He was practicing what he preached to the Ephesians: "Praying always with all prayer and supplication in the Spirit...for all saints" (Eph. 6:18). Just as a woman's birth pangs continue steadily until a birth occurs, so Paul was praying in the Spirit regularly, perhaps several times daily, until Christ's character was fully formed in the Galatians' daily lives.

He also travailed emotionally, as waves of fear and "the anguish of childbirth" (Gal. 4:19, ESV) occasionally washed over him at the prospect of his converts not recovering from their salvation-by-works heresy and thus losing their salvation or rewards. This very real possibility distressed him (Gal. 5:2–4).

Furthermore, he travailed instructionally, by methodically laboring to reprove their errors and reinstruct them in "the truth of the gospel" (Gal. 2:5, 14), point by point, example by example, scripture by scripture. In Galatians he used the Antioch church's experience, the Jerusalem counsel's findings, his rebuke of Peter in Antioch, Abraham's faith-based righteousness, and Sarah, Hagar, and their sons as key teaching illustrations.[1] He continued this instruction in person when later revisiting Galatia (Acts 15:40–16:5).

Moreover he travailed in vigilance, watching diligently over the Galatian flock for evidence of changes in their spiritual condition: "Ye did run well; who did hinder you that ye should not obey the truth?" (Gal. 5:7).

Finally, he travailed in suffering. Paul suffered opposition everywhere but especially in Galatia. There he was maligned, driven from cities, threatened, attacked, and brutally stoned to the point of death! Yet he endured these distressing "birth pangs" so Christ's attitudes and ways would be so well established in the Galatians they would no longer live as spiritual babes but as strong, spiritually mature Christians.

Like Paul, many ministers today are travailing—working and praying intensely with all their emotions and energies fully engaged. But some aren't laboring in Paul's ways. Others aren't laboring for Paul's kingdom goal of spiritual maturity among Christians. Why? They're busy working for other ends.

Some travail for political influence or social causes; others, for personal gain or material things. Still others labor for religious recognition by churches or denominations. Some work for public reputation or ecclesiastical office. Others commit everything to establish or perpetuate institutions. Where are those who follow Paul's selfless, spiritually minded example?

It's time we abandon our own ends and commit to travail for spiritual growth and maturity, "until Christ be formed" in our local church bodies and the larger body of Christ. Why? Without travail there can be no births, new beginnings, or lasting changes for good.

For example, without intercessory travail unbelievers can't be converted to the faith or revivals visit lukewarm, dry churches. Without the political travail of revolution, dictators and their oppressive regimes can't be overthrown. Without the "time of Jacob's trouble" (Jer. 30:7), Israel can't bring forth its spiritual children, the 144,000 Jewish evangelists (Rev. 7:1–8) and the international multitude saved through their ministry (vv. 9–17).[2] And this fallen world can't bring forth a new, righteous world order without the seven-year travail of the tribulation period.

So let's turn from selfish or temporal ends to kingdom goals and begin travailing for them.

Like Paul, let's start travailing for the transformation of our local churches and the worldwide church—by prayer, desire, instruction, watchfulness, and suffering. While this call applies first to pastors and other spiritual leaders, it also summons every disciple to vital spiritual travail. Epaphras responded centuries ago. Paul wrote, "Epaphras, who is one of you, a servant of Christ...always laboring fervently for you in prayers, that ye may stand perfect and complete in all the will of God" (Col. 4:12). If we too will travail in prayer, and the others ways mentioned above, we'll soon see God's hand working more distinctly and persistently in our congregations' attitudes, behavior, relationships, labors, and ministries. The result?

Transformation! Christ's life—His compassion, truth, boldness, faith, surrender, etc.—will begin manifesting in us with growing regularity. Let's get busy travailing for transformation.

Chapter 59

TOUCHED BY GOD

*I*N TRYING TIMES human touches can bring deep reassurances and comfort. God's touches, however, produce far great blessings than any mere human pats, hand clasps, or hugs can impart. Lydia was a soul touched by God.

Luke writes, "Lydia...whose heart the Lord opened" (Acts 16:14). To "open" something, whether a door, container, or envelope, we must touch it. So to open Lydia's heart, the Lord had to touch her—His Spirit contacting hers. It was a saving touch. When Lydia heard "the things which were spoken by Paul," she believed, received Jesus, and was baptized (vv. 14–15). Thus she was spiritually reborn (John 3:5, 7–8). This saving touch was new to her, but not to Jesus.

Touching was a vital part of His ministry. Everywhere people "pressed upon him" not just to see and hear but also "to touch him" (Mark 3:10). And whenever they touched Jesus or He touched them, a life-changing transmission of supernatural divine life occurred. This always resulted in a healing experience.

When a leper came begging Jesus' help, "Jesus put forth his hand, and touched him...And immediately his leprosy was cleansed" (Matt. 8:3). When a deadly fever gripped Peter's mother-in-law, "he touched her hand, and the fever left her" (v. 15). When two blind men came seeking sight, "Then touched he their eyes...And their eyes were opened" (Matt. 9:29–30). When people brought the diseased to Him, "as many as touched [him] were made perfectly well" (Matt. 14:35–36). When at the Transfiguration the apostles "fell on their face...afraid," Jesus "touched them, and said, Arise, and be not afraid," and they rose, no longer afraid (Matt. 17:6–7). When the people brought a deaf-mute to Jesus, He "put his fingers into his ears, and...touched his tongue," and the man immediately heard and spoke freely (Mark 7:32–35). When Jesus encountered the funeral procession of a widow's only son, "he came and touched the bier [funeral litter]," and "he that was dead sat up, and began to speak" (Luke 7:14–15). Besides these physical healings, Christ's touches also heal figuratively.

His touch cures spiritual leprosy, or moral corruption and uncleanness, and restores healthy New Testament morality. His touch breaks soul fevers—burning obsessions with worldly goals, sinful desires, or other distracting, spiritually hindering interests.[1] His touch heals spiritual blindness, the inability to see God's hand working in our lives or detect Satan's temptations, traps, and hindrances. His touch heals spiritual diseases, or causes of chronic discontent (dis-ease), and enables us to be thankfully content in every situation (Phil. 4:11–13). His touch heals all fears, from daily anxieties to paralyzing terrors, and leaves us reassured of His faithful love, power, promises, and presence. His touch heals spiritual deafness, or inability to hear His voice, and frees us to discern Him speaking to us through scriptures, sermons, or our consciences. His touch heals spiritual muteness, or inability to testify or evangelize freely, leaving us free to say whatever is necessary to whomever we need to speak. And His touch heals spiritual death, raising us from the soul deadness that's caused by unbelief, lukewarmness, or holding offenses.

These and other healings are ours whenever we touch Jesus. But we won't "press...to touch him" unless we realize we're needy.

Spiritual dependents, we all need Jesus' touches. His initial touches come in the new birth and the baptism with the Spirit. But we need more to grow and thrive. We need daily, hourly re-touches. Every time He touches us, we reenact the account of the woman with the chronic hemorrhage: "virtue," or life-giving healing power, flows from Jesus into us and we sense He's touched us (Mark 5:29–30). But not automatically.

We must ask and seek Christ's touches. When Jairus' daughter lay dying, Jairus could easily have given up. Instead, he asked Jesus, "Come and lay thy hands on her" (Mark 5:23). When the various local crowds heard Jesus' ministry was nearby, they too could have done nothing. But most chose to act. Believing in His compassion and power, they "pressed upon him...to touch him" (Mark 3:10). To receive His reviving touches, we too should actively petition and press.

Will you ask Jesus to touch you again—with new life, strength, emotional healing, grace, wisdom, mercy, or physical healing? Will you press to touch Him—taking more time with Him in Bible reading, prayer, or worship along with self-examination, confession of sin, and any necessary changes? If so, He'll touch you. James promises, "Draw near to God, and he will draw near unto you" (James 4:8). Are you full or needy? Lukewarm or longing for another touch? Don't procrastinate.

Act! Like Jairus, Lydia, and so many others, rise, ask, and press, until you're touched by God.

Chapter 60

EXCEPTIONAL LEADERS EMERGING!

*A*T THE LOWEST moment of a dark, dangerous crisis among despondent, desperate men, the apostle Paul "stood forth" to lead a large, helplessly adrift ship through a deadly hurricane (Acts 27:21). This wasn't ordinary leadership.

But Paul was no ordinary leader. His character and leadership skills were in every way exceptional. He was full of the very qualities his shipmates lacked most: clear vision, unshakable faith, cheerful hope. Luke describes their depressed condition:

> When neither sun nor stars in many days appeared, and no small tempest lay on us, all hope that we should be saved was then taken away.
>
> —ACTS 27:20

But when others were spent, Paul stood, served, and shined.

He reproved the ship's owner for disregarding his previous Spirit-inspired warning (v. 21). Yet, lest the ship's company be dejected, he encouraged them: "Be of good cheer!" (v. 22). Twice he boldly prophesied everyone would survive the vicious storm, though by shipwreck (vv. 22–24, 26, 34), and openly confessed his confidence in God's faithfulness: "I believe God, that it shall be even as it was told me" (v. 25). Detecting sailors abandoning ship, he warned the centurion, Julius, to stop them, since their sailing skills would be needed to beach the ship (vv. 30–31). And he wasn't finished.

Knowing everyone was weak from fasting or seasickness, he wisely urged everyone to prepare for the demanding swim ashore by taking nourishment (vv. 33–34). Leading by example, he ate bread in their sight and again encouraged them to trust God (vv. 33–35). His leadership was so effective, "all [were] of good cheer," though they were still in grave danger and without proof they'd survive (v. 36). Once safe on Malta, Paul continued leading by gathering wood for a bonfire to warm and dry them—only to be snakebit and condemned by the Maltese for so much suffering (Acts 28:1–4). He rendered all this leadership while weak, weary, apparently God-forsaken, and thoroughly drenched by cold autumn rains! It all began when he "stood forth."

After that moment Paul guided every key decision. Whatever he advised, Julius did. Though normally Julius would have killed the prisoners during a shipwreck to prevent any escaping, he spared them "to save Paul" (Acts 27:42–43). Paul's assumption of leadership is especially remarkable considering his status as a prisoner. But, as Jesus prophesied, the last became first! Christ's humble messenger began the stormy fortnight as an insignificant prisoner and ended it an indispensable pilot. His promotion also blessed others.

Since everyone aboard, including Julius, had abandoned hope—a survivalist's chief requirement—Paul's leadership and intercession saved everyone (Acts 27:24, 37, 44). How wonderful, his faith saved even the faithless! That's exceptional leadership emerging in an exceptional trial.

Again, Paul's exceptional leadership came in the worst circumstances, at the lowest moment, and when hidden from public view. After Paul so faithfully ministered in this cruelest, most obscure adversity, God let him testify before Nero and even lead some of his "household" (Phil. 4:22)—guards, servants, or relatives—to Christ. This wasn't accidental.

It was, and still is, the way God raises exceptional leaders. He teaches them to lead in the lowest, humblest, darkest, most unknown places on earth, knowing if they'll lead well there, they'll lead well anywhere, including palaces! Where do we look for exceptionally strong leaders?

Do we expect to find them at the top of thriving churches, expanding businesses, mushrooming institutions, or other entities at the apex of visible success? Many are there. But many others are in circumstances paralleling Paul's in Acts 27. They're hidden away, struggling to lead divided churches, embattled ministries, maligned prayer groups, split families, troubled institutions, or failing businesses through dark storms of adversity. With clear vision, unshakable faith, and cheerful hope, their leadership, faith, and prayers are bringing their ship's company through to relief (Malta) or higher service (Rome). When God withholds visible encouragements for many days, they continue showing the highest leadership in the lowest trials. These are God's emerging leaders—and they're exceptional. Want to be one?

If like Paul you'll faithfully care for those who sail with you in your present distresses, you'll be able to lead anyone, anywhere, anytime, in any distress. That's why God took Joseph, Moses, David, and Paul from the humblest to the highest ministries. They led humble, faithful flocks through the dullest, lowest seasons and direst, most troubling tests. Then God called them to higher service. Where are our Pauls?

The world today is strange, dark, and hopeless. Like Luke, many Christians feel all hope is gone. Many churches are adrift, their faith ready to founder. Who will "stand forth" to reassure, cheer, guide, warn and feed us? Help us overcome? Prepare for Jesus? Safely land on heaven's shores?

I'm looking for exceptional leaders emerging!

Chapter 61

ELIMINATING ENVY

THE APOSTLE PAUL ordered the Galatians to "not be…envying one another" (Gal. 5:26). He wanted them to get serious about eliminating not only their errors but also their envy. Why?

Paul realized wrong attitudes are dangerous, but especially envy. Envy—angry discontent at another having what one keenly wants oneself—is a root sin that causes troublesome behavior. How did Paul know this?

God's Word repeatedly warns of envy's destructive power. Envy divided the first siblings, caused the first murder, and grieved the first family (Gen. 4:1–8). It "moved" Joseph's brothers to betray him (Acts 7:9). Jewish leaders crucified Jesus "for envy" (Matt. 27:18). And Paul himself was persecuted by envious Jews in Antioch and Thessalonica (Acts 13:45; 17:5).

Insightful, Paul understood envy resides in our sin nature and can quickly arise and spoil any relationship—between siblings, friends, coworkers, spouses, Christians, even ministers. The slightest perceived advantages can stir the comparisons and contentions of envy: parental approval, favor with superiors, pastoral attention, wealth, popularity, wisdom, answers to prayer, ministry success, to name some. These carnal contentions sometimes divide churches (1 Cor. 3:3). Thus Paul ordered the Galatians to eradicate the leaven of envy. God wants us to also.

He knows envy is satanic. Before creation, Lucifer (Satan) envied[1] God's unique greatness and rose rebelliously to replace Him. It's inspired by demons. James warned envy's "wisdom" (rationale) is "demonic" (James 3:15, NKJV). It's divisive. Envy spawns rivalrous comparisons, petty criticisms, and bitter contentions, making fruitful cooperation impossible. It's the opposite of love. "Love envieth not," and envy loves not (1 Cor. 13:4). Thus envy prevents what God desires most among believers: loving unity and the character growth and ministry fruit it produces. As long as we hold envy, God withholds revivals, since Christ's greatest petition that we be "perfect in one" remains unfulfilled (John 17:21, 23). God refuses to rain showers of blessings and power upon roots of "bitter envying and strife" (James 3:14). He releases the Spirit's "dew" and "oil" only where "brethren dwell together in unity" (Ps. 133:1–3). So the Head wants His church to eliminate envy.

We can comply in four simple steps.

159

First, we must frankly confess our envy. Jesus taught that truth liberates: "The truth shall make you free" (John 8:32). Envy is aroused so subtly we often initially miss it. But the Holy Spirit doesn't! When after seeing or hearing of someone's blessings, gifts, or advantages we gradually lose our peace, that's the Spirit's way of convicting us. If we'll humbly tell God the liberating truth—whom we're envying and why—He'll immediately forgive, cleanse, and free us from envy[2] (1 John 1:9). But if we deny the truth, envy will remain and trouble us and others.

Incidentally, if we haven't spoken or acted wrongly toward those we envy, we needn't confess to them. That might offend them unnecessarily.

Second, we should firmly reject envy, and say so! "I refuse to let envy rest in my heart!" This confession releases the full power of Christ's nature and Spirit within to save us from envy's control (Rom. 10:10, NAS). Why be so adamant? Envy is deadly; it's better to drink poison than harbor envy.

Third, we should thank God for our blessings in the very area in which we've been envious. By exciting us to want other people's blessings, gifts, or advantages, envy implies ours aren't good enough. Thus we discontentedly disrespect and neglect our blessings as Hannah did her wonderful husband and meal portions (1 Sam. 1:5, 4–8).[3] Persistent thanksgiving alone cures this. The more thankful we are, the less envious we'll be. But if we won't "be content with such things as ye [we] have," we'll be envious of everything we don't have (Heb. 13:5).[4]

Fourth, we should thank God for blessing the very people we envy. "Thanks for doing that for him (or her), Lord!" Envy implies God has erred to bless those we envy. He should have blessed us instead! Thus envy misjudges God as having blessed the wrong person! Joseph's envious brothers subtly misjudged God and Jacob for giving Joseph rich spiritual and natural gifts respectively. Had they instead praised God and Jacob for blessing Joseph, they would have escaped envy's grip and never hated or harmed their innocent sibling. God never errs in granting blessings, gifts, or favors. So whenever He does, "rejoice with those who rejoice" (Rom. 12:15, NKJV). Then you'll be free from envy and its devilish, divisive power—and a joy to God!

Now you know Paul and Christ want you "not envying one another," and how to comply. There's only one thing to do: get serious about eliminating envy.

Chapter 62

PASSIONATELY FREE!

COUNTLESS PATRIOTS HAVE passionately cried for political freedom—and died for it! Patrick Henry famously declared, "Give me liberty, or give me death!" The apostle Paul realized Christians possess an even more precious liberty.

Spiritual freedom! Rather than join the first-century Jewish Zealots' growing call for insurrection against Roman authority, Paul advocated a revolt against all spiritual bondage. He passionately urged the Galatian Christians, and us, to "stand fast" in our spiritual freedom:

> Stand fast...in the liberty with which Christ hath made us free, and be not entangled again with the yoke of bondage.
> —GALATIANS 5:1

Like political freedom, our spiritual freedom was purchased by blood (Jesus'), preserved by blood (martyrs'), and forged in a revolution—the early church's spiritual revolt against Christ-rejecting, legalistic, Pharisaic Judaism and its brutal attempt to suppress Christianity as it spread rapidly from Judea to Rome.

Paul taught that these two peoples—Christ-rejecting Jews and Christ-worshipping Christians—have two different capitals, one present and the other yet to come. Present Jerusalem is "in bondage with her [disbelieving Jewish] children" (Gal. 4:25), but the future or New Jerusalem and its redeemed inhabitants[1] are "free" (v. 26). Thus Jesus also promised that believers who continue in His Word will become "free" (John 8:31–32). Free from what?

Christians are free from every detrimental spiritual, mental, and emotional yoke or entanglement afflicting Adam's children. Let's get specific.

We're free from atheism, the dark wisdom of fools who by declaring "there is no God" (Ps. 53:1) render their lives meaningless and souls hopeless. We're free from false gods, no longer calling on sun, stars, idols, or other lifeless deities to save us. We're free from false religion, loosed from the futility of trying to win salvation by observing Jewish laws, ecclesiastical rites, or other religious rules and rituals. We're free from heresy, as the discerning Spirit and inerrant Scriptures help us detect every false teaching. We're free from fearing death, assured now by Jesus' resurrection that we too will rise when He appears. We're free from the dread of terrorism, knowing our loving, omnipotent heavenly Father guards our every breath, hair, and step. We're free from asceticism, no longer neglecting or abusing our bodies in hopes of saving or improving our souls. We're free from presumption, sure now that indulging "works of the flesh" or any sin causes us to lose God's approval and fellowship and our kingdom rewards (Gal. 5:19–21). We're free from condemnation, no longer hindered in our fellowship, growth, or service by guilt over sins already confessed and forsaken (Rom. 8:1). We're free from people-pleasing, no longer burdened with a yoke of anxiety over others' opinions of us. We're free from materialism, no longer bound to feverishly accumulate monies and goods that ever seduce but never satisfy. Besides being free from, we're also free to.

We're free to be single-minded, having only one motive—pleasing Christ!—for every thought, word, and act. We're free to understand God's Word ever more clearly with the Spirit's help, as we study, believe, and obey it. We're free to abide in close, loving fellowship with Jesus, our Vine, thus producing the Christlike, Christ-honoring "fruit of the Spirit" (Gal. 5:22–23). We're free to live a quiet, humble life, "hid with Christ in God" (Col. 3:3), no longer driven by pride's desire for recognition or popularity. We're free to "stand fast" in our biblical beliefs and lifestyle, unmoved by contradictions, criticisms, or persecutions. We're free to walk in Jesus' light, easy yoke, serving Him in restful divine strength and ability in whatever works or ministries He appoints. We're free to reject carnal temptations and, by the Spirit's grace, choose what pleases God. Once free, Paul urges us to stay free. Why?

Our old master, Satan, is waiting to take us back under his malicious manipulation and misery. And he'll do it if we yield to sin, fear, or false teaching. We mustn't let that happen. Jesus and many martyrs shed blood and the early church endured hellish persecutions so we could enjoy spiritual freedom daily. So "stand fast"! Determine to let nothing and no one—especially your sin nature—hinder your soul's freedom and spiritual growth. Abandon passivity and adopt the patriot's zeal. Like political freedom, spiritual freedom is neither gained nor held without passion.

The Jewish Zealots adamantly believed that, as God's children, He alone should govern them, not men, and certainly not pagan Romans! Thus they rebelled against Rome's authority in AD 66—and died by the thousands at Gamla, Jerusalem, and Masada rather than surrender their liberty. May God give us an equally fervent determination to refuse every yoke of spiritual bondage. Be free! Passionately free!

Chapter 63

SEEKING ANOTHER COUNTRY

OR SEVERAL DECADES now American evangelicalism has been changing its focus. We've turned from our New Testament commissions—evangelism, discipleship, and being Christ's witnesses—to a new goal: controlling American politics for Christ. Though very sincere, we're very wrong.

Three monumental witnesses confirm this: the Gospels, the Book of Acts, and church history.

Nowhere in the Gospels did Jesus mandate that His church govern now in this time. To the contrary He asserted, "My kingdom is not of this world...not of this realm" (John 18:36, NAS). He didn't teach or seek political influence, nor did He order His apostles to do so. Acts confirms that political power was not one of the early church's goals. Neither Peter, Paul, nor John donned a Roman toga, strode in the Senate, and protested the policies of Caligula, Claudius, or Nero, much less presumed to run the empire. Church history shows that every time the Roman or Protestant churches tried to control the state, they caused national or international confusion, hindered their kingdom work, disillusioned thousands, and dishonored God. Indeed, from Constantine forward, the more Christianity quested for power and wealth instead of salvation and holiness, the further it fell into the bondage of error and corruption and the abyss of spiritual failure. These three witnesses are loudly warning us. Are we listening?

Apparently not, because we're feverishly praying, campaigning, and unashamedly slandering opponents to gain political power and make America God's visible kingdom on earth...something biblical prophecy decrees won't happen.

According to Daniel, Revelation, Jesus' Olivet discourse, and the Epistles, nations will grow "worse and worse" in the last days (2 Tim. 3:13), not better and better. Sinfulness, not saintliness, will increase in the world. Secularity, not spirituality, will rise in the public sector. The gospel will be preached but not practiced in all nations. Christ's perfect righteousness, justice, and love will not rule nations until He returns to earth—*after* the present apostasy grows, the true church departs, and the seven-year Tribulation ensues and ultimately ends in the cataclysmic judgment of this fallen order at Armageddon. Then Christ and overcoming Christians and Jews will rule this and every nation—from Jerusalem, not Washington.

Meanwhile, God has charged the church to change the spiritual and moral hearts of nations, not control their governing bodies. The methods He gave us to create believing individuals, assemblies, and movements within unbelieving nations are powerful: evangelism, intercession, Bible teaching, Christlike living, and a public witness against our generation's sins. These methods are simple, not sophisticated; supernatural, not conventional; heavenly, not worldly. They exist to promote the present hidden kingdom of God—Christ's church and body worldwide—not any nation, party, ideology, or political leader. They don't require a Christian president, congress, or judiciary.[1] But they do require a humble, faithful, and godly church. Such an *ekklesia* understands its dual citizenship.

Sadly, too many American Christians don't, because so many ministers practice "America preaching"—constantly addressing messages to America rather than the church. This, along with our innate national pride, has caused many American Christians to confuse the church with America. Many now consider them the same. They see only their citizenship in America, from which they look for a president to save them. But Paul taught, "Our citizenship is in heaven, from which also we look for the Savior" (Phil. 3:20). This doesn't mean it's wrong to love our country, understand current issues, vote our consciences, respect and pray for our leaders even when we disagree with them,[2] or enter politics if so called. But it means we shouldn't mistake politicians for panaceas or confuse political dreams with biblical prophecies.

To a person, our original forefathers in faith agree. Enoch, Noah, Abraham, these all realized their first and abiding citizenship was in heaven and "confessed that they were strangers and pilgrims on the earth" (Heb. 11:13). They looked away from the chaotic capitals of their times, opting to fix their hopes instead on their heavenly country and capital:

> If they had been mindful of that country from which they came out, they might have had opportunity to return. But now they desire *a better country,* that is, an *heavenly*; wherefore, God...hath prepared for them a city.
>
> —HEBREWS 11:15–17

Wisely, they sought a "better country" that's "heavenly." Blindly, we seek only this one. They accepted their country wouldn't be perfect. We insist ours will be. They confessed they were "strangers and pilgrims" in their nations. We say we're patriots and partisans. They sought heaven's gate. Like Lot, we aspire to Sodom's gate. Obviously one of us is wrong.

And it's time we get right. While praying for our country, let's begin seeking another country.[3]

Chapter 64

NEVER SAY NO!

FTER FORTY YEARS in Midian Moses was suddenly recalled to Egypt: "Come now...and I will send thee unto Pharaoh, that thou mayest bring forth my people...out of Egypt" (Exod. 3:10). But his response to God's surprising call was surprisingly negative.

Uncharacteristically uncooperative, Moses resisted with a flurry of questions and protests. He questioned God's choice in selecting him: "Who am I, that I should go unto Pharaoh?" (v. 11). He claimed he lacked sufficient knowledge, such as God's proper name: "[When] the children of Israel...shall say to me, What is his name? what shall I say?" (v. 13). He argued the people would not believe God had visited him and sent him: "They will not believe me...[but] will say, The LORD hath not appeared unto thee" (Exod. 4:1). He contended he was a poor public speaker: "I am not eloquent...I am slow of speech" (v. 10). Finally, he politely but flatly refused God's orders: "Lord, send, I pray thee, by the hand of him whom thou wilt send" (v. 13). Or, paraphrasing, "No, God, I don't want this assignment. Please send someone else."

Understandably, God was angry (v. 14). There was no time for haggling! God's people were in desperate need, fainting with hopelessness under Pharaoh's cruel lash. Moses was God's man, God had prepared him, and his time had come.

In all Moses' inexcusable excuse-making, he forgot one huge fact: when God calls us to a task, He's already considered everything. Omniscient, He knows us—our abilities, knowledge, training, experience, strengths and weaknesses—far better than we do. He also knows every adversary and adversity we'll meet. Questioning His executive decisions implies He doesn't know what He's doing—which only proves we don't! Resisting God's call, whether for fear or selfishness, is always the wrong response.

A. W. Tozer articulates perfectly the right response to a divine call:

> My God, I shall not waste time deploring my weakness nor my unfittedness for the work. The responsibility is not mine, but Thine. Thou has said, "I know thee—I ordained thee—I sanctified thee," and..."Thou shall go to all that I shall send

thee, and whatsoever I command thee thou shalt speak." Who am I to argue with Thee or to call into question Thy sovereign choice? The decision is not mine but Thine. So be it, Lord. Thy will, not mine, be done.[1]

"So be it, Lord" wisely recognizes God's wisdom is always best and humbly submits to it. It also shows faith in God's ever-sufficient grace.

When God called Paul to accept harrying sufferings for His higher purposes and the church's greater good, He promised unfailing grace. No matter how thorny Paul's troubles, Christ assured him, "My grace is sufficient for thee" (2 Cor. 12:9). Indeed, God's commands are His enablings. Every time we believe and act on His surprising call, we find His grace surprisingly adequate. Christ in us can master "all things," including duties we fear may baffle, overtax, or overwhelm us (Phil. 4:13). It's this Christ life God calls and places His confidence in, not our natural strength, wisdom, or abilities. If we'll believe this, stay close to Christ, and pursue His call in childlike trust, we'll find, as Joseph did, that the Lord will ultimately make everything we do prosper (Gen. 39:3). Now back to Moses.

The instant Moses stopped objecting and started obeying, God sent help. His assistance was embodied in Moses' brother, Aaron, whose name means "a shining light; a mountain of strength."[2] When Aaron arrived, new strength girded Moses and his old weakness fled (Exod. 4:27). New hope illuminated his heart and his dark doubts dissipated. Now he understood how his mission impossible was possible. God's grace incarnate in Aaron would provide everything Moses lacked, speaking skills, ministry assistance, companionship, etc. Once linked, they proved an irresistible divine team—and Pharaoh fell and Israel went free!

But things could have turned out very differently. If Moses had considered the natural prospects of God's call—delivering two million weak, discouraged people from powerful, merciless masters—doubt would have paralyzed him. He never would have obeyed God's call. Or met Aaron. Or delivered Israel. Or glorified God. Or taught us this lesson.

Namely, that when the ministry, mission, job, duty or responsibility to which God calls you seems too great and your ability too small, don't resist. Abandon all claims of inability, surrender your selfishness, and begin agreeing with God: "So be it, Lord. Yes, I can do all things, *this* thing, through Christ!" The moment we act, God will begin assisting, sending "Aaron," sustaining light and strength. Has the Savior summoned you?

Never say no!

Chapter 65

HOLY HASTE

*I*N ACTS 20 Paul sailed by Ephesus because "he hastened," if possible, to get to Jerusalem by Pentecost (v. 16). His plan? Go directly to Jerusalem, avoiding distractions yet discharging any responsibilities God brought along the way. This was holy haste.

Conversely, the Bible has much to say about our typically human "headlong" haste, that is, rushing or hurrying. And it's mostly bad. Why? Haste almost always breeds impatience, and this sinful mood inevitably prompts other sins, such as inconsiderateness and offensive words, actions, and reactions. When hasty, for example, we are much more prone to:

- Get angry with others without cause (Eccles. 7:9)
- Rush to judgment (Prov. 18:13)
- Reply too quickly and curtly (James 1:19–20)[1]
- Panic, as our faith, which is supported by patience, lapses (Heb. 6:12)[2]
- Foolishly accuse God of ignoring our prayers (Ps. 31:22)
- Oppressively pressure others to work too hard or fast to satisfy our selfish desires (Exod. 5:13)
- Impulsively and irresponsibly make promises or guarantees that we can't or won't keep (Eccles. 5:2–5)

Thus, unchecked or uncontrolled, haste makes waste, hurry havoc, and rush ruin! Every day haste breeds mistakes, accidents, foolish decisions, strife, hindrances, and other offensive and self-opposing actions. It also causes us to overlook and neglect the duty at hand. When doing things hurriedly, we don't do them "heartily, as unto the Lord," or as excellently and thoroughly as we would if Jesus personally asked us to do them (Col. 3:23). These are the follies of haste. But Paul shows us an alternative.

Sometimes we need to make haste without making havoc. The good news is, by God's grace we can. How? We refuse to be anxious about the problem or task in question, but instead commit it to God by prayer with faith and thanksgiving (Phil. 4:6–7). Then, confident God will help, we move without delay toward our objective with a calm, patient disposition, stopping only for necessary interruptions. Why did Paul hasten toward Jerusalem?

He was zealously pursuing God's will, delivering a love donation from the Gentile churches to the Jewish Christians in Jerusalem. Also, thousands of Jews would crowd Jerusalem during Pentecost, making it ripe for evangelism. Furthermore, Pentecost—the church's birthday—was a perfect time to fellowship with the Judean Christians. After visiting Jerusalem, Paul planned to eagerly pursue the next part of God's plan: Rome! (Acts 19:21). These godly motives, all in God's will, spurred Paul.

But he didn't rush headlong. Spirit-led, he was ready to stop and attend to whatever God placed before him. His running was not a mad sprint but a controlled pace. He moved steadily forward quickened by desire but tempered by a readiness for God's intermissions—like stopping in Miletus to exhort the Ephesian elders (Acts 20:17–38)! Jesus also practiced sanctified swiftness.

Once Jesus planned to pass through Samaria to minister in Galilee (John 4:3–4). Yet near Sychar the Father interrupted Jesus' plan with His plan: to help a needy Samaritan woman and city (vv. 5–42)! Spirit-led, Jesus immediately halted and addressed His Father's business. Then without delay He resumed His swift journey to Galilee (v. 43). What kinds of things require our righteous rapidness?

We should always quickly avoid sin; confess sins when they occur; obey scriptural instructions; show hospitality; give to the needy; share good news with weary hearts; reconcile divided Christians; receive God's correction; obey divine guidance; take the escapes God provides; relieve God's suffering people whenever possible; dissuade others, especially Christians, from seeking vengeance; thank God for new blessings; share our blessings with others; rejoice with others over their blessings; turn away from gossip or slander. In these or any other matters in which we ardently pursue God's will, we should practice holy haste, first asking God's help and then moving promptly, avoiding distractions while remaining sensitive to biblical orders, the Spirit's prompts, and others' needs. Then we'll do God's will expeditiously but without the follies of human haste. Why learn this discipline?

We're in the last days of the church age. In these fast-changing times there will be many occasions when "the king's business [requires] haste" (1 Sam. 21:8). In such scenarios we'll need to ponder and practice Paul's sanctified swiftness, pursuing God's will fervently but never frenetically.

Then we'll "run with patience the race" set before us without running roughshod over fallen runners or innocent bystanders (Heb. 12:2). We'll pursue our plans earnestly, yet never obsessively, ever ready to yield, "if God will[s]" (James 4:15–16). And we'll "run through a troop" of hinderers (Ps. 18:29), yet promptly stop and serve in every Miletus or Sychar God puts before us. Why?

We've learned how to practice holy haste.

Chapter 66

HIS WAY IS PERFECT

*W*HY DO WE sometimes try to do things in every way but God's? Could it be we've never learned, as David taught, "His way is perfect" (Ps. 18:30)? If so, we may take comfort in knowing we're not alone in our folly.

Before the flood Adam's rebellious children determined not to do things God's way—and didn't! God lamented that "all flesh had corrupted his way" (Gen. 6:12). Later the Jews could have walked in God's ways in the wilderness but stubbornly refused to learn them. Again God lamented, "They have not known my ways" (Heb. 3:10). Moses' protégé, Joshua, knew God's will should always be done in God's way, yet he failed to do so when first attacking Ai. Even David did his own thing once. When bringing the ark of the covenant to Jerusalem, he transported it in the Philistine, not the scriptural, way. But there's hope in these dark stories.

While the pre-flood world and Jews of the Exodus stubbornly persisted in their own ways, Joshua and David didn't. Realizing their errors, they reattempted God's will in God's way—and received God's blessing and great joy. Though better, this still wasn't the best.

The best way is doing things God's way the first time. Three barriers prevent this:

1. Worldliness

2. Stubborn pride

3. Ignorance

We often refuse God's way because we want to imitate the ways and means of the world around us—traditional, institutional, religious, or popular methods of operation, or other innovations that differ from biblical ways. Or we're ensnared by our strong personal preferences. We want our way so stubbornly that we simply won't change, even if we discover a better way. Or, like the Hebrews in the wilderness, we may be ignorant of God's modus operandi. The cure for spiritual ignorance is biblical information, and lots of it. So let's explore God's biblical ways of doing things.

When we're working, He wants us doing "whatever" we do "heartily," not halfheartedly, obeying our superiors "as to the Lord, not unto men" (Col. 3:23). Concerning money, He would have us use but not crave it, trust our unfailing God rather than uncertain wealth, and labor to meet our needs and others' rather than to accumulate "treasure upon earth" (Matt. 6:19). In ministry, His way is to aspire to bless others, not ourselves, to seek "not to be ministered unto" through rewards and honors but "to minister and to give" to whomever we meet (Matt. 20:28). In sexuality, God's way is faithful monogamous marriage, not fornication, homosexuality, polygamy, or invalid or repetitive divorces and remarriages. Concerning authority, God's way is that we respectfully "be subject" to all governmental, church, occupational, organizational, and domestic authorities so we may enjoy peace, order, and progress and spread the gospel. Concerning problems, God's way is that we never worry but ever lean on Him "by prayer and supplication, with thanksgiving," and rest in His unfailing guidance and help (Phil. 4:6–7).

Concerning salvation, His way is "by grace…through faith" in Christ alone (Eph. 2:8). In thinking, His way is that we be not carnally but "spiritually minded," applying His Word to all our situations and enjoying the "life and peace" of spiritual insight (Rom. 8:6). Concerning adversaries, His way is never vengeance but instead that we "overcome evil with good" (Rom. 12:21). In victory, His way is that we freely praise Him and acknowledge our helpers, never boasting or gloating. In defeat, His way is to humbly learn from our failures, neither excusing ourselves nor blaming others, so we don't repeat them. In adversity, His way is to "give thanks" and never complain, focusing instead on trusting and obeying Him until He releases us (1 Thess. 5:18). In duty, His way is to always be faithful, no matter how small our job or its visible results. In witnessing, His way is to speak when He creates opportunities, not to force biblical truths or testimonies on divinely unprepared hearts. In worship, His way is to offer heartfelt praises "in spirit and in truth," not conduct cold and lifeless rituals (John 4:23–24). These are just some of His ways.

Scripture reveals many more. But are we ready to learn them? Ready to do things God's way?

Whenever we insist on doing things our way—in worldliness, stubborn pride, or ignorance—we regret it. Like Joshua and David, we eventually realize His way is best—or as David noted, "perfect." So why waste precious time, effort, and opportunities? Let's humbly do everything God's way the first time and receive God's blessing and great joy. Every other way is flawed and must disappoint. Only His way is perfect.

Chapter 67

MORE "ACTS" ARE COMING!

HOUGH A SKILLED writer, Luke ended his record of the early church with only a brief description of Paul's Roman ministry and no formal closing statement (Acts 28:30–31). This abrupt termination seems to leave Acts incomplete.

By contrast, Luke's Gospel is not only complete, describing Jesus' life from Annunciation to Ascension, but also ends more appropriately with "Amen" (Luke 24:53).[1] Why then does Luke's second scroll, Acts, end without a fuller closing, benediction, rhetorical flourish, or even an Amen? We're left wondering about the outcome of Paul's trial. Peter's Roman ministry? What became of the fledgling Gentile churches?

The natural explanation is Paul's trial hadn't occurred, so Luke couldn't record its decision. Therefore he released Acts to bless the thousands of hungry Christian readers rather than await a verdict that may have been years coming. There's also another perspective.

Luke's writing was inspired. So the Holy Spirit, for His own reasons, prompted Luke to stop writing precisely when he did. By thus leaving Acts somewhat unfinished, the Spirit was saying:

> The notable deeds of the Christian era aren't fully recorded.
> More "Acts" are coming. Additional chapters will be added to
> this, the church's official history.

Indeed the glorious work God began at Pentecost wasn't terminated with Paul's Roman ministry, nor the Spirit's mighty river quenched. The grand story went on. Christlike living and ministry continue today on an ever-grander scale. God still raises empowered messengers, initiates Spirit-led missions, and prompts mass conversions worldwide. Miraculous healings and angelic deliverances persist. The risen Jesus, who appears and speaks throughout Acts, is still controlling His body and "acting" through its members. And He's still the central theme and glory of Christianity's story.

At core Acts describes Christ's deeds through His body's members by His Spirit's energy. There's a marked absence of dependence on worldly ways, strength, and wisdom and a beautiful emphasis on simple reliance on God. As God's model for Christian devotion, life, and ministry, Acts sets a very high yet tantalizingly attainable standard for all generations—including ours.

When we compare our typically lukewarm, materialistic, spiritually impotent, "Laodicean"[2] churches today with Acts, it seems we'll never match those first Christians' devotion and fruitfulness. So we content ourselves to look back to the glory days of the Peters, Pauls, and Stephens. Or we review church history's great movers and movements.

We reminisce about the continuing miracles of the first three centuries, the primitive church's perseverance, the martyrs' courage, the church fathers' wisdom, the hermits' separation, or the monks' commitment to prayer. We marvel at pre-Reformation reformers like the Waldensians, who suffered terribly yet stood firm in their faith. We admire the acts of God's stars in the long night of medieval apostasy, Wycliffe, Hus, and other spiritual light-bearers. We marvel at the Reformers' boldness—Luther's resolve, Knox's zeal, and Tyndale's courageous translation labors. We laud the acts of brave, small groups—the Pietists, Moravians, Puritans, Separatists, and original Protestant missionaries. We wonder at the nation-turning acts of revivalists, such as Wesley, Whitefield, Finney, and Moody. We esteem the purity and simplicity of the Holiness and Apostolic Faith movements and the supernatural *charismata* of the Pentecostal, Charismatic, and Third Wave movements. Make no mistake, as in Acts, Jesus was "acting" through all these members of His body by the energy of His Spirit. But even this wistful view of victorious vistas past disappoints. Why? We're looking in the wrong direction.

We should be looking forward. As noted, the Acts' Inspirer has hinted there's more glory coming, that God's best for His church is better than anything Luke or we have seen. After Acts 28 we've seen many wonderful things—but sporadically, never steadily. We've never witnessed a lasting return to all the key elements of the original church's truth, devotion, grace, and power. But we will.

The church's finest hour is yet to come. In these last days Jesus will re-baptize us with the Spirit and release a visitation eclipsing, perhaps dwarfing, Pentecost. Just as the glory of Christ's presence and ministry in Israel's latter temple (Herod's) exceeded its former glory, so the glory of Christianity's latter house will exceed that of its beginnings and subsequent history (Hag. 2:9). New acts of saving grace and power will break out with missions, messages, mercies, manifestations, and miracles.[3] However, spiritual maturity, not sensationalism, will be emphasized this time, and all opposition, however fierce, will only facilitate it. The world will again be turned upside down,[4] and modern-day Lukes will stand by, recording our amazing story, till its central theme Himself appears...

Then Acts will be properly and permanently closed. Believe it, my friend, more "Acts" are coming!

Chapter 68

READY TO SEEK HIM?

THE ANCIENT PSALMIST is urgently calling God-seekers: "Seek the LORD, and his strength; seek his face evermore" (Ps. 105:4). Do we realize what it means to "seek"?

Not at all passive, "seek" is a very active term. We never seek things accidentally or because they're given us. The two usages of "seek" in this verse are translated from two Hebrew words signifying, "to inquire; investigate; try to find, do, or learn; to care for with desire; require; have a relationship; ponder."[1] "Seek," therefore, implies we believers should:

- Ask God to reveal Himself to us
- Investigate the evidence of Him in His Word and history
- Not merely intend or promise to but start seeking Him
- Desire and crave Him
- Realize we need His presence, strength, and favor
- Develop our relationship with Him
- Think often and deeply of Him

Seeking God implies other actions also. We launch a personal expedition to discover the world's richest hidden treasure: God! We go God hunting, alertly searching for the ultimate prey and prize—knowing God. We follow closely the path of eternal life blazed by the Way, His apostles, and remnant believers who've gone before us. We stop patronizing Jesus and start seriously, prayerfully, and insatiably studying Him with determined effort, ready to sacrifice and suffer, if necessary, to fully discover who He is. We commit to a lifelong quest for more of God—seeking Him with all our heart, energy, faculties, and resources so we may walk closely with Him. That's serious action. That's seeking. That's what the psalmist urges. What should we seek?

We seek "the LORD" (Ps. 105:4), not just Bible facts but a growing personal fellowship with its most lovely character—Jesus! We pursue "his strength" (v. 4), the Holy Spirit's power, which gives us inner fortitude, intellectual sharpness, emotional stability, physical endurance, and influence with souls. We hunt for "his face" (v. 4), which radiates His true character to our hearts and smile of approval on our lives. When do we seek?

"Evermore" (v. 4). We seek Christ early in the morning, at night, and any other available time...the rest of our lives. Thus it becomes not our hobby but our habit. How do we seek?

We search for more of our Master through prayer, praise, and worship, but especially through God's Word. Scripture is the primary, infallible, and indispensable medium through which God reveals Himself. Mary of Bethany gave much free time to worshipfully seek Jesus through His Word (Luke 10:38–42). We'll never know the living Word without steadily searching the written Word. Since humans are born seeking milk, touches, and attention, why don't we naturally seek God's attention, touch, and the milk of His Word?

We're too distracted and entangled with this world's alluring lusts, ensnaring strifes, compelling causes, and amusing trivia. Thus we're religious but not serious, professing but not pursuing Christ. Why? We love our idols more than the Immortal. Which Dagons, Baals, and Molechs are stealing our affections?

Longing, worldly desires rise like burnt offerings from our heart-altars daily to appease various false deities: accumulated riches, consumer goods, entertainment, romantic pleasure, dining, leisure, travel, offices, recognition, achievements, to name a few. Will we abandon these false gods who can't satisfy to seek the only One who can? Will we give Him the time, emotion, energy, and adoration we've given them?

If not, we should expect more of the rewards of non-seekers: spiritual dryness, discontentment, confusion, strife, meaninglessness, and the exact opposite of the blessed objectives mentioned in our text, namely, no divine presence, strength, or favor! But there's an alternative. We may repent and become committed God seekers.

Persistent seekers always receive God's promised presence, strength, and favor: "He is a rewarder of them that diligently seek him" (Heb. 11:6). They also revel in sweet fellowship with Jesus, joy, a full revelation of God's character, luminous biblical insight, thriving works, heart rest, peaceful relations, inspiration, holy boldness, fruitfulness, heart's desires, honors, and Christlike humility, all because they've obeyed God's call to seek Him.[2] Throughout Scripture we find God calling seekers.

When Adam stopped seeking Him, God lamented, "[Adam], where art thou?" (Gen. 3:9). He invited Moses, "Come up to me...and be there [remain near me]" (Exod. 24:12). Jesus challenged us to seek Him "first" (Matt. 6:33). He calls weary believers, "Come unto me...I will give you rest" (Matt. 11:28). Scripture closes with the Spirit urging us to "come" and seek Jesus' living water "freely" (Rev. 22:17).

Like the ancient psalmist, these texts summon us to respond in every way "seek" implies. If you're responding, continue. If not, today repent, pray,[3] and respond. Ready to seek Him?

Chapter 69

TOTAL CONTENTMENT

*T*HE APOSTLE PAUL learned to be content with..."whatever!" "I have learned in whatever state I am, to be content" (Phil. 4:11, NKJV). His instruction came by the Spirit in the school of daily circumstances. And gradually.

Day by day the Spirit repeatedly showed Paul how to be content[1]—"satisfied to the point where I am not disturbed or disquieted" (AMP)—in all of life's scenarios, from its humiliating depths to its exhilarating heights. "I know how to live on almost nothing or with everything" (v. 12, NLT). Most Christians have difficulty being abased, while some stoic or ascetic believers won't accept abounding. But to be spiritually mature, like Paul, we must learn to be satisfied in both settings. For that we need self-discipline: "I know in fact how to discipline myself in lowly circumstances. I know in fact how to conduct myself when I have more than enough" (v. 11, WUEST). Since this self-control is a "fruit of the Spirit" (Gal. 5:22–23), we need to live constantly in the fullness of the Spirit to maintain contentment. But this context holds more.

Philippians 4 reveals these keys to contentment:

- "Rejoice" in your close fellowship-walk with Jesus "always" (v. 4). This is the greatest secret of contented overcomers: "Be content with such things as ye have; for he hath said, I will never leave thee" (Heb. 13:5).[2]

- Never worry but ever pray in faith with thanksgiving about every need (Phil. 4:6–7).

- Continually "think on" spiritually edifying, morally right, and intellectually stimulating things to nourish, exercise, and guard your mind (v. 8).[3]

- When doubtful or discouraged, remember and believe you can meet any challenge with God's grace (v. 13; 2 Cor. 12:9–10).

- When abased, never complain (Phil. 4:11) or covet (v. 17) but ever give "sacrifice[s] of praise" (Heb. 13:15).[4]

- When abased, remember your former blessings, like Paul's, will return to "flourish again" (Phil. 4:10; Job 42:10–17).

- When abounding, be humbly moderate (gentle, forbearing), never boastful, willful, or self-dependent (Phil. 4:5; 1 Cor. 10:12).

Essentially, however, contentment remains a simple moral choice to be satisfied enough with Christ and the sweet inner benefits He gives whatever our worldly successes, troubles, needs, or monotony.

Literally, content means, "self-sufficient; sufficient in oneself."[5] The Stoics used this word (*autarkēs*) to describe those who were proudly self-sufficient and self-reliant, living (or aspiring to live) independently of others' help.[6] Paul uses it, however, for humble Christians who realize joyfully we're "self-sufficient in Christ's sufficiency" (Phil. 4:13, AMP).[7] Truly, the more truth, life, and joy we have within, the less outward pacifications we need. Of all people, Christians, who possess God's marvelous Son, Spirit, and Word, should be the most content. Paul was.

The Spirit also taught him how to be full (satisfied) and hungry (seeking) simultaneously: "I am fully initiated into all the mysteries both of fulness and of hunger, of abundance and of want" (Phil. 4:12, WEY). Surprisingly, the great apostle sometimes suffered temporary physical hunger (2 Cor. 11:27). At other times he feasted on royal fare (Acts 28:10). Yet—and here's the great lesson—he was perfectly unmoved from his close walk and work with Jesus by either experience. Why did the divine Shepherd allow Paul's brief shortages? Perhaps to deepen his compassion for poor Christians, whose needs he learned to minister to faithfully.[8]

Figuratively, Paul learned to be satisfied (full) with whatever material things he had, yet always seek (hungrily) more spiritual things. Are we satisfied with what God has given us yet always seeking more of Him and His truth, wisdom, presence, and power? If so, we're learning contentment.

If not, we'll never know it. Whatever we have materially, we'll always be vexed wanting more, always more. Matthew Henry said, "What can a man desire more than enough?...A covetous worldling, if he has ever so much, would still have more; but a heavenly Christian, though he has little, has enough."[9] If we refuse to be content, the circumstances and people in our lives will continually dictate our disposition and productivity and thus our destiny. We'll be up or down in our emotions and work when they are. It's impossible to maintain a steady good attitude and work output if we're discontent with adversity or distracted by prosperity. Content believers march straight forward in devotion and duty daily regardless of conditions (1 Cor. 15:58). Christ and His heavenly purpose, peace, strength, and joy are enough. Period. "Whatever!" That's total contentment.

If Paul learned it, so can you. By the Spirit's personalized instruction. In your daily circumstances. Gradually, one decision at a time: "Lord, I'll be satisfied today." This is the only truly rich life.[10]

So enrich yours. Practice total contentment.

Chapter 70

AS STRONG AS YOUR DAYS

*B*OASTING ON CHRIST'S assistance, the apostle Paul declared, "I can do all things through Christ, who strengtheneth me" (Phil. 4:13). His perfect positivism was rooted in God's perfect grace.

"My grace is sufficient for thee," was Christ's response when Paul prayed for release from his unrelenting sufferings (2 Cor. 12:9). Thus Paul learned that while he remained in vital union with Christ, whatever his challenge, the Lord's "grace"—divine ability, strength, or graciousness imparted without merit—would be "sufficient," or enough to handle it.

So by testifying he could do "all things" through Christ who "strengtheneth[1] me," he was expressing confidence in the unfailing, multifaceted grace of God, as if saying, "I can do all things through the strength of God's grace."

"All things" refers to things in God's will. Paul, who lived only for God's will (Phil. 3:10–14), understood that Christ doesn't supply grace for works outside His will. Christ taught, "Apart from Me you can do nothing" (John 15:5, NAS). So Paul's complete thought was while pursuing Christ's will he could meet any challenge by the strength of Christ's all-sufficient grace. How often? Daily—which brings another grand promise to mind!

In the Spirit Moses promised the Asherites, "As thy days, so shall thy strength be" (Deut. 33:25). Or, "God will give you strength equal to your days."[2] These "days" are literal and figurative: days of our weeks, days of our trials, and days of our lives.[3] God promises strength lasting to the end of our longest day, hardest trial, and lengthiest lifetime. Whenever these "days" demand more strength, He'll supply it. What kinds of strength?

God provides every kind of strength, specifically:

- SPIRITUAL POWER. Our spirit is our core, the nucleus of our whole person. God provides inner spiritual strength by the anointing of His Spirit. We receive fresh anointings as we "wait upon the LORD" daily in private fellowship, prayer, and Bible reading—and then rise in His power to soar in spiritual mindedness, run without weariness, and walk without fainting…all day long (Isa. 40:31). That's how John the Baptist and Jesus "waxed strong in the Spirit" (Luke 1:80; 2:40). Is our spiritual strength waxing or waning?

- PHYSICAL STRENGTH. Though not all, most strong individuals enjoy good health. Thus God's promise of strength implies normal health. That doesn't mean we'll never get sick, but that God will faithfully heal and restore wholeness, thus sustaining our bodily strength until our days end.[4]

- INTELLECTUAL VIGOR. To be strong, we must be strong-minded. Weak-minded, double-minded, fearful, or confused Christians won't fulfill God's will. God's Spirit gives us "sound mind," and we perfect our intellectual strength through regular reading, study, and reflection (2 Tim. 1:7).

- STRENGTH OF WILL. We need strong will to overrule our sinful and selfish desires and will our way through long, hard days, tests, and seasons of adversity. So God imparts strength "to will…his good pleasure" (Phil. 2:13), thus helping us want to do His will and remain resolute until it's finished.

- STRENGTH TO ENDURE. Endurance is the strength to hold on and go on when we feel we can't do either. It's the courage to bear, tolerate, or hold out till God's help arrives.[5] The Philadelphians obeyed Christ's "command to endure patiently" (Rev. 3:10, NIV). God promises if we're willing to endure, "so shall thy strength be"—we'll be able to endure, vigorous, fruitful, and gracious till our trial ends.

- LONGEVITY. Moses was strong and active for 120 years! "His eye was not dim, nor his natural force abated" (Deut. 34:7). Or "He never lost his physical strength" (GW); "he was as strong as ever" (NLT).[6] God offers us the same strength until our work is finished.

These manifestations of divine strength belong to all who faithfully do His will. How long?

To the end of every day, trial, and life span. Nehemiah's laborers repaired Jerusalem's walls from dawn to dusk. Moses endured forty years until his preparatory tests ended. The apostle John was strong in spirit, mind, body, will, and endurance well into his nineties.[7] For what kind of "day" do you need God's strength?

Are you facing new, harder challenges? Long, difficult workdays? A trying "day of trouble" season (Ps. 20:1)? Aging with all its aches, pains, and decreasing physical resilience? Afraid you haven't enough strength for these "days"? Think again! God promises, "As thy days, so shall thy strength be!" Ask for His strength and live in it by faith. Move forward in duty in your challenging workdays, days of testing, and the latter days of your life, expecting to be as strong as your days.

Chapter 71

SPIRITUAL LEADERS GIVEN AND RAISED

*W*HILE EVANGELIZING IN Antioch of Pisidia, the apostle Paul made a passing statement with profound meaning. While summarizing Jewish history, Paul recalled that when the Jews pleaded for a king in Samuel's day, the Lord "gave" them Saul: "They desired a king; and God gave unto them Saul, the son of Kish...for forty years" (Acts 13:21). In the next breath he described Saul's successor, David, differently. Paul said God "raised" David: "When he had removed him [Saul], he raised up unto them David" (v. 22). Why did Paul state God "gave" one leader and "raised" another. What's the difference?

Plenty! These terms reveal God chose both leaders for office but only one was prepared.

Though divinely chosen, Saul was not divinely prepared. He was selected but not trained by God, tapped but not transformed to habitually think and act spiritually. Consequently Saul consistently failed God and His people under pressure.

Conversely, God both selected and shaped David for use. After Samuel anointed him, young David began learning about ruling and warfare as Saul's court musician and personal armor bearer. After this initial training, his faith and skills were further tested, purified, and seasoned in a decade of difficulty in the wilderness—not after but before he was enthroned as king of Judah.

Once crowned as Judah's ruler, his experiential education continued. For seven years he ruled only Judah, not Israel's other tribes, while further perfecting his wisdom, grace, courage, and other abilities necessary to lead with excellence.[1] Thus thoroughly raised by God, David's character—his predictable way of thinking, living, working, and reacting—became completely prepared to lead all Israel. Consequently, for the next thirty-three years David consistently accomplished God's will and didn't buckle, compromise, or rebel in adversity.[2] Paul also mentions this: "He [God] gave testimony...I have found David...a man after mine own heart, who shall fulfill all my will" (Acts 13:22). Saul also could have been divinely raised.

He was a true Jew, not an impostor. He was divinely called and initially touched by God's Spirit, who gave him a new heart, a prophetic anointing, and several key military victories (1 Sam. 10:5–6, 9). But Saul was not fully tested, deeply purified, or thoroughly transformed in character prior to his rule. Thus during his reign he had tragic latent faults—pride, envy, impatience, rage, fear of man, lying, a habit of partial obedience—which surfaced to his and his nation's undoing whenever he faced strong temptation or trouble. Yet if Saul had trusted and obeyed God in his crises with the Philistines and Amalekites,[3] God's Spirit would have graciously purged these faults and gradually transformed Saul's character during his reign as He had David's before his reign. But Saul consistently refused to react with trust and obedience. What do David's and Saul's biographies tell us?

Saul represents spiritual leaders who are sovereignly called and empowered by God's Spirit, yet not thoroughly changed in character by ongoing teaching, testing, and correction (Ps. 94:12–13). David represents those who are called and anointed, and afterward thoroughly changed by the Spirit's inner workings during years of continuing preparation. All ministers, and all Christians, are either becoming Davids or Sauls.[4]

God has called and given millions of Christian leaders worldwide, but the question is how many have also let Him raise them? Many are trained in religious academic institutions, ordained by churches, denominations, or missionary organizations, and placed in leadership positions. Like Saul, they may serve initially with undeniable fruitfulness. But to be deeply changed leaders molded after David's Christlike image, they must continue responding to God's dealings post-ordination. Tests, temptations, troublemakers, persecutions, defeats, disappointments, delays, betrayals—these are our developmental Philistine and Amalekite crises, our formative years in the ministerial wilderness. These crises visit not to destroy but to deal with us. They are fiery forges carefully designed to melt, reshape, and remold our characters. Saul didn't react well in his forges. But we can.

Our consistent reactions to our fiery tests determine if we'll become leaders who ultimately resist or fulfill God's will—and bless or harm His people. David fulfilled God's will and blessed Israel greatly. Saul stubbornly resisted God's plan and his successor, David, and thus deeply troubled Israel.[5] Jewish leaders in Paul's day did the same, blindly resisting God's Messiah and gospel: "They that dwell at Jerusalem, and their rulers...desired...that he should be slain" (Acts 13:27–28). What kind of spiritual leaders do we want to become? Or follow?

Davids? Or Sauls? Deeply prepared, spiritually powerful ministers? Or shallow, unchanged divine appointees? The welfare of our churches and times hang in the balance. Let's seek, and become, spiritual leaders—given and raised.

Chapter 72

PASTOR, PEOPLE, BE LOOSED!

EWARE THE BINDINGS of excessive religious rules! One straightjacket is the unwritten ministerial decree, "Never repeat sermons!" Another is congregations' Athenian demand for "some new thing" every meeting (Acts 17:21). From these bonds pastors and people need loosing.

Admittedly, it isn't good to present old or new material constantly. It's deplorable when pitifully unscholarly pastors bore their people to death by constantly preaching a few favorite texts, topics, or experiences. Conversely, it's liberating for more studious pastors to discover they may occasionally repeat messages in part or whole. When? As the Spirit leads—or as our souls need! To God, preaching isn't about homiletics.

Sermons aren't meant to prove pastors can study, write outlines, and orate. They're God's preferred medium of delivering timely biblical truths to nourish, correct, and guide our walk with Christ. And though many ministers loathe repeating messages, Jesus doesn't.

To induce Peter to accept Gentile believers equally with Jews, Jesus preached a timely sermon: "What God hath cleansed, that call not thou common" (Acts 10:15). He repeated this "three times" (v. 16, NKJV). Thus the Master Minister set a precedent for us: "When My Spirit prompts, you may freely repeat teachings previously delivered." This wasn't the living Word's first repeat sermon.

Consider His ancient written Word. There He duplicated key portions of Israel's law in the Pentateuch. Some psalms are repeated almost verbatim. Selected proverbs are fully or partially restated.[1] Key biblical themes are repeated frequently. Seven times God says, with various wordings, He's "no respecter of persons" (Acts 10:34). Four times He asserts, "The just shall live by his faith" (Hab. 2:4). Three times He promises, "Whosoever shall call upon the name of the Lord shall be saved" (Rom. 10:13). The apostles followed this example.

Peter duplicated his doctrines to the church at large: "I will not be negligent to put you in remembrance of these things, though ye know them" (2 Pet. 1:12). Paul repeated his end-time teaching to the

Thessalonians: "Remember ye not that, when I was yet with you, I told you these things?" (2 Thess. 2:5). John redundantly insisted Christians walk in love: "This is the message that ye heard from the beginning, that we should love one another (1 John 3:11).[2] Why did the apostles keep representing truth to us? Our souls need it.

The uncomplimentary truth is we don't always receive instruction the first time. We understand Bible concepts clearly enough but are often slow to surrender and change our ways to obey them, especially when they cross our will. So God and His tuned-in messengers persist—till we not merely know but yield. This lesson brings two benefits.

First, it releases ministers from unbiblical restrictions when selecting sermons. Yes, it's still preferable they present freshly studied material each meeting, but it's far more important that they minister what the Spirit wants and our souls require, whether novel or familiar. He who alone knows every congregant's heart always points praying pastors to what's needed most at the moment.

Second, it urges congregants to receive whatever biblical teaching a praying pastor or teacher brings as coming from the Lord. If the topic announced is new, our natural curiosity will sustain our interest and the message will also be timely. If it's old or familiar truth, it too will prove timely, and more beneficial than any newer but untimely material. While not informing us with "some new thing," it will nevertheless motivate us, cleansing and reviving us by redirecting us to truths we've heard but not obeyed or recently let slip. Pastors and people who walk in this Spirit-led way will enjoy an invigorating new freedom: "Where the Spirit of the Lord is, there is liberty" (2 Cor. 3:17). And they'll be wiser.

Wisdom is the timely application of knowledge to the spontaneous and fluid situations of life. The wisest preacher, Christ, spoke to each of Asia's seven churches "what the Spirit saith" (Rev. 2:7). His messages spoke directly to their current condition, whether of faithfulness, failure, need, sin, error, or challenging tests. Unchanging, He gives the same kind of informational, motivational, or corrective messages to ministers today if they stay close to Him, prayerful, and immersed in His Word. By God's grace I've learned to practice this.

For years now, as the Spirit prompted or circumstances plainly required, I've periodically retaught familiar but vital passages from the Old or New Testament, especially the Epistles, to those I pastor.[3]

These talks—loosely structured, verse-by-verse, reality checks—probe, correct, and reconnect our branches with the Vine. Invariably, they're convicting, corrective, liberating, and reviving. Are excessive religious rules binding you?

Pastor, people, be loosed!

Chapter 73

THE INTELLIGENT DESIGNER

O ONE CAN consider the wonders of creation—from the distant galaxies to the human body to the amazing cell—without acknowledging its amazingly intelligent design. Unless they're pitifully ignorant. Or a stubborn Darwinist!

Why do so many deny their Creator? To acknowledge Him is to admit moral accountability to Him—something they refuse to do.[1] While debating, evangelizing, and praying for these adamant secularists, let's be sure we're not denying the Intelligent Designer[2] His rightful place of honor in our lives.

God's Son designed not only the creation[3] but also the church. Christ's declaration "Upon this rock I will build my church" (Matt. 16:18) reveals He owns and is presently building the church. If Christ is the church's owner and builder, He's also its Designer. The New Testament discloses His design,[4] or master plan, and reveals what it orders, omits, and suggests. Let's explore these three subjects.

Our Designer mandated obedience to His Word: "If ye love me, keep my commandments" (John 14:15). No body functions without obeying its head. To ensure unity, fruitfulness, and the success of our commission, He ordered us to "love one another; as I have loved you" (John 13:34). To empower us to do these things and endure tests and sufferings, He planned for us to receive the fullness of the Spirit: "Ye shall receive power, after the Holy Spirit is come upon you" (Acts 1:8).

Wisely, the Designer knew we would need discerning, stable leaders to strengthen and guide us. So He gave us five kinds of gifted ministers: apostles, prophets, evangelists, pastors, and teachers (Eph. 4:11). Since no Scripture foretells these offices ceasing, they all continue throughout this age.

Besides gifted ministers, the Designer ordained "gifts" of the Spirit (1 Cor. 12:1–31). These supernatural operations of the Spirit, seen first in Christ's Spirit-filled ministry, now work through us "as he will[s]" (v. 11)—which often means when tests create special stresses and needs in our lives not specifically or fully addressed by Scripture. When supervised by mature elders, these gifts are vitally important, convicting (1 Cor. 14:25–26), converting (Acts 9:34–35), correcting, guiding (Acts

16:6–7), forewarning (Acts 21:10–11), and encouraging us and others in adversity (1 Cor. 14:3).

One key gift is "tongues," or our spiritual prayer language. The eminent apostle Paul taught this "praying in the Spirit" edifies our spiritual core (1 Cor. 14:4).[5] Personally he prayed and sang in his prayer language often, was very grateful for it, and testified it was an excellent means of thanking God (vv. 15–18). Though the Designer thus recommended tongues through Paul, He doesn't require it, leaving us free to pursue or neglect this wonderful blessing.[6] But not denounce it!

Perfectly foreseeing, the Designer included all these spiritual resources because He knew we would need them. No New Testament text predicts their cessation or obsolescence in this age. Old Testament typology confirms this.[7] If we reject or belittle the Spirit's gifts, we grieve Him and insult our Designer's intelligence by calling unnecessary what He deemed necessary.

Conversely, the Designer's plan omits some things we consider important. The New Testament doesn't explicitly order the days, times, or places we must meet; whether we must sing psalms, hymns, or more modern songs; the order of our worship; how ministers must preach, teach, or dress; nor did He establish a central binding tradition or liturgy. He only mandated two ordinances, Baptism and Communion, and that we worship "in spirit and in truth" (John 4:23–24). The rest is up to us. But He also dropped some hints.

While not requiring them, the Designer's New Testament recommends other practices. It suggests we worship the first day of the week (1 Cor. 16:2), baptize by immersion (Acts 8:38–39), let congregants participate in meetings (Acts 14:26), and permit women to minister (Phil. 4:2–3), though men should typically lead (1 Tim. 3:2). While mentioning these things, our Designer stops short of mandating them.

Are we wise enough to follow His intelligent design, distinguishing His orders, omissions, and suggestions? Or are we acting like Darwinists? We criticize evolutionists for stubbornly denying creation's Intelligent Designer, but are we frustrating His plans for His church?

Let's start valuing, practicing, and teaching everything He put in His ecclesiastical design. If He put it in His plan, let's not throw it out. Let's stop judging other Christians over things He omitted from His plan. If He left it out, let's not insist on it. Let's follow His suggestions, as best we understand them, while remaining patient with those who see these issues differently. And let's trust our Designer's wise guidance in our lives and ministries. Why?

We want to honor, not insult, the Intelligent Designer.

Chapter 74

WE WILL BELIEVE IN MIRACLES!

*T*HANKS TO A praying church and angelic intervention, Peter stood knocking at Mary's gate, freed from prison only hours before his scheduled execution (Acts 12:13–17). Not only the way he escaped but also Peter himself was a miracle.

A young servant girl, Rhoda, "came to hearken" (v. 13). Of childlike heart and faith, Rhoda, recognizing Peter's voice, immediately believed the miracle, and "ran" (v. 14) joyfully to tell the others. But instead of rejoicing, they reproached her: "Thou art mad" (v. 15). This came from fellow believers, mind you, who had been praying nonstop for seven days…for Peter's release! After witnessing James' shocking execution (v. 2) and Peter's continuing imprisonment despite many prayers, their faith was weak. Peter's earlier incarceration ended after only one day (Acts 5:19–21). Why was this one continuing? While they nevertheless kept praying, they stopped expecting, probably because the "things seen" were so very discouraging.[1] They believed in miracles generally, and witnessed many, but failed to believe for this one.

These doubting intercessors at Mary's house symbolize true Christians who disbelieve in miracles due to their reasoning or doctrine; believe in and pray for miracles but lack expectancy in specific discouraging scenarios; or speak discouragingly to those who hope for miracles. Rhoda wasn't one of them.

Utterly convinced, Rhoda kept testifying of the miracle: "She constantly affirmed that it was even so" (Acts 12:15). She knew what she knew and wouldn't deny it because others did. Did her confidence convince them?

No! Men of stronger reasoning than faith, they quickly devised a probable explanation justifying their disbelief: "It is his angel" (v. 15). They concluded Peter's guardian angel had come to announce his impending death. Or Peter had sent a human messenger to do so. Or, like James, Peter had already died and his disembodied spirit was visiting. By acknowledging Rhoda heard something, they were close to faith, but not in faith. Did Jesus leave this praying church halfway between faith and unbelief?

No! He prompted Peter to persist: "Peter continued knocking" (v. 16)! Christ was in Peter insisting that His prayerful but doubtful children understand that, yes, He had miraculously released Peter in response to their persistent prayers and they should believe it. Jesus showed the same insistence when the apostles doubted the report of His resurrection.[2]

Finally, the believers believed! When they saw Peter at the door, they were "astonished" (v. 16) and never again doubted that God works miracles, even in the most discouraging situations! Note Peter's reaction.

When his brethren didn't open the door, he patiently "continued knocking." When they opened it, he didn't rebuke them for reproaching Rhoda or being slow to believe. Perhaps this kind humility sprang from remembering how graciously and frequently Jesus had corrected him and the other apostles for their doubts.

This brief incident parallels something that will occur in our generation.

In these last days God will answer our persistent prayers for the church and the nations with miracles—awakenings, outpourings, healings, deliverances, changed lives! Like Rhoda, Christians of childlike faith will joyfully recognize and testify of these works of Christ. Others, like those at Mary's house, will deny or doubt them. Though they're deeply devoted to Jesus and given to prayer, their belief that the age of miracles is past will hinder them from accepting the wonders standing at their "gates." Like Peter, we who believe must be humble, not haughty, toward these deniers, forgiving them for calling us "mad" and praying Christ will revive their faith—as He has ours! Meanwhile, Christ will "continue knocking" at their hearts until, "astonished," they praise Him for His compassionate, end-time works of power. Thereafter they'll profess faith in a Christ who works miracles not only in the past and future but also present. End-time prophecy confirms this.

Immediately after the Rapture the Antichrist's rise to worldwide prominence will be partly the result of false miracles—his supernatural resuscitation from a deadly wound and many other miracles his false prophet will perform publicly to wow the world into submission.[3] Why will he emphasize the miraculous? Satan's age-old envy of God, stirred again by the miracles of Christ in the last-days church, will prompt his "son" to competitively imitate them after the church's departure. Even so, come Lord Jesus!

Indeed, Jesus will soon come knocking at our gates with miracles "exceeding abundantly above" anything we've asked for, seen, or imagined (Eph. 3:20). Before we leave this world, we won't deify miracles, selfishly demand them, or reject God's humbler providential means of assistance. But know this, like the church at Mary's house, when we see supernatural interventions standing at our gates, we will believe in miracles!

Chapter 75

AFTER EVERY MOWING

*I*N PSALM 72 David prophesied of Messiah, "He shall come down like rain upon the mown grass" (v. 6). What does this reveal?

First, the reviving rain of God's Spirit falls on "mown grass." Second, Messiah Himself—King Jesus—descends and visits us in these spiritual showers: "*He* shall come down like rain…" The blessings of Messiah's reign follow, reviving us and our works: "May the king's rule be refreshing like spring rain on freshly cut grass" (NLT). David describes this.

Messiah's justice brings righteousness, peace, deliverance, and the fear of God (vv. 1–5). Souls are saved everywhere as "the righteous flourish" (vv. 7–8). Messiah's enemies bow to His authority and will (v. 9), and His kingdom works are well supported and grow (vv. 10, 15). Heads of state are converted and their nations influenced (v. 11). Messiah rescues and avenges His oppressed, praying servants, giving other sufferers hope (vv. 12–14). Together they praise and worship Him "daily" (v. 15). Agriculture thrives, cities flourish, and congregations increase (v. 16). Messiah's redemption blesses all nations and they all bless His name (vv. 17–19)—until "the whole earth" glorifies Him (v. 19).

While manifesting fully in the millennium, these blessings appear in individual lives, churches, and nations to a lesser degree whenever King Jesus rains His Spirit on freshly mown hearts. Let's consider the key symbols.

The "rain" and "showers" represent the fresh releases of the Holy Spirit Christ gives to bring us and our churches new spiritual life, growth, beauty (Christlikeness), and fruit (James 5:7). These rains fall only when Christ is reigning in us.

"Grass" represents our flesh, or old nature, and our universal mortality. Isaiah cried, "All flesh [humanity] is grass, and…the grass withereth" (Isa. 40:6–7). In antiquity, mowers cut grass with scythes.

"Mowing" symbolizes the cutting back or mortification of our old nature's sins and selfishness so the Spirit can have His way in our lives consistently. A mown heart speaks of a humbled, purified heart and a selfish will that's broken and ready to respond to Christ's will.[1]

Though not described, our "mowers" are the trying people and circumstances God uses to humble us, ranging from brief tests of patience to long, severe persecutions. As we consistently respond to them by continuing to trust God and carefully obey His Word, they "mow down" or remove our old, unspiritual ways of thinking and reacting. Or they cut back some of our blessings, constraining us to seek more satisfaction in our fellowship with our Blesser. Or they bring mortifying injustices that wound us, driving us to seek more of the Spirit's healing wine and oil in prayer.

Thus, as ancient mowers used scythes to mow grass, our troublers and troubles:

- CUT US BACK—reducing our numbers, funds, works, and influence

- CUT US DOWN—in our self-view until we're sober-minded, not self-centered; contrite, not conceited (Rom. 12:3)

- CUT US AWAY—separating us from people, interests, and activities that hinder our spiritual life or work

- CUT US DEEP—inflicting deep wounds that, as God's grace heals and helps us, create in us a new, larger capacity to help other sufferers (2 Cor. 1:3–6)

When this mowing ends, we're thoroughly humble—meek toward God, patient and kind with others, given to devotion, restfully relying on God, worshipful, and free of the flesh of recurring sins or selfishness.[2] Like David, Isaiah also promised God would send revival rains upon such hearts: "I dwell in the high and holy place...to revive the spirit of the humble, and to revive the heart of the contrite ones" (Isa. 57:15). There's more good news.

This pattern may be repeated. Every time we're freshly mowed, yet continue trusting, obeying, and serving God despite the humiliation, we receive more of the Spirit's rain, King Jesus' presence, and the blessings of His reign.

After Jesus' original disciples were laid low by His strange, humiliating crucifixion, He rained on them at Pentecost (Acts 2:32–33). After Stephen's shocking execution and the following persecution, Messiah sent more spiritual rain, this time also in Samaria and Antioch (Acts 8:11). Noting this persisting pattern in church history, Tertullian warned Roman persecutors, "The more often we are mown down by you, the more often we grow."[3] Every subsequent rain of the Spirit—upon Moravians, Methodists, the Great Awakenings, Pentecostals, Charismatics, the Chinese—was preceded by God's mowing, especially upon leaders. But rather than rebel, they received God's preparatory work, examining themselves, receiving correction, and persevering in humble duties.

Are the King's mowers cutting you back, down, away, and deep? Are you still letting Christ reign in your life? Then expect more rain, more of Jesus, and more of His kingdom blessings... after every mowing.

Chapter 76

STAND AGAINST THIS CORRUPTION

$\mathcal{W}$HEN CONFRONTED WITH societal corruption, most Christians stand firmly against it. While there's a lot to protest in these last days, the apostle Paul wants to redirect our righteous indignation.

"Let no corrupt communication proceed out of your mouth" (Eph. 4:29). Note Paul's audience, "your mouth." Since he's writing to believers, Paul is forbidding not pagan but Christian corrupt communications. Also note his language. "Corrupt" is taken from the Greek *sapros*, meaning "rotten, decayed, or bad,"[1] as in spoiled food, drink, or fruit, or in decaying flesh. As a scholar familiar with precise word meanings, Paul's word choice reveals our corrupt communications, like a rotting carcass or spoiled food or drink, are:

- Offensive to observe
- Sickening to smell
- Deadly to ingest

Thus we shouldn't speak or listen to them. Not at all! "*No* corrupt communication..." Are we participating in or condoning any form of corrupt speech?

Broadly speaking, "corrupt communications" are all kinds of unworthy speech. Some common forms are complaining, self-pitying, prejudice, false accusations, unfounded suspicions, gossip, scorn, mockery, slander, misrepresentations, false testimony, plotting, cursing, sexually provocative talk, covetous conversation, boasting, unbelief, anxiety or panic, threats, despair, false teaching, blasphemy, mean-spirited or futile debates,[2] rude or abusive language, rage, flattery, insubordinate comments, and so forth. Why forsake these noxious words?

As *sapros* suggests, they're offensive, sickening, or deadly. Unholy communications displease and offend the holy One. They also offend or stumble people: "to the subverting [spiritual downfall and ruin] of the hearers" (2 Tim. 2:14). Additionally, they reveal our spiritually unhealthy condition, or worsen it, and make others sick. And sometimes they're deadly.

Sinful words de-spiritualize us by grieving and quenching the Holy Spirit whose refreshing refillings and strength we need regularly. They defile our souls, troubling our thoughts, souring our dispositions, stirring unrighteous emotions, and rendering us unfit for God's fellowship or use (Matt. 15:18–20). They're also highly contagious. Like a virus, their negative effects spread rapidly,[3] corrupting others' souls by turning them from right attitudes and actions to wrong ones, thus adversely affecting their relationships with God and people. They stir troubles, sometimes large and deadly, as when the "mixed multitude's" murmurings and later Korah's rebellious accusations caused the deaths of thousands of Jews.[4] Sharply cutting, evil words wound souls: "There is he that speaketh like the piercings of a sword" (Prov. 12:18). Rotten, they sicken our hearts, spoil the fruit of the Spirit, and hinder God's work in and through us. Thus Paul's call to abandon them. And he doesn't stop there.

Wisely, Paul gives us some effective countermeasures. The only way to stop speaking wrongly is to start speaking rightly, to replace corruptive talk with constructive speech: "Let no corrupt communication proceed…but [permit] that which is…edifying" (Eph. 4:29); or speak "only what is helpful, for building others up according to their needs" (NIV); or, "Let everything you say be good and helpful" (NLT).

The constructive communications Paul goes on to cite in Ephesians are thanksgiving (Eph. 5:4, 20), praises or hymns sung to God (Eph. 5:19), exhortations or other "edifying" counsels (Eph. 4:29),[5] kind words (v. 32), the truth spoken in love (vv. 15, 25), prayers (Eph. 6:18), boldly (freely) presenting the gospel or other timely biblical truths (Eph. 6:19–20), reproof (Eph. 5:11), cooperative words (v. 21, implied), loving or respectful words (v. 33, implied), instruction (especially to children, Eph. 6:4), confessions of sin (Eph. 4:32, implied), and confessions of God's Word in faith (Eph. 6:16–17). These words have the opposite effect of those Paul forbids.

Rather than kill, they give life. Instead of corrupting souls, they nourish them. Instead of ruining Christlike character, they build it. Rather than wound hearts, they heal them. Instead of cursing lives, they bless them. Rather than causing others to stumble, they help them stand upright and walk more closely with God. Instead of causing spiritual sickness, they improve spiritual health: "The tongue of the wise is health" (Prov. 12:18); that is, it "promotes health" (NKJV) or "brings healing" (NIV). Thus, in Ephesians, Paul faithfully sets before us corruptive and constructive Christian communications. Yet he goes further, urgently pleading with us to make the right choices and grow spiritually: "Let no corrupt communication proceed out of your mouth," but "speaking the truth in love...grow up." This doesn't mean we shouldn't speak out when necessary against the corruption pervading our culture.

Abortion, sexual perversion, human trafficking, illegal drugs, violence, atheism, pollution, heresy, infidelity, corporate greed, child predators, government mismanagement—these and many other rotten things offend God, poison souls, and sicken society, and we should graciously but firmly reject them.

But not without dealing with the rottenness in our own mouths and ears that also offends, sickens, and kills. So get stirred! Stand against this corruption.

Chapter 77

SURRENDERED TO GOD'S TIMING

SURELY THE HOLY Spirit would never order a minister *not* to preach God's Word! Yet that's exactly what He did, not once but twice!

As Paul's ministry team traveled west across Galatia, they decided to go south toward Asia Minor. But, suddenly, "they...were forbidden by the Holy Spirit to preach the word in Asia" (Acts 16:6), so they continued westward to Mysia. Then they turned north, intending to minister in Bithynia. But, again, "the Spirit allowed them not" (v. 7). How odd! We'd expect Jewish rabbis, pagan priests, sorcerers, idol makers, or Roman officials to ban Paul's ministry, but not the Holy Spirit! Why did He?

Though this biblical context states no reason, others reveal:

- BITHYNIA WASN'T PAUL'S FIELD. All evidence indicates Jesus, the "Lord of the harvest" (Matt. 9:38), sent others, not Paul, to Bithynia.[1]

- IT WASN'T GOD'S TIME TO EVANGELIZE ASIA. Asia wasn't ready for God's Word. God was still preparing hearts there, clearing and plowing His gospel "field."

- IT WAS GOD'S TIME TO EVANGELIZE MACEDONIA. Paul's subsequent vision revealed Macedonia was ready for spiritual planting: "Come over into Macedonia, and help us [now!]" (Acts 16:9). That the Macedonian in Paul's vision was "beseeching" (begging) him indicates the need was urgent!

- GOD'S PLANS WERE LARGER THAN PAUL'S. Paul's intentions were to reach two nearby provinces, Asia and Bithynia. But God wanted "exceedingly, abundantly" more (Eph. 3:20)—for Paul to cross the Aegean Sea to open a new nation (Greece) and continent (Europe).

Thus the Lord of the harvest directed His most prepared sower to His most prepared field. This incident reveals Christ in full command of all His workers and fields of service. Though eager to serve God in Asia

202

and Bithynia, Paul wisely yielded to God's timing. He knew well the Old Testament truth, "To everything there is a season, a time to every purpose under heaven" (Eccles. 3:1, NKJV). Also, "He has made everything beautiful in its time" (v. 11, NKJV); or, "He does everything just right and on time" (NCV). Paul's obedience produced many positive results.

He didn't waste time preaching to unprepared people in Asia. Nor did he presumptuously try to minister in someone else's appointed territory (Bithynia). Instead he faithfully returned to the port of Troas, ready to return to his home church in Antioch if he received no further call to ministry (Acts 16:8).[2] When called, however, he promptly pursued the pressing need in Macedonia, where he founded the outstanding Philippian church. Afterward the Spirit led Paul to more fruitful ministry stops in Thessalonica, Berea, and Corinth. Thus Paul's obedience opened new continents, nations, and cities, all in God's time. And that wasn't all.

Paul's subsequent three-year work in Asia Minor was his most fruitful period of ministry because it too was in God's time (Acts 19:1-20). All Asia heard Christ's gospel and witnessed His compassion through "special miracles" (vv. 11-12). Paul trained many disciples (vv. 9-10). Thousands renounced occultism (vv. 19-20). Thousands more turned from idolatry to Christ (v. 26). What does this teach us?

The Lord's sovereign checks and prompts, and Paul's submissive obedience, demonstrate just how wonderfully the Lord of the harvest works whenever we let Him guide us. It also exemplifies Christ's lordship and Christian servantship in action. If Paul had been impatient, self-willed, or stubborn, these remarkable results wouldn't have occurred. Like Paul, others wisely yielded to God's timing.

After waiting thirty years Jesus began His ministry in "the fullness of time" (Gal. 4:4). Noah waited for God's time in both entering and exiting the ark. Joseph submitted to God's timing for his release from prison. Philip spoke to the Ethiopian eunuch in God's time. Moses and David waited many long years before God used them. Like Paul, all these surrendered to the Lord's exquisitely wise timing, realizing that though waiting is often hard and sometimes long, its rewards are very sweet. Let's follow their example.

When God says don't preach, teach, or counsel just yet, let's obey. When He shows us a field, position, pastorate, or mission is for someone else, let's leave it to them. If He doesn't call us away, let's stay where He has put us and grow stronger, faithfully discharging our duties in our home church. If He calls us to serve in another place, let's do so promptly and joyfully, expecting fruit even if our "Philippi" is as humbling and difficult as Paul's.[3] And let's remember God's plans are often bigger than ours. If He closes our "Asia," He may soon open other rich fields and then, when He's ready, make "Asia" our most fruitful work.

That is, if we're surrendered to God's timing.

Chapter 78

A FAR BETTER LIFE

WAITING TRIAL AND possible execution in Rome the apostle Paul wrote, "For to me to live is Christ, and to die is gain" and "to depart and to be with Christ...is far better" (Phil. 1:21, 23). "Gain?" "Far better?" Is this text altered?

No, with full inspiration Paul affirms that for Christians, dying is "far better" than living. Why? Upon death, we'll "be with Christ," personally, visually, forever! That's "far better" than continuing to endure this evil, deceptive, hostile, troubled world. Paul's word choice is illuminating.

In the Greek, "depart" means "to unloose, undo, or break up [for departure]."[1] All these aspects of the departure of death are positive.

We break up the tent of our mortal body and move into a better, permanent temple, our glorified body. We loose the anchor of our life ship, leave the harbor of this world, and embark on a better voyage on the sea of eternity, where new explorations, adventures, and victories await. We break up and cast off the chains of bodily limitations to rise, eternally freed spirits, to a better, higher life. We undo and remove the heavy yoke of our worldly vocation to roam and graze heaven's better, greener pastures, forever liberated from our rigorous labors. Thus, like Paul, we can face death, life's greatest fear and foe, with a positive attitude, "always confident" that to be "absent from the body" is to be "present with the Lord" in the eternal world (2 Cor. 5:8).[2] The contrast between the two realms, this world and the next, is stark.

In this world there's darkness, deception, and rebellion; in the next there's light, truth, and submission to God's will. Here we experience pain, grief, and tears; there we'll have no sorrows (Rev. 21:4). Here we have sickness, weakness, and death; there, health, strength, and irrepressible life. Here we have a sin nature; there it won't exist. Here there's frequent strife, unrest, and war; there, only sweet, peaceful unity among all people and nations. Here God is misrepresented, rejected, and denied His rightful authority; there all will know, worship, and serve Him joyfully. Here Christians suffer for their faith (Phil. 1:29); there we'll be honored for it. Here we labor continuously for kingdom rewards; there we'll enjoy them—forever.

Now we have limited knowledge; then we'll have access to omniscience, knowing everything past, present, and future as fully as God knows us. Now we rarely enjoy manifestations of Christ's nearness; then we'll bask in His presence constantly (Rev. 22:3–5). Now we work long hours to produce or buy our food; then we'll dine at will without exhausting labors. Now millions starve; then we'll all be satisfied with monthly fruits (v. 2) and year-round harvests (Amos 9:13). Now Satan's demons tempt, harass, deceive, and oppress daily; then they'll trouble no one. Now prejudice, envy, and rivalries separate us and weaken our efforts; then we'll live and labor in blissful, productive harmony. Now sin corrupts our creation; then all creation—land, sea, air, space—will be newly remade, unimaginably beautiful, and ours to enjoy.[3] Now earth is subject to astrological, meteorological, and geological catastrophes; then the new earth will be tranquil and undisturbed. Now men rule unjustly, selfishly, and without concern for our welfare; then Christ will rule with justice and love, and always for our good—forever.

Let's remember this the next time we, loved ones, or fellow Christians face prospects or visitations of death. As Paul mused, ours is not a win or lose situation. It's win or win even more: "Life versus even more life! I can't lose" (Phil. 1:21, THE MESSAGE). If our work is finished here, it's time to move on. If we've overcome life, it's time to overcome death. If we've endured this world, it's time to enjoy the next. Though rarely stated so bluntly, it's comfortingly true that "dying in God's timing and will is only victory for a believer."[4] We have a loving Father, sacrificial Savior, and resurrecting Spirit to thank for that.

Not just euphemisms for funerals, these are firm facts for the faithful. The moment we stop breathing, we're "in His presence"[5] in a world and life "far better" than ours. So while grieving over the passing of believing friends and family, we may also deeply rest, knowing they've "departed"—folded their tent, weighed their anchor, loosed their chains, removed their yoke—only to "be with Christ," fully conscious, unimaginably joyful, today "in paradise" (Luke 23:43). And we'll see them again at our passing or Christ's appearing—forever.

Paul wasn't mistaken. Christian death is gain, not loss; triumph, not defeat. Rest, knowing there awaits us a far better life.

Chapter 79

LET'S EPHESIANIZE!

*W*HEN SOME OVERZEALOUS magicians' attempt to use Jesus' name to exorcise a demon backfired, all Ephesus—then a center for occultism—saw the gospel's superiority over the occult (Acts 19:13–17). Magicians couldn't stand before the Messiah!

The response was overwhelming. Convicted of practicing magic themselves, many Christians repented, ridding themselves of it in every form. Their contrition was so great they spontaneously burned all their occult paraphernalia, including small scrolls inscribed with magical formulas (vv. 18–19). This shows that, even after conversion, Christians may become entangled with occult interests or activities.

Occult means "hidden, covered, concealed."[1] It refers to any attempt to use hidden supernatural powers to practice divination or magic. Want more specifics?

Divination is the unauthorized attempt to discover hidden and often humanly undiscoverable knowledge from a (purportedly) divine source through people or objects. Common diviners are astrologers, fortune-tellers, necromancers, clairvoyants, false prophets, psychics, channelers, or other mediums. Objects typically used for readings are the stars, cards, tea leaves, fortune cookies, hands (palms), branches, animal organs, and so forth. While these diviners seek knowledge, magicians seek changes.

Magic (sorcery, witchcraft) is any unauthorized attempt to harness supernatural powers to effect changes that impose one's will upon people or situations. Spells, incantations, potions, dolls, and other means supposedly serve this end. Other borderline magic practitioners or practices are stage magicians (illusionists), spiritism, ghost hunting, charms, hypnotism, and (especially hallucinogenic) drug abuse (Rev. 9:21). Some of these "magical arts" (Acts 19:19) are the acts of frauds.

However, others truly engage the supernatural. Many occultists are assisted or possessed by deceptive, malevolent demons that supernaturally power their dark craft (Acts 16:16–19). Knowing this, God forbids Christians to have any involvement in occultism, redirecting us instead to the truly divine knowledge of God's Word and the biblically authorized operations (gifts) of His Spirit.[2] This suggests that all occult works are satanic counterfeits, Satan's cheap imitations of God's priceless revealed knowledge and accessible power. But which supernatural help will we seek?

The relentless pressures of life—fear, injustice, jealousy, sickness, bereavement, war, disaster, business competition, lawsuits, curiosity—eventually drive us to seek help from a source greater than ourselves. Why not from occultists? Here are some reasons.

Since His Word bans them, all forms of occultism are acts of rebellion to God. They seek knowledge God wisely hasn't revealed. They try to impose our will on people or situations we have no right to control. Ironically, they sell us short: we seek Satan's limited help, when God's greater knowledge and power are available! They imply the lie that God isn't enough, thus revealing and increasing our unbelief. They ignore the sufficient means God has already graciously given us to obtain extra help and knowledge in trouble: prayer and the gifts of His Spirit (1 Cor. 12:1, 4-11). They hook us, leading us by curiosity into more dark works, deception, unbelief, and sin—and farther from faith, truth, liberty, and God. They open us up to demonic oppression, possession, or attacks (Acts 19:16). But there's something far more vital we must grasp.

The worst form of occultism is our disobedience to God! When King Saul partly obeyed God's orders to kill "all" the Amalekites, leaving only the king and best animals, he was satisfied with his incomplete obedience. After all, his disobedience was so small! But God wasn't happy. Through Samuel He informed Saul his partial obedience was "rebellion" and as heinous to Him as occultism: "Rebellion is as [abominable as] the sin of witchcraft" (1 Sam. 15:23). Israel's sovereign was shocked.

Are we shocked, or still sleeping? Still assuming God doesn't mind a little disobedience, or awake to the witchcraft of our rebellion? May this bolt from the blue strike us: while all forms of divination and magic are despicable, our stubborn disobedience—the hidden rebellion or occultism in us and our churches—is far more grievous to God and hindering to His work! If jolted sufficiently, we'll "Ephesianize."

That is to say, like the Ephesian Christians we'll abandon our occultism. How?

Obviously, we'll cease participating in any overt occultism. We'll destroy any occult books or materials we own. We'll turn away from everything glorifying occultism (TV shows, movies, exhibitions, websites). We'll warn fellow Christians involved in any form of occultism to abandon it, and if they continue, we'll break fellowship.[3] But most importantly, we'll zealously attack that most abominable occultism, the disobedience remaining in our lives! The results will be dynamic. And ironic.

We'll work a little holy magic. By God's grace working in our hearts, we'll harness the supernatural power of His Word and Spirit and, *abracadabra,* make our rebellion disappear. Let's Ephesianize!

Chapter 80

KINGDOM COLONISTS

*T*HROUGHOUT HISTORY GROWING empires and nations— Phoenicia, Greece, Rome, Britain, Netherlands, Spain—have established colonies for military or commercial purposes. Philippi was a Roman colony (Acts 16:12).

Roman colonies were "little Romes," "Romes away from Rome,"[1] or models of Rome. Military outposts, these newly founded or adopted foreign cities were strategically located for the empire's defense or expansion. They were often located in seaports and always linked to Rome and other colonies by Roman roads for easy access. Every colony had a core population of retired Roman soldiers. As colonists, they retained the rights and privileges of Roman citizenship and received retirement benefits of land, tax exemption, and the right to elect local judges. Experienced soldiers, they also constituted a citizen militia ready to fight uprisings in their territories. Loyal to Roman emperors, laws, religion, and culture, colonists helped "Romanize" the subjugated peoples they lived among, modeling the Roman lifestyle for their adoption.

The Philippian colonists valued their citizenship. Paul's enemies in Philippi claimed their citizenship compelled them to oppose Paul's unauthorized religion: "These men...teach customs which are not lawful for us to receive...being Romans" (Acts 16:20–21). Indeed colonists had special duties and rewards. One commentator notes:

> Though living on foreign soil, the citizens were expected to be loyal to Rome, to obey the laws of Rome, and to give honor to the Roman emperor. In return, they were given certain political privileges...
> This was their reward for leaving their homes in Italy and relocating elsewhere.[2]

Although many Philippian Christians were also colonists, Paul charged them with a new, higher duty: "Let your conduct be as it becometh the gospel of Christ" (Phil. 1:27); or, "behave, live, or conduct your life as a citizen of heaven"[3] who honors Christ and His gospel and kingdom. As they had been model Romans in faraway Macedonia, always loyal first to emperor and empire, they were now to be model "Christians" (Christ's loyalists), seeking "first" to please and promote Christ in this foreign world

(Matt. 6:33). Their primary citizenship was no longer in Caesar's realm but in God's heaven: "Our citizenship is in heaven…" (Phil. 3:20). Not later but now: "*is* in heaven." Indeed the Philippian church was a "colony of heaven" (MOFFATT) in a city of Rome. And one day they'll be suddenly taken "home" to report to the King concerning their lives as His colonists: "…in heaven, from which also we look for the Savior" (v. 20).

Like these Philippians, believers today are kingdom colonists.

We're transplanted on foreign soil—this unbelieving world. We're located on a major road—the new and living "Way," linking us to our King, capital (New Jerusalem), and other colonists (John 14:6). We're to be loyal to our Emperor—Jesus. On this foreign soil we're to live by His laws—the Bible. We're His soldiers—ready to fight His spiritual battles. Through evangelism we enlarge His kingdom—His authority over lives. We hold dual citizenship—in our nation and heaven. Yet our greater loyalty is to the land of our spiritual birth: "Our [first, enduring] citizenship is in heaven." Thus every local church is a kingdom colony.

Churches are "little kingdoms of God," "kingdoms away from the kingdom," or earthly models displaying God's heavenly kingdom. They're founded by the King, who personally guides and sustains them. They're His strategically located outposts in this spiritually hostile foreign world. Our godly living increases our Emperor's honor and silences His critics: "With well-doing ye…put to silence the ignorance of foolish men" (1 Pet. 2:15). We enlarge His kingdom by testifying of Him and His Way, "ready always to give an answer to every man that asketh…of the hope that is in you" (1 Pet. 3:15). As His "good soldiers" (2 Tim. 2:3) we fight the "rulers of the darkness of this world" (Eph. 6:12) in daily intercessions and suffer periodic counterattacks for doing so. But, loyal to our King and kingdom, we refuse to conform to the surrounding culture. Instead, by consistently trusting and obeying our King, our life-examples "kingdomize" individuals, families, and cities, drawing them into our King's salvation, Word, and ways.

For this loving loyalty our King gives us special privileges: full access to His sweet presence and fellowship daily; clear insight into His Word and plan; help with every worldly problem; full financial provision; protection in every conflict; supportive fellowship with other kingdom colonists; the stimulating hope of our King's appearing to take us home and later return to rule this world; and many other rewards in His eternal kingdom.

What privileges! What a kingdom! What a King! Don't be a disloyal citizen of heaven. Be one of Christ's faithful kingdom colonists.

Chapter 81

POWER TEACHING

*A*FTER EVANGELIZING EPHESUS, the apostle Paul "separated the disciples" and began teaching them daily in Tyrannus' lecture hall (Acts 19:8–9). This teaching and evangelism continued for two years until "all they who dwelt in Asia heard the word of the Lord Jesus" (v. 10). Thus Luke discloses what happened in Asia.

Then he reveals how. The gospel spread throughout Asia not only because Paul had an open door in Ephesus, the world's fourth largest and Asia's most influential city, but also because he practiced power teaching—excellent Bible teachings accompanied by attesting miracles. Luke says:

> God wrought special miracles by the hands of Paul, so that from his body were brought unto the sick handkerchiefs or aprons, and the diseases departed from them, and the evil spirits went out of them.
> —ACTS 19:11–12

These "special" miracles remind us of Jesus' ministry. Why? It *was* Jesus' ministry—through Paul! Luke insists not Paul but "God" worked them. They were exceptional even for miracles! "God gave most unusual demonstrations of power through Paul's hands" (Acts 19:11, PHILLIPS). Sweat cloths or work aprons that Paul had used were laid on the sick or possessed, and God's healing power, transmitted through them from Paul's body, was so potent it repelled diseases and demons. During Jesus' ministry God's power so pervaded His body that it healed whoever touched His clothes in faith (Mark 5:27–29). These distinctive miracles now manifesting through Paul proved Jesus was still alive and, by His Spirit and servant, ministering in Ephesus as He had in Israel. Their effects were also similar.

Jesus' powerful, compassionate miracles drew people from all Israel and beyond to become His disciples, or utterly committed student-followers. Thus His power drew them to His teaching. Matthew presents this power-teaching connection most clearly. He remembers Jesus "went about all Galilee...healing," and as His "fame" spread, "great multitudes" followed—then He immediately began teaching them (Matt. 4:23–5:2). In Ephesus the heavenly Christ did the same through Paul, an anointed member of His earthly body. Paul's miracles drew seekers from all Asia—whom Paul promptly began instructing in Tyrannus' school and later sent throughout Asia to evangelize and train still more disciples.

These years in Ephesus were glorious, the apex of Paul's ministry and the gospel's influence as recorded in Acts. Ephesus was a large, influential center of Satan's twin strongholds of idolatry and occultism,[1] yet God's power triumphed magnificently even there! Of all the summary statements[2] Luke includes in his history of the early church, only the one describing Paul's Ephesus ministry says God's Word not only grew but also "prevailed." "So mightily grew the word of God [in Asia], and prevailed" (Acts 19:20), or "had a powerful effect" (NLT). He specifies that all Asians "heard the word," and many "turned" from idols to God (vv. 10, 26). Without special miracles, the gospel wouldn't have reached this spiritual summit.

Jesus' anticipated this by promising believers would do "greater works" than His (John 14:12–14). He also manifested them initially in Jerusalem by healing many through Peter's shadow (Acts 5:15–16). Like Paul's special miracles, Peter's also led to more teaching, so much that Jewish leaders later admitted, "Ye have filled Jerusalem with your doctrine" (v. 28). Eventually many Jewish priests converted. Luke records triumphantly, "A great company of [even] the priests were obedient to the faith" (Acts 6:7). How dynamic power teaching was!

If wise, we'll neither deny nor imitate it. To deny it is to rationalistically reject the immutability of Christ's promise and power. To presumptuously imitate it may create dire consequences, as Sceva's sons soon discovered in Ephesus (Acts 19:13–16). If Christ foretold power teaching, and fulfilled it not once but twice in Acts, He's likely to fulfill it again.

Indeed we'll see a revival of power teaching before the Rapture. Jesus will show His people and the world once again that He's still alive and working compassionate miracles aplenty—through not Paul or Peter but chosen members of His current earthly body. Christianity also needs His miraculous mercies to again "prevail" over Satan's strongholds of idolatry, witchcraft, and false religion that blind and bind billions. As in Ephesus, this power teaching will prompt imitation miracles, by not Sceva's sons but Satan's son, the Antichrist.[3] But Christ will judge him in due time.

Meanwhile, we desperately need another Ephesus season! Not charlatans peddling phony gospels and prayer cloths for donations, but humble ministers teaching Christ's truth and working merciful miracles no scientist can explain, magician duplicate, rationalist explain away, or atheist deny! When Jesus releases them, these miracles will, again, bring multitudes under His teaching and among His disciples—forever!

Let's pray for, and expect, power teaching.

Chapter 82

STRANGE, STRANGER, OR STRANGEST

*E*VER WONDERED WHY God allows strange turns of events? Studying the apostle Paul's experiences helps us remain believing, faithful, and focused when situations become strange, stranger, or strangest.

It was strange when God's best minister, Paul, was suddenly surrounded in Jerusalem's temple courts, beaten by the Jews, arrested by the Romans, and narrowly escaped flogging and death.[1] Paul was there only at James' request to demonstrate to Jewish Christians that, contrary to rumors, he didn't teach Jews to disrespect Moses or the law. Even the non-Christian Jews shouldn't have objected to Paul fulfilling a Jewish vow. But they did. Violently! We'd also think God, who led Paul to Jerusalem to deliver a peace-making financial gift from the Gentile churches to the Jewish churches, would've given him success. Or an award. But not an arrest! Why did God allow his arrest?

Then it got stranger. The Jews falsely charged Paul with sacrilege and insurrection, and he wasn't quickly vindicated. Instead he was nearly assassinated, whisked away to Caesarea, and detained two years without trial or release. The Roman governor consulted Paul frequently, but only hoping for a bribe. Finally, to avoid returning to a biased Jerusalem courtroom, Paul, a Roman citizen, appealed his case to Caesar.[2] Why did God allow this prolonged unjust detention and judicial misbehavior?

Finally, the strangest things happened. During Paul's ensuing voyage to Rome, he experienced a hurricane, shipwreck, snake bite, and three-month delay.[3] Why did God allow such adversity on what should have been a quiet passage?

While in Acts Luke doesn't specify God's purposes, hindsight illuminates several. Let's review them.

The gift Paul delivered helped reconcile the Gentile and Jewish churches. His vow and subsequent sufferings helped many Jewish Christians stop misjudging him and thereafter feed eagerly on his epistles. During his years in Caesarea, Paul taught and counseled many Christian visitors, and news of his faithful cross-carrying inspired many others.[4] His audiences with Governors Felix and Festus, King Agrippa II, and later Nero fulfilled his destiny to witness before "Gentiles and kings" (Acts 9:15). His tumultuous voyage to Rome, like his overnight flight to Caesarea, showed how God can use anyone, even pagan authorities, to support or shield believers. While in Roman custody, Paul was fully provided for, transported, and protected from the Jews. His shipwreck opened a door to minister Christ to the Maltese (Acts 28:1–11). After Paul's initial "Don't sail" warning was vindicated and his excellent character seen in the hurricane, God turned the centurion, Julius, to trust Paul's judgment—and perhaps his Lord! Julius' recommendation to Rome's warden gave Paul an "open door" in the world capital from which for two years he ministered God's Word and wrote four epistles without anyone interfering (Acts 28:16, 30–31).[5]

Together these strange situations reveal several sure truths. God's justice ultimately prevails despite even the longest injustice. Paul was eventually released to minister again. Adversity doesn't affect God's faithfulness. He still kept His promises, saving Paul's shipmates from a watery grave (Acts 27:22, 44) and getting him safely to Rome (Acts 23:11; 27:24). God causes "all things," even sinners, storms, snakebites, and sovereigns, to work His good purposes (Rom. 8:28, NAS). Paul's amazingly Christlike faith, humility, and grace under sustained intense pressures prove God can indeed conform us to Jesus' "image" and help us "do all things" by His strength (Rom. 8:29; Phil. 4:13).

Also, the Spirit always guides and controls our lives with perfect wisdom. Though Paul's path seemed so unreasonable, it ultimately produced fruit, honored God, blessed others, and rewarded him. And we see prophecy's value. Through prophecy the Spirit showed Paul several "things to come" (John 16:13)—he'd witness to kings, be arrested in Jerusalem, survive the hurricane, and arrive in Rome—and fulfilled them all! Finally, our perplexing tests will inspire others to overcome theirs. The Spirit prompted Luke to close Acts with Paul's strange test to inspire future generations to overcome their strange tests. Are you inspired? Overcoming?

Has your life taken a strange turn lately? Several? "Do not think that something strange is happening" (1 Pet. 4:12, NCV). Instead believe these lessons from Paul's life and follow his ways. Accept your adversity.[6] Stay very close to Jesus in it. Maintain your inner peace. Soak and revive your spirit in God's Word daily. Carefully obey God's Word and guidance. Quickly confess and forsake all sins. Forgive constantly. When hindered or persecuted, remember, Paul's God is yours, and He's still overruling storms, sinners, and sovereigns. So remain believing, faithful, and focused. Rest, knowing God has clear purposes in your confused circumstances. You're still on course to fulfill your destiny—even when situations become strange, stranger, or strangest.

Chapter 83

AMBASSADORS IN CHAINS

*W*HILE CLOSING HIS very heavenly, revelation-laden Epistle to the Ephesians, the apostle Paul disclosed his very low, earthly condition: "I am an ambassador in chains" (Eph. 6:20, NKJV). How surprising, God's ambassador "in chains"?

Appointed by heads of state to represent them in foreign capitals, ambassadors are highly honored to be chosen to convey their nation's messages and conduct its negotiations. They also serve their fellow citizens visiting or working in their host country when problems arise. Typically ambassadors are treated with the utmost dignity, and even given diplomatic immunity in their host countries. But not this country! Not this diplomat!

Paul was personally tapped by King Jesus near Damascus to represent Him before Gentile nations and "kings" (Acts 9:15). He was subsequently highly honored to represent the King of kings and His kingdom, speak for Him to the Roman Empire, and present His terms of salvation to Romans, Greeks, and Jews. But instead of granting Paul honors and diplomatic immunity, the Romans, spurred by false Jewish allegations, dishonored him by unwarranted arrest, delayed prosecution, and unjust detention for over four years "in chains."[1] How undiplomatic!

Thus, paradoxically, Paul was both distinguished and despised. As heaven's representative, he was honored to share Christ's gospel with the lost and His biblical instructions, prophecies, and mysteries with the redeemed. Yet when writing his Ephesian letter in Rome, Paul was chained to a Roman guard, without liberty to even walk outside or explore the city—a privilege the humblest Romans and even many slaves enjoyed. Acts 28:30–31 describes Paul's humble Roman "embassy." Thus honored and humbled simultaneously, Paul was an ambassador yet a prisoner, privileged yet persecuted.[2]

The same thing happened on the Isle of Malta. There for three months the Maltese officials received Paul as Christ's royal diplomat. Yet, while Paul's healing ministry flourished, he remained chained and subject to a centurion (Acts 28:1–11). Why this mix of exaltation and mortification?

No accident, God intentionally permitted Satan to harass Paul throughout his ministry with a "thorn in the flesh"—a demonic messenger sent to repeatedly stir troubles and afflictions (2 Cor. 12:7). God ordained this relentless adversity for one purpose: to keep Paul humble (vv. 7–10). As Paul reacted to his adversities with an accepting attitude and consistent obedience to Christ's teaching, he remained spiritually minded. Spiritually strong and free, he continued receiving the Spirit's anointings for more revelations, epistles, visions, prophecies, and messages of wisdom and comfort for Christians! Thanks to his Christlike acceptance of God's higher purposes in his lowly humiliations,[3] Paul's diplomatic service flourished—despite his chains.

Firmly faithful, he remained spiritually unmoved. Daily he continued:

- PURSUING HIS DEVOTIONAL LIFE—seeking "first" the King and His Word every morning and His will in every decision (Matt. 6:33)

- PRAYING—"ceasing not" to pray for every church, minister, and disciple he served (Eph. 1:16)

- MINISTERING—sharing God's Word with "all that came in to him" (Acts 28:30–31), witnessing to Caesar and his household, and dictating his crowning ambassadorial communiqués to the Ephesians, Philippians, Colossians, and to Philemon

- STAYING ON MESSAGE—"preaching the kingdom of God and…Jesus Christ" (v. 31) as he always did, rather than becoming entangled with political agendas, nationalistic goals, social strifes, or religious fads

Indeed Paul accepted God's higher purposes so fully that he asked the Ephesians to pray not for his release but only for more inspired words, doors, and boldness to continue faithfully delivering the King's words in his confinement (Eph. 6:19–20).[4] The King also prompted Paul to charge the Colossians, "Remember my bonds [chains]" (Col. 4:18). He wanted not just the Colossians but all believers to remember His ambassador's faithfulness, how Paul, though greatly limited, continued spreading His King's liberating truth and helping heaven's citizens overcome their troubles in this foreign, spiritually hostile world. Why? So we'll do the same in our "chains."

While our bindings may be literal, they're more likely to be figurative: long trials of faith, unrelenting harassments, implacable critics, difficult marriages, slander, financial constraints, false charges, defeats, failures, rejections, or other adversities that humble us, limit our sphere of influence, or leave us feeling like lowly prisoners. When these sobering trials visit, let's neither complain nor rebel but remember.

Remember that "we are ambassadors for Christ" (2 Cor. 5:20). Like Paul, we're honored to represent our King, present His terms of peace to the lost, and help His citizens—our fellow believers—in this foreign land. Wisely, our Father sends "thorns" to keep us humble, close to Him, and fruitful. Instead of only seeking release from them, let's also pray for grace to finish our mission well, as Paul did, faithful ambassadors in chains.

Chapter 84

A SPIRITUAL BATTLE BRIEFING

*T*O WIN CONFLICTS or contests, we must know our adversary and his objectives, methods, agents, weapons, strengths, and strategies. For that we need battle briefings.

Before battles, officers inform their soldiers about their enemies and everything they expect them to do. Before athletic contests, coaches inform their players of their opponents' strengths and weaknesses and how they plan to check or exploit them. Before political campaigns, strategists brief campaign staffers on their opponent, his message, voter base, and how they plan to sway undecided voters. Thus briefed, military, athletic, and political warriors go forth to battle. Jesus understood this.

He briefed His disciples before sending them out to speak and minister in His name. Matthew 10 describes Him briefing the twelve and Luke 10 the seventy. Following Christ's lead, Paul briefed the Ephesian elders at Miletus on the challenges they faced leading Christ's flocks (Acts 20:17–38). All these mission briefings discussed believers' natural adversaries and adversities.

In Ephesians 6:10–20, however, Paul gave a different kind of briefing. He revealed not the human but the spiritual side of our warfare as bearers of Christ's redeeming Word, works, and life in this dark, sin-bound world. His spiritual battle briefing revealed:

- OUR ENEMY—"the devil" (v. 11)

- HIS OBJECTIVES—to stop our Spirit-led intercessions (v. 18), evangelism (v. 15), sharing of God's illuminating Word (v. 17), and courageous stands as witnesses for Christ's truth and righteousness in churches and nations (vv. 13–14)

- HIS METHODS—to use craftiness, "wrestling,"[1] or sudden attacks to move us from our Savior, supplications, sharing, and stands

- HIS AGENTS—evil spirits in "heavenly places" (v. 12, NKJV), or the spiritual realm, especially the "rulers" of the world's spiritual darkness (v. 12). These spirits work through people who, by yielding to sin or selfishness, come under their influence or control.[2]

- HIS WEAPONS—specifically, his "wiles" (tricks) and "fiery darts" (fearful, provoking, or tempting thoughts sent to trouble, offend, or deceive us)

- HIS STRENGTH—be advised, "the unseen power that controls this dark world" (v. 12, PHILLIPS) is supernatural. To defeat him we must "put on" God's "whole armor" and "be strong in the Lord" and "his might" (v. 10).

- HIS STRATEGIES—to deceive, provoke, or intimidate us (v. 11). Thus we need discernment, grace, and, as Paul prayed, boldness (vv. 19–20).

Though sufficient, Paul's spiritual battle briefing isn't exhaustive. Elsewhere he and other biblical writers give further information on our enemy and his typical strategies, wrestlings, and attacks.

The devil is God's "adversary"[3] and opposes us because we love God and do His will. He's a rebel, having launched the first rebellion against God in heaven. He's a tempter, urging us to indulge desires that displease and dishonor God. He's a thief, always trying to steal whatever blessings God gives us: truth, provisions, relationships, peace, ministries, answers to prayer, and so forth. He's the "accuser of the brethren," inspiring others to accuse us of faults to defame us and God. He's a liar, inspiring gossips to spread false representations about truth-loving Christians. He's a murderer, instigating killings by homicide, feticide, suicide, or character assassination. He's a hinderer, always trying to weaken or slow God's work. He's a deceiver, misleading hypocrites, false prophets, and disobedient Christians who then mislead others. He's an "angel of light," inspiring false visions, prophecies, and errors purportedly given by the true Light of the world. He's the "prince of this world," founding, innovating, and guiding its highly developed but coldly Christless culture. He seeks prey like a roaming "lion" and wisely and patiently awaits unsuspecting victims like a deadly "serpent."[4] Has he been working in your circumstances?

For embracing Jesus and His will, have Satan's demonic agents moved through people to wrestle against you? Rebel against your authority? Tempt you? Steal your material or spiritual blessings? Accuse you falsely? Try to kill your good name—or you? Hinder your work or ministry? Deceive you? Convince you to compromise with this world's unbiblical values? Don't surrender.

Stand! As Paul urges, "Strong in the Lord" (Eph. 6:10)! Strengthen your heart with God's nourishing Word. Refill your soul with His invigorating Spirit in prayer and worship. Put on God's complete armor. Be spiritually minded, realizing demons, not people, are your real enemies: "Our struggle is not against human opponents, but against...evil spiritual forces" (Eph. 6:12, isv). Humbly examine yourself frequently, confessing sin and obeying God's Word quickly. Never repay wrongs, but "overcome evil with good" (Rom. 12:21). Then stand.

Stand unmoved by Satan's craftiness, wrestling, or attacks. Don't claim ignorance or inability and faint. You've been sufficiently informed about your enemy and his ways. Yes, fellow Christian soldier, this is your spiritual battle briefing.

Chapter 85

STRONG IN THE LORD!

AUL'S FINAL CHARGE to the Ephesians was, "Be strong in the Lord, and in the power of his might" (Eph. 6:10). To understand this key command, let's first explore what it doesn't mean.

Spiritually strong Christians don't practice sin. Knowing "the LORD" is their "strength" (Ps. 27:1), they recognize sin is their weakness and so quickly confess and forsake it whenever it arises. They're not afraid. They quickly reject tormenting fears, knowing they're not of God (2 Tim. 1:7), and refuse to yield to anxiety, instead praying in faith about "everything" (Phil. 4:6–7, NKJV). They aren't doubtful. Once they have God's Word about a situation, they hold it, realizing doubt, if yielded to, grows until we're hesitant in "all our ways" (James 1:6–8). They're not divided. Realizing spiritual unity is Christ's passionate desire, and unnecessary divisions hurt us and our churches, they "make every effort to keep the unity of the Spirit" (Eph. 4:3, NIV).

Furthermore, they're never offended with God. They've learned from Mary's and Martha's initial reaction to Lazarus' perplexing death to always refuse to be offended with Christ however offensive their tests: "Blessed is he, whosoever shall not be offended in me" (Luke 7:23).[1] They're not offended with people. They always forgive offenders, as Christ taught, so they can always receive God's forgiveness (Mark 11:25–26). They're not discouraged. When disappointed, they acknowledge it in prayer, as David did,[2] but then choose to keep trusting God, be "of good courage," and expect His encouraging responses (Ps. 27:13–14). They're not confused. When doubtful thoughts or mixed emotions arise, they quickly resolve these inner conflicts to remain single-minded—and strong. They're not dull with overindulgence. They avoid excessive eating, sleeping, pleasure, or leisure to keep their spirit strong, mind sharp, discernment quick, and communion with God close. Thus "strong in the Lord" means *not* weak with sin, afraid, doubtful, divided, offended, discouraged, confused, or dull.

These negatives settled, let's examine the positives: what spiritually strong Christians are!

They're confident. They're sure God's faithfulness is unfailing, His Word inspired, His promises true, His warnings sure, His principles universal, His prophecies unstoppable, His ways unchanging, and His miraculous power undiminished.

They're loving. Realizing "God is love," "He first loved us," "love builds up,"[3] and without love all knowledge, gifts, and accomplishments are futile, they willingly keep Love's great commandment, "that ye love one another, as I have loved you" (John 13:34). By patiently walking in love, they grow as strong as Love—and "greater [stronger]...than he that is in the world" (1 John 4:4).

They're faithful. Their devotion is habitual, duty unfailing, prayer constant, ministry steadfast, thanksgiving ceaseless, giving regular, and worship consistent.

They're watchful. Aware that hostile spirits lurk hoping to attack them, they alertly watch their souls, circumstances, churches, and Christian friends for anything that weakens, deceives, corrupts, or harms—ready when necessary to correct themselves, mend divisions, or kindly pray for, assist, or exhort others.

They're disciplined. Avoiding ascetic extremes, they voluntarily choose to discipline their bodily lives to maximize their spiritual strength, fellowship with Jesus, and usefulness to Him.

They're wise. Knowing ignorance and foolish decisions render us weak and ineffective, they prayerfully study God's Word to learn His wisdom. Becoming "wise as serpents" (Matt. 10:16), they more quickly discern Satan's wise tactics and temptations and check them with wiser decisions.

They're spiritually minded. While studying Scripture and receiving its teaching, they focus on doing the Word. Yielding daily to the Bible's spiritual viewpoint changes how they think about everything. Soon they're "spiritually minded," enjoying God's "life and peace" whatever their circumstances (Rom. 8:6), and no longer deceived, stumbled, or even troubled by Satan's servants.

They're patient. Like the overcoming Philadelphians, they submissively keep "the word of my patience [endurance]" (Rev. 3:10). They accept delays, bear crosses of misunderstanding and reproach, and persevere in humble, thankless duties, enduring quietly until Christ releases and rewards them.

They seek perfection—consistent spiritual maturity. Daily they aim, by God's grace, to please the Lord and fulfill His will in all their relationships and activities. If they fail, they confess it and quickly resume their walk, but never stop seeking perfection.[4]

They're spiritually empowered. Paul's charge adds, "[be strong] in the power of His might." "His might" is the unique power of God's Spirit. Strong Christians seek and rely on the omnipotent Spirit, who energizes their walk, witness, prayers, ministries, and perseverance in persecution—and, when necessary, grants miracles.

Paul's charge to the first-century Ephesians is the Spirit's challenge to twenty-first-century Christians. Why settle for being weak or average in our spiritual strength? Let's pursue being strong in the Lord!

Chapter 86

ABOUT FIERY DARTS

THE APOSTLE PAUL urged us to "quench all the fiery darts of the wicked one" (Eph. 6:16, NKJV). Let's investigate these "fiery darts" by interrogative analysis—asking questions to help us probe and understand this subject.

What are "fiery darts"? They are flaming arrows used in warfare from ancient to recent centuries. While conventional arrows were used to injure, maim, or kill people, flaming arrows were incendiaries shot to enflame and destroy fortifications, buildings, and houses. Pieces of hemp or other materials soaked in oil, pitch, or resin were tied around arrow shafts just behind their arrowheads. Many such arrows were then lit and quickly shot at enemy positions. Destructive fires, or quick, efficient quenching, followed.

What do "fiery darts" symbolize? They represent evil thoughts that, like flaming arrows, are swift, piercing, troubling, and potentially destructive. These wrong thoughts enter our minds through words we hear, read, or think[1] and start burning agitations (spiritual fires) of sin in our hearts and lives. The context indicates[2] they're often thoughts of doubt or disbelief in God or His promises that create fear, anxiety, or even panic— powerful emotions that, if unchecked, will move us to compromise our biblical beliefs or moral stands or stop pursuing God's will. But these incendiaries may also be other kinds of thoughts: anger, misjudgment, strife, envy, unforgiveness, pride, impatience, indecision, covetousness, discontent, unthankfulness, deception, unfaithfulness, or sexual lust.[3]

Additionally, fiery darts are hurtful words other people speak against us—lies, reproaches, innuendoes, plottings, insults, or mockery. These are spoken (shot) to start fires of misjudgment, anger, and rejection in those who hear them and agitations of fear or anger in us when we hear reports of them.[4] Like their ancient counterparts, these flaming arrows fall suddenly on our heads (minds), descend from above (the heavenlies), and often strike in bunches. Even one, if not quenched, may consume God's work in us, spoiling our "excellent" spiritual walk and ministry (Ps. 62:4) and harming others.

Where do they come from? "The wicked one" (Eph. 6:16, NKJV) uses his spiritual archers, the "rulers of the darkness of this world," to shoot fiery darts through anyone—unbelievers or Christians—presently subject to his influence (v. 12). So our warfare isn't merely with these adversarial people but with the "wicked spirits" prompting their behavior.

Why do they come? Ephesians 6 reveals three reasons. First, we're effective intercessors, "praying always...in the Spirit" for unbelievers, believers, and ministers (v. 18). Second, we're spiritual light-bearers, receiving the light of God's Word in Bible study, releasing it in daily living, and spreading it through ministry, thus diminishing the darkness of sin and falsehood in this satanic world. Third, we're obedient, fruitful branches in Christ's church vine.[5]

How do we extinguish fiery darts? We put on God's "whole armor" daily (Eph. 6:10–17). Every gap in our spiritual armor gives Satan an "advantage" (2 Cor. 2:9–11). We use our "shield of faith," choosing to trust God's faithful Word whenever tempted to doubt or fear. We also use the "sword of the Spirit" by speaking God's Word in faith, as Jesus did (Matt. 4:4, 7, 10).

What if we don't extinguish them? We invariably sin or fail, and dishonor God—to Satan and his invisible archers' delight! Realizing this, Jesus solemnly warned "evil thoughts" would defile us (Matt. 15:19–20). Solomon wisely urged, "Keep your heart with all vigilance" (Prov. 4:23, esv), or "be careful what you think" (ncv). The apostle Paul ordered us to "examine" ourselves,[6] reject "imaginations" [unscriptural reasonings, imaginary predictions], and humbly align "every thought" with God's Word (2 Cor. 10:5). But this wisdom is often forgotten.

Sadly Scripture describes many of God's people and works being hindered, harmed, or destroyed by fiery darts of doubt, fear, anger, threat, unbelief, lust, envy, revenge, greed, pride, and other swift, piercing, troubling thoughts or words.[7] But we needn't be.

We can quench "all" Satan's mischievous missiles (Eph. 6:16)! Then we'll continue standing, fully armored and interceding effectively. We'll continue spreading, radiating the light of God's truth through our lives, churches, and ministries. We'll continue bearing, producing "fruit of the Spirit" (Gal. 5:22–23) and of good works. And Christ will be honored—and delighted!

So delighted that He'll shoot "his arrows" (Ps. 7:13) at Satan's servants—sudden, swift vindications, breakthroughs, deliverances, conversions, exposures of hypocrites, silencing of false accusers, unravelings of plots—until they and their malicious works are ruined.[8] It's amazing just how much evil God's arrows, released on time and target, can undo, and how much good they can do: "And Esther said, The adversary...is this wicked Haman" (Esther 7:6). Understand this subject better?

Then practice what you've learned about fiery darts.

Chapter 87

DOORS, UTTERANCE, BOLDNESS

INISTERS NEED PRAYER as much as congregants. Perhaps more! The apostle Paul asked Christians to pray for him often, especially for doors, utterance, and boldness.

He solicited the Colossians' prayers "that God would open unto us a door" (Col. 4:3) and gratefully informed his Corinthian prayer partners[1] God had opened a "great and effective door" in Ephesus (1 Cor. 16:9, NKJV). He implored the Ephesians, "[Pray] for me, that utterance may be given unto me," adding, "that I may open my mouth boldly" (Eph. 6:19).

"Doors" are divinely appointed speaking opportunities for ministers or any Christian. Paul realized only the doors Jesus opens bear lasting fruit (Rev. 3:7–8). Christ gave Paul a vision expressly opening a door in Macedonia (Acts 16:9). Once there, Paul met Lydia in Philippi, "the Lord opened her heart," and she received Paul's message (Acts 16:14, NIV). Soon the outstanding Philippian church was founded in Lydia's home. Thus through one door, the light of Christ's Word shined into a heart, home, city, nation, and continent.[2] But not without a fight.

For spreading this gospel light, its bearer, Paul, was falsely accused, wrongfully convicted, and illegally beaten and jailed by locals opposing his ministry. One commentator notes:

> The focus of all spiritual warfare is ultimately the opening of doors...so that the ministry of the gospel may be advanced.[3]

Truly, the demonic "rulers of darkness" (Eph. 6:12) resist all our divinely arranged opportunities to spread the light of God's truth. But we overcome them when, despite their sudden attacks, subtle wiles, and sharp arrows of reproach or persecution, we persist in using our doors to share God's Word with unbelievers and believers. Paul did this in Rome.

For over two years before his arrival the spiritual "rulers" fiercely resisted Paul's mission to Rome. When he finally arrived, however, God faithfully gave him a door, utterance, and boldness. For the next two years Paul preached and taught God's Word freely to whoever visited his "hired house" (Acts 28:30–31) and wrote four epistles that still enlighten, inspire, correct, and guide us! So though it seemed the "rulers" had defeated Paul by causing his detention, he was the victor and they the vanquished. Why? A door was opened, God gave Paul utterance, he spoke it boldly, and the light of Christ's Word saved and trained many disciples—and the rulers couldn't stop it!

By asking prayer for "utterance" (Eph. 6:19), Paul was requesting that the Holy Spirit reveal what to say when Christ opened doors, to bring to mind "the right words" (NLT). This Spirit-given "utterance" consists of inspired thoughts, convicting words, motivating sermons, timely instructions, life-changing writings, and wise counsels given "in season" (Isa. 50:4), all coming straight from the Father's heart through the minister's words to the believer's heart.[4] So, wisely, Paul depended on God for his messages and their delivery, realizing nothing blesses the King's people and builds His kingdom like the utterance He gives. He wanted God not only to speak to him but also through him.[5] And Christ did so regularly.

By requesting prayer for "boldness" (Eph. 6:19–20), Paul sought courage and inner strength to speak freely the utterance the Spirit gave him, without holding back for fear of reproach, rejection, or persecution. Many responded.

They prayed for Paul faithfully, God answered them faithfully, and Paul commended them faithfully: "Ye also helping together by prayer for us" (2 Cor. 1:11). And Christ will one day reward them faithfully.[6] Are we following their example faithfully?

If we don't pray for our ministers, we, they, and others will suffer. Our Pauls will have fewer opportunities to speak to us, other churches, or divinely appointed Lydias; less boldness in speaking; and less God-given insights, messages, and counsels to share.[7] Consequently, less life-giving, clarifying Word-light will be released, since many doors will remain closed that prayer would have opened. We won't be as well informed, inspired, or prepared for our daily tests. Our ministers may grow less confident, even timid, when presenting corrective or unpopular truths, or omit weightier subjects altogether (Matt. 23:23). Some will quietly compromise, watering down their messages until they're powerless, boring, dead. This somber prospect prompted Paul to request prayer for doors, utterance, and boldness. Often!

If we'll pray often for our ministers, we'll all benefit. Christ will open new doors for them. They'll enlighten new hearts, homes, cities, nations, the world! Their messages will become noticeably more timely. We'll sense Christ Himself speaking to us through them. They'll hold nothing back, thus ensuring we learn God's "whole counsel," widely, deeply, and accurately (Acts 20:27, NKJV). Why wait?

Start praying today for your ministers' doors, utterance, boldness.

Chapter 88

KEEP PRAYING, PAUL'S COMING!

$\mathcal{W}$E TYPICALLY CONSIDER Paul's call to Philippi an answer to his prayers for guidance (Acts 16:6–10). But it was also an answer to the Philippians' prayers.

Before Paul's arrival, Jewish women had been gathering outside Philippi every Sabbath for prayer (v. 13). While all Macedonia needed Paul's "help," as Paul's vision revealed (v. 9), his arrival in Philippi was apparently a specific answer to these women's prayers, much as Peter's mission to Caesarea was to Cornelius' petitions (Acts 10:2, 4–5).

For what had they been praying? Spiritual "help" (Acts 16:9)? To discover, as locals were discussing, "the way of salvation" (v. 17)? Or if, as some Jews claimed, Jesus of Nazareth was that way (Acts 28:22)? Or simply for ten Jewish men so they could start a proper synagogue? We're not sure.

But we're sure of some things. We know they prayed in purity. Their outdoor chapel was located beside a river for baptizing proselytes and other ceremonial washings. These Jewish women and their converts knew from the Torah that God, desiring holiness, commanded, "Sanctify yourselves...be holy; for I am holy" (Lev. 11:44). To please Him and ensure His response to their prayers, they washed regularly. The river Gangites was just over a mile from Philippi. That they walked this distance to pray in purity showed commitment, a diligent dedication to purity.

Whatever this prayer group's petitions were, we know:

- They desired purity and dedicated themselves to it.

- They believed God answers prayer.

- They were faithful, meeting regularly.

- They were separated—meeting outside their pagan city—to seek God.

- They were not popular, since idolatry and occultism, not Judaism, prevailed in Philippi.

- They were humble, being women and without a synagogue.[1]

- They were few, not enough for Luke to number.

Their ritual purity symbolizes spiritual purity. They represent Christians who "wash" their souls often to please God's desire for holiness.

Such believers wash in the river of the Word frequently. As they read, meditate on, and study Scripture, Jesus sanctifies and cleanses them "with the washing of water by the word" (Eph. 5:26). They further wash away the defilement of sin and self by obeying the Word. Peter describes this fuller washing: "Ye have purified your souls in obeying the truth" (1 Pet. 1:22). They also wash by quickly confessing and forsaking their sins whenever they occur. John describes this cleansing in the river of Jesus' blood: "The blood of Jesus...cleanseth us from all sin...If we confess our sins, he is faithful and just to forgive...and to cleanse us from all unrighteousness" (1 John 1:7, 9).

Besides these "washings," they submit to God's most invasive and effective purifier: spiritual fire! When reproach, rejection, or trouble for Christ's sake heats their circumstances with pressures, they let the river of the Spirit's conviction thoroughly search their consciences. As they confess their wrong attitudes, motives, or thoughts, God cleanses their spiritual core.

To further please Christ, these Christians honor "his righteousness," not emerging trends, in their churches (Matt. 6:33). They bravely stand against sin and, when necessary, impenitent sinners in their assemblies, knowing sin is highly contagious and Christ's churches must maintain holiness.[2] Such believers, female or male, are cut from the same cloth as the praying Philippians.

Summarizing, the Philippians were a separated, sanctified, humble, small but faithful prayer group, as Matthew Henry noted, a "little meeting of good women."[3] Had they prayed for a long time? Were they weary? Discouraged by delays? Ready to give up? We don't know.

But we know God answered—awesomely! He sent His best man! Paul was appointed, anointed, discerning, compassionate, and filled with apostolic wisdom. He taught them how to be saved and established in Christ, as individuals and as a church. And that's just what followed. Philippi's humble little women's prayer meeting was transformed into the outstanding Philippian church—established, fruitful, honored, and blessed with many more than ten men![4] Whatever these praying women had asked, God answered them "exceedingly, abundantly above" their petitions (Eph. 3:20)!

Is your prayer group a "little meeting of good women" or men? Don't underestimate it, however unimportant you feel. If you're seeking God's "help," He'll give it. He'll send "Paul"—an awesome answer! It may be a very insightful minister who helps establish your church on a new level of spiritual maturity. Or other greatly needed answers—breakthroughs, revivals, reconciliations, healings, deliverances, open doors, new converts, favor, needed resources, and so forth.

So follow the Philippian pattern. Even if you're few and unpopular, commit to holiness, humility, and godly separation. Keep washing regularly in the rivers of God's Word, blood, and cleansing fire. Meet faithfully and keep praying: Paul's coming!

Chapter 89

THE LORD IS MY ROCK!

HE LORD IS my rock," proclaimed David triumphantly (Ps. 18:2). Many biblical writers confessed the same. To understand them, let's review what nature and Scripture reveal about rocks.

In nature, large rocks are ancient, unmovable, immutable, immense, adamant, and impenetrable. Carbon dating affirms their great antiquity. The swiftest winds and streams can't budge them. They weather, yet don't visibly change in our lifetimes. Their immensity is evident and sometimes immeasurable. They are among the hardest naturally occurring substances. And they can't be pierced and probed by mere human strength. Thus nature teaches us about our Rock.

Like a rock, our God is ancient. The "Ancient of Days" is the oldest, wisest, most enduring, and only infallible source of knowledge and wisdom. Immovably stable, God is never shaken by disasters, wars, or unrest. All who trust Him are stabilized by His stability, and their unmovable beliefs, values, and lifestyles stabilize others (Ps. 62:6). Immutable, He is the only unchanging character in our constantly changing culture. His fixed ways of working make us confident in our unpredictable world.[1] Holy, He is uncompromising with sin; we must abandon it to have Him. Immeasurably immense, His biblical thoughts are unmatched in depth, scope, weight, and beauty. Impenetrable to all human opposition, He is a secure, safe defense, an unbreachable fortress and shelter, in every spiritual battle and storm. His Spirit, presence, and angels preserve all who abide close to Him with perfect protection, provision, inspiration, guidance, and hope. This describes our awesome supernatural Rock. But not completely.

The Bible adds God is our:

- SAVING ROCK. Only Jesus' Saviorship is effective and His salvation sure. He alone is "the rock of my salvation" (Ps. 89:26).

- FOUNDATION STONE. God's Word is the only enduring thought base—solid, spiritual bedrock and life-building stones—on which we can build godly character, relationships, families, churches, and societies (Matt. 7:24–25).

236

- ROCK OF FAITHFULNESS. As boulders remain reliably in their place, so God and His Word remain reliably true. He is our only utterly faithful promise keeper, performer of prophecy, and answerer of prayer: "Unto thee will I cry…my rock" (Ps. 28:1).

- ROCK OF RESTORATION. Eagles nest on rocky cliffs, travelers rest under great rocks, David lived in a rocky cave during his persecution, and Moses rested on a stone seat during a battle.[2] Similarly, when wearied with rigorous trials, battles, and burdens, Christ's disciples nest, rest, recover, and refresh their spirits daily in the "cleft of the rock" of devotional reading, prayer, and personal worship.

- FOUNT OF LIVING WATER. In the wilderness God "opened the rock, and the waters gushed out" to sustain and delight His people (Ps. 105:41). Christ our rock was smitten on Calvary so the living water of the Spirit could fill and delight us with heavenly life in this worldly wilderness.

- SOURCE OF SWEETNESS. Knowing bees built hives in the clefts of rocks, God promised Israel satisfying "honey out of the rock" (Ps. 81:16). Our rock-honey is the sweet, deep, soul satisfaction we draw from personal fellowship with Jesus that contents us, even in rocky times and stony trials.

- HIGHER PERSPECTIVE. High atop a rock Balaam gained God's perspective toward His people: "I see him [Israel] from the top of the rocks" (Num. 23:9, NAS). By believing the Word of our rock, our viewpoint rises. We become "spiritually minded" (Rom. 8:6) toward people, problems, and life. David asked for this top-of-the-rock viewpoint: "Lead me to the rock that is higher than I" (Ps. 61:2).

- CRUSHING WEAPON. When rolled, slung, or dropped, rocks were formidable weapons in ancient combat. Little David defeated large Goliath with a stone! Christ is our smiting stone, who breaks our prideful, impenitent enemies to save us from oppression.[3]

- SHARP CIRCUMCISER. Joshua used sharpened rocks to circumcise God's people ("flint knives," Josh. 5:2–3, NAS; cf. Exod. 4:25). Sharply and steadily, our rock's penetrating Spirit convicts us until we cut off all our "flesh," or old nature and its sinful and selfish ways.

- BOUNDARY SETTER. Large rocks often marked property boundaries in ancient times (Prov. 22:28). God our rock sets and changes all our "boundaries"—the seasons of our lives and borders of our influence (Dan. 2:21; Exod. 23:31).

So proclaiming, "The Lord is my rock," means He's your enduring wisdom, unshakable stability, unchanging character, uncompromising Holy One, profound word, impregnable fortress, saving rock, life foundation, faithful One, restorer, refreshing water, sweet honey, crushing weapon, sharp circumciser, boundary setter, and higher viewpoint. That's a very full confession of faith. In faith confess it so you may more fully possess it.

With David, say triumphantly and thoughtfully, "The Lord is my rock!"

Chapter 90

The Evil Day

*T*HE APOSTLE PAUL'S inspired writings reveal many vital truths: salvation by grace, the mystery of the church, the fivefold ministry, the gifts of the Spirit, and the Rapture, to name some. Ephesians 6 discloses another.

There Paul warned us to prepare to stand fast in "the evil day" (Eph. 6:13). What's the "evil day"? Well it's not good times—when things go our way, every need is met quickly, no one opposes us, our churches are growing, cities safe, nations peaceful, and economies booming. Then what is it?

It's "evil in its day of power" (PHILLIPS). Or the "day of trouble" (Ps. 20:1).[1] In such adverse times God permits us to experience evil—adversity, opposition, injustice, or other hardships. Our loving heavenly Father steps back and, strangely, lets evildoers have their way and evil run its course, though limiting its severity and duration. Why? Only to test and strengthen our faith, loyalty, endurance, and character. Evil days are times of personal, church, national, or global adversity.

Personal troubles are the most trying. Easy living goes and hardships come, then multiply. We experience difficulties in our work or ministry. We lose our job or house. People reject or mistreat us without cause. Our businesses, projects, or finances fail. Sin, drugs, hatred, or unjustified divorce split our families. Close friends betray us. Loved ones or beloved spiritual leaders pass. Radiant health fades and we experience bouts of weakness or sickness. Or the frail "evil days" of old age come (Eccles. 12:1, 2–7).

Or our church experiences troubles. Scandal engulfs one of our leaders. Heresy invades and spreads like leaven. Envy, money matters, personality conflicts, or political issues divide us. New leaders prove disappointing. Our church is publicly denounced, mocked, protested, or sued. Visitors stop coming, supporters cut funds, and other churches turn away.

Or national troubles come. Greed grows, poverty rises, immorality proliferates, and government ignores these problems. Citizens grow apathetic, then cynical. Our economy sputters, and then plummets. Biblical faith and values decline and faithless leaders rise. They persecute godly believers as Pharaoh did the enslaved Hebrews, Nero the early Christians, and Hitler the European Jews. Terrorized, many Christians compromise—but others forge convictions and stand fast in the evil day.[2]

Or worldwide troubles suddenly erupt. For persistently rejecting Christ, teaching amoralism, and sinning grossly, nations experience wars,[3] disasters, unrest, terrorist attacks, economic turmoil, or other divine chastisements. Thus this Christless world culture reaps the evil it's sown.[4] These calamities awaken sleeping believers and humble arrogant atheists, release those captive to false religions, and turn sinners to the Savior.[5] The last evil day, the Tribulation, will occur just after the true church departs.

These evil days—personal, church, national, and global—always begin with bad breaking news. It was a dark day when David heard of Ahithophel's betrayal and, later, Absalom's death. Many Jews fainted when they heard Eli, Hophni, and Phinehas perished the same day. Notorious evil days are seared into the average American's psyche: December 7, 1941; November 22, 1963; September 11, 2001. Who can forget 1968, the evil year marred by the assassinations of Robert F. Kennedy and Martin Luther King Jr., the Tet Offensive in Vietnam, riots nationwide, the tumultuous Democratic convention, and near anarchy? Is there any good news in all this bad news?

Yes! God uses evil days for His higher purposes—if we accept they're part of His wise, loving plan and trust and obey Him till they pass! Joseph held to this: "Ye thought evil against me; but God meant it unto good" (Gen. 50:20). If we embrace Joseph's attitude, our evil days will work for, not against, us. Mightily! They'll humble us, shatter our immature misconceptions, and teach us to fear, love, and seek God more. They'll develop our faith, purify our hearts, forge better habits, establish spiritual thinking, sharpen our discernment, enlarge our compassion, increase our endurance, prove our loyalty to Christ, and mold His character in us. We'll emerge from our adversities like Paul, strong in the Lord, covered with God's armor, unmoved by Satan's strategies, and "praying always" for others (Eph. 6:10–18). But these higher purposes won't be fulfilled if we reject Paul's warning.

When little children are taught things they dislike, they sometimes close their eyes, put fingers in their ears, and naughtily rant, "Na-na-na-na-na-na," to drown out the unpleasant truth. But it remains true. And needed! Let's be good children of God, open our eyes and ears, and fully accept this inspired truth: evil days must come. God's Word says so.

Are you ready? Has your evil day already come? If not, prepare now to stand in the evil day.

Chapter 91

IT'S TIME FOR MIRACLES

OFFENDED, DISCOURAGED, AND puzzled by Israel's long absence of miracles, Gideon asked: "If the LORD be with us...where are all his miracles?" (Judg. 6:13). He didn't know, but it was time for miracles again—through him! What's a miracle?

Precisely it's "an effect or event in the physical world that surpasses all known human or natural powers and is ascribed to a supernatural cause."[1] Put simply, miracles are wondrous occurrences humans can't explain. Scripture affirms that God and Satan work them[2] and that there are many kinds.

There are miracles of healing, when a sick or injured body is instantly restored to health. Peter's prayer in the temple enabled a lifelong cripple to suddenly stand, walk, and leap. There are miracles of creation. In the beginning God created the heavens and earth and all life forms. There are miracles of re-creation. Jesus re-created Lazarus' decaying body after four days of entombment. There are miracles of provision. God gave Israel manna from heaven and Jesus multiplied bread and fish to feed thousands. There are miracles of protection. God shielded the three Hebrew boys from deadly flames and will use fire to slay those who attack the two witnesses in the Great Tribulation (Rev. 11:5).

There are miracles of revelation. Jesus appeared in visions to give Peter and John key revelations. There are miracles of judgment. God suddenly took Ananias' and Sapphira's breath and removed Elymas' eyesight when they went too far in testing His forbearance. There are miracles of deliverance from oppression, as in the Exodus; storms, as when Jesus commanded peace on Lake Galilee; demons, as when He freed the madman of Gadara; persecution, as when Jesus' appearance halted Saul of Tarsus' anti-Christian campaign; war, as when God's angel decimated Sennacherib's army. Why should we study miracles?

Jesus was a great miracle worker. Frustrated, His enemies acknowledged, "What do we? For this man doeth many miracles" (John 11:47).[3] Jesus' disciples praised Him for His "mighty works" (Luke 19:37), and He's the same "today" (Heb. 13:8). So to reject miracles is to reject Jesus!

Moreover, despite the advances of medical science and technology, we still need miracles. Also, God wants us to believe in His miraculous power. Paul prayed we'd discover "the exceeding greatness of his power" (Eph. 1:19). Studying the Bible's testimony about miracles strengthens our faith in these extraordinary divine acts—and prepares us for seasons of miracles.

Before Moses returned to Egypt, the Hebrews hadn't seen God's miracles for hundreds of years. After he arrived, a forty-year season of wonders commenced during which the supernatural became natural. Similar "beginning[s] of miracles" (John 2:11) occurred in Mary's life, when for three months she observed her long-barren cousin's amazing pregnancy; at Cana, in Jesus' ministry; at Paphos, in Paul's ministry; by the Jordan, in Elisha's ministry; and recently, in the Healing and Charismatic revivals.[4] How does God use miracles?

Miracles:

- Reveal His existence to atheists and skeptics[5]
- Display His great compassion (Mark 1:41; 5:19; 8:2–8; 9:22)
- Authenticate His messengers and messages
- Convert sinners who receive, witness, or hear of His miracles
- Lead these converts into discipleship, as in Jesus' ministry (Matt. 4:23–5:2)
- Restore doubting Christians to faith (John 20:27)
- Show God's power exceeds Satan's[6]
- Found new churches or grow existing ones[7]
- Turn families, tribes, cities, regions, or nations to God

But Scripture reveals miracles may be hindered by certain things, especially doubt, unbelief, being offended at God, or not confessing and forsaking sin.

For example, Christ said His miraculous "signs" follow believers, not doubters. And surprisingly even the most astounding miracles won't convince people who are stubbornly determined to disbelieve (John 11:46). Offended at Jesus, His fellow Nazarenes received "no mighty work" from Him (Mark 6:3–6). Samson's sin ended his miracles, but his repentance restored them. We too can help release or restrain miracles.

All true Christians assume the validity of biblical miracles—Creation, the virgin birth, new birth, Jesus' miracles, His resurrection—yet many reject miracles today. Some believe science has rendered them unnecessary. Others believe God works miracles, but not for them. Some hold doggedly to doctrinal prejudices against miracles. Intellectual pride moves others to dismiss miracles as the foolish imaginations or myths of overexcited, undereducated fanatics. Where do you stand?

God's Word stands firm: God put the rare but valid gift of "working of miracles" in His church and nowhere recalls it (1 Cor. 12:10). Church history and current experience continue confirming this. Until we believe God works miracles, we'll have none. Once Gideon believed, God showed "where all his miracles were"—through him! He wants to do so again through us. It's time for miracles.

Chapter 92

PASS ON THE LOVE...

*H*EARING OF DIVISION among the Philippians, Paul pleaded passionately for them to live together in loving unity (Phil. 2:1–4). Phillips translates the first two verses:

Now if you have known anything of Christ's encouragement and of his reassuring love; if you have known something of the fellowship of his Spirit, and of compassion and deep sympathy, do make my joy complete—live together in harmony...in love, as though you had only one mind and one spirit between you.

Paul's thought here seems to be:

If [or since[1]] you have received and experienced firsthand Christ's personal encouragement and "reassuring love"; if [or since] you have also received and experienced the Holy Spirit's tender mercies and compassions, don't let the love stop with you. Pass it on to other believers by living together with them in the harmony of patient love and humble cooperation.

—AUTHOR'S PARAPHRASE

The Philippian church was outstanding in many respects (Phil. 1:3–5; 4:10, 14–19). However, they still had disunity lingering in their ranks. So Paul exhorted them to walk in loving unity three times in this letter, the last reference addressing two leading women who, despite being his valuable helpers, were apparently disagreeing regularly (vv. 1–3).[2] If they and the other Philippians would respond, their sweet unity would "fulfill" not only Paul's joy but also that of Jesus, for whose heart he spoke. Paul's appeal is fully authorized by God's Word.

Scripture reveals on the eve of Jesus' crucifixion He commanded us to love one another and prayed earnestly for our loving unity.[3] So for His sake, whether financially poor or wealthy, we all "owe" each other love. The apostles Paul, Peter, and John taught our loving unity should "increase more and more," become "fervent," and always be practical, never hypocritical. Like Christ's, our love should be free of pride, envy, and prejudice. It must forget others' past sins and, when necessary, be sacrificial. The more we practice loving unity, the more our confidence in prayer, answers to prayer, and enjoyment of God's presence increases, until His love is "perfected" in us. But not by our natural goodness or willpower alone.

Paul's appeal is based squarely on God's work of grace in us. We know Jesus' "tender mercies and compassions" because we're "in Christ" and experience daily the "fellowship of the Spirit" (Phil. 2:1). Since we know His love, we can and should show it. In the following verses Paul tells us how to begin.

"Lowliness of mind," "esteem," "look...on" (Phil. 2:3-4), these words refer to our thoughts. They reveal love begins in our thoughts.[4] Then it's released through our choices and manifested in our words, acts, and re-actions. So to behave lovingly we must think lovingly. Are we ready to reject "every" unloving thought (2 Cor. 10:5)? To obey Paul's appeal, we must pass on the love we're receiving from Jesus daily.

He never condemns but ever corrects us, truthfully but always with hope. Will we do this? He provides all our needs. Will we help provide others' needs? He sends us encouragers. Will we "exhort one another daily" (Heb. 3:13)? When we confess sins, He immediately forgives us. Will we forgive offenders when they confess their sins? He patiently leads us into new depths of biblical truth. Will we patiently instruct others as they're able to receive? He's long endured our bad attitudes and habits. Will we persevere with stubbornly carnal or worldly Christians? He leads us to excellent advisors when we need them. Will we patiently counsel those seeking our knowledge or expertise? He answers many prayers we don't deserve. Will we help bless or deliver undeserving ones? He "ever liveth" to intercede for us (Heb. 7:25). Will we intercede for others daily? He remains faithful even when our faith lapses.[5] Will we continue loving others even when they doubt us? He often withholds punishments due us. When the Spirit prompts us, will we forbear punishing others? Our answers will determine if we'll apply or abandon Paul's appeal, pass on Christ's love or let it stop with us.

If we pass it on, everyone wins. We'll be blessed "more" by giving love than by receiving it (Acts 20:35). Others will return our love.[6] We'll be strengthened spiritually, since "love edifies" (1 Cor. 8:1, NAS). Our church's unity will grow and we'll receive new anointings of the refresh-ing "oil" and "dew" of the Spirit (Ps. 133:1-3). Our joy, like Paul's, will be full. Chiefly, Jesus' joy will be full—His great commandment obeyed, high priestly prayer answered, and plan for His church prospering!

All this will follow if we'll pass on the love...

Chapter 93

READY TO BE A NOBODY?

$\mathcal{J}$N DESCRIBING JESUS' *kenosis*—His relinquishing of divine glory, privileges, and powers to become human and accomplish His Father's will—Paul emphasized Jesus' humility.[1] He "made himself of no reputation" (Phil. 2:7), or "nothing" (NIV).

How amazing! The One who was everything became nothing—a nobody! Unnoticed, unappreciated, overlooked, not sought, without honorable reputation, that's a nobody—and exactly what our Lord became! Isaiah foresaw Jesus' utterly ignorable condition centuries before the Incarnation:

> He grew up like a small plant before the LORD, like a root growing in a dry land. He had no special beauty or form to make us notice him; there was nothing in his appearance to make us desire him.
>
> —ISAIAH 53:2, NCV

Isaiah foresaw Messiah as a "small plant," not a mighty Lebanon cedar in the religious, academic, or political landscape. He was a root grown in "a dry [barren] land," such as Galilee, not a spiritually fruitful garden like Jerusalem, Spirit-watered with the messages of prophets, priests, and Levites. Not exceptionally handsome or physically strong, Jesus was so ordinary that nothing about His "appearance" impressed or attracted anyone. Many of God's own Jewish people "esteemed him not" and some "despised and rejected" Him (Isa. 53:3). The Gospels fully confirm Isaiah's shocking prediction.

Jesus of Nazareth was born of a scandalous conception, despised people, and poor family—and in an animal pen.[2] He grew up in a tiny village a considerable distance from His nation's worship center and in a region not known for producing rulers, prophets, or scholars. He enjoyed no formal education or tutelage, though His mother taught Him diligently[3] and He attended synagogue worship regularly, gleaning scriptural knowledge from Torah readings and rabbinic homilies (Luke 4:16–20). For most of His adult life He worked manually for low wages as a common carpenter and stone worker. He never married and had no children to preserve His name. He never owned a house but rented one for His headquarters and borrowed another at festivals. He never owned a donkey, though He once used one, preferring instead earth's humblest transportation—feet! He never owned any property, except His clothes, and thus wasn't a respected land owner in Nazareth. He never joined a religious sect or political party, and so was overlooked or rejected by many who did. He never rose to a higher socioeconomic class but remained a materially poor, socially low, politically weak man...until His meteoric three-year ministry. After it suddenly ended in a stunning national rejection, He took the world's lowest exit—crucifixion! Had the Spirit not miraculously empowered His ministry, no one outside of His hometown would have ever heard the name Jesus of Nazareth.[4]

Thus Paul concluded, from this world's perspective, Jesus became "nothing." To Roman eyes, He lived in the world's basement, less than nothing, a nobody's nobody. Since then many Christians have experienced their own *kenosis* by accepting a humble position to do God's will, pursuing their divinely predestined works or ministry. They've become of no reputation, nothing, a nobody!

The zealous young Pharisee, Saul of Tarsus, stripped off his religious ambition and humbly made tents in obscurity in Tarsus for a decade. Philip and Peter risked their ministerial reputations to obey God's call to "go down" to minister to despised Samaritans and Gentiles (Acts 8:5; 10:20–21, 28). Paul's apostolic reputation declined when he was arrested and held for years on false charges. Some Christians abandoned him.[5] Others, however, understood his lowness. Why?

They too were nobodies. For the first three centuries Christians were either overlooked or looked down on throughout the Roman Empire. Most Romans considered them an ignorant, antisocial, unpatriotic sect with superstitious beliefs, questionable morality, secret meetings, and strange rituals—founded by a crucified Jewish criminal! But these believers, confident of their high calling and position in Christ's kingdom, meekly accepted their low position in Roman society and continued in the footsteps of Jesus' self-emptying. Countless others have followed them throughout church history. Will we?

What if God lets our personal lives, ministries, or churches experience a humbling *kenosis* for a season? What if we're hidden, unknown, small, or ignored? Utterly ordinary? Seemingly foolish, weak, or hopelessly defeated? Misrepresented by hateful slanderers and misunderstood by the public? Pride feeds on reputation, recognition, and special treatment. Will we let our pride die? Humility feeds on Christ's recognition, approval, and fellowship. Will we let our humility grow? Be content in the world's basement? Finish our Father's will quietly, without any worldly glory?

Are we so confident that in Christ we're somebody—God's dear children, priests, kings, citizens of heaven, developing co-rulers and judges—that in this world we're ready to be a nobody?

Chapter 94

MISLED!

ATAN REALIZES HE doesn't have to destroy Christians to defeat us. He just has to distract us.

He doesn't have to violently assault us, as in the long, vicious Roman persecution. He just stirs us to focus on the wrong objective or fight the wrong battle. Similar strategies are used in war, athletics, and the Bible.

Military strategists have long used diversions. Aggressors launch a diversionary action to draw out their enemy. Once he commits to the wrong battle, they move elsewhere to take their real objective. When a football team wants to rush the ball to the right, it fakes motion to the left, momentarily distracting the defense. While they're out of position, the offense quickly executes its play and scores.

Of incomparably greater consequence was Satan's attempt to misdirect Jesus in the temptation (Luke 4:1–13). Knowing Jesus was sent first to His cross, not his kingdom, Satan offered Jesus the kingdom first, without any cross. Thankfully Christ discerned and rejected Satan's diversion.

But Satan's successfully diverting many American Christians today. We're fighting the right battle—to save our nation—with the wrong methods. We're trying to change society our way, not God's. Our way is politics, politics, and when all else fails, more politics! We're convinced that to save this nation, we must become politically aggressive and gain political power. But the New Testament doesn't call the church to aggressive political action. Not once. Why? It's not God's method of changing a nation.

His method is threefold:

1. THE CHURCH. God changes His people first, then their society. Our repentance, not that of atheists and liberals, begins the healing of the land: "If my people, who are called by my name [born-again Christians!], shall humble themselves, and pray, and seek my face, and turn from their wicked ways, then will I...heal their land" (2 Chron. 7:14).

2. THE HEART. When God begins working in society, He does so from the inside out. He changes sinners' hearts, minds, and lives first, before changing their political leaders, legislators, and laws. God's new covenant is founded not on new laws, judicial precedents, or even social reforms, but on new hearts: "A new heart also will I give you...a new spirit will I put within you" (Ezek. 36:26).[1] Then, gradually, people with divinely transplanted hearts craft political agendas and societal changes reflecting God's heart.

3. THE SPIRIT. God's method depends on His Spirit's mysterious but mighty work, never on this world's conventional wisdom and ways. God's work is done, "Not by [human] might, nor by [human] power, but by my Spirit, saith the LORD" (Zech. 4:6). However diligently and astutely we analyze, strategize, and campaign, one huge fact remains: nothing short of a supernatural work of God's Spirit—a true visitation or outpouring of the Spirit, whether sudden and spectacular or quiet and steady—will exalt Jesus, change hearts, stop abortions, curb violence, convert homosexuals, and restore respect for the authority of God's Word and morality. And only our sustained prayers, life witness, evangelism, and bold but love-driven protests against sin can facilitate this.

This three-pronged method is scriptural and slow but sure.

Our current methods are also sure—to fail! Why? They're the opposite of God's methods. We're trying to cleanse society first, before purging our churches. We're attempting to work from the outside in, trying to legislate righteous behavior among citizens with unredeemed hearts. We're relying on human intelligence—demographic studies, polls, pundits—not the sovereign wisdom of the Spirit, the power of God's spoken Word, and the influence of our righteous living and witnessing. We've forgotten that God's method once built the early church from a mustard seed to a mighty movement that infiltrated and influenced the entire Roman world. Don't we believe this can happen again?

Could it be that in this sophisticated, technological, politically charged culture we've become ashamed of the simple, unsophisticated, unpopular gospel and abandoned it as a viable method of societal change? Paul clung to the gospel, knowing it alone releases God's power to save souls and nations: "I am not ashamed of the gospel of Christ; for it is the power of God unto salvation to everyone that believeth" (Rom. 1:16). How did we get here?

Unquestionably, our leaders led us here. They didn't mean to mislead us any more than David meant to mislead Israel when he transported the ark to Jerusalem by the wrong method. Nevertheless, Satan has diverted them, and they have unwittingly misled us. It's time we save our nation God's way.

So if you're a leader, don't mislead. Stop preaching politics. If you're a congregant, don't be misled. Stop listening to endlessly politicized sermons. Let's never again be misled!

Chapter 95

IN TROUBLE?

*I*N TROUBLE? A "day of trouble"? Yet, despite your difficulties, are you still committed to God? If so, David wants to encourage you.

In Psalm 20 David described committed believers in a crucible of adversity. They were anointed,[1] praying, giving, praising, sacrificing, and yet still enduring a harrowing "day of trouble" (v. 1). But, though troubled, their triumph was sure. Why? They had an excellent history with God. David describes it.

They were true believers. While others sought deliverance by human strength and wisdom alone, these trusted in God's "name," or faithful, loving character (v. 7). They were redeemed. Their anointing (v. 6) was the seal of God's Spirit signifying His ownership, workmanship, and approval. These saved ones were also sold out to their Savior.

Consistently obedient, they walked "upright," conforming to biblical standards of morality and justice (v. 8). Strong in faith, they believed in God's "right hand," or supernatural delivering power (v. 6). They worshipped regularly, with "offerings" and "burnt sacrifices" (v. 3). These numerous offerings imply they were sacrificial and charitable, ready to give up anything to please God and generous in sharing their wealth with the poor. They were hopeful, not pessimistic, always "rejoicing" in the Lord's all-sufficient "salvation" and expecting to raise new victory "banners" to rally around (v. 5). They prayed often, reciting God's promises to prompt Him to grant their "counsels" (plans) and "petitions" (v. 5). They were bold, not timid, asking Him to honor "all" their petitions. But despite this spiritual excellence, things weren't going well. They were still in trouble and struggling.

Enemies were persecuting them with false accusations. Thus they needed protection and vindication: "The LORD...defend thee" (v. 1). They needed help—people, provisions, and favor—to continue God's work: "send thee help" (v. 2). Wearied with long tests, they needed spiritual refreshment and physical vigor: "strengthen thee" (v. 2). Chiefly, they needed rescue, or God's EMS: "Save, LORD" (v. 9). Despite this persecution they were still blessed. How?

God counted them worthy to suffer for Him. The pressures they faced constrained them to "remember [recall and ponder] the name of the LORD" (v. 7), creating a deeper, wider, and more enduring experiential knowledge of God. Their greatest privilege, however, was divine favor in prayer. While the Bible teaches us to conform our prayers to God's will,[2] David's words reveal a complimentary thought: God also delights to grant our personal wishes—"The LORD...fulfill all thy counsel...all thy petitions" (vv. 1, 4–5). Jesus' teaching confirms the Father loves to do this for His committed ones.[3] Thus our loyalty prompts His. Our loving conformity elicits His loving generosity. David, God's consecrated servant and this psalm's author, was one of these privileged petitioners— and about to receive a life-changing experience.

Somewhere in his trouble David had a "now I know" moment, a seismic shift from merely hoping to knowing: *"Now know I* that the LORD saveth his anointed" (v. 6). We don't know what prompted this powerful, pivotal conviction, but it deeply assured David of God's faithfulness, and he emerged utterly convinced God always keeps His promises and answers every prayer offered in faith according to His will. Maybe it was the Spirit's strong inner witness to a scripture, a powerful prophecy, a vision, or an open answer to another long-awaited secret prayer. Or some other breakthrough showcasing God's amazingly reliable and powerful help.[4]

It's also possible David's assurance sprang solely from a brave decision to trust God's faithful character no matter what—despite persisting contradictions, stubborn enemies, heavy burdens, and strange, long delays. Under similar circumstances Job vowed, "Though he slay me, yet will I trust in him" (Job 13:15). Whatever David experienced, it permanently convinced him God always delivers His believing, praying people. This gave him immediate rest in his long "day of trouble" and prompted him to write this psalm to encourage us to build our own excellent history with God.

Are you building? Are you anointed, believing, upright, prayerful, praiseful, giving, hopeful, and yet still harassed, rejected, or hindered in your distressful "day of trouble"? Keep petitioning God's help in faith and expecting His faithful responses daily from "the sanctuary [above]" (Ps. 20:2). A. W. Tozer wrote:

> Invariably where daring faith is struggling to advance against hopeless odds, there is God sending "help from the sanctuary."[5]

And if your spiritual history isn't as excellent as David's, don't despair. God inspired this psalm to inspire you.

So today resume building your history with God. Confess all unfaithfulness and ask forgiveness. Follow David's model in Psalm 20. However things look, commit to rely on God's faithful character and promises. Expect God's loving responses to your loving commitment. Expect your "now I know" moment. Not later but at this time, while you're still in trouble.

Chapter 96

POURING OUT ... GLADLY!

FTER EXHORTING THE Philippians to humbly "work out" their obedience, Paul said if Christ permitted his execution, he would gladly be "poured out" as a libation for Him (Phil. 2:17, NKJV). What did he mean?

A common rite in ancient worship, libations were drink offerings, liquids ceremoniously poured out to one's deity.[1] Since drink is vital to life, pouring out one's drink to a god demonstrated he was the source of one's life and therefore more important than life and all its blessings (Ps. 63:3, NLT). When offered in thanksgiving for blessings, libations exhibited a conviction that one's god alone was worthy of such blessings, and, since rightfully his, they were offered to him (2 Sam. 23:13–17).[2] Jewish drink offerings typified Christ, who "poured out his soul unto death" to redeem us (Isa. 53:12).[3] While sometimes offered alone, Jewish libations usually accompanied animal or meal offerings, upon which they were poured (2 Kings 16:13).

Therefore Paul fittingly described his life as being "offered" along with or upon the Philippians' "sacrifice and service" (Phil. 2:17). He saw their personal and corporate obedience as a living sacrifice[4] ready for heaven's altar and his execution as an accompanying libation. As they yielded, "always obeyed" Christ, and did "all things without murmurings and disputing" daily (vv. 12, 14), they became "obedient unto death" like their Lord (v. 8). This continuing wholehearted devotion, prayer, labor, giving, and suffering became "a sweet smell, a sacrifice acceptable, well-pleasing to God" (v. 18). Thus their service was the sacrificial meat or meal and Paul's readiness for martyrdom the accompanying wine poured out to the Lord. And not reluctantly.

Completely abandoned to his Savior, Paul was glad, even enthusiastic: "I joy, and rejoice" (v. 17). And he urged the Philippians to follow suit, rejoicing with him over his offering of himself to Christ as he rejoiced with them at their self-sacrifice: "I want all of you to share that joy ... and I will share your joy" (vv. 17–18, NLT). Humbly, Paul considered their sacrificial obedience as valuable to God as his. He also believed what he taught, that "in Christ" they were all seated, worshipping, serving, growing, and now pouring themselves out "together" (Eph. 2:6; 4:16). Are we thinking and living like Paul?

Are we pouring out to the Lord or holding back in the reserve of self-interest, self-comfort, unbelief, or lukewarmness? Christ, who redeemed us with wholehearted devotion to His Father's will, wants us to do the same, pouring out everything we are, have, and hope for to serve Him. Are we?

Are we pouring out in intercession, praying for others to be saved, blessed, or delivered?[5] In our jobs, using our vocational gifts "heartily, as to the Lord" (Col. 3:23)? In giving, donating generously to churches, ministries, or the poor? In submission, obeying God-ordained authorities? In thanksgiving to God?[6] Songs of praise? Time spent with Jesus? Support of missions? Rendering "helps" to ministers or others in need (1 Cor. 12:28)? Fellowship with believers? Church leadership? Ministry? Exercising spiritual gifts that strengthen believers? Bible study? Pastoral watchfulness and counsel? Training converts? Let's probe deeper.

Do we rejoice with those who pour themselves out for Christ or criticize their efforts, as Judas did Mary's, as a foolish "waste" (Mark 14:4; John 12:4–5)? Do we humbly value others' sacrifices as much as ours or downplay and overlook their devotion? Our answers reveal if we're becoming like Paul, who by his life's end was completely poured out, utterly spent, like a fighter utterly punched out or a marathon runner unable to take another step. As his execution drew near, he testified, "My life has already been poured out as an offering to God...I have fought the good fight, I have finished the race" (2 Tim. 4:6–7, NLT). This is nothing new. We see devotees pouring themselves out for other ends every day.

Athletes leave it all on the field or court, expending maximum effort. Entrepreneurs use all their resources to launch their businesses. Fallen soldiers, in Lincoln's words, give the last full measure of devotion. Countless Christian martyrs, like Paul, have spilled their blood to loyally worship and serve Christ. Let's join the ranks of the outpoured.

Let's slay our desire for easy living, flay our proud selfishness, tip over the libation bowls of our hearts, and pour out our mental, physical, and emotional energies—our very souls—to lovingly serve Jesus' pleasure, people, and honor. He spent all for us. Let's spend all for Him, rallying our last bit of strength, endurance, generosity, forgiveness, Bible study, burden-bearing, praise, prayer, and ministry. And joyfully!

Then every day we'll live not withholding or dribbling out but, like Paul, pouring out...gladly!

Chapter 97

FAITHFUL IN THE DARK

HOUGH AN EXTRAORDINARY spiritual light-bearer, Paul was in the dark in Rome. He didn't know what would happen next, his execution or release. So he waited, patiently and trustfully, to "see how it will go with me" (Phil. 2:23). How odd!

Paul was an exceptional prophet. He often received "visions and revelations" of Christ and His will, plans, and guidance, as well as prophecies of coming events in Paul's and the church's future (2 Cor. 12:1).[1] So Paul was accustomed to the Spirit giving him "light" (insight) on perplexing situations and "things to come" (John 16:13). But not in Rome. There Christ left him in "the dark" of unknowing (Isa. 50:10).[2] But, experienced and mature, Paul stayed close to Jesus, calmly awaited His direction, and faithfully pursued his duties. Paul's "darkness" lasted approximately two years (Acts 28:30–31). Many others were faithful in the dark.

Moses spent six days in deep silence on Mount Sinai before God began revealing His plan for Israel's way of life and worship. For over three years Elijah awaited guidance for his ministry at Cherith and Zarephath. After the earth's surface dried, Noah waited fifty-eight more days until God ordered him from the ark (Gen. 8:13–16). Simeon waited decades to discover the Messiah's identity. For one and a half years the apostle John didn't know when or if he would leave Patmos, but he remained faithfully "in the Spirit" every Lord's day (Rev. 1:10). Philip didn't know why God ordered him from Samaria's revival to an empty desert road—until he saw an Ethiopian official's caravan and was told to approach. Their experiences, and Paul's, brightly illuminate a key truth.

It is this: however trusting, obedient, spiritually minded, close to Christ, and insightful we are, Christ will occasionally put us in darkness to test our faith, patience, and loyalty, and grow in us the grace of faithful living and enduring service. Five times Scripture hammers home this truth: "The just"—from the least to the most spiritually mature—must learn to "walk by faith."[3] God accomplishes wonderful things in us as we live and labor by faith in the dark. Let's identify some.

In the dark we learn:

- To TRUST GOD'S FAITHFULNESS. When for long periods we can't see the light, yet the Lord repeatedly sends it just in time—to us late, but never too late—we realize God is always faithful. Always! This valuable experience-born assurance is "gold tried in the fire" (Rev. 3:18).

- CHRIST PURIFIES OUR HEARTS. While waiting for the light, impatience, discontent, complaining, and other sins surface in our lives. Confessing and forsaking them purifies our hearts (1 John 1:7, 9).

- DEEPER CONTENTMENT. By staying near Jesus and His Word when deliverance seems far away we soon discover just how satisfying life can be close to Him—in darkness or light.[4]

- CHRIST TRULY TURNS "ALL THINGS" FOR GOOD (ROM. 8:28). This insight grows every time we see God turn our mysterious, dark valleys into clear mountaintop victories.

- WHILE WE WAIT HE WORKS. After we stop questioning and resisting and start accepting our darkness, we realize every day of it is proof of God's love, and necessary, so He can finish preparing our approaching blessings.[5]

- GOD'S SOVEREIGN CONTROL NEVER CHANGES. As we trust and obey, we still see Christ's providential hand working for us daily, even in our darkest circumstances. Soon we realize He rules both darkness and light equally: "The day is thine [in your control], and the night also" (Ps. 74:16).[6]

- NEW, DEEPER BIBLICAL INSIGHTS. He reserves His richest jewels of truth for those who persistently study His Word in the "darkness" (Matt. 10:27). Thus their darkness becomes a "secret place" of biblical illumination and ministry preparation (Ps. 18:11).

These "treasures of darkness" (Isa. 45:3) prepare us to minister to God's people much more effectively than we could before we experienced the darkness. Consequently, when other believers enter their long, dark "valley of the shadow" (Ps. 23:4), we can help keep their hearts filled with the light of God's Word that brings them hope and guidance, illuminating their steps until they too emerge, tested, proven, deeply changed, strong in character, and spiritually rich.[7] What a joy!

Are you, like Paul, in the darkness of unknowing? Don't grumble.

The light of the world has put you there! Don't rebel. Submit! Don't be offended. Offer thanks! Don't droop. Move forward! Don't doubt. Keep believing, hoping, knowing daylight always follows night: "Unto the upright there ariseth light in the darkness" (Ps. 112:4).

And when your new day dawns, you'll emerge wiser, stronger, and ready to help others become faithful in the dark.

Chapter 98

LOOK BEYOND THE DARKNESS

ITTINGLY, THE GREAT Tribulation will close with a great termination—a deep darkness, brilliant light, and huge gathering (Matt. 24:29–31).

Immediately after the final "bowl" judgment God will suddenly remove all celestial light. The sun will lose its radiant power. Consequently, the moon will "not give its light" (Matt. 24:29). An awesome creation-quake, or violent disordering of all the galaxies and stars, will follow: "The stars shall fall from heaven, and the powers of the heavens shall be shaken" (v. 29).[1] Deep darkness will then pervade the world. Why the darkness? God will be dimming the lights in the world's theater to prepare its center stage for His feature attraction, the full, brilliant, sustained shining of Jesus' glory.

That "sign of the Son of man" is Jesus' bodily appearance in the sky in "power and great glory," the light of the world gleaming "as the sun shineth in its strength" (Rev. 1:16)—but just above earth's atmosphere, not 93,000,000 miles away! He may hover there for as much as twenty-four hours to enable "every eye" and "all the tribes of the earth" to see Him (Rev. 1:7; Matt. 24:30). (After this, He'll descend as suddenly and lethally as a lightning bolt, in God's "blitzkrieg," or lightning-war, against the Antichrist at Armageddon; Matt. 24:27–28.) Releasing light waves as strong as the sun's, this stunning sign will likely blind many who gaze too long at it (Acts 9:8–9).

Meanwhile, angels will blow trumpets to signal two huge gatherings: one, of the "elect" saints and angels in heaven to take their place in Jesus' army bound for Armageddon; the other, of His "elect" birds to feast on Armageddon's bloody carnage.

A similar pattern—great darkness, great light, great gathering—marked Jesus' first advent. The Roman world was pitch dark with pagan idolatry and emperor worship. Israel was covered with the darkness of Herod's evil rule and the Pharisees' blind leadership. It was in this spiritually darkened "theater" that God revealed Israel's and Rome's greatest light. Matthew describes Jesus' arrival in Galilee as a bright sun rising in a very dark region: "The people who sat in darkness saw great light, and to them who sat in the region and shadow of death, light is sprung

260

up" (Matt. 4:16). This was the long-awaited "sun of righteousness" arising "with healing in his wings" (Mal. 4:2). As the glory of Jesus' eternal truth and compassionate ministry hovered over the land, God's elect gathered around the light. "They came to him from every quarter" (Mark 1:45). This pattern is developing again.

Today the world is growing grossly dark with atheism, Darwinism, unchecked immorality, rising occultism, disbelief in Jesus' divinity, the discrediting of God's Word, and the early signs of an approaching unified worldwide system of commerce, religion, and government. Many churches are growing dark with a diluted gospel, feel-good preaching, a sin-friendly atmosphere, nationalism, and a growing desire to conform to secular culture. Increasing weapons of mass destruction, unchecked terrorism, rogue leaders and nations, global warming, rising petroleum prices, political confusion, a weak economy, spiraling national debt, wars and fears of wars, and, yes, the old Israeli-Palestinian conflict—all these dark clouds cast a pall of unprecedented darkness over our troubled world. Why the darkness?

God is sovereignly dimming the world's lights again so the brightness of Christ's last rising (revival or movement) among His people will shine with maximum brightness. Like the stunning illumination of Jesus terminating the Tribulation, this one will be awesome. And powerful—it will blind, destroy, and proliferate.

It will deeply impress millions with the knowledge of who Jesus truly is, leaving them blind to the glory of mere humans. It will inspire a holy fear that breaks, and thus destroys, the control of sin in millions of penitent souls. It will produce new life abundantly, as millions previously uninterested in Jesus will ask Him to save them. And "whosoever shall call upon the name of the Lord shall be saved" (Rom. 10:13).

A massive twofold gathering of the elect will follow: initially, Christian converts, returning prodigals, and mature disciples will unite on earth to form new or renewed assemblies of developing overcomers; later, in God's time, these taught, tested, transformed ones will be "caught up" with resurrected believers "to meet the Lord in the air," in the final Christian clustering, the Rapture (1 Thess. 4:16–18). Then, literally, "unto him shall the gathering of the people be" (Gen. 49:10).

Fittingly, then, this great church age will have a great closing—with a deep darkness, brilliant light, and huge gathering. Rejoice, history's greatest Light and gathering are coming! So today, look beyond the darkness.

Chapter 99

APPRECIATING ANONYMOUS ASSISTANTS

*H*ISTORY SHOWS THAT behind most great men there's a good woman. Scripture reveals behind most effective Christian leaders, there's a good assistant. Or two. Or more! Paul commended two of his faithful helpers to the Philippians.

First he lauded Timothy, his most famous disciple, aide, ministerial trainee, and friend, for being a faithful, selfless minister utterly committed to Christ's interests (Phil. 2:19–24). Then he praised Epaphroditus, with whom most Christians today are not familiar (vv. 25–30). Comparatively speaking, Timothy was acclaimed and Epaphroditus anonymous. But though he wasn't a first-line leader, Epaphroditus was a first-rate Christian; what he lacked in prominence he made up for in spiritual excellence. Let's examine and appreciate him.

Epaphroditus' name means "lovely, handsome, charming,"[1] implying his character was lovely to God and charming or winsome to men. God apparently saw the inner "beauty of the LORD" in Epaphroditus (Ps. 90:17). And sinners, seeing the Savior's image "lifted up" in his character, were drawn to Christ (John 12:32). Though not widely applauded, Epaphroditus was divinely approved, a "vessel unto honor" (2 Tim. 2:21). So Paul recognized him: "He nearly died for the work of Christ, risking his life to complete what was lacking in your service to me" (Phil. 2:30, ESV). Furthermore, Paul instructed the Philippians to honor him and others like him: "Honor men like him" (v. 29, NIV).[2] Epaphroditus wore many hats.

Paul called him a "brother" (v. 25), his grace-related, born-again, spiritual sibling in God's family, with whom he enjoyed sweet fellowship as a personal friend. He was Paul's "companion in labor" (v. 25), a "co-worker" (NLT) in Paul's apostolic ministry. He was Paul's "fellow soldier" (v. 25), a spiritual warrior who by prayer, fasting, suffering, and other labors helped Paul fight the good fight against hostile Jews, Romans, demons, occultists, and false apostles. He was a faithful "messenger" (v. 25) whom the Philippians entrusted to deliver financial gifts and messages to Paul and other ministers and churches.[3] Paul testified he was a "minister" to "my need" (v. 25), giving not only the monetary support but also the fellowship, prayer, and other assistance Paul sorely needed while detained in Rome. As stated above, Epaphroditus had also recently been "sick," even "near to death" (vv. 26, 30), apparently due to exhaustion or illness caused by excessive labor in Rome, rigorous pedestrian travel,[4] exposure to the elements at sea,[5] abusive enemies, extreme fasting and prayer, or a combination of these. Whatever the cause, this shows Epaphroditus was willing to sacrifice himself, if necessary, to serve God's ministers and people (v. 30).

Thus he was a love-driven servant of Jesus Christ. Paul's words confirm Epaphroditus had a strong (*agape*) love for his fellow Christians. He "longed" for fellowship with his Philippian brothers and was "distressed" that they were distressed over his life-threatening illness: "He longed after you all... [he] was full of heaviness ["distressed," NIV] because ye had heard that he had been sick" (v. 26). While Paul lamented of many ministers, "all seek their own" (v. 21), it refreshed and comforted him to remember Epaphroditus' humble, loving heart. He served not for recognition, wealth, office, or rivalry, but for love of Christ and Christians alone. His passionate longing to bless and serve God's people mirrored Paul's (Phil. 1:7–8). This implies his heart was determined to keep Christ's great commandment, "that ye love one another, as I have loved you," and fulfill His high priestly prayer for loving unity to prevail among believers (John 13:34; 17:21–23). Thus he incarnated what many Romans said of the early church, "Look, how they love one another."[6]

Because Epaphroditus thus honored God, God honored him, prompting Paul's order, "Honor men like him." Paul's glowing description and request that Epaphroditus be highly regarded shows not only God but also Paul appreciated his anonymous assistants. Do we?

They're love-driven servants of God whose continual, dutiful "helps" keep our churches and ministries alive, strong, and growing (1 Cor. 12:28). Rarely seen or heard, their devoted labors are usually overlooked and undervalued. Though we know their names, compared to our fivefold ministers they're anonymous. These hidden Epaphrodituses are faithful intercessors, aides, armor bearers, secretaries, deacons, elders, messengers, and other helpers. Though not highly visible parts of our local body—its mouth, hands, arms, or ears—they're its hidden vital organs. Though not first-line leaders, they're first-rate Christians, spiritually excellent, honorable, and priceless. Without them pastors don't minister effectively, nor do churches grow or ministries spread Christ's Word, ways, and worship. Do we appreciate them and their unheralded daily labors? Why not?

We have pastor appreciation days. We acknowledge gifted ministers, worship leaders, missionaries, and scholars. Let's also remember those who stand behind them, our Epaphrodituses! Let's get busy appreciating anonymous assistants.

Chapter 100

THE CHIEF OF ZEAL

FTER RECALLING JESUS' self-emptying, Paul described his own—how he forsook his old religious life and ambitions and adopted new spiritual desires (Phil. 3:4–9, 10–14). It began when he was suddenly converted near Damascus.

Immediately Paul stopped longing for Pharisaic recognition, rank, and rewards and began hungering only for more of Jesus: "Now I long to know Christ" (v. 10, PHILLIPS). He jettisoned his cheap religious assets to seek the richest spiritual asset—knowing, pleasing, worshipping, and being loved by Jesus.[1] It was a notable miracle when Pharisaism's most enthusiastic advocate turned from religion to relationship, institutionalism to intimacy, seeking religious recognition to craving Jesus' approval. Despite this new goal, Paul's former core enthusiasm remained.

The record proves his zeal survived his conversion. Paul the Christian was just as enthusiastic, driven, unwavering, and indomitable as Saul the Pharisee. Aflame with unwavering ardor, he had not one lukewarm bone in his body. Philippians 3:4–14 describes the ultimate switch: a man all-out for Jewish legalism suddenly becoming all-out for Christianity. Thus to be Pauline is to be zealous.[2]

Even Paul's best students may forget this. We glory in Paul's doctrine, lauding and lecturing from his epistle to the Romans. We celebrate his missions and design ours accordingly. We're awed by his miracles and power to endure mistreatment and pray to have them. We marvel at his tender love and recite it reverently (1 Cor. 13). We envy his revelations and wish we had them. Yet despite our endless praise of Paul's gifts and virtues, we sometimes overlook his zeal.

Apparently he did too! Since he had formerly persecuted Christians, Paul self-deprecatingly labeled himself "chief" of sinners (1 Tim. 1:15). At the time, however, he was the church's unofficial but undisputed chief of zeal. His language betrays an insatiably hungry heart incessantly driving him forward in God's truth and cause. Listen to his pulsating passion: "Now I long to know Christ" (Phil. 3:10, PHILLIPS); "I follow after," "reaching forth," "press toward" (vv. 12–14, KJV). This hints how Paul overcame his most dogged adversaries, the Judaizers. Zealous as they were, he was even more zealous!

Surprisingly, Paul's "switch" has occurred more often than we think. Many sinners who were utterly zealous for a vocation, profession, pastime, art, trade, sport, or religion have become equally zealous for Christ upon conversion. This should also be our aim: to be all we can be (not as little) for Christ's joy, people, kingdom, and honor. Numerous biblical characters displayed such zeal.

For instance, God declared Phinehas morally "zealous for my sake" (Num. 25:11). Paul called the Jews "zealous toward God" (Acts 22:3) and the Corinthians "zealous of spiritual gifts" (1 Cor. 14:12). He taught all Christians should be "zealous of good works" (Titus 2:14). Though Paul warned the Galatians that heretics were "zealous to win you over," he affirmed zeal is good only "provided the purpose is good" (Gal. 4:17–18, NIV). Wisely, he recognized almost everybody's zealous for something.

Scholars are zealous for knowledge, athletes and fans for sports, geeks for new technologies, readers for great books, entertainment buffs for classic movies, music lovers for memorable songs, greedy souls for more profits, political enthusiasts for rising candidates, and pleasure seekers for more indulgence. But these temporary pursuits are worthless compared to God's eternal ends. And His zeal.

You see, God Himself is zealous. He performs His promises zealously and commands us to be enthusiastic in heart and work.[3] He wants us to be zealous not only for Him but also His church, Word, correction, and calling.[4] He honors zeal and challenges us, as He did the Laodiceans, to "be zealous and repent" of all apathy toward Him and His will (Rev. 3:19).

Vital as it is, however, raw zeal alone can't please God or fulfill His plan. To reach that lofty goal, our zeal must be:

- Knowledgeable, not ignorant (Rom. 10:2)
- Controlled, not hasty (2 Sam. 18:19–32), reckless (2 Sam. 21:1-2), or excessive[5]
- Fueled by love, not rivalry or animosity[6]
- Tempered with rest, to avoid burnout (Ps. 69:9)

Let's pause and check our spiritual temperature.

Are we Pauline or passionless? Hot or cold? Ardent or apathetic? Revived or just religious? Deeply devoted to Christ's interests or ours?

Is our zeal knowledgeable or ignorant? Controlled or hasty, reckless, or excessive? Driven by love or lower motives? Wisely limited or harmfully self-consuming? Let's not fool ourselves. To overcome our adversaries' fervent opposition to our Christlike walk and work, our zeal, like Paul's, must excel theirs. So let's jettison our apathy, stir our ardor, and rouse our minds to be Pauline.

Freely, joyfully, energetically, steadily imitate the chief of zeal.

Chapter 101

TURNED FOR GOOD AGAIN!

*B*Y TRYING TO stop Jesus' foremost messenger, the Jews only spread His message further—all the way to the Roman capital! Paul triumphantly testified, "The things which happened unto me have fallen out rather unto the furtherance of the gospel [in Rome]" (Phil. 1:12).

This turning of adversity into advantage has always been a hallmark of God's favor upon His people and work. Having seen it repeatedly in Scripture, history, his own experiences, and others' lives, Paul believed and confidently taught this pervasive principle:

> We know that God causes all things to work together for good to those who love God, to those who are called according to His purpose.
>
> —ROMANS 8:28, NAS

Let's review two significant divine turnings in Paul's life.

Earlier, in Philippi, God turned Paul's cruel injustices to favor the Philippian Christians' cause. He spread news of Paul's and Silas' miraculous deliverance through the testimonies of the jailer, his family, and the prisoners who witnessed it (Acts 16:25–34). It's also likely He used reports of the powerful city magistrates' humiliation before Paul to intimidate other would-be enemies (vv. 35–39). After hearing this, who would defy the Christians' God or dismiss their message as idle Jewish rumors?

Now, in Rome, God turned Paul's guards into unofficial evangelists. Paul's imprisonment for his faith was known "in all the palace" (Phil. 1:13). How? The soldiers guarding him, probably in six-hour shifts, were members of Caesar's imperial bodyguards, the Praetorian Guard (Acts 28:16). After guarding Paul, and being freshly soaked in his gospel teaching, they returned to palace duty each day and shared with others Paul's Spirit-empowered message about Jesus (vv. 30–31).[1] Undoubtedly Paul's message and manner—joyfully continuing his work despite being falsely charged and detained—impressed and won them, just as Christ's amazing non-resistance on the cross won His executioner (Mark 15:39). Besides infiltrating "the palace," their reports reached "all other places" in Rome (Phil. 1:13). So Nero's bodyguards, servants, perhaps family, and the Roman Christians and public heard of Paul's adversity, ministry, and Messiah. Paul also had the time and quietness to produce four New Testament epistles that still bless Christians worldwide![2] So though the messenger was bound, his message was loose and running swiftly from Rome's lowest to highest circles (2 Tim. 2:9)![3] God's wisdom is so amazing! He used the Jews' narrow-minded hatred to open Paul a wide door for compassionate ministry! And more.

Paul's Roman detention (AD 61–63) became another divinely arranged sabbatical, like the one he had recently experienced on Malta.[4] For "two whole years" his physical stress was greatly reduced in Rome (Acts 28:30). He had no long pedestrian travels, hasty flights from persecutors, stormy voyages, or mountain roads to climb.[5] Sufficiently well fed, and thus free from the privation he occasionally suffered while traveling (2 Cor. 11:25, 27), his strength was fully replenished. So he enjoyed full physical recuperation. His psychological stress was also minimized, since his Roman guards shielded him from plotting Jewish assassins. And he was replenished spiritually. He had lots of time to refill his soul by studying God's Word and praying.[6] Thus Paul's inner "cup," his soul's cistern, overflowed—while imprisoned! Therefore Rome became a vital pit stop, where Paul was spiritually, psychologically, and physically resupplied just before the final leg of his epic ministry "race" (2 Tim. 4:6-7, NIV).[7]

So in Philippi and again in Rome God turned Paul's adversity into advantage. This wasn't novel.

Bible history is full of it. God used the patriarchs' envy, Haman's anti-Semitism, the Sanhedrin's injustice, and Domitian's persecution to give us the wonders of Joseph's saving reign, Esther and Mordecai's rescue of the Jews, Christ's triumphant resurrection, and John's towering Revelation. The more these believers were persecuted, the more they multiplied and grew. God faithfully turned all their curses into blessings. In Joseph's words, what their adversaries meant for evil God transformed into good.[8] So every attack on God's people advanced them—in the Bible. Will our adversities advance us?

Absolutely! The universal principle of Romans 8:28 still operates for every Christian who loves God and follows His call. Will you believe it today, in your "Rome" of sudden strange adversities, injustices, misunderstandings, hindrances, or rejections for Christ's sake? If so, it will refill you with invigorating hope, flowing joy, and unshakable confidence in God's faithfulness. You'll remember your past "Philippis" where God turned adversity into advantage, and give thanks. You'll encourage others experiencing difficulties to restfully trust Romans 8:28 and worship God. In prayer and testimony, you'll offer professions of deep faith as Job and Habakkuk did.[9] Whatever's challenging you, you'll confess triumphantly, "Lord, I believe to see *this* situation turned for good—again!"

Chapter 102

SPREAD THE HEAT!

*I*N PHYSICS, HEAT transfer is "the flow of heat from one body at higher temperature to another body at a lower temperature, until the two temperatures are equal."[1]

These transfers of warmth through solids, liquids, or gases occur by direct contact, flowing of liquids, or electromagnetic waves.[2] For example, heating pads warm our sore muscles, hot drinks warm our shivering bodies, and sunlight warms our cold houses. This science parallels life.

Ardent personal and social interests spread similarly. When someone with inner heat—passion, fervor, zeal, love, excitement—for a subject, activity, or vocation speaks about it, other hearts are warmed with their passionate interest. Soon they too are ardent lovers of music, art, law, medicine, or whatever else has been promoted. When committed social leaders describe their passions, others begin glowing with desire for their ideals and goals—and fires of social or political reform burn. Sin also transmits this way.

Ancient writers described sexual lust as a burning. Paul wrote, "It is better to marry than to burn [with lust]" (1 Cor. 7:9). Anger is a raging fire. Covetousness creates a heat for goods or wealth. Envy is a zealous fire to outdo or undo those who have what we want. Contention is a bed of hot coals flaring up to consume relationships. Words radiate all these sinful heats: "The tongue is a flame of fire…a whole world of wickedness…It can set your whole life on fire" (James 3:6, NLT). These ungodly fervors spread by sustained contact with sinners, their flowing words, or the silent radiation of their bad examples. But there's good news.

Spiritual heat—saving faith, fervent love for Jesus, and zeal to know, serve, please, and honor Him—is also transferable. God wants to transfer these heavenly passions from fervent believers to lukewarm and cold souls. The Trinity is our heat source. Our Father is a "consuming fire," His Son the "Sun of righteousness," and His Spirit like "seven lamps of fire burning."[3]

This heavenly heat warms men through contacts, liquids, and radiation. God's angel touched Isaiah, and his sin was purged and heart reignited with passionate prophecies. Warm blood and water flowed from

Jesus' pierced side. His blood draws, washes, and warms sinners with saving faith; His water—the river of Spirit first released at Pentecost—revives and reheats our cold, discouraged hearts. Near Emmaus ("hot springs"[4]), Jesus' inspired teaching warmed two doubting disciples' core temperatures: "Did not our heart burn within us...while he opened to us the scriptures?" (Luke 24:32). This wasn't the first time spiritual heat spread.

The first major spiritual heat transfer occurred when God appeared in a burning bush to reignite Moses' faith and later, in a fiery pillar, to lead and warm the Hebrews' hearts through many long, cold desert nights. For centuries Jews came to rewarm their souls in the Shekinah-indwelt temple during festivals.

At Pentecost this heat flowed when God's Spirit fell as "tongues of fire" on 120 Jewish believers (Acts 2:3). Their ardent devotion and missionary zeal warmed hearts from Israel to Rome—where the fire of Christianity burned long before the fire of Rome! When Antioch caught spiritual fire, Barnabas fanned its converts' flames with passionate exhortations to "cling to the Lord" (Acts 11:23). Christian history continues this heart-warming story.

While meeting with fervent Moravians, John Wesley felt his heart "strangely warmed" with a glowing faith that subsequently heated the world. The Second Great Awakening lit fires of devotion and zeal in thousands who then warmed a callous nineteenth-century America with desperately needed social changes.[5] Twentieth-century healing revivals brought the warmth of Christ's compassion to thousands of sick people frozen in hopelessness by the lie, "The age of miracles has passed."[6] Today the heat flows on.

Evangelism is still "strangely warming" sinners' hearts worldwide. Devotional writers are rekindling Christians' heart fires daily. Christian martyrs' testimonies are radiating courage to other sufferers. Spirit-filled praise and worship is melting denominational and generational barriers. Committed, generous, wise, merciful, and studious Christians are igniting others to imitate their virtues. The fervent prayers of righteous intercessors are releasing warm rivers of faith worldwide, melting icy atheists, frozen dogmatists, cold intellectuals, frigid individualists, and lukewarm churchgoers. Want to spread this heat?

Get hot! Draw near the Sun of Righteousness. Stay close, so His spiritual heat—passionate faith, devotion, love, holiness, hope, compassion, wisdom, zeal—can transfer to you daily. Learn, worship, fellowship, and pray with other ardent believers regularly. Then your words, works, and life example will radiate Jesus' warmth everywhere you go. It's time for a temperature check.

Are you close to the Sun? Receiving His heat? Warming your spiritual core? Then go spread the heat!

Chapter 103

OUR HIGH CALLING

PAUL SPOKE OF our "high calling" in Christ (Phil. 3:14). The Christian calling is indeed high, so high it's above all others.

This world has many elevated vocations: medicine, politics, philanthropy, social service, scientific research, education, and so forth. People pursuing these callings are ennobled and lifted by the thought that they're serving something greater than themselves and leaving individuals, families, and nations better than they found them. But there's something higher.

Every born-again Christian, even the lowliest, has a far loftier calling. He (or she) is summoned to live and labor daily on the rarest heights inhabited by mortals. These spiritual highlands are characterized by, for instance, a heavenly viewpoint, a close walk with Jesus, clear biblical insight, holiness, the Spirit's guidance, divine love, sweet Christian fellowship, selfless ministry,[1] and the overarching hope of Jesus' appearing. Living steadily in these heavenly things gradually elevates our thoughts, habits, and works until one day we reach the highest possible elevation—Christ's presence and kingdom forever! Unless Satan defeats us.

Not surprisingly, his plan is to pull us down from our high calling: "They [Satan's agents] only consult to cast him down from his excellency [excellent spiritual walk and work]" (Ps. 62:4). Or, "They plan to topple me from my high position" (NLT). How?

Satan uses numerous ways, weapons, and wiles to keep us from steady heavenly living and ministry.

Distance is one way. The adversary discourages us from seeking God daily, encouraging us instead to live by our old strength and wisdom. Why? So that, detached from Christ, we'll follow Him "afar off" (Mark 14:54).

Disposition is another way. If we constantly yield to anger or fears, we'll sink in the frustrating quicksands of agitation or timidity—and Satan wins.

Doctrine may hinder us. Many Christians substitute a cold, dead, intellectual pursuit of doctrine for a warm, living, personal fellowship with Jesus—and die in the desert of Spiritless orthodoxy.

Self-deception may sink us. If we never seriously practice God's

Word but instead constantly judge others with it, we become "hearers only, deceiving your own selves" (James 1:22).

Disbelief is an ever-present danger. If we doubt we or others can live higher, especially in difficulties, unbelief will keep us from walking triumphantly upon our "high places" (Hab. 3:19).

Worldly distractions allure. There are many interesting, humanly compelling issues, activities, and causes that, though good, are not what God has called us to pursue (2 Tim. 2:4).

Disobedience devastates us. Stubbornly refusing to obey any of God's Word or guidance leaves us grounded and plodding a circular path in the lifeless valley of disobedience.

Division is perilous. Fostering unloving attitudes, offenses, revenge, or envious competitiveness leaves us "yet carnal" and far from the heights of Christlike living (1 Cor. 3:1–3).

Degeneration may defeat us. If we neglect restoring our souls daily, we'll degenerate—lose spiritual strength and gradually revert to our old ways of thinking and living, including fleshly sins or indulgences.

Disloyalty will test us. A friend, family member, or fellow Christian will eventually betray us in difficult times. We'll also be tempted to abandon fellow Christians in their trials. If we forgive our betrayers and stand true to embattled brothers,[2] we'll never fall to a lower plane.

Discouragement will visit. Confession is good for the soul, but never condemnation.[3] Self-condemnation over confessed sins and failures is pride refusing to receive God's gracious forgiveness.

Defiance will arise. Eventually an adversary will openly defy us, attacking our beliefs or work "for the Word's sake" and tempting us to defy God by rebelling against our hard circumstances (Matt. 13:21). Accepting our hardened adversaries and hard adversities will keep us soaring in the Spirit.

Even godly desire can be problematic. Excessive zeal must be controlled. If it prompts fanatical behavior or a hasty running ahead in ministry,[4] we'll misrepresent Jesus, misinterpret His Word, mislead His sheep, and dishonor the Father.

Any of these things may hinder us from spiritual elevation—rising steadily higher in heavenly thinking, living, and ministry every day. We must discern and dispatch them and continue seeking "those things which are above" (Col. 3:1). Sometimes that's not easy.

Our spirits occasionally become low and hearts heavy due to long trials, sudden attacks, bitter defeats, or unbroken monotony. It's easy then to come down to unspiritual thinking and living, because that's the default position of fallen human beings. But however low situationally, we must refuse to come down spiritually, instead redoubling our determination to persevere in our high calling: "I keep going on, trying to grasp that purpose for which Christ Jesus grasped me" (Phil. 3:12, PHILLIPS).

So keep climbing higher. Never step down from our high calling.

Chapter 104

REJOICING IN THE LORD...ALWAYS!

*H*AVE NOTHING TO rejoice about, my fellow Christian? Perhaps you're forgetting something.

Three times the apostle Paul urged the Philippians, and us, "Rejoice in the Lord" (Phil. 3:1, 3; 4:4). His inspired repetition implies this practice is important and should be continuous: "Continue to rejoice that you are in Him" (Phil. 3:1, AMP).[1] Therefore he instructs us to rejoice "always" (Phil. 4:4), not in our blessings in the world but "in the Lord"—in our marvelous Savior and salvation, in all that's ours as born-again believers in Christ. Let's explore the full range of our rejoicing.

We rejoice in Jesus' forgiveness. By God's grace alone we're forgiven and saved from sin's power and eternal punishment. We rejoice in Jesus' peace. Released from our former restlessness, we can enjoy supernatural inner tranquility daily—peace with God, the peace of God, and peace with others who are at peace with Him. We rejoice in Jesus' fellowship. While many won't come to Christ, we can draw near and spend time in close, satisfying, private fellowship with Him in prayer and worship day or night. We rejoice in Jesus' Word. We may nourish our hearts and minds by prayerfully studying Christ's sayings and the entire Bible. We rejoice in Jesus' favor. The ultimate advocate, Christ turns people's hearts to trust, befriend, or help us and our work. We rejoice in Jesus' training or discipleship. Through pastors and elders He steadily instructs and exhorts us to walk in His "ways," or daily spiritual life disciplines. We rejoice in Jesus' faithfulness. Our unchanging Rock of reliability, He always fulfills His promises, warnings, and prophecies, and faithfully controls and releases us from every trial.

We rejoice in Jesus' assemblies. Not alone, we have the stimulating and sustaining support of our local church's fellowship, worship, prayers, and when necessary, charity. We rejoice in Jesus' body. Our lives are meaningful now as living cells and active parts in Christ's earthly body, the mystical, ministering union of believers worldwide. We rejoice in Jesus' gift, the Holy Spirit. The Good Shepherd guides us by the staff of His Spirit, who personally convicts, strengthens, teaches, and leads us, and who manifests Christ's nearness, and activates spiritual gifts in us to bless others. We rejoice in Jesus' strength. Knowing His strength never fails, we're confident we too "can do all things" by His strength within (Phil. 4:13). Thus we stand strong against stubborn opposition, confident in our powerful Source, beliefs, hope, and God-appointed work. We rejoice in Jesus' provision. Our royal Shepherd makes all grace abound so all our need is provided sufficiently and we don't lack any necessities of life.[2]

Moreover, we rejoice in Jesus' protection. Whatever enemies, weapons, and wiles we face, we're perfectly safe as long as we abide in Christ our impenetrable "shield" (Ps. 28:7). We rejoice in Jesus' order. He commands us to be submissive to "all authority" in our nations, churches, workplaces, and homes so we may enjoy His favor, peace, and prosperity, and promote His gospel. We rejoice in Jesus' sufferings. Though deeply tried by the same sharp thorns and heavy crosses He faced—misunderstanding, rejection, reproach, injustice—we're honored to experience them so we can fully know Him, minister powerfully, and ultimately rule with Him. We rejoice in Jesus' ministry. By exercising our gifts and pursuing our callings, we help continuously enlarge the ministry Jesus only "began" on earth (Acts 1:1). We rejoice in Jesus' appearing. While others anxiously look around, confused, we're "eagerly waiting" for Jesus—our blessed, purifying hope—to appear (Phil. 3:20, NLT) and suddenly take us to be with Him forever (1 Thess. 4:17). We rejoice in Jesus' kingdom. Whatever distresses may grip our nation, we're registered citizens of Christ's heavenly city-state, New Jerusalem, where we'll reside and rejoice forever with our Redeemer and His redeemed ones. Why rejoice continuously in these blessings "in the Lord"?

They're untouchable joys: trouble can't spoil them unless we let it. Whatever adversity we experience in the world, these blessings abide "in the Lord." Delighting in them enables us to face dull days, mundane duties, and even ruinous, hopeless losses, and still declare with Habakkuk, "Yet I will rejoice in the Lord" (Hab. 3:18).[3] While thus rejoicing, we're revived, strengthened, and restored to our fullness of life and effectiveness of labor in Christ. The result? We become overcomers—like Habakkuk, David, Hannah, and Paul![4] The adversary hates this.

He touches us frequently with worldly troubles, hoping we'll let them eclipse our untouchable joys "in the Lord." Don't let that happen! Never forget what's yours as a Christian. Remember, whatever your circumstances, you may overcome and honor God by rejoicing in the Lord...always![5]

Chapter 105

PRACTICING GOD'S PEACE

IN PHILIPPIANS 4, Paul teaches us to "stand fast" spiritually by, among other things, practicing God's peace (vv. 1, 6–7). For this, we must:

- Firmly refuse to be anxious about anything. However important or urgent our needs or troubles, we must, "Be anxious for nothing" (v. 6).[1]

- Petition God about every problem: "Tell God every detail of your needs" (v. 6, PHILLIPS).[2]

- Believe God hears us and rely on His faithfulness to answer.

- Give thanks for His answers by faith, praying "with thanksgiving" (v. 6).

Admittedly, this is a challenge since, strangely, we often prefer to fret and complain our way through problems. If practiced diligently, Paul's "anxious for nothing, praying in everything" discipline produces overcomers who consistently rest in God's surpassing peace whether their circumstances are triumphant, trying, or terrible. One commentator notes, "Prayer and peace are closely connected. One who entrusts cares to Christ instead of fretting over them will experience the peace of God to guard him from nagging anxiety."[3] When practiced habitually, this exercise forms a strong, secure, "sound mind" (2 Tim. 1:7) well guarded and ready to handle Satan's constant psychological warfare.

Thus God urges us to form a new habit or routine for handling adversity. Our old way of worrying, reasoning, depending solely on human wisdom and ways, and complaining, insults and grieves our heavenly Father who has so repeatedly promised to care for us (1 Pet. 5:7). We must replace it with a new habit of utter God-reliance through simple, spontaneous prayers of faith and thanksgiving. One source states, "Do you want to worry less? Then pray more! Whenever you start to worry, stop and pray."[4] This exercise brings wonderful benefits.

We release all our anxieties to God, our great Psychologist, thus sparing us their harmful effects (Ps. 62:8). God consequently releases His peace afresh to "keep" (guard) our hearts with its supernaturally sustaining strength: "The peace of God which surpasses all power of comprehension" (Phil. 4:7, WUEST). Our faith also releases God's hand to help us in His time and way, providentially or supernaturally (Acts 12:7, 11). God is honored by our reliance, confidence, and praise (Phil. 4:7). Finally, our example inspires others to trust Him and practice His peace.[5]

But this won't happen if we don't change our old ways. "In everything" adverse, we'll continue reasoning, fearing, and complaining. If humble and wise, we'll change these bad habits to please and honor God. And enjoy His peace.

Remember, the peace Paul describes is "the peace of God" (v. 7)! This is not human but divine serenity, the marvelous, indescribable tranquility and blissful absence of agitation that fills God's own heart and heaven.[6] This He promises us and nothing less. This explains how some of God's saintliest servants—Joseph, Daniel, Jeremiah, Esther, Paul— were so miraculously kept and remained steady, clear-minded, and fruitfully active in the most turbulent, cruel, or terrifying moments. It was amazing, a miracle, nothing less than God and His heavenly peace in them! "They glorified God in me" (Gal. 1:24).

God's peace is our legacy from Jesus (John 14:27) and a fruit produced in us easily and naturally when the Spirit is present and having His way with us (Gal. 5:22). We're called to live in it (1 Cor. 7:15), and it marks us as authentic citizens of God's kingdom (Rom. 14:17). It comes to us through God's Word (John 16:33) and whenever we choose to interpret the events of our lives in light of that Word (Rom. 8:6). God releases it to us every time we do "good"—His good will or good deeds to others (Rom. 2:10)—and choose to "trust in Him" in trials (Rom. 15:13, NIV). Every fresh visit of God's presence in our lives brings fresh peace, especially when we're in fearful situations (John 20:19, 26). Christ imparts this peace whenever we receive the Holy Spirit or His call to service (vv. 21–22). We should pray often for one another and our churches to be filled with God's peace.[7] We should let God's peace "rule," or judge, our spiritual lives, determining when we're in or out of God's will (Col. 3:15). We should diligently maintain God's peace so we'll be found living "in peace" when Jesus appears (2 Pet. 3:14). So the choice is yours.

You may keep your old habit or form a new one, suffer your old anxieties or enjoy your new peace—God's peace that supernaturally strengthens you, guards your mind, relieves your stresses, pleases and honors God, and inspires others. OK, you've had your devotional lesson.

It's time now for action. Whatever problems you're facing today, get busy forming new habits and practicing God's peace.

Chapter 106

God's Waiting Room

*T*HE APOSTLE PAUL told the Philippians he would send Timothy to them "as soon as I shall see how it will go with me" (Phil. 2:23). Clearly, then, he wasn't sure if his trial before Nero would end in his release or execution.[1] Why?

He was in God's waiting room. God sometimes keeps us waiting for answers to prayer or divine guidance, fulfillments, or insights. Scripture speaks often of these periods.

Moses had to wait six days on the summit of Sinai before God began revealing His plan for Israel's tabernacle, worship, and law (Exod. 24:15–16). Jeremiah had to wait ten days for God's guidance for the survivors of the fall of Jerusalem (Jer. 42:7). Abraham had to wait twenty-four years to discover who his son of promise would be, when he would be born, and by which wife (Gen. 17:21). Ruth, Boaz, and Naomi had to wait one long day—their longest!—to discover if indeed God's blessing would be on Boaz's proposed marriage to Ruth (Ruth 3:13, 18). These waiting ones were not alone.

Samson had to wait weeks, perhaps months, for his hair to regrow and to discover if God had given him another chance to redeem his ruined ministry (Judg. 16:22). Paul had to wait approximately a decade before knowing when, where, and how the Spirit's saving work among the Gentiles would begin.[2] He had to wait over two years in prison in Caesarea to discover when and how he would travel to Rome, as God promised.[3] The aged apostle John had to wait in gloomy exile on Patmos until "the Lord's day" dawned with the awesome visions and prophecies recorded in the Revelation (Rev. 1:9). He waited another year and a half to learn if he would be released.[4]

All these and many more spent time—days, weeks, months, years—in God's waiting room. Why did God keep them waiting?

He was doing a deep work in their souls. We easily forget that what God does *in* us is even more important than what He does *for* or *through* us. Seasons in God's waiting room make us more patient, perfect in character, dependent on God, pliable (easily led) in His hand, sensitive to His voice, aware of His providential work, Christlike, faithful, and at one with God. There we learn the Bible's most profound spiritual truths, the great vital lessons of spiritual maturity. Here are some of them.

We learn that God richly rewards those who wait patiently for Him. After waiting in doubly difficult trials Job received a double portion (Job 42:10–17). We learn not to rebel by abandoning God or impatiently rushing ahead of Him to kindle "fires" of self-led works (Isa. 50:10–11).[5] We learn how to occupy ourselves well, using our waiting times efficiently by steadily pursuing our God-given work. We learn to nourish our faith and cultivate closeness to Jesus every day to keep our love hot, faith strong, and hope alive however discouraging our circumstances. We learn God's blessing always follows His leadings, not ours. We learn God never wastes time. When He asks us to wait, it's only because He's doing many other things, working "all things" together for His good plan and our good blessing (Rom. 8:28). We learn His times for deliverances, fulfillments, or revivals are always best, though we often misjudge them as being late. We learn He never forgets where we are, regardless of how inactive and uninterested He seems.[6]

We learn the immense value of receiving even one word, leading, or answer to prayer from God—almighty God! We gladly wait for visits, counsels, or assistance from doctors, politicians, experts, and other important people; how much more then from Him? We learn God is utterly faithful to fulfill all His promises, even those that seem utterly impossible (Acts 27:23–25, 44; 28:16). We learn it's better to suffer where God places us rather than abandon our appointed place and work to obtain relief (1 Kings 17:1–7). We learn God greatly strengthens us—especially our enduring faith and patience—as we submissively wait for Him in loving fellowship, patient hope, and faithful labors: "Be assured that the testing of your faith leads to power of endurance" (James 1:3, WEY), "but let the process go on until that endurance is fully developed, and you will find you have become men of mature character, men of integrity with no weak spots" (v. 4, PHILLIPS). It's time we learn these towering truths.

Waiting for God to speak, guide, deliver, work, or open doors? Then, like Paul, you're in God's waiting room—and in good company. Learn deeply the vital lessons of God's waiting room.

Chapter 107

ORDERED TO THINK!

*T*HE APOSTLE PAUL realized most actions arise from preceding thoughts. So before ordering the Philippians to "do" the biblical truths he taught and modeled (Phil. 4:9), he first urged:

> Whatever things are true...honest...just...pure...lovely ...of good report...[of] virtue...[causes of] praise, *think on these things.*

—PHILIPPIANS 4:8

Or paraphrasing, "Think the right things; then you'll do the right things."[1] Even after a powerful conversion, we won't consistently act righteously unless we first think righteously. If our Christian walk is to thrive, we must give ourselves to devotional reading and Bible study (2 Tim. 2:15). It all starts here—or doesn't start!

Filling our minds with God's words saturates our minds with God's thoughts—powerful spiritually active agents, Spirit-filled intellectual and volitional drivers that prompt righteous living. We "meditate day and night" in Scripture and then, stimulated by it, "do all that is written therein" (Josh. 1:8).

Thus spiritually right thinking is fed by Scripture, as we pursue Bible study and receive biblical teaching. It's cultivated by meditation, as we recall and slowly reflect on biblical thought stuff, considering what it means and how it applies. It's guarded by self-examination, as we screen our minds to identify and reject wrong thoughts.

Instead of limiting our field of thought to God's Word, Paul throws our intellectual windows open to a wide world of worthy thoughts: "Whatever" is true, noble, right, pure, admirable, virtuous, or praiseworthy! Conversely this begs us *not* to think on whatever's opposite. But we can't live in a thoughtless vacuum. If we don't obey Paul's command to think worthily, we'll inevitably feed unworthy thoughts, whether trivial or evil, into our minds—and risk corrupting them![2] Paul's advice is an excellent TV, movie, Internet, or entertainment guide!

When pondering worthy subjects, ask God to help you detect His biblical laws, principles, providential hand, plans, mercies, and decisions in them (2 Tim. 2:7). Then by the Spirit's illumination even secular topics—biographical, historical, scientific, social, cultural—come alive with surprisingly edifying spiritual insights. Pause also to consider how they apply to your life, tests, and times. That's inspired thinking.

Paul's order here is inspired by our spiritual Head, Christ. Not just Paul but also Christ wants thoughtful Christians: intelligent, curious, contemplative, growing in vital biblical and human knowledge. Didn't He teach us to love God with "all thy mind" (Matt. 22:37)? Why?

Thinking sharpens our minds, enabling us to analyze information, form opinions, and converse or share better (Prov. 27:17). And discern! While thoughtless Christians are easy prey for Satan's liars and deceivers, thoughtful ones are much less vulnerable.[3] Hence, Scripture repeatedly bids us meditate.

Meditating on God's Word cultivates awareness of and closeness to God. Isaac got alone with God to "meditate" (Gen. 24:63).[4] This also develops scriptural memory, while not meditating fosters forgetfulness. Meditating on God's promises creates deep, peaceful trust and stability (Ps. 26:3, NLT). Meditative thinking in general develops the "sound mind" the Spirit gives and we need if we are to fulfill God's will in the face of persisting opposition (2 Tim. 1:7).[5]

Therefore Scripture urges us to ponder a wide range of subjects: God's Word, doctrine, goodness, and work; His creation, miracles, wisdom, and providence; human life, adversity, dreams, and fulfillments; neglecting God's will, past lessons, and others' needs.[6] It also rebukes us for thoughtlessness, or not reflecting on God's sovereign lordship and loving acts in our lives: "Even an ox knows its owner...but...my people don't recognize my care for them" (Isa. 1:3, NLT).

So Paul issues not a negative but a very positive order: "Think!" He understood by accentuating the positive, we avoid the negative (Gal. 5:16). Persistently "thinking on" whatever's excellent is the most effective, really the only, way of "bringing into captivity every thought" to obey Christ (2 Cor. 10:5). Wherever right thinking is being steadily cultivated, wrong thinking is being steadily eliminated—and can't root, grow, and trouble or corrupt our minds. This is also the only way to overcome the inner emotional turmoil caused by unspiritual (unbiblical) thinking. Will you obey this apostolic order to "think on" worthy things?

A. W. Tozer wrote:

> Thinking about God and holy things creates a moral climate
> favorable to the growth of faith and love and humility and

reverence. We cannot by thinking regenerate our hearts...but we can by Spirit-inspired thinking help to make our minds pure sanctuaries in which God will be pleased to dwell.[7]

So take the initiative! Fully develop your mind, asking and expecting the Spirit's help. Discipline your thought life by studying whatever's excellent, praiseworthy, spiritually edifying, or intellectually stimulating. Then you'll be ready when Christ, our thoughtful Judge, asks, "How think ye?" (Matt. 18:12). So don't sit intellectually idle. Get busy!

You've been ordered to think!

Chapter 108

ORDERED TO OBEY!

FTER ORDERING THE Philippians to "think on" biblical and other excellent topics, the apostle Paul added: "Those things which ye have both learned…and seen in me, *do…*" (Phil. 4:9). To him biblical thinking wasn't enough. It must produce biblical living.

Paul realized if we fail to put our excellent biblical and ethical thinking into action, all of it—our reading, study, meditation, notation, discussion—is futile. What's worse, we're foolish, like the "silly" Christians he described who were "ever learning" but never living and thus never fully knowing God's truth and who therefore never received His approval for service (2 Tim. 3:6–7). Succinctly, then, the Lord insists we not only know but also do His will. And not just once. Or occasionally.

"Do" here refers not to a single act but rather to a continuous practice. Paul was saying, "Keep putting into practice all you learned and received from me—everything you heard from me and saw me doing" (Phil. 4:9, NLT). Why is persistence important?

Steady obedience is the only way to perfect godly living. We perfect every human activity by practicing it, usually daily. We practice our singing, instruments, and musical ensembles. We practice our baseball, tennis, or golf swing. We practice our speech, dance, or art. We practice our physical exercises, hand crafts, or other hobbies. We practice our cooking, floral, and decorating skills. We practice law, medicine, and accounting. In all these activities we would never consider our abilities or gifts as being perfected after one act—or two, five, or ten! We accept that only continuous practice will fully develop them.

Yet as Christians we forget this is also true of our walk with Christ. He said, "If ye continue in my word, then are ye my disciples indeed" (John 8:31). Continuing in Jesus' Word involves persistence in not only its study but also its practice. Diligently. Daily. With determination.

So though we shouldn't wonder why God tests us in the same area of obedience over and over, we do, and pray for release from our repetitive trials. After all, we've obeyed God before in these matters, so why doesn't that suffice? Simply because to become spiritually mature (perfect or complete) we must trust and obey God many times over many years.

Thus the wise apostle commands his students, and us, "Practice what you have learned" (Phil. 4:9, AMP). The reverse is equally true.

If we're not practicing obedience daily, we're practicing disobedience. Jesus described only two types of Christians, one who hears His words and "doeth them" and another who hears and "doeth not" (Luke 6:47–49). Both Christians are practitioners, but God approves only one's practice. Here's a stark contrast with the pagan religions of Paul's day.

The mythological Greek and Roman gods didn't demand that their worshippers change their moral or ethical conduct. They only asked them to observe various religious rites, festivals, feasts, and offerings.[1] Theirs were "worship as you are" religions. Thus the Spirit impressed Paul to stress to the Philippians and us that the true God is different. He demands we change, conforming our ways of living to His. We're not merely to study, discuss, and imitate Christianity weekly. We're to live it every hour of every day of every year—if we're serious about knowing Jesus and walking closely with Him.

If so, our obedience will be varied. Every day we'll maintain our devotional fellowship with Christ and execute our duties unto Him. But we'll render other obedience "as the occasion demands" (1 Sam. 10:7, NKJV), or in whatever areas of obedience Christ chooses to test us in our ever-changing situations: mercy, submission, diligence, holiness, sacrifice, courage, faith, giving, self-control, and so on. We'll complete some kinds of obedience in a day; others in months or years.[2] Some types of obedience will be easy; others will demand heartrending sacrifices and suffering. Some acts of obedience will be seen; others will be hidden. Will we repeatedly practice obedience or disobedience in all these various scenarios?[3] Our response is important—really, imperative.

Thus Paul's brief exhortation, "do," is in the imperative mood. He's giving us orders, not suggestions; requirements, not options. "You must practice the biblical life truths you've learned and observed if you hope to become a peaceful, Christlike Christian."[4] There's no other way. If you don't respond, you'll never be Christlike. So don't forfeit spiritual maturity.

Yield to Paul's apostolic exhortation and thrive. If challenged by great difficulties, ask for more grace. You'll find you can do "all things" and practice all God's words and ways through Christ's strength (Phil. 4:13). Today embrace the fact that you've been ordered to obey!

Chapter 109

PERFECT POSITIVISM

ATURALLY WE EACH lean toward optimism or pessimism. Pessimists frequently insist they're negative because they're realists, while optimists are often idealists, uninformed, or naïve. What about Christians?

After we're converted, our faith breeds positivism and our doubts negativity. Optimistic believers brim with hope because they trust God's faithfulness, that all His words are true and promises sure (Acts 27:25). Pessimistic Christians cling to rationalistic doubts. Thus, like Thomas, they joyfully believe God only after seeing His fulfillments or blessings, never before. Which core attitude should we adopt?

I recommend the apostle Paul's view. He asserted unequivocally that, whatever the challenge, he was ready for it in Christ: "I can do all things through Christ who strengthens me" (Phil. 4:13, NKJV). Or:

> I am ready for anything and equal to anything through Him Who infuses inner strength into me; I am self-sufficient in Christ's sufficiency.
>
> —PHILIPPIANS 4:13, AMP

Three clarifying thoughts are needed.

First, while "all things" includes all possible scenarios, pleasant and unpleasant, as Paul vividly describes (vv. 11–12), his adverse circumstances (imprisonment) subtly emphasize the unpleasant. Very unpleasant! Can we handle being "abased" in life's most humiliating, despised, unjust, painful, or burdensome conditions as Paul was? Unaided human strength can't experience these adversities very long without complaining, raging, or fleeing. But with Christ and His Spirit within, Christians can be "content [satisfied enough]" (v. 11), productive, and even joyful in them. How?

We learn that whatever our pain, grief, unfairness, or perplexity, Christ's grace is always "sufficient"—enough to meet our present need—if we'll remain humble and willing (2 Cor. 12:7–10). Therefore we can fulfill any humbling task or endure any hardship optimistically because our faith, hope, and love are supernaturally renewed by Christ's grace as we seek Him daily.[1]

Second, this biblical optimism is just as vital when we're in prosperity. The same Christ who gets us through low, dark valleys helps us handle high, heady triumphs. In such seasons we need His grace to remain sober minded, God fearing, spiritually hungry, and focused, keeping Christ and His call "first" (Matt. 6:33). Why? Good times create unique temptations to become lax, abandon our spiritual disciplines, or turn from God to pride, greed, worldly pleasures, or other ways of putting self first. Scripture repeatedly warns of these unsuspected pits.[2]

History confirms many great individuals, ministers, churches, and nations have failed on mountaintops, not in valleys. Adversity forced them to rely wholly on God, but in success they forgot Him and began relying on their wealth, power, or popularity. David, Solomon, Uzziah, and Hezekiah were strong and honored, not weak and reproached, when lust, idolatry, pride, and unthankfulness toppled them.[3] In our seasons of favor and fulfillment, will we remain close to Christ, prayerful, watchful, and dutiful? Paul affirms we "can" be as focused and spiritually minded in prosperity as in adversity.

Third, Paul's optimism must be counterbalanced with Jesus' warning, "Apart from Me you can do nothing" (John 15:5, NAS). We can do "all things" in union with Christ, but "nothing" without Him—nothing God approves. Why? He gives grace to accomplish His will, not ours; His kingdom agenda, not our worldly ambitions. Says one commentator, He "does not grant us superhuman ability to accomplish anything we can imagine without regard to His interests."[4] Whatever we accomplish outside His will will eventually come to "nothing."

But if, like Paul, we're committed to Christ's will, we should be the most positive people on earth. Whether presented with victory or defeat, praise or persecution, we should respond, "Can do!" Why? We're confident whatever we need—favor, ability, wisdom, patience, meekness, resources, strength, assistance, guidance, or protection—Jesus' supernatural grace will supply it.

Thus we can love unlovable people, endure long tests, and accomplish difficult assignments—or receive blessings, honors, or gain. We can be faithful in a day of small things—or while growing larger, more influential, even famous. We can execute new jobs, fulfill larger responsibilities, and overcome harder tests. We can be received or rejected, enjoy health or endure sicknesses, celebrate freedom or accept limitations. We "can do" all these things and anything else in God's will with excellence and contentment—unless we focus on our natural limitations, weaknesses, or past failures.

Thus focused, Moses initially responded negatively to God's challenging call to deliver Israel. But after God graciously promised His assistance, Moses repented, became positive, and prevailed. If we follow Moses' footsteps, we'll discover we too "can do" whatever we face. That's Pauline positivism.

And it's perfect—a spiritually mature attitude perfectly balanced between unbridled optimism and unbelieving pessimism, neither too bold nor too timid. Let's embrace and walk in Paul's perfect positivism.

Chapter 110

SHARING WITH OUR SOVEREIGN

SCRIPTURE ASSERTS THE Lord is a great Sovereign who owns everything and everyone: "The earth is the LORD's, and the fullness thereof; the world, and they who dwell therein" (Ps. 24:1). Jesus demonstrated this.

He used Peter's boat as a platform for teaching: "He entered into one of the boats, which was Simon's... And he sat down, and taught the people out of the boat" (Luke 5:3). When Peter found a shekel in a fish's mouth, Jesus unapologetically claimed and used it. He sent messengers into a village to borrow a man's donkey to ride when entering Jerusalem. He also sent messengers requesting to use another believer's home during Passover week: "The Master saith... I will [desire to] keep the passover at thy house" (Matt. 26:18). Or, paraphrasing, "I'd like to use your house for My purpose, sir."

That house was in Jerusalem, and Christ's purpose was the hosting of His Last Supper. But it wasn't the last time He used believers' houses. He still asks to use our houses today for a variety of kingdom purposes. Let's explore them.

Homes are an ideal setting for Bible studies. Scripture commands, "Study to show thyself approved unto God" (2 Tim. 2:15), but where shall we study? Besides typical church structures, schools, and office buildings, private homes make excellent classrooms for hungry disciples.

Many prayer meetings are held in private homes. One very famous one was held in Jerusalem in "the house of Mary," Mark's mother, where many Christians gathered to pray. Their petitions delivered Peter, the church's primary leader, from certain death (Acts 12:12).

Private residences are excellent settings for youth meetings. I know one couple who added an indoor gymnasium, swimming pool, and sound system to their home to serve as an activity center for not only their four sons but also their church's vibrant youth group.

Fellowship meals fit the home setting well. Soon after Matthew's conversion, he "made him [Jesus] a great feast in his own house" (Luke 5:29). Mary of Bethany famously anointed Christ during another honorary dinner, and countless early Christian love feasts were held in homes.

Leaders' meetings are sometimes held in homes. Pastors, deacons, elders, or board members can gather there for confidential discussions, prayer, and praise and worship (Acts 13:1-3).

Private homes make thrifty lodgings for traveling believers, especially ministers. Priscilla and Aquila opened their home to Paul many times. A Shunammite woman built prophet's quarters onto her home for Elisha's periodic use. In England, John Wesley slept in fellow Methodists' homes far more often than his own!

Chiefly, our homes may serve as worship centers, or house churches. The first Christians met exclusively in homes for over two centuries.[1] Believers have periodically returned to this primitive trend down the centuries due to persecution or preference. Today millions of Christians worldwide meet exclusively in homes, preferring small, informal house meetings to larger, more formal church services.[2] Others worship secretly in homes for safety, since their governments or cultures strongly oppose Christianity.[3] The amazingly fruitful and enduring growth of Christianity in China during the twentieth century occurred almost exclusively in house churches. Christ's uses of our humble domiciles may be short or long term.

Jesus held a brief luncheon at Zacchaeus' house on short notice and as far as we know never used it again. But He used the Upper Room in Jerusalem much longer. Besides hosting the Last Supper, it was likely the site of Jesus' post-resurrection appearances to His secluded apostles (John 20:19, 26), the ten-day prayer vigil preceding Pentecost (Acts 1:13-14), the "pulpit" for Peter's first sermon, and initially the early church's headquarters. All this time the "owner of the house" (Mark 14:14), whoever he was, yielded his private home for his Sovereign's kingdom purposes—and paid a price. His decision disrupted his privacy and leisure time, created additional work preparing and cleaning the residence, caused wear and tear on his furnishings, and incurred additional expenses for maintenance. Would you do the same, if asked?

What if Jesus should speak to your heart asking, as He has so many others, "I'd like to use your house for My purposes"? Or, I need your "donkey," "boat," or "shekels"—automobile, business property, or money respectively? Would you gladly share your things with your Sovereign and pay the price of kingdom progress? That requires much grace.

When "much grace" rested on the first Christians, "no one claimed that any of his possessions was his own, but they shared everything they had" (Acts 4:32, NIV). They were truly "ready to give, willing to share" (1 Tim. 6:18, NKJV). Are we?

Let's prepare our hearts for sharing with our Sovereign.

Chapter 111

THE PERFECT PROVIDER

*U*NHESITATINGLY AND UNEQUIVOCALLY the apostle Paul promised the Philippians, who had so faithfully supported him, that God would faithfully support them:

> My God shall supply all your need according to his riches in glory by Christ Jesus.
>
> —PHILIPPIANS 4:19

This was the ultimate creature comfort!

Consciously or unconsciously we all seek material security. Daily we work, seek, inquire, and pray to satisfy our present and foreseeable human needs. Ultimately we trust in one of two sources, the Messiah or mammon,[1] "his riches in glory" or our riches on earth. One provider is uncertain, the other unfailing. One is imperfect, the other perfect. One is subject to our economy, the other supersedes it. Back to Paul's precious promise.

He pledged God would meet not some or most but "all" the Philippians' financial needs. Hudson Taylor said, "When God's work is done in God's way for God's glory, it will not lack for God's supply."[2] How wonderful! All our earthly material needs—for our person, family, church, ministry, or business—may be supplied by our heavenly Shepherd's "riches in glory" (v. 19).

This provision is complete and wide-ranging. Whatever our present need, God's grace is always "sufficient," or enough to fully supply it (2 Cor. 12:9). But are we mature enough to let enough be enough, or are we still craving more? God's provision also covers every human need. "All your need" includes spiritual, social, and emotional needs.[3]

Primarily, however, the "need" promised is financial, since money was the gift the Philippians gave Paul and thus the recompense he expected for them (Phil. 4:10, 14–18). How does God provide?

Our providential Provider is endlessly creative. He may increase our finances or decrease our expenses; decrease the cost of needed items or have people buy them for us; prompt people to lend us property or goods or donate them; reduce or eliminate our needs; or, if necessary, send manna or fish with coins! Will we humbly receive however He provides? What are His resources?

"His riches in glory" are also "the riches of his glory" (Phil. 4:19; Eph. 3:16). They are the vast spiritual and natural resources of heaven and earth available to Jesus now in His glorified condition. He always supplies "according to" these unfathomable resources (Phil. 4:19).

So God's supply is regal in nature, like the lavishly generous gifts or favors given by monarchs or the very wealthy.[4] Paul taught Timothy God gives to us "richly," not just to meet needs but also "to enjoy" (1 Tim. 6:17). How comforting! If God gave "according to" our means, we'd barely be supplied; but if "according to" His bounty, we'll be supplied liberally, though never so excessively as to stir greed, pride, trust in our bounty, or the illusion we no longer need our Supplier. This suggests a companion truth.

Since our heavenly Father-King gives generously, shouldn't we, His royal children, do likewise? If not in amount, then proportionately? Matthew threw an expensive banquet for Jesus, but the widow's two mites were a more generous gift since they were all her assets.[5] So, though poor, she was a regal giver. And faithful!

Just like the Philippians! They supported Paul not only in their city but also wherever he ministered (Phil. 4:10, 14–18). When teaching this verse, we must emphasize how faithfully they gave. To own their promise, we must own their obedience. Then, whatever our trials, we'll know confidently God will provide "all" our needs from His unlimited heavenly resources. Non-givers aren't promised this. Why?

Divine reciprocity. God promises we'll reap what we sow and in the measure we sow it (Gal. 6:7; 2 Cor. 9:6, 8). Because the Philippians fully[6] met the needs of God's minister, God fully met their needs. Paul vowed, "My Master will fully repay you; I cannot."[7] Giving to God's work or servants, therefore, assures us He'll always repay us, and in the measure we give. Conversely, as His servants we may always receive freely (Matt. 10:8), knowing God will faithfully repay our donors in His time and way.[8] But not make them wealthy.

This text doesn't promise material prosperity—large supplies of excess wealth or property. Rather it guarantees material provision—we'll never lack life's necessities (Ps. 23:1). Though God often gives us "richly," or generously above our needs (Phil. 4:18), this text doesn't promise affluence. Mature Christians are "content" (v. 11) with whatever He provides because their fellowship with Jesus is so rich they don't need excess wealth to be secure or satisfied (Heb. 13:5).[9] They've found eternal wealth.

Are you praising God for meeting your needs or whining for more? Idolatrously loving and trusting your imperfect mammon or thankfully relying on the perfect Provider?

Chapter 112

BRING YOUR OFFERING!

O LD TESTAMENT JEWISH priests presented God sacrifices for the people and for themselves. As New Testament believer-priests, all Christians should also bring the Lord offerings.[1] And often.

Jewish sacrificial worship was continuous. Daily burnt offerings ascended from the altar and incense from the holy place. There were special offerings for Sabbaths, dedications, vows, healings, and other occasions. During festivals so many offerings were presented the priests were almost overwhelmed with their duties. But they discharged them faithfully.

Do we offer worship faithfully? Acceptably? For that, and to avoid offering self-appointed "Cain" worship,[2] we must first know which offerings God desires. So let's examine His Word to identify some of them.

Since we present all our offerings in our bodily temples, we should first offer up our "temple" itself. Paul requests a "living sacrifice," our redeemed bodies and renewed minds wholly yielded to Christ daily, hourly (Rom. 12:1). Then all day long our joyful walk with Jesus becomes a living demonstration of God's good will for mankind (v. 2).

Every act of obedience rendered in our yielded bodies further "slays" our self-will, rendering our compliance an offering. Thus to obey is to offer worship.

We should offer a "sacrifice of praise to God continually...the fruit of our lips giving thanks to his name" (Heb. 13:15), whether by songs[3] of praise and worship or by the simple but powerful habit of giving thanks (1 Thess. 5:18; Eph. 5:19–20, Col. 3:17).[4]

Offerings of intercession are vitally important, sustaining our families, fellow believers, churches, ministries, and leaders. Paul and Peter urged us to offer these "spiritual sacrifices" for others (1 Pet. 2:5; Eph. 6:18–19; 1 Tim. 2:1–4).

Our service is an offering. "Whatever" we do "heartily, as unto the Lord" (Col. 3:23) is thereby sanctified as a sacrifice, whether it's our vocation, profession, ministry, or duty: "Your faithful service is an offering to God" (Phil. 2:17, NLT).

Monetary and material gifts given to God's work or the poor are offerings. Paul compared the Philippians' financial gift to incense accompanying a sacrifice: "A lovely fragrance, a sacrifice that pleases the very heart of God" (Phil. 4:18, PHILLIPS).[5]

All good deeds—hospitality, assistance in distress, mercy, etc.—rendered for love of the Savior and souls are acceptable sacrifices: "Do not forget to do good...with such sacrifices God is well pleased" (Heb. 13:16, NKJV).

All Christian fellowship, including loving communications, is a worthy offering to God, especially when our fellow Christians are suffering or lonely: "To share [communications]"[6] with others pleases God (v. 16).

The Christians we faithfully evangelize, disciple, counsel, or pray into a close walk with Jesus are an offering to Christ (Rom. 15:16). With Paul, we'll rejoice when our believer-offerings are presented to Him in heaven (1 Thess. 2:19; Col. 1:28).

Every cross carried—or unjust rejection accepted for the sake of Christ's righteousness, Word, or call—becomes a sacrifice of suffering (Phil. 1:29). Every cross rejected—by resisting it or compromising to avoid opposition—becomes an offering refused.

Martyrdom is the ultimate offering. Paul described his approaching execution for Christ's sake as a "drink offering" (Phil. 2:17, NIV). Thousands since have quietly poured out their last breath to Christ rather than deny His deity, truth, or call. All these offerings are sacrificial acts.

They cost Christians something. Assisted by God's grace, ordinary believer-priests just like us surrender things they love to please, serve, and glorify by worship One they love more. To show their supreme adoration for Him, they abandon things they value: their rights, time, energy, preferred activities, money, goods, privacy, leisure, people's approval, easy circumstances, a peaceful life, or their very existence on earth! Though costly, they willingly pay these sacrifices to show how much they cherish their King. Thus they let go of something near and dear to draw nearer their dearest One in worship.

These sacrifices are offered voluntarily, never forced. They're offered to please God, not impress men. They win not worldly recognition but divine favor, re-anointings, intimacy, insights, and power. While not saving our souls, they nevertheless help transform our characters into the image of our High Priest, who "gave Himself" to His Father on the cross to save us all (Titus 2:14). Having free wills, we don't have to offer them—but we'll never be like our High Priest unless we do so. And often.

So as believer-priests serving in the temple of the church, let's offer God these sacrifices daily: our bodies, obedience, praise, thanksgiving, intercession, money, material gifts, good deeds, fellowship, converts, disciples, crosses, our earthly lives. Are you disregarding or discharging this sacred duty? Are you a forgetful or faithful believer-priest? Today be faithful. Bring your offering!

Chapter 113

STRENGTH TO SUFFER WELL

*P*AUL PRAYED THAT the Philippians would be "strengthened" according to God's "glorious power" (Col. 1:11). "Power," or (Greek) *dynamis,* describes God's miraculous power, strength, or ability. Why this request?

We need God's power to consistently overrule our old nature, obey God fully, serve Him effectively, and, for those so gifted, work miracles— all to advance the gospel, build the kingdom, and honor Christ. But Paul requested a different manifestation of power, the strength to be patient, joyful, and thankful while suffering—or the strength to suffer well: "[That you might be] strengthened with all might, according to his glorious power, unto all patience and long-suffering with joyfulness; giving thanks..." (vv. 11–12). Today we wouldn't ask for this.

We would want a more positive power. We want strength for success—in our business, professional, ministerial, political, athletic, or other desirable pursuits. We certainly need this, but Paul knew we also need strength for suffering.[1] Why?

Without it we'll falter in our trials, dishonor Christ, and be disapproved for greater service. With it we'll "stand fast" as Scripture repeatedly urges,[2] unmoved by adversities and adversaries, and set good examples, be transformed into Christ's image,[3] qualify for greater authority, and honor and delight Christ, who loves overcomers!

Since such "stands" honor Christ, Paul calls the strength that fuels them His "glorious power"—the suffering strength that glorifies Jesus. The Bible, Israel's history, church history, and current Christian experience outside America[4] spotlight this grace. Paul incarnated it and glorified Christ by suffering well often.[5] As we suffer well, consistently trusting and obeying God in hard situations, our heart is purified, loyalty proven, devotion enhanced, commitment to Christ strengthened, discernment sharpened, ministry gifts honed, besetting sins purged, and Christlike characters forged. This prepares us to live and reign with Christ forever.

That's why Jesus and His apostles urged us to suffer well.[6] It's also why Jesus ordered the church to receive the Spirit's fullness. He knew only "power from on high" (Luke 24:49) would give us His strength on earth—to suffer or succeed. Acts repeatedly confirms this.

The apostles' power gift successfully healed a lame beggar. Moments later the same *dynamis* enabled them to suffer well while wrongfully arrested, jailed, and threatened by Israel's most powerful council (Acts 3–5). Repeatedly Acts shows empowered Christians both ministering effectively and suffering well, as conversions or miracles led to adversity, and adversity, when endured well, led to more conversions and miracles. Let's go deeper.

Specifically, God's power enables us to suffer:

- PATIENTLY. At Cherith Elijah waited patiently for God's guidance, even after his brook dried up—because of the very message he had faithfully proclaimed (1 Kings 17:1, 2–9)!

- PEACEFULLY. Daniel's peace was so deep he slept in an enclosed underground cell—filled with anxiously hungry lions!

- POWERFULLY. Psalms promises God will enable those who steadily seek and praise Him to grow ever stronger—even in "valleys" of sorrow (Ps. 84:4–7)!

- PERSEVERINGLY. The Philadelphian Christians had such fortitude they persevered in their Christian walk and work for years—despite the ongoing slander of local Jews (Rev. 3:10, NAS)!

- PRAISEFULLY. In Philippi Paul and Silas lifted their voices to again praise God late one night—while illegally humiliated, beaten, lacerated, and jailed in a dark, filthy dungeon (Acts 16:16–25)!

- PROLIFICALLY. As the early church endured centuries of periodic Roman persecutions, many pagans, deeply impressed by their strength in suffering, converted.

- PRODUCTIVELY. While imprisoned by the Nazis, Corrie and Betsie ten Boom faithfully led secret, inspiring Bible studies daily—in flea- and lice-infested barracks![7]

- PROPHETICALLY. Joseph, Daniel, Jeremiah, and the apostle John continued receiving powerful prophecies—while enduring prisons, exile, pits, and other indignities!

- WITHOUT PANIC. Without the Spirit's full strength Peter
  panicked under pressure during Jesus' trial; with it he
  remained perfectly poised—sleeping deeply the night
  before his scheduled execution (Acts 12:4–6)!

With the Spirit's help, we too may suffer well. Sadly, many good Christians suffer poorly.

They complain, lash out at others, become offended with Christ, and indulge self-pity. Or they worry constantly, doubt God's faithfulness, and turn from devotion and duty to worldly distractions or sins. If we're still manifesting these symptoms in adversity, it's time we pray to be "strengthened with all might" with God's glorious suffering power.

What are you suffering today? Whatever difficulties, injustices, hardships, griefs, burdens, pains, or delays try you, God's strength for suffering is greater.[8] You already seek God's strength for success, but that's mostly self-serving. Broaden your concept and experience of the power of God. Begin asking for and receiving the additional Christ-honoring strength to suffer well.

Chapter 114

QUAKEPROOF!

G OD HAS PROMISED to shake everything in these last days so that only what He has made—quakeproof things[1]—may remain:

> Yet once more I shake not the earth only, but also heaven... [signifying] the removing of those things that are shaken, as of things that are [man-]made, that those things which cannot be shaken may remain... a kingdom which cannot be moved.
> —HEBREWS 12:26–28[2]

Thus men's temporal works and kingdoms will fall and God's eternal kingdom and works remain—in the last days. But not only then. In the first century, Colossae was also about to be rocked.

When the apostle Paul wrote the Colossians, unbeknownst to him and them, a powerful earthquake was soon to level their city, leaving it a small village without a significant Christian presence.[3] (This explains why Jesus didn't address the Colossians among the churches of Asia Minor thirty-five years later; Rev. 2–3.) Though Paul didn't know devastation was coming, the omniscient Holy Spirit did. So let's review how the message He inspired Paul to send to the Colossians prepared them for impending disaster.

Initially He prompted Paul to refute the various heresies troubling them, knowing their houses of character, family, and worship couldn't stand if built on error (Col. 2:1–23).[4] The rest of his epistle gives practical instructions and warnings that, if heeded, would make them spiritually quakeproof, strong and stable enough to withstand any shaking.

Paul commended their faith, hope, and love so they would continue growing in these key Christian virtues (Col. 1:3–8). He prayed they would be "filled" with the knowledge of God's plan, wisdom, and spiritual insight, live "worthy" lives full of good works, and be "strengthened" to endure long tests with joy and thanksgiving (vv. 9–12).

He reminded them the goal of Christ's passion was to "present" them to Himself in heaven, mature, "holy, and unblamable" (Col. 1:20–22).[5] Therefore, they should "walk" in union with Him now on earth (Col. 2:6), not apathetically but joyfully, "abounding with thanksgiving"

(v. 7). Since Christ is holy, they should "mortify" illicit sexual activity and covetousness—or face God's anger (Col. 3:5–6). They should also "put off" wrong emotions, attitudes, and speech and steadily "put on" the knowledge, attitudes, and ways Christ taught (vv. 7–10).

Since there are no class distinctions in Christ, they should humbly love and respect all Christians (Col. 3:11–14). They should be thankful for God's peace within and let it rule their life decisions (v. 15). They should stay full of God's Word, exhort one another, praise and worship Christ in song, and do everything "heartily," as if Christ requested it (vv. 16–17, 23). They should discharge all family and occupational duties for Christ's honor (vv. 18–23). Knowing they'll face Christ's judgment, employers should treat their employees fairly (Col. 4:1).

They should use their time well, speak with grace and wisdom, and faithfully fulfill their ministries (Col. 4:5–6, 17). They should "continue in prayer" daily, watching and giving thanks for answers (v. 2). They should ask for opportunities to share Christ and His Word—especially for their ministers (vv. 3–4)—and grace to "stand perfect and complete" in all God's will (v. 12). All these preparations were driven by Paul's central theme.

Faithfully he aimed that arrow of truth at their hearts. To be quakeproof, they must fix and refix their innermost desires and thoughts on heavenly, not worldly, things: "Seek those things which are above, where Christ sitteth…Set your affection on things above, not on things on the earth" (Col. 3:1–2). Only these life-goals would carry them through great distresses and prepare them to be "with him [Christ] in glory" when He appeared (v. 4). Why did the Spirit order them not to love or crave the things of this world but seek first the eternal goals of Christ's kingdom? Their world, with all its possessions and cherished lifestyle, was about to be shaken. Suddenly. Strongly. Without recovery.

Though two thousand years removed, the Colossians' situation parallels ours. We too are about to be rocked in these last days.

God's going to shake His churches until our errors, sins, and love of this world fall away—or we fall. He's going to shake America until it again acknowledges His existence, creatorship, and authoritative Word and stops justifying abortion and celebrating homosexuality—or it collapses. After the church is taken, He'll shake the world for seven years until sinners come to Christ—or fall with the Antichrist. When the shaking finally stops, only Christ's kingdom will remain standing—and quakeproof Christians! Feel the tremors beginning?

Don't be afraid. God's sending this rumbling. He'll use every ecclesiastical, national, and international distress to ultimately accomplish His good plan. Meanwhile, obey the Spirit's detailed instructions to the Colossians. Be quakeproof!

Chapter 115

GET PRESENTABLE!

*I*KNOW MY PASSION and you know yours, but what about Jesus? What's His passion—the burning desire and eager hope that drives Him?[1]

It's the presentation of His bride church in heaven. Jesus died to not only save us but also make us ready for eternal union with Him. This highest bliss begins when the Holy Spirit officially presents the church to Christ in heaven. Nine New Testament references describe this, the great climax of church history.

The apostle Paul revealed the presentation will occur after the resurrection of Christians at the Rapture: "He who raised up the Lord Jesus shall raise up us also...and shall present us with you" (2 Cor. 4:14). All presented Christians will be chaste and pure: "I have espoused you to one husband, that I may present you as a chaste virgin to Christ" (2 Cor. 11:2). This presentation is the goal of the teaching, testing, and sanctification processes we're presently undergoing: "That he might sanctify and cleanse it with the washing of water by the word; that he might present it to himself a glorious church, not having spot, or wrinkle...but...holy" (Eph. 5:26–27). Again, Christ expressly reconciled us "to present you holy and unblamable and unreprovable in his sight" (Col. 1:22). Paul taught Christians God's wisdom, hoping to "present every man perfect in Christ Jesus" (v. 28).[2] As if anticipating our fears that we'll never become ready for presentation to Christ, Jude asserted Christ was "able to keep you from falling, and to present you faultless before the presence of his glory" (Jude 24). Fivefold ministers, who are Christ's love-gifts given to mature His church, will stand by at the presentation, rejoicing and receiving rewards for their labors: "For what is our hope...or crown of rejoicing? Are not even ye in the presence of [or being presented to] our Lord Jesus Christ at his coming?" (1 Thess. 2:19). There's more.

Jesus added we should watch, pray, and live spiritually worthy lives so we can "stand before the Son of man" at the presentation (Luke 21:36). The apostle John foresaw the presentation preceding or accompanying the joyous, heavenly "marriage supper of the Lamb" (Rev. 19:7–9). We must trustingly and obediently cooperate with God's grace to "make ourselves ready" for this presentation (Rev. 19:7).[3] Are we ready? Are we presentable?

If guests visit at odd hours of the night, they may ask us, "Are you presentable, or sufficiently dressed and groomed to receive us?" Our royal guest and bridegroom, Jesus, will appear "at an hour when you do not expect him" (Luke 12:40, NIV). So we need to always be presentable. All brides, ancient and modern, want to be at their very best when presented to their grooms. Thus motivated, they go to work on themselves.

They protect their purity by remaining faithful, rejecting other suitors and, in ancient times, veiling themselves in public. They diligently cleanse their skin to remove blemishes and soften it with oils and creams.[4] They give special attention to their hair, washing, trimming, and brushing it to perfection. Modern brides often get physically fit, dieting and exercising to shed excess pounds. Most brides choose a beautiful white dress, sometimes embroidered with silk, silver, or gold thread.[5] They adorn themselves with their best jewelry[6] and apply sweet fragrances.[7] Ancient Jewish brides watched eagerly round-the-clock for their presentation time—the sudden, unannounced appearing of their beloved.

How can we, like these Jewish and Gentile brides, "make ourselves ready"? Here are some suggestions.

Cultivate devotion to Jesus and keep your heart pure. Abandon all besetting sins. Soften your heart by showing God's mercy. Shed the distractions and hindrances that weigh you down. Weave a beautiful wedding dress embroidered with your righteous acts of obedience to Christ's teachings. Mine the jewels of Bible truth and gold of proven faith and adorn yourself by living and sharing them. Commune and worship in Christ's presence regularly until you're bathed in the sweet fragrance of His graciousness. Watch daily and eagerly for the signs of His coming. Then you'll be prepared for presentation—and a delight to the Holy Spirit. Why?

His prime responsibility in this age is to make Christians presentable.[8] He's on a mission, passionately focused and diligently working toward this great goal. Sadly, too many Christians are on vacation, living for themselves, maximizing their personal pleasures, and minimizing their spiritual duties. Tragically, some have retired. They've abandoned God's call to the presentation, given up hope, and given themselves over to wasting time. Don't waste yours.

Seek the Spirit's passion. End your spiritual vacation. Come out of retirement. Launch your own mission. Get presentable!

Chapter 116

THE COHERER

COHERER IS SOMETHING or someone that holds things together. Paul reveals all creation is being held together, or sustained, not by random force but by Redeemer force: "By him [Jesus] all things consist" (Col. 1:17), or "all coheres in Him" (MOFFATT). The original language is illuminating.

The Greek word for "consist" means, "hold together in proper place or arrangement."[1] So Jesus is personally holding "all things" together—the universe, natural world, spiritual world, social order, and the church—in the place and arrangement God has ordained for this time (v. 16). Why? To fulfill His Word, specifically His promises, prophecies, and plan.[2] Omnipotent, nothing escapes His benevolent control (Rom. 8:28, NAS). History agrees.

Repeatedly history shows the Coherer holding things together when it seemed certain they would fall to pieces. The Gospels and Acts showcase this.

When Jesus' disciples were divided as to who would be the greatest, He reunited them by teaching them their need for humility. When their faith collapsed while crossing a stormy Lake Galilee, He reestablished them by halting the turbulence and exhorting them to keep trusting His presence, promise, and power even when He seemed indifferent. When they were offended, frightened, and scattered after His crucifixion, He regrouped them with a series of special appearances, messages, and miracles. When the young church's unity unraveled due to their old prejudices, He moved the apostles to quickly restore unity by correcting the injustices. When the Judaizers spread their divisive "Jews-only" teaching in the churches, He used Paul's skilled teaching and brave peacemaking to mend the growing Jewish-Gentile rift. Down the centuries, whenever the church was on the brink of utter sinfulness, confusion, impotence, and dryness, He intervened with reformations or revivals to restore its life and fruitfulness. He's still holding His true body together, despite all our superficial divisions. And He's always held the world and its nations together.

When proud kingdoms or nations aggressed others, He eventually defeated them. When despots oppressed their subjects, in due time He removed or overthrew them. When America experienced great crises—the Revolutionary War, Civil War, Great Depression, civil rights movement—He carefully controlled events to sustain this nation as a sanctuary for Christianity and force for good in the world. When two great world wars erupted, He turned key battles at crucial moments to keep His worldwide prophetic plan on schedule.[3] When chemical, biological, and nuclear weapons emerged, He moved world leaders to limit their development to avert global annihilation.[4]

On a more personal level, He holds individuals, marriages, families, and churches together.

For instance, when the pressures of continuing multiple trials make us feel we're coming unglued, He rebinds our souls with timely Scripture readings, sermons, counsels, fellowship, good news, answers to prayer, renewed hope, and refillings of His Spirit. When our marriages are troubled, He has older, wiser believers offer words of wisdom that help us recover the unselfish love that fosters sweet marital unity. When bad attitudes and arguments spoil our family's peace, Christ convicts troublemakers and prompts peacemakers to prayerfully and patiently work things out.[5] When sin, heresy, insubordination, or other factors divide churches, Christ inspires spiritually minded leaders to point out biblical solutions, urge humble cooperation, and take the necessary steps, however challenging, to heal the divisions.[6] Unchanging, His cohesive work continues.

Today He's still holding everything together to facilitate His grand end-time plan. Remember this the next time a sudden crisis, loss, defeat, or disillusionment, from nearby or distant causes, makes you feel your life is coming unglued.

And if to further test and perfect your faith, He lets things come apart,[7] He'll still be there, faithfully holding *you* together and making your faith an inspiration to others until restoration comes (Isa. 41:10). Thus you will become a little coherer, like Peter, and "strengthen thy brethren" (Luke 22:32). Remember, you're the key—your decision to trust the Coherer's unfailing faithfulness is crucial.[8] But you're not the Coherer!

So when everything is "shaken to the core" (Ps. 82:5, NLT), don't try to hold it together with your wisdom, strength, and influence alone. Go to Christ, who "holds everything together" (Col. 1:17, GW). He's sustaining the world; can't He also hold your life, marriage, family, church, or ministry together? Ask Him to restore whatever's failing to its "proper place or arrangement" to honor Him and serve His plan. Then trust Him. "Let not your heart be troubled, neither let it be afraid…believe also in me" (John 14:1–2). Rest, knowing, "The one who trusts [Him] will never be dismayed" (Isa. 28:16, NIV). And one more thing.

Whenever He calls, guides, prompts, or checks you, cooperate with the Coherer.

Chapter 117

WANT TO MINISTER?

*W*ANT TO MINISTER? Every Christian should want to share Christ and His Word with others. But we're not all equally effective ministers.[1]

When sharing scriptural truths, some of us only inform; others inspire. Some dispense God's living truths with deadness of spirit; others teach the same with spiritual life. Some explain only the letter of the Word; others open encouraging insights. Some are polished yet powerless speakers; others aren't so polished, yet release reviving power. What's the difference? Why is one's ministry so ordinary and the other's so extraordinary? What makes one's so dead and the other's so dynamic and nourishing?

While there may be many reasons, here's one. One minister has academic biblical preparation only—and may we all become biblical scholars! The other has this plus something more: a deep, thorough, experiential preparation in biblical living in the divinely accredited School of the Spirit. The apostles formed the first graduating class in this institution of higher learning and deeper character formation.

Jesus called Peter and the other apostles to minister, or "Feed my sheep" (John 21:16). With what did the original apostles feed His people? They taught and counseled Christ's sayings, parables, prophecies, life experiences, and the Old Testament as He had often opened it to them (Luke 24:27, 32). But that wasn't all. They themselves—their exemplary devotion, disposition, love, faith, patience, diligence, long-suffering, joy, and faithfulness to Christ's teaching—became spiritual food and drink for Christ's sheep. Admittedly, this is mystical. How can Christians "feed" on their ministers?

To clarify, let's see how the preparation of essential Jewish foods parallels God's preparation of spiritually nourishing ministers, whether clergymen or laymen. Let's revisit first-century Jewish culture.

To produce large quantities of flour for bread, Jewish farmers ground wheat kernels between two heavy millstones often turned by donkeys.[2] To generate oil, they placed olives in a stone basin and split them under a rolling millstone. Then they extracted their pits, wrapped the olives in cloths, and placed them under a large, stone pillar ("olive press") whose crushing weight gradually pressed out all their precious oil.[3] To make wine, they placed grapes in a stone winepress and trampled them under their bare feet. Grinding, crushing, trampling—these processes were necessary to nourish the Jews with bread, oil, and wine. The apostles, and all the other Christians who ministered so effectively in the early church, experienced their own grinding, crushing, and trampling experiences.[4] So did Joseph centuries earlier.

Betrayal by his brothers, separation from his father, forced emigration, slavery, injustice, a lengthy prison stay, loneliness, abandonment—these powerful processes prepared Joseph for powerful ministry. Driven by stubborn (mulish) enemies, these mills ground his human pride, crushed his natural hopes, and trampled his human rights. Yet because he refused to be offended and kept trusting and obeying God, God used these destructive experiences to construct the character of "Zaphenath-paneah" (Gen. 41:45), "the giver of the nourishment of the land."[5] Thereafter he ministered exceptionally, giving life-saving interpretations, insights, counsel, leadership, and nourishment. His granaries fed the world, and his example and words have nourished believers' faith, refreshed our hope, and gladdened our hearts for centuries.[6] Thus his experiential preparation—the grinding, crushing, and trampling—made him a dynamic minister.

Are you undergoing experiential preparation? Are mulish people grinding on your nerves daily? Are heavy griefs, sorrows, or troubles "pressing" you? Are stony-hearted people trampling your rights at home, work, church, or in the courts? Don't rebel! Submit under God's mighty hand. Without grinding, crushing, and trampling, modern Christians, like ancient Jews, will starve! Your reaction is crucial. Joseph, the apostles, and the early Christians all learned to see God in their "mills" and kept patiently trusting and obeying Him.

So accept your adversities as being God's way of forming Christ's character in you and preparing you to minister dynamically. Don't fret over when they'll end. Just be sure to please God, carefully obeying His Word, guidance, and correction in your experiential "schools." Learn your lessons well and make excellent grades in your daily tests. Then, whether you're a layman or cleric, your teachings, counsels, fellowship, and life example will nourish, sustain, and inspire Christ's sheep. Exceptionally!

The exceptional Oswald Chambers said it best: "Pain must ever be the price of power."[7] Indeed we must bleed to bless, suffer to succor, die to impart life, and bear burdens to relieve them. So don't just study and lecture Bible truths; live them every day. Endure your grinding, crushing, and trampling however long God chooses to educate you, confident a wonderful graduation day is coming.[8]

Now that you're better informed, I ask again, want to minister?

Chapter 118

BACK TO BETHEL!

RISE, GO UP to Bethel, and dwell there"—with these words God called Jacob to return to full fellowship with Him (Gen. 35:1). Why this command? Let's review Jacob's history.

Though well born and bred in a godly home, Jacob's life didn't begin well. After stealing his father's blessing from his brother Esau, he fled to Syria. But on the way God appeared at Bethel[1] to graciously offer Jacob a wonderful relationship with Him (Gen. 28:10–22). Instead of walking with God, however, Jacob wandered from Him spiritually...for twenty years.

Then family trouble arose (Gen. 31:1–2). Immediately God called Jacob to return to Bethel (v. 3).[2] Jacob responded, but then stopped short. After God helped him through the terrifying crisis of facing Esau, Jacob settled down, first at Succoth, then in Shechem, well north of Bethel. There disaster rudely awakened him from his sleep of procrastination.[3] His daughter, Dinah, was raped, and his sons retaliated, killing all Shechem's men (Gen. 34). Suddenly Jacob's comfortably independent, self-constructed world was collapsing around him. Then God spoke, "Arise, go to Bethel." Why did Jacob wander? And why do we?

Believers have two natures. Our new Christ nature, humble and loving, hungers to draw near God and live spiritually dependent upon Him. Our old nature, proud and self-centered, is habitually reluctant to draw near, preferring to wander independently and keep God at a distance—unless we need Him. If so, we return for help, and after God graciously helps us with our "Esaus," we wander away again. This was Jacob's problem, and it's ours. What awaited Jacob at Bethel?

Bethel, meaning "house of God," represents living very close to God, in Him really, a life steadily immersed in fellowship with God. Let's examine the Bethel life.

Jacob found God there by grace. While fleeing his shameful sin, seeking escape, not God, God sovereignly met him, revealing Himself in a genuine conversion experience (Gen. 28:13). Bethel became Jacob's "gate of heaven," where he envisioned Christ, our "new and living way" of life and prayer, represented as a ladder from heaven to earth (vv. 12, 17).[4]

Jacob found new hope, as God promised him a much better future (vv. 13–15). His dreams changed. For the first time this self-centered young man dreamed of fulfilling God's purpose, not his, in life (vv. 12–15). God gave him precious promises of a good land, large family, and world-blessing destiny (vv. 13–15). And Jacob believed God's promises and began recognizing His presence, hand, and voice (v. 16; Gen. 35:15). Awestruck in God's presence, Jacob began fearing God and worshipping Him (Gen. 28:17–19). He also committed his life to God (vv. 20–22).[5] Thus at Bethel all the essential elements of walking with God—saving grace, personal conversion, faith, prayer, promises, worship, and commitment—appeared in this wayward wanderer. But they didn't last. Jacob preferred wandering to worshipping—and he kept clinging to idols.

But after God's shock treatment at Shechem, Jacob promptly expelled the idols from his life and family and returned straight to Bethel (Gen. 35:2–6). God responded as quickly, restoring Jacob's authority (v. 4), neutralizing his enemies (v. 5), pardoning his sons (v. 5), reappearing to him (vv. 9–13), increasing His promised blessings (v. 11), and changing Jacob's name to confirm his change of character: the untrustworthy wanderer Jacob was now the princely worshipper Israel (v. 10). He remained so, walking closely with God, the rest of his life. God's message to us?

Like Jacob, through our stubbornly independent pride, we tend to wander first and worship later—until God scares us with Esaus or shocks us at Shechems.[6] Then we stop procrastinating and begin pursuing the Bethel life. But we don't have to relive Jacob's folly.

Have you:

- Heard God's call to the Bethel life but procrastinated?

- Become comfortable living near God—dutifully attending church—but not in Him, not seriously pursuing close fellowship with Him?

- Often felt you should seek the Lord more in Bible study, prayer, and worship…yet you've repeatedly chosen to continue wandering in selfish independence, worldly idol-loves, or shallow, do-as-little-as-possible Christianity?

If so, like Jacob, you're living in the dangerous self-deception of Shechem and endangering yourself and your family by spiritual procrastination. It's time to put away your idols and go all the way home to the Christ of your conversion. And "dwell there"—believing God's promises and seeking Him, praying, worshipping, and keeping your commitments daily—until He returns for His "Israel," or princely,[7] church. Ask God to circumcise your wandering nature and strengthen your worshipping heart.

Or, if you're already living the Bethel life, pray with Abrahamic persistence for friends and loved ones still wandering until they return from Shechem...or Sodom.[8] And don't delay.

It's time to get back to Bethel!

Chapter 119

REVIVAL READINESS

*E*VERYWHERE CHRISTIANS DESIRE revival. We want God to revisit us with His Spirit's abundant life and power. We want
to experience His glory—Jesus ministering among us by His
Spirit through His body as in the early church. But revival power requires revival readiness.

For that we need a "broken and contrite heart" (Ps. 51:17). This condition alone enables God to come and breathe new life and power into
our lifeless walk, listless work, and lukewarm churches. Yearning to do
so, God calls us to revival readiness:[1]

> I dwell…with him also who is of a contrite and humble spirit,
> to revive the spirit of the humble…to revive the heart of the
> contrite ones.
>
> —ISAIAH 57:15

No random condition, the contrite heart is a direct result of a "broken spirit," and God greatly desires it: "Thou desirest not [animal] sacrifice…the sacrifices of [desired by] God are a broken spirit; a broken and
a contrite heart…thou wilt not despise" (Ps. 51:16–17). Some may wonder,
does God really want us "broken"? Does He prefer shattered, depressed,
aimless Christians?

Absolutely not! It's our stubborn pride, with all its self-assertive resistance to His will, that God seeks to shatter and crush.[2]

We see the defiant obstinacy of this unbroken spirit in Pharaoh, who
wouldn't obey God; Thomas, who wouldn't believe God; Nebuchadnezzar,
who wouldn't credit God for his success; King Saul, who wouldn't confess
his sins; Ahimaaz, who wouldn't wait God's time to serve; and the unjust
judge, who wouldn't help an oppressed woman. Unwilling to approve or
use such spiritual adamancy, God urges us not to follow their examples.

"Be ye not like the horse, or like the mule, that have no understanding" (Ps. 32:9). Unbroken horses are typically unruly and self-willed.
Many mules are stubborn with a mind of their own. Neither responds
well to their owners' authority. Therefore they're hard to guide and use
effectively (v. 8)—until they're broken.

Like them, our selfish pride, with its tendency to assert its will against

God's, must be broken—until we consistently respond easily to God's authority. God uses human authorities to break our resistance to authority and train us for His use. While we're children, He uses parents; while students, principals and teachers. As citizens, we find He uses government leaders and policemen; as employees, employers; as Christians, ministers. Why these providential trainers? God knows if we resist human authorities, we'll resist heavenly authority (Rom. 13:1–7). He also sends other "breakers," or divinely designed breaking processes.

Conviction of sin leaves us contrite. Job testified of this.[3] The defeat of self-chosen plans shatters self-confident pride. David was humbled when God struck Uzzah. Failing under temptation breaks us. Peter wept bitterly after denying Christ. Impending judgment shatters us. After seeing God's angel with drawn sword before him, Balaam meekly vowed to reverse his steps. God's full, manifest presence breaks us. Beholding the Holy One, Isaiah wailed over his unclean lips. Long-suffering, with its many wounds, griefs, and oppressions, grinds us to dust. After years of suffering, Joseph emerged thoroughly meek in thought and word: "It is not in me; God will give Pharaoh an answer."[4] Identification with the suffering of God's people softens us. Upon hearing of Jerusalem's disrepair and reproach, Nehemiah was undone with brokenheartedness.

These situational breakers leave our old man finished and our new man "free...free indeed" (John 8:32, 36). With our high-minded pride worn down to a healthily low meekness, we can now "walk humbly with thy God" (Mic. 6:8), totally surrendered to His will, ready to fully trust and obey Him, and sensitive and responsive to whatever pleases Him. It's this resulting condition God desires, not the breaking; not the shattering, but the sweetness of spirit that follows. Why? It enables Christ to minister through us.

With the husk of pride broken off, the Christ-kernel in us produces spiritual bread-truths that feed others' faith. With our thin grape skin of vanity broken, the Spirit's sweet water gushes out and becomes wine that satisfies others' spiritual thirst. With the hard pit of self-will removed, the healing oil of powerful ministry flows out. If we're broken!

That can occur easily or not so easily. We can voluntarily smash our stubborn pride by consistently obeying God, as Jesus did (Phil. 2:5–8, NAS). If not, God's breakers will continue visiting us. But even this is His love; He wants to revive us!

Experiencing a breaking process? Reacting to your breakers or authorities with horse-like or mulish attitudes? Or with a "broken and contrite" spirit? Your deliverance—and path to revival power—needn't be hard. Surrender now! Yield wholly to God's will and obtain revival readiness.

Chapter 120

CONSTANT COMFORTERS

*J*ESUS REPEATEDLY CALLED the Holy Spirit "the Comforter" (John 14:16).[1] Therefore the more the Spirit fills us, the more we become comforters—Christians who relieve others' sufferings.

Twice the apostle Paul wrote of comforting the Colossians: "I would that ye knew what great conflict I have for you, and for...Laodicea...that their [and your] hearts might be comforted" (Col. 2:1–2); and, "All my state [situation] shall Tychicus declare unto you...whom I have sent...that he might...comfort your hearts" (Col. 4:7–8). No isolated example, Paul regularly comforted others.

He risked persecution to bring Gentile churches' donations to Jerusalem to comfort their poor Jewish brothers. When greatly needing Epaphroditus' help himself, he sent him instead to the Philippians to relieve their fears that Epaphroditus had died (Phil. 2:25–28). Though exhausted, wet, and cold, Paul helped build a fire on Malta's beach to warm his fellow shipmates (Acts 28:1–3). To prevent the panicking Philippian jailer's suicide, he quickly informed him no prisoners had escaped (Acts 16:27–28). Once released, he went straight to Lydia's house to calm the church's fears for his safety (Acts 16:40). These examples reveal Paul the constant comforter.

Similarly, God wants us to steadily exert comforting influence. Truly Spirit-filled Christians do so.

Their faith restores doubters. Their intercessions refresh overburdened ones. Their hope cheers the discouraged. Their spiritual thinking soothes the agitated. Their friendliness consoles rejected ones. Their insights clear up the perplexed. Their patience steadies the impatient. Their peacemaking calms contentious ones. Their assistance relieves the overworked. Their knowledge satisfies truth seekers. Their loyal friendship heals the betrayed. Their honesty reassures the defrauded. Thus the comforting Spirit in them comforts others.

Knowing the Comforter is the "Spirit of truth," and "the truth shall make you free," they often comfort others by simply presenting the truth—God's Word or the facts of the matter at hand—which, when obeyed or accepted, frees from stress and creates peace (John 14:16–17, 26; 8:32).

By calling the Comforter the "Spirit of truth," Jesus implied truth comforts. Just to know the truth (God's Word) relieves us from the burden of ignorance and bonds of false teaching. Obeying the truth further strengthens our God-confidence, thus reducing our unsettling uncertainties.

The Spirit also comforts by teaching us deeper insights from God's Word (Luke 24:27, 32). "Understanding [insight] shall keep thee" calm and sure in turbulent situations (Prov. 2:11). So biblical insight comforts.

The Comforter also brings God's comforting Word[2] to mind just when we need it. So biblical recall comforts.[3]

Paradoxically, conviction comforts. By convicting us when we sin, the Spirit leads us straight to repentance, where the sweet relief of restored fellowship with God replaces the uneasiness of sin. And there are many more "comfort[s] of the Holy Spirit" (Acts 9:31) that save us from the agitations of sin and self-centered living—if we abide near Christ.

If we don't, instead of receiving and ministering comforts, we fret and agitate others by our bad attitudes, ungracious speech, selfish decisions, and offensive actions and reactions. Sadly, not the Comforter but the troubler works through us. And our commission is unfulfilled.

We're called to represent "the God of all comfort" who faithfully "comforteth those that are cast down" (2 Cor. 1:3; 7:6). So comforting others is part of our mission mandate: as we preach the gospel, teach all nations, and bear witness of Christ, we comfort sinners and saints daily by:

- Fellowship, especially in trying times
- Sharing God's Word
- Teaching biblical prophecy
- Sharing experiential insights
- Reconciling with penitents seeking our forgiveness
- Exhorting discouraged Christians
- Assisting suffering Christians
- Quickly sharing good news
- Prophecy, if so gifted
- Reassuring others of Christ's appearing[4]

This consoling work is doubly rewarding. First, we're comforted by seeing our words or works relieve others (2 Cor. 7:13). Second, we reap what we sow: God gives faithful comforters many faithful comforts.[5] Are you faithfully comforting others?

As there are different levels of the Spirit's fullness,[6] so we have different kinds of influence—compassionate, callous, cruel. Our influence is determined by the regularity with which we yield to the Spirit or to sin and self. What's our characteristic influence?

Are we usually cruel—hurting instead of comforting others? Callous—indifferent to others' sufferings? Or compassionate—promptly relieving others' stresses whenever possible? Clearly, Jesus wants us so full of the Comforter that compassionate rivers of relief flow through us daily. Hourly. Constantly.

So ask the Comforter to refill you. Stay full by staying close to Jesus—full of God's Word, prayer, worship, thanksgiving, and by quickly confessing sins. Ease others' sufferings whenever possible. Then, like Paul, you'll be one of Jesus' constant comforters.

Chapter 121

SPIRITUAL MATURITY—IN DETAIL

AUL INFORMED THE Colossians his overarching purpose in ministry was to "present every man perfect [spiritually mature] in Christ Jesus" (Col. 1:28). Thus his entire ministry, including his epistles, was aimed at this lofty ideal of spiritual maturity.

Colossians highlights this. Paul's opening prayer unquestionably targets spiritual maturity (Col. 1:9–14). His description of Jesus' awesome creatorship and preeminence (vv. 15–19), his revelation that the same One lives "in" us (v. 27), and his preview of our coming presentation to Him in heaven (vv. 22–23, 28) inspires the kind of faith and obedience that produces spiritual maturity. The rest of Colossians (chapters 2–4) expounds this theme, giving us a detailed description of spiritual maturity as Paul lived and taught it.

Christians who are "perfect"—consistently spiritually mature—are "knit together" with other Christians by brotherly love (Col. 2:2). Rich biblical insights have richly assured them of God's faithful character and perfect plan (v. 2). They're confident all wisdom is hidden in Christ, not other philosophers or religions (v. 3). They're not fooled by heretics' persuasive arguments (v. 4). They live and worship in divine order, or God's ways and priorities (v. 5). Rooted, nourished, and established in faith, they're habitually confident in God (vv. 5, 7). Honoring Christ's lordship, they "walk" what they're taught (vv. 5–6). They're constantly, worshipfully thankful to God and also grateful to people (v. 7). They're unspoiled by unbiblical philosophies and religious traditions (v. 8). They're convinced Jesus is no mere extraordinary man—God's very fullness indwells Him, and He rules the natural and spiritual realms (vv. 9–10, 15).[1] They've circumcised, or cut off, their love of the "things of the world" (vv. 11–13).[2] They're free from Jewish and all other legalism (vv. 14, 16–17, 20–22). They duly appreciate but never venerate angels (v. 18). They believe Christ alone, and no man, is Head of the church (v. 19). Though self-disciplined, they avoid extreme asceticism (v. 23).

Most importantly, they regularly contemplate eternal things and passionately seek heavenly goals first (Col. 3:1–2). They live humble, self-effacing lives, contentedly "hidden" in Christ in this egotistically driven world (v. 3). They eagerly and joyfully anticipate Jesus' appearing (v. 4). They accept God's wrath is as real and necessary as His grace (v. 6). They mortify[3] sexual lusts and financial greed, knowing practicing these sins brings God's discipline (vv. 5–6). They consistently "put off" their "old man" nature with its sinful attitudes and behavior (vv. 8–9) and consistently "put on" Christ by increasing their knowledge of Him and obedience to His will (v. 10). They disavow and disallow all their former prejudices, realizing now "there is no respect of persons" (vv. 11, 25). Ever mindful of their undeserved election, they cultivate humility, forbearance, forgiveness, and unity (vv. 12–14). Wisely, they let God's peace, not circumstances or others' opinions, assess their spiritual condition (v. 15). They're "rich" in the fullness of God's Word—and always seeking more (v. 16)! They sing worshipfully "to the Lord" often, for His pleasure and their refreshment (v. 16). They do everything "heartily," as if Christ asked them to do it (vv. 17, 23). They faithfully discharge their marital and family duties, as defined by God's Word (vv. 18–21).

Expecting Judge Jesus to reward or punish them fairly, they're obedient employees or fair employers (Col. 3:22, 24–25; 4:1). They persevere in prayer, with vigilance and thanksgiving (Col. 4:2). They intercede for "doors of utterance,"[4] boldness, and grace for their ministers (vv. 3–4). They interact with unbelievers wisely, never naively (v. 5). They use their time and opportunities efficiently (v. 5). They speak thoughtfully, with grace (v. 6).[5] They practice and encourage comforting brotherly fellowship (vv. 7–9). They take parental oversight of younger believers (v. 10). They develop mercy, not malice, for those who failed, abandoned, or betrayed them (v. 10). They commend zealous intercessors (vv. 12–13). They encourage churches to spread and share excellent teaching (v. 16). They encourage discouraged ministers to fully discharge their responsibilities (v. 17). They pray often for grace for God's people (v. 18).[6] These are the specifics of spiritual maturity. Why did Paul enumerate them in such detail?

He understood an ideal or goal is not enough. We need more. We need a plain path of practical instructions to guide us into the full possession of our ideals. So after informing us we'll be "presented" one day "perfect in Christ Jesus," Paul described how we may reach this spiritual ideal—the things we should practice to fully develop the spiritual maturity Christ desires. Ready for examination?

Is Paul's goal in ministry your goal in life? Are you willing to steadily learn, live, and share these ways of spiritual maturity to prepare yourself and others to be presented "perfect in Christ Jesus"? Now that you've seen the ideal, grasp it. Meditate on Paul's instructions and imitate them until you radiate them. Rise and possess spiritual maturity—in detail.

Chapter 122

LET HIM BE REVEALED IN YOU!

OR CENTURIES PHILOSOPHERS and theologians have mused, "Who is God?" We would never know unless God chose to reveal Himself. The good news is, He has…passionately! Consider these ways.

Chiefly, all creation reveals Him. "The heavens declare the glory of God," exclaimed the awestruck psalmist (Ps. 19:1). The innumerable exquisitely perfect wonders present in space, earth, sea, sky, plants, birds, animals, microorganisms, and, yes, God's greatest work, man, openly display God's power, order, wisdom, and love. Creation makes it obvious: there's an awesome Intelligence, Designer, Builder, Technician, Artist, Musician, and Craftsman somewhere.[1] He's been here before us and left His distinctive signature on all His creations. They declare the truth, "He is" (Heb. 11:6), and God holds us responsible to acknowledge it (Rom. 1:18–23). Yet there's a clearer revelation.

God has described Himself in His Word. "The entrance of thy word giveth light"—or intellectual understanding of God's nature, mind, plans, and purposes (Ps. 119:130). Knowing man's vast intellectual capacity, God gave us a record of inspired words to more precisely and fully paint His self-portrait in our minds. Anyone anywhere anytime who with an open mind reads God's self-revelation in the Bible will see God for himself. But a more focused revelation was coming.

The incredible Incarnation! Not content for us to read about Him, God chose to let us see and hear Him in action. That history-changing demonstration of God on our level, in our world, in our flesh occurred in Jesus of Nazareth, who exhibited "all the fullness of the Godhead bodily" (Col. 2:9). In Jesus' life, teachings, works, and sufferings, Jews, Greeks, and Romans could see for themselves God alive, acting, and spotlighted on the world's stage. We too may gaze at the Wonder through four inspired historic telescopes: Matthew, Mark, Luke, and John. Perfect as this was, God wanted a larger revelation of Christ.

So He chose to expand the Light through a new company of people, the church. His plan was, and still is, simple: to implant Christ's life in every believer, feed it with His Word, empower it with His Spirit, train it through His ministers, and grow and purify it through testing until the light of His self-revelation in Christ shines through the church's world-wide witness, teachings, and works. Thus its name, the earthly "body"—living manifestation, hard evidence, tangible representation—of the heavenly Christ! Christ knew this broader manifestation would convert nations (John 17:21-26). Unsatisfied still, God chose to disclose Himself in a smaller, more personal way.

That micro-disclosure is the Christian. Every believer is to study, obey, and worship Christ our Glory until He illuminates us—each individual living cell in Christ's larger body—with His glorious truth, grace, holiness, and good works. Until Christ returns, the only Jesus our loved ones, neighbors, and countrymen will likely see is in us. They may not ponder creation, read Scripture, study Jesus' life, or heed the church's witness, but they will wake up and take note when the Spirit changes *us* to think, forgive, give, live righteously, serve God, and suffer adversity as Jesus did. When they see "Christ in you," the "hope of glory" will surge in their despairing hearts, giving them faith that they too can change (Col. 1:27).[2] This smallest but perhaps most effective God-revelation is in our hands. Will we release or veil Him?

This matters tremendously to God. From the beginning He's wanted to reveal Himself…passionately! Just as passionately Satan has tried everything imaginable to distort, confuse, or hide God's self-revelation.

He's inspired naturalists to deny creation's intelligent design and promote the fantastic lie that we've developed by chance without God's intervention—thus preventing us from seeing our Creator. He inspired medieval clergyman to resist releasing the Bible to the public and today uses liberal theologians to deny its inspiration and infallibility to undermine its authority—and conceal its Author. He's inspired secular scholars to deny the facts of Jesus' divinity and miracles and present Him as a mere man mythologized by His followers—thus blocking our view of the amazing Incarnation. He's corrupted the church's witness by power and wealth seeking, sin, and heresy—distorting the beautiful image God intended Christ's body to project. He relentlessly opposes and tempts Christians to separate us from the Vine—so the sweet fruit of Christlikeness won't be seen in us. Thus God's nemesis still casts his dark spiritual "covering" and "veil" (Isa. 25:7)[3] over this world to prevent God's glorious self-revelation—and grieve God.

So don't stand by idly. Help satisfy God's heart! Draw near Christ daily, walk closely with Him, and let Him be revealed in *you.*

NOTES

PREFACE

1. In the unforgettable words of Ezekiel, when describing the Millennial river of God, "Every thing shall live where the river cometh" (Ezek. 47:9).

CHAPTER 1
THE WAY OF PEACE

1. For biblical quotations in this paragraph, see Romans 10:15; 15:33; Luke 10:6; Ephesians 2:17; Romans 5:1; Philippians 4:7; Romans 3:17.

2. See Romans 14:17.

3. For the points in this sentence, see Luke 7:50; 8:48; Romans 2:10; Psalm 55:18; Matthew 4:11; Luke 2:29–30.

4. See Psalm 37:11, 37; Isaiah 54:13.

CHAPTER 2
SOW RIGHT, SOW NOW, SOW MUCH, SOW ON!

1. God strongly establishes the ageless, universal principle of personal responsibility for personal sin in Ezekiel 18:20.

2. Here in North Carolina, for instance, lettuce typically matures in thirty days, corn in sixty, and cotton in ninety.

CHAPTER 3
BY HIS SPIRIT

1. The Spirit's work through Paul's ministry was so pervasive vast numbers turned to Christ not only from Diana (Artemis) but also from many other Greek gods whose shrines filled Asia Minor.

2. That Nicodemus risked his leadership to care for Jesus' body after His crucifixion implies the Spirit had given him saving faith in Jesus and the vital teaching He had given him (John 3:1–8; 19:38–42).

3. See John 4:16–30; 1 Corinthians 6:9–11.

4. Contrast John's initial hasty call for the Samaritans' judgment with his later ministry to them (Luke 9:52–56; Acts 8:14–17).

5. See Acts chapters 6, 8, 10–11, 15.

CHAPTER 5
PREACHING AND PRACTICING THANKSGIVING

1. And the fourth (Heb. 13:15), if he authored Hebrews.

2. The opposite is also sadly true. The more we murmur, the more we want to murmur.

3. Again, the opposite is also true. It's impossible for us to endure very difficult or long tests unless we form and nurture the thanksgiving habit.

4. For these examples, see Matthew 11:25; 15:36; 26:27; John 11:41.

CHAPTER 6
ARE YOU CLINGING?

1. J. Strong, *A Concise Dictionary of the Words in the Greek Testament and the Hebrew Bible* (Bellingham, WA: Logos Bible Software, 2009), s.v. "*prosmeno.*"

2. As Paul did in his personal *kenosis* or self-emptying (Phil. 3:4–14).

CHAPTER 7
IT'S TIME WE FEAR HIM

1. We do so just as Christ's first disciples desired to "be with him" (Mark 3:14), Mary and the Bereans searched His Word (Luk 10:38–42; Acts 17:10–12), and Paul passionately pursued God's call (Phil. 3:12–15).

2. A. W. Tozer, *The Root of the Righteous* (Harrisburg, PA: Christian Publications, 1955), 38–41.

3. For texts supporting the rich blessings listed here, see in order: Proverbs 14:26, 27; 19:23; 2 Kings 4:1–7; Proverbs 22:4; Psalm 145:19; Exodus 1:21; Psalm 33:18; 103:11, 13; 115:11; Job 1:8; Psalm 25:14; 34:7; Nehemiah 7:2; Proverbs 10:27.

CHAPTER 8
JESUS' INTERESTS

1. See Ephesians 2:19–22; 4:13–16; 5:25–27.

2. See Mark 16:15–18; Matthew 28:18–20; Acts 1:8.

CHAPTER 9
GOD HAS A PLAN!

1. When Paul's plans were not God's, the Spirit faithfully checked him (Acts 16:6–7).

CHAPTER 10
HOW HE MAKES CHAMPIONS

1. The terms *champion* and *overcomer* are remarkably similar. The English word *champion* means "a person who has defeated all opponents in a series of competitions," whereas the New Testament word "overcomer" (or he who "overcometh," Rev. 2:7) is a translation of the Greek *nikao*, meaning "to subdue, conquer, prevail," or a Christian who subdues or conquers all challengers and challenges. See *Webster's Encyclopedic Unabridged Dictionary of the English Language* (New York: Gramercy Books, 1996), s.v. "champion." Also see James Strong, *A Concise Dictionary of the Words in the Greek Testament and the Hebrew Bible* (Bellingham, WA: Logos Bible Software, 2009).

2. See Revelation 2:7, 11, 17, 26; 3:5, 12, 21.

CHAPTER 12
LIKE THE CORNERSTONE

1. See also Psalm 118:22–23; Matt. 21:42; Mark 12:10–11; Luke 20:17–18; Acts 4:10–11; Rom. 9:32–33; 1 Pet. 2:6, 5–8.

2. "Them that honor me I will honor" (1 Sam. 2:30) is a soaring, repeatedly demonstrated biblical truth confirmed by Jesus' teaching (John 12:26).

3. Animals or humans were often sacrificed and their bodies buried beneath the corner-stones of temples or gates in pagan cities. Though God never approved of such abominations, it nevertheless happened that His Son's death founded His new temple, the church.

4. J. F. Walvoord, R. B. Zuck, and Dallas Theological Seminary, *The Bible Knowledge Commentary: An Exposition of the Scriptures* (Wheaton, IL: Victor Books, 1985), note on Ephesians 2:20.

CHAPTER 14
MESSIAH PLEASERS

1. For more on this, see Matthew 9:16–17.

CHAPTER 15
THOSE POSITIVE CHECKS!

1. For the examples of divine checks in this paragraph, see Acts 16:6–10; Genesis 26:1–3; 48:17–19; 1 Samuel 16:6–7; Matthew 1:19–20.

2. In our example above, Paul's two checks (Acts 16:6–7) probably came through prophecy, since both he and Silas had prophetic gifts (Acts 15:32).

CHAPTER 16
APOSTOLIC ANGER MANAGEMENT

1. For excellent renderings of this passage, see the NIV, NAS, NLT, and *The Message*.

2. See also the ESV and NAS. Other versions read: "Anger is typical of fools" (GW); "Anger labels you a fool" (NLT); "Getting angry is foolish" (NCV).

3. J. P. Louw and E. A. Nida, *Greek-English Lexicon of the New Testament: Based on Semantic Domains* (electronic edition of the 2nd edition) (New York: United Bible Societies, 1996), s.v. "*topos*."

4. God's supernatural power is in His Word. When we surrender to the Bible's commands regarding anger and sincerely confess agreement with them, the power of God's Word is released in us "unto salvation" in our immediate situation (Rom. 10:10).

5. For biblical examples of these, see Luke 15:28; 2 Kings 5:11; John 7:23; Exodus 16:20.

CHAPTER 17
THE RECORD KEEPER

1. These renderings are from the NLT, NAS, and NIV respectively.

2. For these examples, see Job 1:8; Genesis 18:19; 1 Samuel 15:10–11; Exodus 32:7–9; 1 Samuel 3:13–14. For others, see John 1:47–48; Revelation 2:2–3; 3:10; 3:17.

3. One recently reported case is the wrongful conviction and twenty-five-year imprisonment of Michael Morton (Williamson County, Texas). See Josh Levs, "Innocent Man: How Inmate Michael Morton Lost 25 Years of His Life," December 4, 2013, http://www.cnn.com/2013/12/04/justice/exonerated-prisoner-update-michael-morton/ (accessed August 17, 2014).

4. Peter echoes this (1 Pet. 2:19–20; 4:12–16).

5. Christ assured us of this in Matthew 10:26.

CHAPTER 18
DREAMING...

1. See Job 33:14–18.

CHAPTER 19
FRIENDLY FIRE

1. Among the most divisive attitudes are envy, judgmentalism, prejudice (denominational, racial, social, etc.), and vengeance.

2. This is why Paul reminds us to walk in love just before warning us to not devour each other with friendly fire (Gal. 5:14–15).

3. During the American Second Great Awakening, the Stone-Campbell movement chose as its motto: "In essentials, unity; in non-essentials, liberty; in all things, charity." The body of Christ would do well to remember and practice this today.

CHAPTER 21
LYDIA CHRISTIANS!

1. See S. Smith and J. Cornwall, *The Exhaustive Dictionary of Bible Names* (North Brunswick, NJ: Bridge-Logos, 1998), s.v. "Lydia." Some scholars believe "Lydia" was her nickname, not proper name, referring to her native land (Lydia) in Asia Minor, where the purple dye, cloth, and garments sold were made. If so, she was called "the Lydian."

2. See Luke 24:45.

3. See 1 Peter 1:22; Ephesians 5:26.

CHAPTER 22
DECLARE THE UNKNOWN GOD!

1. C. S. Keener, *The IVP Bible Background Commentary: New Testament* (Downers Grove, IL: InterVarsity Press, 1993).

2. There He reveals Himself most intimately, fully, and sweetly. (See Daniel 3:25; John 9:35–38; Acts 23:11).

CHAPTER 23
BE BEREAN!

1. P. J. Achtemeier, Harper and Row, and Society of Biblical Literature, *Harper's Bible Dictionary*, 1st ed. (San Francisco: Harper and Row, 1985).

2. See Romans 8:29; cf. Acts 4:13.

3. See 2 Timothy 3:12.

CHAPTER 24
GOD, HIS GOLD, HIS GLORY

1. The Maluku (Moluccas) Archipelago, especially the Banda Islands, in the Southwest Pacific within Indonesia where nutmeg, mace, and other spices were found in abundance.

2. Wikiquote.org, "Pope Leo X," http://en.wikiquote.org/wiki/Pope_Leo_X (accessed August 19, 2014).

CHAPTER 25
RECKON, YIELD, AND WALK TO VICTORY

1. See Romans 6:1–2; Galatians 5:13.

CHAPTER 26
BEEN REFILLED LATELY?

1. Peter's spontaneous anointing (Acts 4:8) and this one on the Jerusalem Christians (v. 31) were refillings, since both he and they had previously been baptized with the Spirit.

2. See Acts 8, 9, 10, and 19, remembering while earthly agents were often involved, the real Baptizer was the heavenly Christ.

3. The visionary John the Baptist introduced the first mention of the baptism with the Holy Spirit and repeatedly identified Jesus as the Baptizer (Matt. 3:11; Mark 1:8; Luke 3:16; John 1:33). The combined further testimonies of Jesus (Acts 1:4–5) and Peter (Acts 2:32–33) make it indisputable: Jesus is the Baptizer with the Holy Spirit!

4. The Spirit does, however, still work in our lives, speaking in our consciences to woo us to repentance (Rom. 2:4).

CHAPTER 27
BE FULLY OBEDIENT

1. Admittedly this obedience is rare and hard, but Christ unequivocally warned us there would be such "crosses," or seasons of separation, in every disciple's life (Matt. 10:34–39; Luke 14:25–27).

2. Oswald Chambers and Harry Verploegh, *Oswald Chambers: The Best from All His Books* (Thomas Nelson Publishers; Nashville, 1987), 228.

CHAPTER 28
OUR DOCTOR'S ORDERS

1. In order, these references are John 13:34 (15:12, 17); Mark 11:22; Matthew 6:33; 11:28; 7:7; Mark 13:33.

2. These are: 2 Timothy 2:15; 1 Peter 2:17; Philippians 4:6–7; Ephesians 4:26–27; 1 Thessalonians 5:17.

3. If, on the other hand, the pastoral counsel you're receiving is consistently errant, apathetic, or abusive, you should prayerfully seek another pastor and church. But never leave just because your "doctor's orders" are convicting, unflattering, or challenging.

CHAPTER 29
GOD'S BELIEVER-TEMPLES

1. See 1 Peter 2:5; Revelation 5:10.

2. Specifically, the second Jewish temple, known as Herod's temple (19 BC–AD 70).

3. These waters flowed from the ancient Gihon Spring.

4. In 2 Corinthians 6:14–7:1 God commands Christians to not be "unequally yoked" in close associations with unbelievers and, not stopping there, to cleanse ourselves from "all filthiness of the flesh and spirit" so we may experience the fullest degree of His intimate, Fatherly fellowship.

CHAPTER 30
THE POWER OF SONG

1. See Exodus 15:1–21; Numbers 21:16–18; Revelation 5:8–10.

2. See Exodus 15:1; Judges 5:1; 2 Samuel. 22:1.

3. Testimonies confirm the singing of the gospel is often as effective as the preaching of the gospel.

4. See 1 Kings 4:32.

CHAPTER 31
THE PROPER POSITION FOR PRAYER

1. See Acts 21:5.

2. For the examples cited in this paragraph, see in order: 1 Kings 18:42; 19:4; Daniel 6:10; 10:10, 15–17; 2 Samuel 7:18; Psalm 41:3–4; Joshua 5:14; Mark 14:35; Exodus 3:5; 3:6; 2 Kings 20:2; Matthew 14:30; Jonah 2:1; Mark 11:25; Ephesians 6:11, 14, 18; 1 Kings 8:22; Genesis 24:11–13; Luke 3:21; Genesis 3:8–10; 5:22.

3. "This [standing] was the characteristic Christian attitude in prayer... For early Christians, standing meant one had special privileges to come to God as Father, through Christ. To stand in the presence of God meant to be accepted by him and to have the right to speak freely." [Everett Ferguson, "How We Christians Worship," Worship in the Early Church, *Christian History*, issue 37, page 5 (PDF version).]

CHAPTER 32
PASSING BY THIS WORLD'S WONDERS

1. Some scholars hold the statue, comparable to the Statue of Liberty, stood on two marble pedestals astride the harbor entrance. Others assert it stood on one beside the harbor entrance, since the first position would have required the harbor to be closed during the Colossus' construction and later blocked by its massive fallen pieces.

2. See Acts 20:16; 24:17.

CHAPTER 34
INSPIRED INTERCESSIONS

1. He makes the same assumption in Mark 11:25.

2. To this day, every great blessing the church has ever received has been birthed out of periods of sustained prayer offered according to God's will by committed believers.

3. See Daniel 6:10.

4. Besides prompting petitions for us to pray, the Holy Spirit Himself prays for us and others independently within our bodily temples according to the Father's perfect will (Rom. 8:26–27).

5. This petition for us to "stand" perfectly in God's will, while it echoes Paul's charges in Ephesians 6:10–14 and Philippians 4:1, was Epaphras' constant prayer.

CHAPTER 35
NO REST UNTIL HE RESTS!

1. See Exodus 25:8; Psalm 132:13-14.

2. Jesus promised to take us in John 14:1-3, prayed for this in John 17:24, and foretold it through Paul in 1 Thessalonians 4:16-18 and 1 Corinthians 15:49-53.

3. For glimpses of God's, and our, final rest, see Revelation 4:1-5:14; 19:7-9; 21:1-22:17.

CHAPTER 36
SPEAKING OF LEADERS...

1. See Paul's orders for Christians to respect government and church leaders, Romans 13:1-7; Titus 3:1; 1 Thessalonians 5:12-13.

2. See Exodus 22:28.

3. Interestingly, God did "smite" the high priest, Ananias, in a providential judgment. In the Jewish revolt that began a few years later (AD 66), zealots hunted Ananias down and killed him for his collaboration with the Romans and other corruptions, including stealing tithes from priests. See W. W. Wiersbe, *The Bible Exposition Commentary* (Wheaton, IL: Victor Books, 1996).

CHAPTER 37
VISION VENGEANCE

1. As was the case when Elisha was surrounded at Dothan (2 Kings 6:16).

CHAPTER 38
HE FAITHFULLY HELPS THE HELPLESS

1. See in order: Acts 21:31-32; 23:10; 23:12-35.

2. The notorious, heretical "Judaizers," who, to appease Jewish sensibilities, insisted falsely that Gentile Christians had to first become Jewish proselytes in order to be saved (Acts 15:1-2).

3. A careful reading of Acts 21:10-14 reveals God's voice through prophecy only warned Paul of his approaching trouble in Jerusalem, while it was his friends and associates, wishing to spare him, that "besought him not to go up."

CHAPTER 39
READY FOR TERTULLUS

1. Smith and Cornwall, *The Exhaustive Dictionary of Bible Names*.

2. This was the legal strategy the Corinthian Synagogue attempted unsuccessfully to use against Paul (Acts 18:12-13).

CHAPTER 40
PROACTIVE PROVIDENCE

1. This was probable if Paul's hearing were held in Jerusalem and ended in an unpopular acquittal. Tensions were high in Jerusalem between Roman officials and Jewish zealots, as the infamous "*sicarii,*" or dagger men, were stealthily cutting Romans' and

Jewish collaborators' throats. Lysias wanted no part of a Jewish rebellion or on the other hand, of losing a Roman citizen (Paul) to assassins. Either could end his career.

2. See Acts 9:24; 9:29; 14:5; 20:3; 23:12–13; 25:3–4, 9–11.

CHAPTER 41
UNREASONABLE!

1. See John 18:38; 19:4, 6.

CHAPTER 42
YOU'LL NEVER FAIL

1. See 1 John 4:8, 16.

2. See John 13:34–35; 17:26.

CHAPTER 43
THE GOADS OF GOD

1. J. M. Freeman and H. J. Chadwick, *The New Manners and Customs of the Bible* (North Brunswick, NJ: Bridge-Logos Publishers, 1998).

2. Paul's Christ-centered, Spirit-filled, Word-rich ministry harvested Jewish and Gentile souls all over the Mediterranean and conquered false prophets, false teachers, idols, errors, occultism, and other enemies of God in many a spiritual battle.

CHAPTER 44
LOST YOUR FOCUS?

1. In the Bible, "waters" speak figuratively of troubles and "deep waters" great troubles (Ps. 69:1–2, 14–15).

CHAPTER 45
TARGET CHURCHES

1. See Acts 5:3; 6:1; 15:1–2.

2. Matthew Henry, *Commentary in One Volume* (Grand Rapids, MI: Zondervan Publishing House, 1961), 1693.

3. See Acts 11:25–26; 15:35; Gal. 2:11.

4. See Acts 11:27–28; 13:1–3; 14:26–27; 15:32.

5. See Acts 11:19–23; 11:27; 15:2.

6. In following centuries, Antioch became an important center of Christian learning, promoting the literal interpretation of the Bible as a corrective against the excessively allegorical interpretations advanced by the Origen-led Alexandrian school.

CHAPTER 46
BOUND FOR A CERTAIN ISLAND

1. Though not explicitly stated, this is implied. It's unthinkable that Paul would hold healing meetings in Jesus' name among unbelievers without also sharing the gospel (Acts 28:7–10).

2. It would be exceptional for a Roman officer to unnecessarily delay his mission for seven days, especially to accommodate the wishes of a prisoner. This suggests faith was growing in Julius' heart. Furthermore, David Wilkerson believed God used the soldiers' and prisoners' testimonies of Paul's extraordinary faith, leadership, ministry, and Lord to seed Rome with the gospel once they arrived.

3. Paul uses this name for Satan, who rules the invisible demonic hosts surrounding earth's atmosphere (Eph. 2:2).

CHAPTER 48
PRISON MINISTRY—PAUL'S WAY

1. These are the Books of Ephesians, Philippians, Colossians, and Philemon.

CHAPTER 49
ANGELS STAND BY

1. David expressed this grief in Psalm 55:12–14.

2. See Exodus 23:20; Acts 12:8–9; 10:1–7.

CHAPTER 50
REMEMBER THE HUGUENOTS!

1. The Roman persecution of Christians began in AD 64 with the fire of Rome and ultimately ended with the Edict of Toleration in AD 311.

2. "The Huguenots and the Wars of Religion," *Christian History* XX, issue 71, no. 3 (2001); 9.

CHAPTER 51
GET BACK TO GOD'S WORD!

1. "Right" is taken from the Hebrew *yashar*, meaning, "to be straight." Strong, *A Concise Dictionary of the Words in the Greek Testament and The Hebrew Bible.*

2. "Simple" here means dull, naïve, untaught. If even these receive God's Word, it will make them increasingly wise.

3. See Psalm 51:6.

4. Solomon's and John's warnings are most memorable (Eccles. 1:1–11; 12:13–14; 1 John 2:15–17).

5. See Proverbs 6:20–22; John 14:26.

CHAPTER 52
ESTABLISHED TO GROW

1. "Established" (Acts 16:5) is taken from the Greek, *stereo*, meaning "solidified, made stiff or firm," thus fully set up or founded.

2. Originally, the "mixed multitudes" were Gentiles who mingled with Jews in Israel's congregation (Exod. 12:38; Num. 13:3). Today they are unconverted churchgoers who infiltrate congregations of born-again believers.

3. For the points listed, see: the gospel (Rom. 16:25); faith (Acts 16:5); hope of Christ's appearing (James 5:7–8); love (John 17:26; Eph. 3:17); thanksgiving (Col. 2:7); pastoral

focus (Acts 6:4); sound doctrine (Heb. 13:9); holiness (1 Thess. 3:13); obeying God's Word (2 Thess. 2:17); good works (2 Thess. 2:17); godly separation (2 Thess. 3:3); prayer (Eph. 6:18; Acts 12:5); praise and worship (Acts 13:2; 16:25); right attitudes (Prov. 4:23; 23:7); fair judgment (John 7:24; Matt. 18:15–17).

4. As He has done from the inception of the church (Acts 2:47).

CHAPTER 53
GOD'S OPPORTUNISTS

1. See note 1, chapter 48, "Prison Ministry—Paul's Way."

2. David's men guarded Nabal's sheep free of charge (1 Sam. 25:14–16).

3. As in Reinhold Niebuhr's famous prayer, "God, grant me the serenity to accept what I cannot change, the courage to change the things I can, and wisdom to know the difference."

CHAPTER 54
CHARACTERISTICS OF THE HOLY SPIRIT

1. Genesis 24:1 note, in *The New Scofield Study Bible* (New York: Oxford University Press, 1967), 34.

2. Jesus' high priestly prayer for His people is His last will and testament and the blueprint for the church's construction (John 17:13–26). As executor of Christ's estate and builder of His holy temple, the Holy Spirit remains focused on fulfilling everything Jesus requested in that prayer.

CHAPTER 55
MASTERFUL PATIENCE

1. People came from all over the world to worship and deposit their riches in the bank of the massive temple of Artemis, one of the wonders of the ancient world.

2. The Great Check is described twice (Luke 24:49; Acts 1:4–5).

CHAPTER 56
HIS SHINING FACE

1. "Presence" is taken from the Hebrew *paneh*, meaning "face." [J. Swanson, *Dictionary of Biblical Languages with Semantic Domains: Hebrew (Old Testament)*, electronic ed. (Oak Harbor, WA: Logos Research Systems, Inc., 1997).]

2. On God turning, hiding, and setting His face, see Deuteronomy 23:14; 31:18; Jeremiah 44:11.

CHAPTER 57
THE WORLD WILL KNOW

1. See Isaiah 37:20.

2. See Ezekiel 38:16; 39:7.

3. As Moses prayed, "Let the beauty of the LORD our God be upon us" (Ps. 90:17).

CHAPTER 58
TRAVAILING FOR TRANSFORMATION

1. See Galatians 2–4.

2. Isaiah foresaw this (Isa. 66:8).

CHAPTER 59
TOUCHED BY GOD

1. Some common spiritual fevers are preoccupations with covetousness, envy, vengeance, worldly ambition, sex, sports, politics, and social controversies.

CHAPTER 61
ELIMINATING ENVY

1. Envy is a companion sin to pride. Where pride is, envy is; where humility is, envy is not.

2. We must confess the truth about our envy to God and turn from it to be forgiven, cleansed, and freed from its influence (John 8:32, 36; Prov. 28:13; 1 John 1:7, 9).

3. The ancient Greek philosopher Epicurus (341–270 BC) said, "To whom little is not enough, nothing is enough." [William Barclay, *The New Daily Study Bible: The Letters to Timothy, Titus, and Philemon* (Louisville, KY: Westminster John Knox Press, 2003), 145.

4. Epicurus also said, "Nothing is enough for the man to whom enough is too little," and "Do not spoil what you have by desiring what you have not." See http://quotations book.com/quote/140/ (accessed January 21, 2014). Also, see http://quotationsbook.com/ quotes/author/2319/ (accessed January 21, 2014).

CHAPTER 62
PASSIONATELY FREE!

1. To clarify, New Jerusalem (Rev. 21–22) will be the home of the redeemed of all ages, Jewish and Gentile, not just Christians.

CHAPTER 63
SEEKING ANOTHER COUNTRY

1. For proof, we need look no further than the awesome work of God in China during the twentieth century. There the underground house church movement grew spiritually while enduring several persecutions, and then emerged in the late 1970s with explosive numerical growth, all while their government was ruled by Communists.

2. Paul commands us to pray for all government leaders, not just those we prefer, realizing that if government at least maintains law and order, the gospel can spread to the saving of many (1 Tim. 2:1–4).

3. Perhaps no New Testament exhortation underscores this call better than Colossians 3:1–4.

CHAPTER 64
NEVER SAY NO!

1. A. W. Tozer, "The Prayer of a Minor Prophet," in *The Best of A. W. Tozer* (Harrisburg, PA: Christian Publications, 1978), 77.

2. Smith and Cornwall, *The Exhaustive Dictionary of Bible Names*.

CHAPTER 65
HOLY HASTE

1. See Proverbs 29:20.

2. See Isaiah 28:16.

CHAPTER 67
MORE "ACTS" ARE COMING!

1. "Amen" closes twenty-five of the twenty-seven New Testament books.

2. By "Laodicean" we mean similar in character to the ancient church of Laodicea Jesus described so unflatteringly yet hopefully in His seventh letter to the churches of Asia Minor (Rev. 3:14–22).

3. To learn much more about God's past and current miraculous works worldwide in this age, I suggest Craig. S. Keener's monumental work, *Miracles: The Credibility of the New Testament Accounts*. (Grand Rapids, MI: Baker Publishing Group, 2011).

4. This was the pagans' description of the early church's work (Acts 17:6).

CHAPTER 68
READY TO SEEK HIM?

1. For Hebrew words *dāra* and *bāga*, see Swanson, *Dictionary of Biblical Languages with Semantic Domains: Hebrew (Old Testament)*.

2. For references to some of the blessings listed in this sentence, see 1 Samuel 3:21; 2 Chronicles 14:7; 17:4; 26:5, 8, 15; Psalms 16:11; 37:4; Proverbs 2:3–6, 9, 11; Matthew 11:28–30; Revelation 3:21.

3. A. W. Tozer offers this prayer to penitent non-seekers: "O God…I am ashamed of my lack of desire…I want to want Thee; I long to be filled with longing; I thirst to be made more thirsty…Begin in mercy a new work of love within me. Say to my soul, 'Rise up, my love, my fair one, and come away.' Then give me grace to rise and follow Thee…In Jesus' Name, Amen." [Tozer, *The Best of A. W. Tozer*, 19.]

CHAPTER 69
TOTAL CONTENTMENT

1. "Content" is rendered from the Greek *autarkēs* (*au-TAR-cāse*), meaning, according to one source, "contented with one's lot, with one's means, thought the slenderest." See J. Strong, *Enhanced Strong's Lexicon* (Bellingham, WA: Logos Bible Software, 2001). A simpler definition is "satisfied enough with what one presently has or is."

2. Warren Weirsbe notes, "Instead of having spiritual ups and downs as the situation changed, he (Paul) went right on, steadily doing his work and serving Christ. His personal references at the close of this letter indicate that he was not the victim of

circumstances but the victor over circumstances: 'I can accept all things' (Phil. 4:11); 'I can do all things' (Phil. 4:13); 'I have all things' (Phil. 4:18). Paul did not have to be pampered to be content; he found his contentment in the spiritual resources abundantly provided by Christ." See W. W. Wiersbe, *The Bible Exposition Commentary*. (Wheaton, IL: Victor Books, 1996).

3. Contentment, or "perfect peace," is only possible if we "stay," or occupy, our minds daily with biblical and other worthy truths (Isa. 26:3).

4. Having authored 1 Thessalonians 5:18 and 1 Corinthians. 10:10, and remembering complaining stumbled even Job (Job 3:1–2), Paul was careful not to murmur: "Not that I complain of want" (Phil. 4:11, MOFFATT).

5. Greek "*autarkēs*." See H. Liddell, *A Lexicon: Abridged from Liddell and Scott's Greek-English Lexicon* (Oak Harbor, WA: Logos Research Systems, Inc., 1996).

6. G. Kittel, G. Friedrich, and G. W. Bromiley, *Theological Dictionary of the New Testament* (Grand Rapids, MI: W. B. Eerdmans, 1985).

7. See 2 Corinthians 3:5.

8. See Galatians 2:10; Acts 11:29–30.

9. Matthew Henry, *Commentary on the Whole Bible* (Grand Rapids, MI: Zondervan Publishing House, 1961), Phil. 4:18, note, page 1867.

10. Paul establishes this in 1 Timothy 6:6–8.Without this contentment, even those with great worldly wealth are pitifully "poor" in heart (Rev. 3:17).

CHAPTER 70
AS STRONG AS YOUR DAYS

1. "Strengtheneth" (Phil. 4:13) is taken from the Greek *endynamoō*, meaning to make one "able, capable, equal to, or strong" to do. See Kittel, Friedrich, and Bromiley, *Theological Dictionary of the New Testament*.

2. Or, "Your strength will equal your days" (Deut. 33:25, NIV).

3. One translation reads, "You will be strong as long as you live" (NCV).

4. God's first promise of physical healing is found in Exodus 15:26.

5. Mrs. C. Nuzum defined endurance as the ability "to move steadily on in the way, work, and will of the Lord, even when things are very different from what we wish them to be." [Mrs. C. Nuzum, *The Life of Faith* (Springfield, MO: Gospel Publishing House, 1956), 45.]

6. Matthew Henry notes this paraphrase for Deuteronomy 33:25: "The strength of thy old age shall be like that of thy youth; thou shalt not feel a decay, nor be the worse for the wearing, but shalt renew thy youth; as if not thy shoes only, but thy bones, were iron and brass." [Henry, *Commentary on the Whole Bible*, Deuteronomy 33:25, note, page 207.]

7. George Mueller began his traveling ministry at seventy and continued till he was ninety-two. One of my most faithful ministry supporters and personal friends, Jack McHugh, labored daily as a skilled and sought after draftsman until his passing at age ninety-one. The founder of the school for which I teach, Dr. Ron Cottle, is still traveling and teaching in excellent health at eighty (and looks sixty!). As their days, so has their strength been. To God be the glory!

CHAPTER 71
SPIRITUAL LEADERS—GIVEN AND RAISED

1. Regarding the length of David's reign, see 2 Samuel 5:4–5.

2. David's two sins, his affair with Bathsheba and numbering of the people, though egregious, were rare demerits on an otherwise outstanding record.

3. For the full description of these two key crises in King Saul's life, see 1 Samuel 13 and 1 Samuel 15.

4. All Christians are ministers of Christ, yet here we speak first of those in the fivefold ministry (Eph. 4:11–13).

5. See Ecclesiastes 9:18.

CHAPTER 72
PASTOR, PEOPLE, BE LOOSED!

1. See these references for examples of repetition in the Law (Lev. 26; Deut. 28), the Psalms (Pss. 14 and 53; Pss. 60 and 108), and Proverbs (Prov. 1:7 and 9:10; Prov. 15:33; 18:12).

2. See his repetition in 1 John 3:11, 23; 4:7, 11, 12.

3. Some sample passages from the Epistles are: Philippians 4; Colossians 3; 1 Thessalonians 5; 1 Corinthians 13; Ephesians 4–6; Romans 12. Other key passages are John 17; Deuteronomy 28; Psalm 37; Matthew 7:1–5.

CHAPTER 73
THE INTELLIGENT DESIGNER

1. See Ron Carlson and/ Ed Decker, *Fast Facts on False Teachings* (Eugene, OR: Harvest House, 1994), 53. Additionally, for a compelling look at the Darwinism vs. Intelligent Design controversy, purchase or view online (Youtube.com) Ben Stein's documentary, *Expelled: No Intelligence Allowed!*

2. By "Intelligent Designer" we mean God, though, strictly speaking, Intelligent Design theory is not identical with Creationism. See http://www.intelligentdesign.org/ (accessed April 22, 2013).

3. Scripture repeatedly teaches the Father created all things by His Son (John 1:3, 10; Eph. 3:9; Col. 1:16; Heb. 1:2).

4. While elements of Christ's design for His church are found throughout the New Testament, Christ's high priestly prayer (John 17) is the most succinct blueprint for the construction and destiny of the church. Thus it's the primary focus of the Holy Spirit's work in, among, and through believers in this age.

5. See Jude 20.

6. The personal ability to speak with tongues available to every Spirit-baptized Christian (1 Cor. 14:2, 4) is to be distinguished from the operation of tongues with interpretations in meetings (vv. 21, 27–28).

7. Abraham's servant seeking Isaac's bride represents the Holy Spirit's mission to find Christ's bride-church (Gen. 24). The gifts Eliezer gives Rebekah as tokens of Isaac's love (vv. 22, 30, 53) represent the gifted ministers and spiritual gifts Christ lovingly gave His church. As Rebekah never gave up her gifts, so the church has never relinquished hers.

CHAPTER 74
WE WILL BELIEVE IN MIRACLES!

1. Since Herod Agrippa I was holding Peter in maximum security, guarded by four shifts of four guards each, there was no means of escape but a miracle (Acts 12:4, 6).

2. See Mark 16:14; John 20:24–29.

3. For this, see 2 Thessalonians 2:3–12, especially verses 9–11; Matthew 24:23–25; Revelation 13:3, 11–15.

CHAPTER 75
AFTER EVERY MOWING

1. This mowing or mortifying of the fleshly nature (Col. 3:5–7) is also called spiritual circumcision (Col. 2:11).

2. A mown heart is also a weaned heart; see Psalm 131:1–2.

3. David W. Bercot, editor, *A Dictionary of Early Christian Beliefs* (Peabody, MA: Hendrickson Publishers, 1998), 428.

CHAPTER 76
STAND AGAINST THIS CORRUPTION

1. Swanson, *Dictionary of Biblical Languages with Semantic Domains: Greek (New Testament)*.

2. See 2 Timothy 2:14, 23–24.

3. Paul uses leaven to symbolize the unseen but rapidly spreading ill effects of any unchecked sin among Christians (1 Cor. 5:6).

4. See Numbers 11:4–10, 31–34; 16:1–50.

5. See Hebrews 3:13.

CHAPTER 77
SURRENDERED TO GOD'S TIMING

1. Perhaps Peter ministered among the Bithynians, since we know he specifically addressed them in his first epistle (1 Pet. 1:1). Andrew or Bartholomew may also have ministered in Bithynia, since tradition says they ministered in the nearby areas of the ancient world (Bartholomew in Armenia; Andrew in Ukraine and southern Russia). See Howard F. Vos, *Exploring Church History* (Nashville: Thomas Nelson Publishers, 1994), 5.

2. At this juncture, Paul's primary mission objective of strengthening the Galatian churches was already accomplished (Acts 15:36, 16:4–5).

3. Paul experienced delayed fruitfulness and humiliating persecution before his great spiritual victory in Philippi (Acts 16:11–40).

CHAPTER 78
A FAR BETTER LIFE

1. J. Strong, *Enhanced Strong's Lexicon* (Bellingham, WA: Logos Bible Software, 2001), s.v. "*analyō*."

2. "Present with the Lord" proves deceased Christians are neither unconscious nor asleep but wide awake and sharing activities with Christ—worshipping, walking, and working "with the Lord." "Sleep" (1 Cor. 15:51; 1 Thess. 4:14) refers only to our bodily appearance when deceased.

3. See Psalm 37:11; Romans 8:19–21 (NIV, NLT); Rev. 21:5.

4. Jack W. Hayford, general editor, *Spirit-Filled Life Bible* (Nashville: Thomas Nelson Publishers, 1991), 1808.

5. When in November 1917 Oswald Chambers passed unexpectedly at age forty-three, his wife sent out word to his friends, fellow ministers, and students: "Oswald in His presence." Her confidence and confession are examples we should follow.

CHAPTER 79
LET'S EPHESIANIZE!

1. Dictionary.com, s.v. "occult," http://dictionary.reference.com/browse/occult (accessed February 13, 2014).

2. See Leviticus 19:31; Deuteronomy 29:29; Isaiah 8:19–20.

3. This is commanded to keep us uncompromised and hopefully shame them into repentance (Eph. 5:11; 2 Cor. 6:14–18; 2 Thess. 3:14–15).

CHAPTER 80
KINGDOM COLONISTS

1. W. W. Wiersbe, *The Bible Exposition Commentary* (Wheaton, IL: Victor Books, 1996).

2. Ibid.

3. R. L. Thomas, *New American Standard Hebrew-Aramaic and Greek Dictionaries*, updated edition (Anaheim: Foundation Publications, Inc., 1998).

CHAPTER 81
POWER TEACHING

1. The huge temple of Artemis drew worshippers from all over the ancient world and supported a large shrine-making business (Acts 19:23–27). The city was also known as a center of occultism, especially the supposedly powerful magic charms and spells inscribed on small scrolls known as the *Ephesia grammata*, or "Ephesian writings."

2. Luke summarizes the progress of the gospel in various regions during the first thirty years of church history in these references: Acts 2:47; 5:14; 6:7; 9:31; 12:24; 19:20; 28:30–31.

3. Ever envious of God, Satan is driven to imitate whatever God does, including the miracles of Christ, which He will imitate through the Antichrist after the church's departure (2 Thess. 2:8–12; Rev. 13:11–15).

CHAPTER 82
STRANGE, STRANGER, OR STRANGEST

1. See Acts 21:17–22:30.

2. These events are described in Acts 23–26.

3. These events are described in Acts 27:1–28:11.

4. Acts 24:23 implies Paul, though detained, freely received anyone wishing to see him. We may assume his inspiring example of Christlike suffering inspired many in Caesarea as we know it did later in Rome (Phil. 1:12–14).

5. See note 1, chapter 48, "Prison Ministry—Paul's Way."

6. One great keynote by which overcomers live is "In everything give thanks; for this is the will of God in Christ Jesus concerning you" (1 Thess. 5:18).

CHAPTER 83
AMBASSADORS IN CHAINS

1. Considering Paul's successive two-year imprisonments in Caesarea (Acts 24:27) and Rome (Acts 28:30–31), three-month stay on Malta (v. 11), and the travel time by sea and land (Acts 27:20; 28:14), his total time in custody was probably four and a half to five years.

2. Very conscious of his ironic condition, Paul referred to his "chains" or "bonds" no less than thirteen times in the New Testament (Acts 26:29; 28:20; Eph. 6:20; Phil. 1:7, 13, 14, 16; Col. 4:3, 18; 2 Tim. 1:16; 2:9; Philem. 10, 13).

3. Remember Paul taught us to "give thanks in all circumstances" (1 Thess. 5:18, ESV), revealed "God causes all things to work together for good to those who love God, to those who are called according to His purpose" (Rom. 8:28, NAS), and testified, "I have learned to be content whatever the circumstances" (Phil. 4:11, NIV).

4. See *Life Application Study Bible* (Wheaton, IL: Tyndale House Publishers, 2004), Ephesians 6:19–20, note, page 2010.

CHAPTER 84
A SPIRITUAL BATTLE BRIEFING

1. As wrestlers grasp, pull, push, trip, and hold down ("pin") their opponents, so Satan tries constantly to grasp us through anger (vexation, offenses, or unforgiveness), pull us with temptations, push us with fears, trip us up with lies, and hold us down with discouragement or unbelief.

2. Satan can use sinners, carnal Christians, or even spiritual Christians whenever we give him "place" or "advantage" through sinful or selfish thoughts, speech, or action (Eph. 4:26–27; 2 Cor. 2:9–11). Thus Scripture urges us to trust, obey, seek God, and examine ourselves regularly (Rom. 6:16; 1 Cor. 11:28, 31; 2 Cor. 13:5; 2 John 8).

3. The names or descriptions of the devil in this paragraph are found in 1 Timothy 5:14; Isaiah 14:12–15; Matthew 4:3; John 10:10; Revelation 12:10; John 8:44; 1 Thessalonians 2:18; 2 Corinthians 11:3, 14; 2 Timothy 3:13; John 12:31; 1 Peter 5:8; Revelation 12:9.

4. I've borrowed some of these points, though not their description, from *The Bible Exposition Commentary* by W. Wiersbe, Ephesians 6:10–12, notes.

CHAPTER 85
STRONG IN THE LORD!

1. The baffling death and surprising resurrection of Jesus' good friend Lazarus is described in John 11.

2. David humbly acknowledged, "O my God, my soul is cast down within me" (Ps. 42:6).

3. For these references, see 1 John 4:8, 16, 19; 1 Corinthians 8:1, NIV; 13:1–3.

4. Anyone serious about any endeavor seeks perfection in it. At his first team meeting with the Green Bay Packers, Vince Lombardi announced, "Gentlemen, we are going to relentlessly chase perfection, knowing full well we will not catch it, because nothing is perfect. But we are going to relentlessly chase it, because in the process we will catch excellence. I am not remotely interested in just being good." Multiple NFL championships ensued. Should Christians be less serious about spiritual excellence?

CHAPTER 86
ABOUT FIERY DARTS

1. God permits Satan to bring sinful suggestions to mind to test us, hoping, though we're free to receive them (John 13:2), we'll reject them (Matt. 4:1–11).

2. Paul's call to "quench" fiery darts with a shield of "faith" imply they are anti-faith in nature, or conducive to fear or unbelief (Eph. 6:16).

3. Craig Keener notes, "Because the Greek and Roman god of passion (called Eros and Cupid, respectively) was said to strike with flaming arrows, some of Paul's readers may have thought specifically of the temptation of lust in this verse." See C. S. Keener, *The IVP Bible Background Commentary: New Testament* (Downers Grove, IL: InterVarsity Press, 1993), note on Ephesians 6:16.

4. See Psalm 64:2–4; 1 Samuel 25:12–13, 21–22.

5. Joseph was "shot at" for this reason (Gen. 49:22–23), but it only made him stronger (v. 24).

6. Paul repeatedly urged self-examination (1 Cor. 11:28–31; 2 Cor. 13:5), as did John (2 John 8).

7. For further study, see Genesis 3:1, 4; Galatians 2:12; 1 Samuel 18:6–8; 25:11–12, 21–22; 27:1–2, 7; 2 Samuel 11:2–4; 13:22, 32; 1 Kings 19:2–3; John 13:2 [Matthew 26:14–16]; Numbers 22:16–17, 19.

8. See Psalms 7:13; 18:14; 64:7.

CHAPTER 87
DOORS, UTTERANCE, BOLDNESS

1. In 2 Corinthians 1:11 Paul gratefully acknowledges the helpfulness of the Corinthians' intercessions for him.

2. Lydia was the first known convert and her house fellowship the first known church in Europe. (We know, however, many converted at Pentecost had carried the gospel home to many parts of the world, though with unknown effect, Acts 2:5–11.)

3. Hayford, general editor, *The Spirit-Filled Life Bible*, Ephesians 6:19–20 note, page 179.

4. For other examples of God showing His messengers what to say, see Exodus 4:12, 22–23, 28–30; 24:12; Proverbs 16:1; Jeremiah 7:27–28; Matthew 21:3; 26:18; 10:27; Luke 3:2–3.

5. Two such outstanding examples of Christ speaking in an extraordinary way through ministers are the messages of Charles H. Spurgeon and Charles G. Finney—both of whom were supported by committed intercessors.

6. "Those shall share in the reward, who bear their part of the burden." [Henry, *Matthew Henry's Commentary in One Volume*. See Philippians 1:7, note, page 1861.] (See Hebrews 6:10).

7. Sometimes we complain about our ministers' powerless preaching or uninteresting teaching when we're partly to blame because we're not asking the Lord to give them utterance!

CHAPTER 88
KEEP PRAYING, PAUL'S COMING!

1. Like slaves and children, women were lightly esteemed in first-century Greco-Roman and Jewish cultures.

2. On the contagiousness of sin, Paul taught, "A little leaven leaveneth the whole lump" (1 Cor. 5:6) and "evil company corrupts good morals" (1 Cor. 15:33).

3. Henry, *Commentary in One Volume*, Acts 16:13, page 1699.

4. In his epistle to the Philippians, Paul lauds their outstanding obedience and charity (Phil. 2:12; 4:10, 14–18)!

CHAPTER 89
THE LORD IS MY ROCK!

1. Because God doesn't change, neither do His distinctive ways of operation (Mal. 3:6; Heb. 13:8).

2. For the examples in this sentence, see Job 39:27–28; Isaiah 32:2; 1 Samuel 22:1; Exodus 17:12.

3. See Daniel 2:34; Matthew 21:44.

CHAPTER 90
THE EVIL DAY

1. The phrases "evil day," "day of trouble," and "times of trouble," symbolize the same adverse seasons called the "hour and...power of darkness" (Luke 22:53) and spiritual "night" (John 9:4). In all these periods God permits the powers of darkness to attack, hinder, or temporarily overrule the children of light for His own higher purposes. For other references to the "evil day" or "day of trouble," see Psalms 9:9; 10:1; 20:1; 27:5; 37:19, 39; 41:1; 50:15; 2 Kings 19:3; Job 2:11; 42:11.

2. When most German Protestant churches succumbed to the Nazis' nationalistic propaganda and supported Hitler, Dietrich Bonhoeffer and other godly pastors rejected Hitler's lies and formed the separate Confessing Church. We should applaud this courageous stand, even if we question Bonhoeffer's later participation in Hitler's assassination plot.

3. Some of the twentieth century's most notable worldwide "evil days" were the First World War, the Second World War, the Cold War, and the Cuban missile crisis.

4. This is the inevitable result of two timeless biblical principles: "Whatever a man soweth, that shall he also reap" (Gal. 6:7); and, "Righteousness exalteth a nation, but sin is a reproach to any people" (Prov. 14:34); or, "Doing what is right makes a nation great, but sin will bring disgrace to any people" (NCV).

5. See Ezekiel 7:7; Amos 6:3; Habakkuk 3:16; Zephaniah 1:14–18.

CHAPTER 91
IT'S TIME FOR MIRACLES

1. *Webster's Encyclopedic Unabridged Dictionary of the English Language* (New York: Gramercy Books, 1996), s.v. "miracle."

2. See Matthew 24:24; 2 Thessalonians 2:9; Revelation 13:13–15.

3. Peter's inspired summary of Jesus' ministry emphasized the miraculous (Acts 10:36–38).

4. The Healing Revival broke out in America in the 1940s and the Charismatic Movement in the 1960s.

5. During Kathryn Kuhlman's miracle ministry, skeptics often arrived suspicious and left converted. See Kathryn Kuhlman, *I Believe in Miracles* (Alachua, FL: Bridge-Logos Publishers, 1990), 129–137.

6. Acts repeatedly reveals that whenever the gospel invaded new territory, it clashed with the occult works of darkness and "prevailed" (Acts 19:20, 11–19), thus turning pagans from the power of Satan to the power of God (Acts 26:18; see Acts 8:5–13; 13:6–12; 16:16–19).

7. Both in the text and extensive footnotes of his two-volume work *Miracles*, Craig Keener repeatedly points to examples of this occurring all over the world wherever God has worked miraculously. See Craig Keener, *Miracles: The Credibility of the New Testament Accounts*, vol. 1 (Grand Rapids, MI: Baker Publishing Group, 2011), 299, 332.

CHAPTER 92
PASS ON THE LOVE...

1. In the original language, "The 'if' clauses...speak of certainties. So in this passage 'if' may be translated 'since.' Paul wrote here about realities, not questionable things." See Walvoord, Zuck, and Dallas Theological Seminary, *The Bible Knowledge Commentary: An Exposition of the Scriptures*.

2. These references are Philippians 1:27; 2:1–4; 4:1–3.

3. The references quoted or alluded to in this paragraph are, in order, John 13:34–35; 17:21, 23; Romans 13:8; 1 Thessalonians 4:9–10; 1 Peter 1:22; 1 John 3:17–18; Philippians 2:3; 1 John 3:10–12; James 2:1–4; Acts 9:10–17; 1 John 3:16; 1 John 3:21–23; 4:11–12.

4. "The apostle knew well that thought and attitudes are the basis of speech and action and so direct the whole course of a person's life (cf. Phil. 2:5; 3:15; 4:8)." [D. A. Carson, R. T. France, J. A. Motyer, and G. J.Wenham, eds., *New Bible Commentary: 21st Century Edition*, 4th ed., (Downers Grove, IL: Inter-Varsity Press, 1994).]

5. So states 2 Timothy 2:13.

6. Love anyone long enough, and they'll eventually love you. Matthew Henry wrote, "Love and you shall be loved." [Henry, *Commentary on the Whole Bible*, 1863.]

CHAPTER 93
READY TO BE A NOBODY?

1. The Greek word *kenosis,* meaning "to empty out; to strip of all things," is used in Philippians 2:7 to describe Jesus making Himself "of no reputation." See Liddell, *A Lexicon: Abridged from Liddell and Scott's Greek-English Lexicon.*

2. See Matthew 1:18; Luke 2:24; Leviticus 12:8. Contrast Jesus' humble upbringing, say, with that of young Moses raised in the lavish palace, excellent education, and doting approval of Pharaoh! Henry notes, "One would think that the Lord Jesus, if he would be a man, should have been a prince. But quite the contrary." [Henry, *Commentary in One Volume,* 1863.]

3. "Made of a woman" (Gal. 4:4) implies ever so subtly not only Mary's birthing but also her ongoing counsel and instruction, all grounded in the Old Testament Scriptures and Sovereign.

4. Again Henry notes, "His whole life was a life of humiliation." Yet He lived it with honor!

5. Paul laments these unfaithful ones in 2 Timothy 1:15; 4:16.

CHAPTER 94
MISLED!

1. See Jeremiah 24:7.

CHAPTER 95
IN TROUBLE?

1. Historically this psalm's "anointed" one is Israel's devoted and victorious king, David. Figuratively, every committed Christian is Davidic—"anointed" with the Spirit, called to reign with Christ, and challenged to become a victorious overcomer. Thus Psalm 20 speaks to us all.

2. Jesus instructed us to pray, "Thy kingdom come. Thy will be done in earth" (Matt. 6:10), and the apostle John said we can pray with confidence when asking "any thing according to His will" (1 John 5:14).

3. See John 14:13–14; 15:7–8; Mark 11:24; 1 John 3:21–22.

4. Noah had a "now I know" moment when he beheld the "olive leaf plucked off" (Gen. 8:11) and Peter experienced the same when God miraculously delivered him from Herod's prison (Acts 12:11).

5. Tozer, *The Best of A. W. Tozer,* 242.

CHAPTER 96
POURING OUT...GLADLY!

1. Under the old covenant, Jews offered libations of wine, oil, and water, but never blood, which was offered in pagan worship (Num. 15:1–10; Ps. 16:4).

2. The water David "poured out before the Lord" conveyed the thought that the risk his men took to obtain it rendered it a sacrifice so costly that only God was worthy of it (2 Sam. 23:13–17). Later, the water Jewish priests poured before the Lord during the Festival of Tabernacles (1) memorialized the water God gave them in the wilderness

from the smitten rock (a type of Christ); and (2) conveyed the thought that the Holy Spirit, obtained by the costliest sacrifice (Christ's death) and given us by grace, was so precious a gift only God was worthy of it (John 7:37–39).

3. David foresaw Jesus praying, "I am poured out like water" (Ps. 22:14).

4. Paul urged the Romans, and us all, to become not dead but "living sacrifices" (Rom. 12:1).

5. Epaphras exemplifies this (Col. 4:12).

6. Giving thanks is the New Testament "sacrifice of praise" (Heb. 13:15).

CHAPTER 97
FAITHFUL IN THE DARK

1. For examples, see Acts 19:21; Ephesians 3:3–6; Acts 16:9–10; 23:11; 1 Thessalonians 4:13–18. Besides these revealed truths, Paul, like John, stood in God's very presence and heard Him speak "unspeakable words" (2 Cor. 12:2–4; Rev. 10:4; Deut. 29:29).

2. This darkness is not the darkness of sin, which occurs when we deliberately disobey God's Word, warnings, or guidance (1 John 1:6; 2:9, 11).

3. See Habakkuk 2:4; Romans 1:17; 2 Corinthians 5:7; Galatians 3:11; Hebrews 10:38.

4. Paul encapsulated this great lesson in Philippians 4:11–13 and Hebrews 13:5.

5. "Therefore will the LORD wait, [only] that he may be [more] gracious unto you" (Isa. 30:18) is vividly seen in Joseph's experience. God had him wait two additional years only because it wasn't yet time for Pharaoh's dream (Gen. 40:23–41:1). One minister said, "For every Genesis 40 there's a Genesis 41 that follows."

6. The psalms assure us, "Even the darkness is not dark to You, and the night is as bright as the day. Darkness and light are alike to You" (Ps. 139:12, NAS).

7. Through Isaiah God promised to faithfully lead his people through darkness (Isa. 42:16). He does so through overcomers who've already passed through it successfully.

CHAPTER 98
LOOK BEYOND THE DARKNESS

1. I make no attempt to explain how these awesome astrophysical events will occur, but merely assert with childlike faith that they will occur just as the Bible describes them by the inexplicable, immeasurable, miraculous power of God.

CHAPTER 99
APPRECIATING ANONYMOUS ASSISTANTS

1. Smith and Cornwall, *The Exhaustive Dictionary of Bible Names*, s.v. "Epaphroditus."

2. James had honored Paul and Barnabas in the church's official statement concluding the first-recorded church council (Acts 15:25–26).

3. See Philippians 4:18. That the Philippians entrusted Epaphroditus with their collections and messages to Paul implies he was one of their elders. See *The Life Application Study Bible*, Philippians 2:25, note, page 2018.

4. Wuest translates, "Having recklessly exposed his life" (Phil. 2:30). One source surmises, "It may have been that 'he fell ill on the road and nearly killed himself

by completing the journey while he was unfit to travel.'" [Caird, *Paul's Letters from Prison*.] See Carson, France, Motyer, and Wenham, eds., *New Bible Commentary: 21st Century Edition*.

5. "Travel conditions were dangerous and harsh, especially at sea in late fall and early spring, and these conditions decreased one's resistance to antiquity's many diseases." [Keener, *The IVP Bible Background Commentary: New Testament*.]

6. For the full quote, immortalized by Tertullian, see http://www.tertullian.org/quotes. htm (accessed September 1, 2014).

Chapter 100
The Chief of Zeal

1. See Psalms 16:8, 11; 17:15; 27:4; 65:4.

2. In the New Testament, *zeal* and *zealous* are translations of the Greek *zēlos* and *zēlōtēs*, which mean "ardor, deep devotion, burning enthusiasm, passionate commitment, and a vigorous striving to reach a desired end."

3. For these points, see 2 Kings 19:31; Revelation 3:15; Colossians 3:23.

4. For these points, see John 2:17; Psalm 119:139–140; Revelation 3:19; Philippians 3:12–14.

5. The Spanish Inquisition exerted excessive zeal in the pursuit of so-called heretics.

6. The Crusades were inspired not by true zeal for Christ but by hatred of long-standing Muslim enemies, false hopes of salvation by works, and ignorance of God's purposes and ways.

Chapter 101
Turned for Good—Again!

1. These guards were chained to Paul as he "prayed without ceasing" (1 Thess. 5:17) for others (and them!), witnessed to visitors about Christ and salvation, taught Bible studies to Roman disciples, preached the gospel to various groups who visited after hearing of his incarceration and message, and dictated letters to Christian leaders and groups around the Mediterranean. Sitting by such an effusive fountainhead of Christian truth and love, surely some, perhaps many, of Paul's guards were saved by his prayers and talks. See "Paul's Chains," Phil. 1:12–14 note, in Wiersbe, *The Bible Exposition Commentary*.

2. Paul's prison epistles are Ephesians, Philippians, Colossians, and Philemon.

3. Nero's Praetorian Guard parallels somewhat our president's Secret Service detail. We could reasonably include others very close to the commander in chief, including his White House staff, cabinet members, or highest leaders of the military. Such high-level individuals could easily influence Washington's officials and citizens.

4. God timed Paul's shipwreck and snakebite (in winter months when sailing was suspended) so He could turn it into three months of rest and easy, adversity-free ministry (Acts 28:1–11).

5. Paul climbed rigorous mountain highways while traversing Cyprus (Acts 13:6) and Pisidia (v. 14).

6. Paul's known contact with Jewish and Christian leaders in Rome implies access to copies of the Old Testament scriptures.

7. Paul had three to five years to live, his execution occurring in AD 67 or 68.

8. See Genesis 50:20; Exodus 1:12; Deuteronomy 23:3–5; Acts 8:1–4; 8:5–13; 11:19–21.

9. See Job 13:15; Habakkuk 3:17–19.

CHAPTER 102
SPREAD THE HEAT!

1. *McGraw Hill Dictionary of Architecture and Construction* (New York: McGraw Hill Co., 2003). See http://encyclopedia2.thefreedictionary.com/Heat+Flow (accessed December 7, 2013).

2. These means are conduction, convection, and radiation respectively.

3. See Hebrews 12:29; Malachi 4:2; Revelation 4:5.

4. The name Emmaus means "hot springs." See Smith and Cornwall, *The Exhaustive Dictionary of Bible Names.*

5. Among them the abolition, temperance, child labor, and women's rights movements.

6. People all over the world who experience miraculous healings often testify of a strong sensation of heat or burning in the part of their body experiencing divine restoration.

CHAPTER 103
OUR HIGH CALLING

1. Christ showed us not selfish but selfless ministry, and said: "The Son of man came not to be ministered unto, but to minister, and to give his life..." (Matt. 20:28).

2. Proverbs emphasizes this: "A friend loveth at all times, and a brother is born for adversity" (Prov. 17:17); or "A friend is always loyal, and a brother is born to help in time of need" (NLT).

3. See Romans 8:1, 34.

4. Ahimaaz models uncontrolled desire to bear the "king's tidings." Though he hadn't waited long enough to receive accurate "tidings" from God, he still insisted on running *now* and ultimately delivered a false, incomplete message (2 Sam. 18:19–33, esp. vv. 22–23, 29). So do others who rush into ministry unprepared.

CHAPTER 104
REJOICING IN THE LORD... ALWAYS!

1. Or, "Be constantly rejoicing in the Lord" (Phil. 3:1, WUEST); or, "Whatever happens...rejoice in the Lord" (NLT).

2. See 2 Corinthians 9:8; Philippians 4:19.

3. Or, "But I will still be glad in the LORD; I will rejoice in God my Savior" (NCV).

4. All these learned to consistently "rejoice in the Lord" whatever their circumstances (Hab. 3:17–19; Ps. 37:4; 64:10; 1 Sam. 2:1; 30:6; Acts 16:24–25; Phil. 4:11–13).

5. "Rejoicing" in the Lord is synonymous with being "glad," "delighting," or "glorying" in Him. See "rejoice in the LORD," Psalms 33:1; 97:12; Isaiah 41:16; 61:10; Zechariah

10:7; "be glad," Psalms 32:11; 64:10; 104:34; "delight," Psalm 37:4; Isaiah 58:14; "glory" 1 Corinthians 1:31; 2 Corinthians. 10:17.

CHAPTER 105
PRACTICING GOD'S PEACE

1. One of Oswald Chambers' favorite sayings was "I *refuse* to worry!"

2. Or, "Let your requests be unreservedly made known in the presence of God" (WEY).

3. Hayford, general editor, *The Spirit-Filled Life Bible*, Phil. 4:6, 7 note, page 1806.

4. *The Life Application Study Bible*, Phil. 4:6, 7 note, page 2022.

5. The strong, calm faith of Moravian pilgrims in a fierce Atlantic storm stirred young John Wesley's heart to desire what they had. George Mueller's amazing faith and answers to prayer have inspired countless Christians to be anxious for nothing but in everything confidently pray.

6. God's peace will be New Jerusalem's atmosphere. Perhaps this is why God chose Jerusalem, His city of peace (Heb. 7:2), as the capital of His ancient Jewish people and a type of the capital of the new world. The meaning of "Jerusalem," though obscure, is very likely, "founded in peace; teaching peace…double peace"—or *founded in and teaching the double or twofold peace of God*. This "double peace" fills its citizens who, redeemed and filled with God's Spirit, live in "double peace"—with God and men. For "Jerusalem," see Smith and Cornwall, *The Exhaustive Dictionary of Bible Names*.

7. The New Testament records many such prayers (1 Cor. 1:3; 2 Cor. 1:2; Gal. 1:3; Eph. 1:2; 6:23; Phil. 1:2; 1 Thess. 1:1; 2 Thess. 1:2; 3:16; Titus 1:4; Philem. 3; 1 Pet. 1:2; 2 John 3; Jude 2; Rev. 1:4).

CHAPTER 106
GOD'S WAITING ROOM

1. Personally, Paul hoped for release (Phil. 2:24), though the issue was not yet fully settled (Phil. 1:20).

2. See Acts 9:30; 11:25–26.

3. See Acts 23:11; 24:27; 25:11–12.

4. Exiled by the Roman emperor Domitian in AD 95, John was released from exile after Domitian's death in AD 96.

5. No easy thing, since even Abraham and Peter succumbed to this temptation to go ahead of God (Gen. 16:1–3; John 21:3–5).

6. For more evidence that God never forgets us, see Genesis 8:1; Daniel 5:10–13; Acts 10:1–4; 11:25; Exodus 3:4; 1 Kings 18:1; 2 Kings 11:4–5; Isaiah 49:14–15.

CHAPTER 107
ORDERED TO THINK!

1. "Whatever is true, whatever is worthy of reverence and is honorable and seemly, whatever is just, whatever is pure, whatever is lovely and lovable, whatever is kind and winsome and gracious, if there is any virtue and excellence, if there is anything worthy of praise, think on and weigh and take account of these things [fix your minds on them]" (Phil. 4:8, AMP).

2. On corrupted minds, see 1 Timothy 6:5; 2 Timothy 3:8; Titus 1:15.

3. This doesn't diminish the Spirit's role in discernment. But even when He prompts or warns, we may fail to detect deceivers, heresies, diversions, and entanglements if we don't prayerfully think through what He shows us.

4. "Meditate" is taken from the Hebrew *śiah*, meaning "to rehearse or go over in one's mind," or reflect and contemplate. See R. L. Harris, G. L. Archer Jr., and B. K. Waltke, ed., *Theological Wordbook of the Old Testament*, electronic ed., (Chicago: Moody Press, 1999).

5. We'll not complete our courses and hear Christ's joyous "Well done!" if we remain weak minded, fearfully minded, double minded, carnally minded, high minded, or incuriously dull minded.

6. For references to the subjects cited in this paragraph, see Psalms 1:2; 119:15, 23, 48, 78, 97, 99, 148; 1 Timothy 4:13–15; Psalms 104:34; 77:12; 143:5; Ecclesiastes 7:13; Psalms 8:1, 3–4; 19:1; 1 Chronicles 16:12; Mark 6:52; Psalm 49:3; Ecclesiastes 9:1; 4:1, 4, 15; 7:14; Daniel 7:8; 8:5; 9:23; Luke 3:15; Haggai 1:5, 7; Deuteronomy 8:2; Hebrews 10:24.

7. Tozer, "To Be Right, We Must Think Right," in *The Best of A. W. Tozer*, 44.

CHAPTER 108
ORDERED TO OBEY!

1. Perhaps we've forgotten this ancient fact. Interesting, isn't it, that the farther Christians get from real Spirit-filled, Bible-ruled, Christ-centered, devotionally driven Christianity, the more we also rely on mere rituals, ceremonies, and rites.

2. Christ commended the Philadelphians for keeping "my command to endure patiently" (Rev. 3:10, NIV), or His orders to "persevere" (NLT) amid their adversities till His appointed time and way of deliverance arrived. Significant time and adversity are required for it to be said accurately one has "endured" or "persevered."

3. Paul commended the Philippians for their repetitive financial support: "You sent me aid again and again when I was in need" (Phil. 4:16, NIV).

4. Paul promises specifically, "The God of peace shall be with you," if you practice obeying Him (Phil. 4:9).

CHAPTER 109
PERFECT POSITIVISM

1. See Isaiah 40:28–31.

2. See 2 Chronicles 26:15–16; 2 Samuel 11:2–5; 1 Kings 11:9–11 (Neh. 13:26); Deuteronomy 8:10–20.

3. Wisely, A. W. Tozer prayed: "If, as sometimes if falleth out to Thy servants, I should have grateful gifts pressed upon me by Thy kindly people, stand by me then and save me from the blight that often follows. Teach me to use whatever I receive in such manner that will not injure my soul nor diminish my spiritual power. And if in Thy permissive providence honor should come to me from Thy church, let me not forget in that hour that I am unworthy of the least of Thy mercies, and that if men knew me as intimately as I know myself they would withhold their honors or bestow them upon others more worthy to receive them." See Tozer, "The Prayer of a Minor Prophet," in *The Best of A.W. Tozer*, 79.

4. *Life Application Study Bible*, Phil. 4:13, note, page 2023.

CHAPTER 110
SHARING WITH OUR SOVEREIGN

1. Thus Peter, Paul, John, the other apostles, and many apostolic church fathers spent the vast majority of their lives ministering in homes. By the third century some wealthy Christians began vacating their large homes and dedicating them entirely for church use, even altering their structure to make larger meeting rooms. Later that century large and sometimes elaborately decorated public buildings (prayer halls) were erected solely for Christian worship. See "Where Did Christians Worship?", *Christian History Magazine*, Worship in the Early Church, issue 37, pages 33–34.

2. A 2009 Pew Research forum found 9 percent of American Protestants worship exclusively in homes. A 2010 Barna study estimated some 6–12 million Americans worship in homes. See http://usatoday30.usatoday.com/news/religion/2010-07-22-housechurch21_ST_N.htm (accessed February 3, 2014).

3. Such persecution prevails today in Saudi Arabia, Pakistan, China, parts of Africa, and many other nations where Islamic or indigenous religions predominate or Communism rules.

CHAPTER 111
THE PERFECT PROVIDER

1. "Mammon" (Matt. 6:24, Gk. *mamōnas*) refers to deposited monies and other assets trusted in instead of God. In Matthew 6:19–34 Jesus warned us we can't serve God and mammon (v. 24) and ordered us not to lay up wealth to trust in it but instead to trust in our heavenly Father's unfailing supply, seek His kingdom will and work "first," lay up heavenly treasure (by good works, including giving, 1 Tim. 6:17–19), and expect God to supply all our present and future needs.

2. Wiersbe, *The Bible Exposition Commentary*.

3. Daily we need spiritual refreshment, strength, and insight; loving social intercourse with Christian friends and family; satisfying peace and joy; and the ability to control emotional agitations, such as, anger, fear, impatience, and envy. Christ also provides "all" these needs.

4. For examples of monarchs' rich or bountiful gifts, see Genesis 12:16; 13:1–2; 41:42–43, 45; Matthew 2:11; Esther 1:7–8; 5:3; 1 Kings 10:13.

5. See Luke 5:29; 21:1–4.

6. Paul testified, "I have all, and abound. I am full" (Phil. 4:18).

7. R. Jamieson, A. R. Fausset, and D. Brown, *Commentary Critical and Explanatory on the Whole Bible* (Oak Harbor, WA: Logos Research Systems, Inc., 1997), s.v. "Php 4:19."

8. See Luke 6:38; 1 Kings 17:10–16; Deuteronomy 15:10.

9. While advocating against human wealth seeking, we must also affirm divine wealth creation. God sovereignly grants some Christians extra financial success or blessings so they can give more to His work and people (Luke 7:4–5; 8:1–3; Acts 16:14–15, 40; 2 Cor. 8:14–15; 9:8).

CHAPTER 112
BRING YOUR OFFERING!

1. While the OT system of animal offerings is obsolete, offerings are not.

2. Cain infamously offered, and God famously rejected, worship on his terms (Gen. 4:1–5). To this day God still rejects Cainish worship, or that which ignores or defies the worship God has specifically requested (John 4:23–24).

3. One of our fellowship's favorite worship songs is "Offering," written by Paul Baloche. See http://www.youtube.com/watch?v=dCh7AFvEVjk (accessed April 2, 2014).

4. Thanking God is very desirable to God, beneficial to us, and essential for overcomers. See Psalms 29:1–2; 69:30–32; 100:4; 29:1–2, 11.

5. Mary of Bethany's extravagant offering of her most valuable material possession to Jesus, despite the criticism she received, filled the atmosphere with a delightful scent that deeply pleased Him (John 12:3; Mark 14:6–9).

6. The Greek word for "share" is *koinōnia*, meaning to "share in common" or fellowship, whether by material property or social intercourse (kind communications). Are we "sharing" offerings of loving messages in letters, telephone calls, e-mails, or text messages, or are we withholding our *koinōnia*?

CHAPTER 113
STRENGTH TO SUFFER WELL

1. By Christian "suffering" we mean our full acceptance of all the unpleasant situations that visit our lives for Christ's sake, from brief, minor irritations to long, painful persecutions.

2. See 1 Corinthians 16:13; Galatians 5:1; Ephesians 6:11–14; Philippians 1:27; 4:1; 1 Thessalonians 3:8; 2 Thessalonians 2:15; Revelation 3:11.

3. A "man of sorrows" and "acquainted with grief," Jesus suffered well among disbelieving half-brothers, in a tumultuous season of ministry, and during His substitutionary sufferings (Isa. 53:3).

4. When late twentieth-century Chinese Christians learned Americans were praying for their release from persecution, they asked us rather to pray for strength to be faithful in their sufferings.

5. See 2 Corinthians 12:7–10; Acts 14:19–23; 16:16–40; 27:9–44.

6. See Matthew 5:10–12; 7:25–26; 1 Peter 1:6–7; 4:12–16.

7. Centuries earlier, the Spirit also strengthened William Tyndale and Martin Luther to continue translating scripture while suffering captivity in Belgium and Germany respectively, Tyndale continuing his Old Testament work and Luther his German version of the New Testament.

8. In the midst of horrific conditions and brutal beatings in the infamous Ravensbruck Nazi concentration camp, Betsie ten Boom affirmed and proved the truth, "There is no pit so deep that God's love is not deeper still." See http://www.corrietenboom.com/history.htm (accessed April 10, 2014).

CHAPTER 114
QUAKEPROOF!

1. "Quakeproofing" involves designing and building structures to withstand or resist the effects of earthquakes. See http://www.thefreedictionary.com/quakeproof (accessed April 17, 2014).

2. The writer to the Hebrews is quoting the prophet Haggai (Hag. 2:6–9).

3. Paul wrote the Colossians from Rome in approximately AD 60. The Roman historian Tacitus states a quake struck Colossae, Laodicea, and Hierapolis in Nero's seventh year (AD 61), while Eusebius assigns it to his tenth year (AD 64). Whichever date is accurate, the fact remains the city was devastated by a quake not long after receiving Paul's letter.

4. These errors included an early form of Gnosticism (which denied the full deity, incarnation, sole Saviorship, and headship of Christ), Greek philosophy, aspects of Jewish legalism, and the veneration of angels.

5. For more on the "presentation," see Luke 21:36; 2 Corinthians 4:14; 11:2; Ephesians 5:27; Colossians 1:28; Jude 24; Revelation 19:7–9.

CHAPTER 115
GET PRESENTABLE!

1. By "passion" we mean what we want above all else, our first or chief love, our most fervent interest, our deepest delight.

2. Paul alluded to the presentation again in Colossians, noting that when Christ appears to take us away, we will "appear with [or be presented to] him in [heavenly] glory" (Col. 3:4).

3. God's grace, for instance, gives us the Christ life, but we must feed it. His blood opens the "new and living way," but we must draw near and pray, worship, and intercede. His grace gives us the Holy Spirit, but we must let Him lead and correct us. His grace gives us teachers, pastors, and counselors, but we must respectfully obey their instruction. His providence gives us tests, but we must prove ourselves in them. Thus we "make ourselves ready" for presentation.

4. Compare Esther's year-long preparation before becoming Xerxes' queen (Esther 2:9, 12).

5. See Psalm 45:9, 13.

6. See Song of Solomon 1:10–11; Isaiah 61:10.

7. See Song of Solomon 1:12.

8. Study Genesis 24, noting that the servant Abraham sent to find a bride for his son symbolizes the Holy Spirit, whom the heavenly Father has sent in this church age to find, prepare, retrieve, and present a bride church fit for His Son.

CHAPTER 116
THE COHERER

1. Swanson, *Dictionary of Biblical Languages with Semantic Domains: Greek (New Testament)*, s.v. "*synistēmi.*"

2. Thus Jesus' monumental promise: "Heaven and earth shall pass away, but my words shall not pass away [unfulfilled]" (Matt. 24:35). See also Mark 14:49; John 10:35.

3. World World II history buffs will remember especially the Battle of Midway Island in the Pacific theater and the Battle of Britain, and later Moscow, in Europe.

4. The Coherer was certainly at work during the Cuban missile crisis in October 1962. Not mere reason but the Redeemer—prompted by the prayers of believers worldwide— moved President Kennedy to refuse his hawkish military advisors, respond to Khrushchev's conciliatory letter rather than his bellicose one, and secretly agree to remove American ballistic nuclear missiles in Turkey rather than provoke a cataclysmic nuclear exchange.

5. Strangely our faithfulness to the Coherer's Word, call, or righteousness may divide our families (Matt. 10:34–39; John 7:1–5; Gen. 37:20–28). But He'll heal these wounds also if we'll stay faithful, bear our crosses of rejection, and pray for our estranged loved ones. Once reunited, the Coherer will make our family stronger and more blessed than before (Job 42:10–12; Acts 1:14; Gen. 45:4–15).

6. Here again, Christ sometimes permits churches to split to test their faithful remnants, purge them of impenitent troublemakers, reestablish biblical truth and order, and restore their fruitful pursuit of His calling (1 Cor. 11:19, NLT; 1 John 2:19).

7. As He did in the lives of Job, Lazarus, and Paul (Job 1:13–19; John 11:14; Acts 27:14–20).

8. Job, Habakkuk, Martha, and Paul made the monumental decision to continue trusting the Coherer when everything around them fell apart (Job 13:15; Hab. 3:17–19; John 11:23–27, 39–41; Acts 27:22–25).

CHAPTER 117
WANT TO MINISTER?

1. I'm not referring to Christian categories, such as clergy or laymen, but rather to the spiritual blessing and power imparted as we share God's Word. Like our Lord, we're here "not to be ministered unto, but to minister" (Matt. 20:28), and all of us should aspire to be "faithful people who will be able to teach others as well" (2 Tim. 2:2, ISV). Scripture affirms God uses laymen as well as clergy (Acts 8:4, 5–8; 11:19–21; 18:26).

2. The smaller "mills" (one eighteen-inch to twenty-four-inch concave stone turning on another fixed convex stone underneath) could be operated by manpower; the larger mills (using four-foot to five-foot stones) were turned by animals, often donkeys. See Merrill C, Tenney and Moises Silva, *The Zondervan Encyclopedia of the Bible*, vol. 4 (Grand Rapids, MI: Zondervan, 2009), 253–254.

3. Crushing weight is also used to make diamonds and marble. Diamonds are formed when carbon is subjected to great pressure and intense heat deep in the earth's crust. Marble is made when limestone is subjected to extraordinary heat and pressure for an extended time.

4. The apostle Paul was "milled" frequently (2 Cor. 4:8–12), yet always found God's grace sufficient (vv. 7–10).

5. While some interpret Joseph's Egyptian name as "the god speaks (and) he lives," others correctly render, and the biblical context soundly supports, "the giver of the

nourishment of the land." See Charles F. Pfeiffer, Howard F. Vos, and John Rea, *The Wycliffe Bible Encyclopedia*, vol. 2 (Chicago: Moody Press, 1975), 1833.

6. Apply this personally. How many times has *your* soul been stirred, nourished, refreshed, and reinspired by reading how amid the worst difficulties Joseph became a man of noble character, enduring faith, beautiful humility, soaring wisdom, Christlike compassion, fatherly benevolence, deep insight, and prophetic knowledge?

7. D. W. Lambert, *Oswald Chambers: An Unbribed Soul* (Fort Washington, PA: Christian Literature Crusade, 1968), 25.

8. And be encouraged; the longer God keeps you in your "mill" or "school," the more powerful your ministry will be when He releases you (e.g., Moses, David, Paul).

CHAPTER 118
BACK TO BETHEL!

1. Bethel was originally called Luz, but after meeting God there, Jacob renamed it Bethel, or "house of God" (Gen. 28:17, 19).

2. That "the land of thy fathers" (Gen. 31:3) meant Bethel is proven by God's later recall, in which He specified, "Arise, go up to *Bethel*, and dwell there" (Gen. 35:1). Thus God intended Jacob to return not near Bethel but to Bethel—and remain there the rest of his life!

3. Procrastination is no small sin. Delayed obedience *is* disobedience, subtle but sure rebellion, and opens us up to shameful troubles, losses, and griefs that God never intended for us, as Jacob soon discovered in Shechem (Gen. 34).

4. In John 1:51 Jesus confirms He is Jacob's ladder, the only way upon which angels carry our prayers to heaven and heaven responds with our answers (cf. Heb. 10:19–20).

5. Though Jacob's vow was laced with selfishness, it was nevertheless sincere. Though still carnally minded, he had been touched by the Spirit and responded in the only way he knew (cf. Exod. 2:11–12).

6. If necessary, God in His love will use not only personal but also national disasters to get the full attention of Jacob Christians and churches in these last days (Rom. 8:28; Amos 3:6).

7. God has repeated this call down through the centuries, ordering Moses to "be there" on the mount of devotion and inspiring Christ to call His disciples to "be with him," and later, "Come unto me" (Exod. 24:12; Mark 3:14–15; Matt. 11:28).

8. Abraham's persistent intercessions delivered Lot from Sodom, even when he "lingered," procrastinating to leave (Gen. 18:22–33; 19:15–22, 29)!

CHAPTER 119
REVIVAL READINESS

1. This call to humility was a central and oft-repeated theme in Jesus' teaching ministry (Matt. 23:12; Luke 14:11; 18:14).

2. In both texts (Isa. 57:15; Ps. 51:17), the Hebrew words translated "broken" and "contrite" are very strong, describing something "broken down, shattered, smashed, crushed to dust, or beaten to pieces." See R. L. Thomas, *New American Standard*

Hebrew-Aramaic and Greek Dictionaries, updated edition (Anaheim: Foundation Publications, Inc., 1998).

3. See Job 42:6.

4. See Genesis 41:16.

CHAPTER 120
CONSTANT COMFORTERS

1. He declared this four times! See John 14:16; 14:26; 15:26; 16:7.

2. Inspired by the Comforter, the Word of God, when believed and received, imparts the strongest possible comfort to believers' hearts (Rom. 15:4; Luke 24:27, 32). This is especially true of the Book of Psalms (Ps. 119:50, 52, 76).

3. See John 14:26; Acts 11:15–16.

4. See Bible references for comfort by: fellowship (Rom. 1:12), sharing God's Word (Rom. 15:4), teaching biblical prophecy (1 Thess. 4:18), sharing experiential insights (2 Cor. 1:4–5), reconciling with penitents (2 Cor. 2:7), exhorting (1 Sam. 23:16–17), assisting suffering Christians (Col. 4:10–11), quickly sharing good news (1 Thess. 3:6–7), prophecy, if so gifted (1 Cor. 14:3, 31; Gen. 40:5–13), reassuring others of Christ's appearing (1 Thess. 5:9–11).

5. Paul, who comforted so many, was comforted by many (Col. 4:10–11; Phil. 4:10, 14, 18).

6. I'm speaking practically here, not doctrinally. Whether we've received one or two works of grace, we must abide close to Christ daily for the sap of the Vine's Spirit to flow fully through the branch of our life (John 15:1–8).

CHAPTER 121
SPIRITUAL MATURITY—IN DETAIL

1. The apostles began to grasp this when Jesus demonstrated command of the winds and waves (Mark 4:41).

2. The apostle John describes these sinful "things that are in the world" as "the lust of the flesh, and the lust of the eyes, and the pride of life" (1 John 2:15–17).

3. A practical definition of *mortify* is to deny something until it dies.

4. "Doors of utterance" are divinely appointed and blessed speaking opportunities (John 4:6–7, 40–43; Acts 10:21–22; 16:14–15; 1 Cor. 16:8–9).

5. See Ephesians 4:15; 2 Timothy 2:24–26; Acts 6:10; Luke 4:22; Psalm 45:2.

6. Paul began and ended all his epistles with prayers for grace.

CHAPTER 122
LET HIM BE REVEALED IN YOU!

1. A fetus moving in the womb, the vast information in a single cell, the perfectly coordinated tissues, organs, and systems of the human body, the awe-inspiring beauty of the sunrise and sunset, the ocean and weather patterns, earth's precise position in our solar system, the food chain, the water cycle, the stunning uniqueness of snowflakes or our finger, foot, voice, and eye prints, these are not the work of chance. They're evidence God has provided for intellectually honest investigators.

2. When Peter and John were filled with Christ's boldness, others noted, "They had been with Jesus" (Acts 4:13). The apostle Paul said others were seeing Christ's life in him: "And they glorified God in me" (Gal. 1:24).

3. See 2 Corinthians 4:3–4.

Contact the Author

Mail:
Greg Hinnant Ministries
P.O. Box 788
High Point, N. C. 27261

Telephone:
336 882-1645

Email:
rghministries@aol.com

Website:
www.greghinnantministries.org

OTHER BOOKS BY THIS AUTHOR

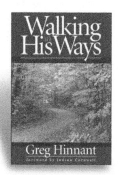

Walking in His Ways

Walking on Water

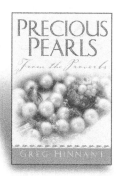

Precious Pearls
From the Proverbs

Word Portraits: Five
Illustrations of the
Mature Christian

DanielNotes: An
Inspirational Commentary
on the Book of Daniel

Not by Bread Alone:
Daily Devotions for
Disciples, Volume 1

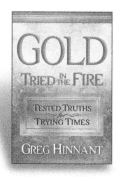

Gold Tried in the
Fire: Tested Truths
for Trying Times

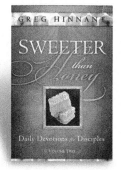

Sweeter than Honey:
Daily Devotions for
Disciples, Volume 2

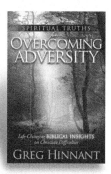

Spiritual Truths
for Overcoming
Adversity

Notes

Notes

Notes

Notes

Notes

Notes

Notes

\

Made in the USA
Coppell, TX
04 May 2021